Struggling with Destiny in Karimpur, 1925–1984

STRUGGLING with DESTINY in KARIMPUR, 1925–1984

Susan S. Wadley

UNIVERSITY OF CALIFORNIA PRESS
Berkeley · Los Angeles · London

University of California Press
Berkeley and Los Angeles, California

University of California Press, Ltd.
London, England

© 1994 by
The Regents of the University of California

Library of Congress Cataloging-in-Publication Data

Wadley, Susan Snow, 1943–
   Struggling with destiny in Karimpur, 1925–1984 / Susan S.
Wadley
      p.   cm.
   Includes bibliographical references and index.
   ISBN 0-520-08407-1 (pbk. alk. paper)
   1. Ethnology—India—Mainpuri (District)   2. Villages—India—
Mainpuri (District)   3. Family—India—Mainpuri (District)   4. Social
change—India—Mainpuri (District)   5. Mainpuri (India : Dis-
trict)—Social conditions.   6. Mainpuri (India : District)—Rural con-
ditions.   I. Title
GN635.I4W33   1994
306'.0954'2—dc20   93-48297
                                                              CIP

Printed in the United States of America

08   07   06   05   04   03   02   01   00
9   8   7   6   5   4   3

The paper used in this publication meets the minimum requirements of
ANSI/NISO Z39.48-1992 (R 1997) (*Permanence of Paper*). ⊚

This book is dedicated to the memory
of three wise men,
Hal, Januki, and Ageha,
whose untimely deaths were both personal
and community losses,

and to my parents, Chet and Ellen

Contents

Tables

Maps and Figures

Note on Transliteration

All italicized technical terms in Hindi and the Karimpur dialect (a blending of Braj and Kanauji) have been transliterated according to the system followed by the Library of Congress, with the exception that the medial and final *a*, which is usually not pronounced, has been omitted from most words. The final vowel has been retained in a few words that have become familiar to English readers in Sanskrit-derived transliterations (*karma, dharma*), except when I am directly quoting a Karimpur speaker, where I have transliterated them in as they are pronounced in the dialect (*karam, dharm*). Likewise, since in Karimpur ज़ is pronounced as a *j* rather than a *z*, I have transliterated accordingly (thus, for example, *ijjat*, not *izzat*).

I have used a different system for proper nouns, including the names of deities. These are given without diacritics and with the substitution of *sh* for both the consonants श and ष, of *ch* for both च and छ, of *ksh* for क्ष, and *ri* for ऋ (thus Kshatriya, Shudra, Krishna). The glossary provides diacritics for those who wish to be certain of pronunciation. In addition, certain common Anglicizations have been adopted (zamindar, panchayat), and place names have been given in their common English spellings (Delhi, Agra).

Preface

> People say that earlier there was someone from America who came here, a
> queen. She built a house on some land here. She sometimes comes, that
> Mem Sahab. She is called the Queen Sahab (*rānī sahab*). She asks the village
> people about their conditions, what are their troubles, what difficulties there
> are. In marriages she may give a little money. And she gives medicine and
> help to people who are poor.

In this way, a man from a village near Karimpur, a community located
150 miles from Delhi on the Gangetic plain in North India, told of the
foreign woman who came to Karimpur and helped people there. When I
first heard this story, in 1984, I was truly astounded, for my village friends
had not told it to me. In fact, I heard it only because the servant of the
superintendent of police had told it to the SP's wife, a close friend of ours.
One afternoon, she asked him to tell it to me. In this story, Charlotte
Wiser, a missionary who lived in Karimpur in the 1920s, and myself, an
anthropologist who worked in Karimpur in the late 1960s and mid-1970s
and then once again in 1983–84, are condensed into one person. Charlotte and I were both white and American, and we helped people with
medicines. I knew that people often thought me to be Charlotte's daughter or granddaughter, but it never occurred to me that local folklore had
collapsed our identities. To me, the differences of missionary and scholar,
of age (Charlotte died over ten years ago, in her eighties), of friendships
within the community, of method and theory all made us distinct. But I
clearly saw differences where people in Karimpur and surrounding communities did not.

The issue of differences notwithstanding, this book is the result of more than sixty years of American contact with Karimpur, contact that undoubtedly makes Karimpur—a pseudonym given the village by Charlotte Wiser and her husband, William—one of the most studied communities in South Asia, and perhaps the world. Whether for the community itself, and the individuals in it, this prolonged intrusion by foreign scholars has been a blessing or curse remains a question. Nonetheless, Karimpur provides a unique opportunity for understanding social change in North India, for it is the site of a truly long-term study.[1]

In 1925, after a half dozen years in India as a teacher in the agricultural college in Allahabad, William Wiser sought permission from the Presbyterian mission to do a survey of a farming community in order better to understand the agricultural conditions and life situations facing his students. With his wife, Charlotte Wiser, and two sons (a third was born during the study period), he pitched a tent in the mango grove at one end of the village he later called Karimpur.[2] The survey turned into a detailed study of Indian village life, extending over six camping seasons from 1925 to 1930 and culminating in four manuscripts. *Behind Mud Walls*, jointly written by William and Charlotte, was first published in 1930; *Social Institutions of a Hindu Village in North India*, a doctoral dissertation in rural sociology, was submitted by William to Cornell University in 1933; *The Hindu Jajmani System*, by William, was published in India in 1936; and *The Foods of an Indian Village*, published in Allahabad in 1936, was originally submitted by Charlotte as a master's thesis in nutrition at Cornell University. These works form the core of published materials on life in Karimpur between 1925 and 1930.

In addition, before his death William Wiser gave his census and land records to Lewis Levine, of New York University, who later passed them on to me while I was a graduate student. An eight-hundred-page collection of oral traditions was given to Norvin Hein, of Yale University: it is this collection that led me to Karimpur in 1967.[3] Cora Dubois received copies of wall paintings, which have disappeared. Other field notes from the 1920s are missing, although many personal notebooks and diaries are in archives at Yale.

From 1930 until 1960 the Wisers had minimal contact with Karimpur, as they were involved instead in setting up the India Village Service, an experiment in rural development that became a model for India's Block Development Program, at Marehra, in Etah District to the north. Then they decided to retire to Karimpur and began to build a house there on land owned by a Brahman family. As the house neared completion,

William became seriously ill; he saw the house only once. After his death, Charlotte returned to live in Karimpur for a month or two a year from 1962 to 1971, continuing to investigate and write about village lives. Her publications from this period include two new chapters to *Behind Mud Walls* (1960, 1971) and the monograph *Four Families of Karimpur* (1978). Her notes and tapes from this period are missing, but a partial census from 1964 has proved a valuable aid.

After Norvin Hein gave me access to the Wiser Collection of Oral Traditions, I worked in Karimpur from December 1967 to March 1969, focusing primarily on oral traditions as keys to Karimpur belief systems concerning religion. I also collected basic core data, including a household census, land records and maps, and data on *jajmānī* relationships, as well as some information on politics and agriculture. (For my published works on Karimpur, see the bibliography.)

In 1974–75 I went to Karimpur with my husband, Bruce W. Derr, who was planning to do research on agriculture and socioeconomic change. This work was originally to be a restudy of land tenure patterns, but difficulty with access to land records transformed it into a study of farming practices and reactions to agricultural change and population growth. He conducted detailed interviews with selected farmers, in addition to collecting a new census, production figures, and other statistics. His findings are reported in *The Growing Abundance of Food and Poverty in a North Indian Village: Karimpur, 1925–1975*, a doctoral dissertation submitted to Syracuse University (1979), as well as in numerous papers (see the bibliography).

Finally, in 1983–84 I returned to Karimpur with Bruce to do a study of social change, focusing on men's and women's life histories. In addition to gathering life history materials from a variety of villagers, we completed a village census, collected retrospective fertility histories from all women who ever married, updated my collection of oral traditions, conducted time studies of men's and women's work, and obtained land records and maps for twelve points in time between 1940 and 1984. The present book is based primarily on research done in 1983–84, although it draws on the previous research done in Karimpur.

Having lived and worked in Karimpur for more than twenty-five years, I have had many and varied experiences there. Let me share just a few. I remember my first visit to Karimpur: it was December of 1967. I had arrived in India a few weeks before and had met Charlotte in Delhi. She sent me to friends of hers in the district town closest to Karimpur, and they contacted a young man, Jageshwar Dube, from the village to take me there. Leaving behind my American clothes, I wore what I thought would be appropriate—the *silvār-kamīz*, or long shirt and baggy pants worn by college girls in Delhi and women in the Punjab—and rode to Karimpur along the narrow country roads on the back of Jageshwar's bike. He took me directly to the house built by the Wisers and now inhabited by the family of Bajreng Prasad Pandey. Bajreng's large family, then numbering some twenty-five adults and children, was to become my Karimpur family, but on that first visit I was the awkward American, spoken to as a child or person hard of hearing, in careful slow Hindi. While the children gathered to stare silently, the women offered friendly greetings—*"namaste miss sahab"*—with a tentative smile. I was led to a cot in the courtyard and fed fried breads and a potato curry. Jageshwar, who was working on his B.Ed. degree, helped translate, his English being comparable to my Hindi. Later he gave me a quick tour of the village. I thought that I would never be able to find my way through the winding lanes. And the dialect! This was not the textbook Hindi that I had been taught in graduate school. Would I ever understand what people were saying?

A few days later, I loaded my bedroll, single suitcase, tape recorder, and camera into a cycle rickshaw and moved to Karimpur. I also wore a sari—and never again, on instructions from Bajreng's wife, Jiya, have I worn anything else. In Karimpur in 1967, only preadolescent girls wore the Punjabi-style dress that I had worn on that first day. Charlotte had asked her semiretired cook, Bashir Khan, to come and look after me. He lived in the "kitchen," a narrow room with a door to the verandah as well as one to the courtyard, furnished with two small tables and a kerosene burner in addition to his cot. During waking hours, I shared the front room (with its long narrow table, few chairs, and the eccentric kerosene fridge left by the Wisers) with children and anyone else who happened by. Jiya assigned me a cot across the courtyard as a sleeping place: I shared a room with sundry grandchildren and other visitors. Except for the month when Jiya's married daughter was there with her newborn son and a cow-dung fire smoldered nightly, it was comfortable. And except for times when the house was overflowing with visitors, I didn't have to share my cot. But the greatest luxury was the latrine built by the Wisers. Not only could I bathe and use the toilet in private, but I could even hide out and read there if the family overwhelmed me.

I had come to Karimpur to study the semantics of social dialects, to explore the differences in vocabulary and meaning among high- and low-caste, male and female speech. I had planned to learn about these social dialects through oral traditions, and my explorations of oral traditions led me to religious songs, stories, and practices. As it turned out, I never completed my original semantic study, although this book approaches some of the same questions. Instead, over the next fifteen months I recorded almost one hundred hours of Karimpur oral traditions.

It was the tape recorder—that instrument of anthropologists and the one thing I had that was unique in the village—that gave me entry and helped me to make friends. Shortly after I moved to Karimpur a young woman of the Bard *jāti* gave birth to a son. The women of my house were attending the rituals associated with the birth, and I and my tape recorder went also. This machine that played back your own voice was an immediate hit: everyone loved to hear their songs or stories. Many Brahman women attended that birth ritual, including the women of the house of Asha Ram, a Brahman landlord whose father had been a village leader. Asha Ram's mother, Panditine, then in her seventies, later became a major source of Karimpur oral traditions: she was always ready with a song or story, and I spent many afternoons in her house while she and the women of the neighborhood sang. Asha Ram's family lived near the Cultivator section of the village, and one afternoon a young man from that group was called to entertain the women and "fill the machine." Thus began one of my most valued friendships in Karimpur: Raghubar has told me stories, sung for me, and answered endless questions about Karimpur ever since.

One day, some months after I had come to Karimpur, I heard a strange ringing din. That, I was told, is *ḍānk*, the ritual of snake possession, during which the snake king, Basuk Dev, "plays" and cures snakebite or answers questions about sickness or missing cattle. I sought out this event and found a group of men gathered in front of the Potter's house. My friend Raghubar was the devotee being possessed, while Januki, a Shepherd known for his ritual knowledge and ability to cure, was the exorcist. The men moved aside so that I, the lone woman there, could squeeze into the front of the crowd with my tape recorder. I recorded *ḍānk* several times and once Basuk Dev was even questioned about my presence: "Was it okay that this American was here taping this?" With Basuk Dev's approval, I remained. But I have not forgotten the power of that experience, nor the necessity of Basuk Dev's approval for my research activities.

One memorable event occurred on a hot June day during the wedding season when I was called to a Brahman household where a new bride had just arrived. Women from the neighborhood gathered to inspect her, and she was asked to sing. As requested, I recorded the event. That night, the young bride's husband came to my door asking to hear the tape. He had not yet seen his wife's face or had an opportunity to speak with her. But if a man can become enamored of a disembodied voice, that young man did that evening. He played the tape again and again, telling all who would listen of the wondrous voice of his bride.

I also remember, with a smile, the evening when the women in my family and I giggled in a corner of the courtyard while Jiya entertained a male relative who had lingered long past normal visiting hours, making the rest of us uncomfortable—for the courtyard, especially at night, is women's territory. We called him "the mouse," after his narrow face and pointed chin, and our comments were variously impolite and outrageous.

There were hard times, too. One day while walking through the village, I was bitten by a dog: fortunately, the many folds of my sari prevented any break in my skin, though the tooth marks and bruise were visible for days. That event taught me about rural grapevines, as people from all over the village came to check on my welfare, and friends from the district town showed up ready to take me for rabies shots. Then there were heat, flies, endless meals of bread and potatoes, and an ear-and-throat infection that persisted for nine months, finally forcing me home in the spring of 1969. Later, there were deaths—of Umesh's daughter in 1975, of Januki in 1983 (the beloved wrestler and curer who had kept putting off getting his photo taken, only to have one made after his death), and of too many other children and adults. The fall of 1983, in particular, seemed to bring one death after another, leading me to realize how insulated we Americans are, especially from the tragedy of early death. There was also the constant barrage of humanity, so "foreign" to my suburban self, used to the privacy of my own room and a house with only four persons in it and no near neighbors. But the pleasures—the fun of events like Holi or a women's song festival, the friendships, however fragile, the attempts on both sides to bridge the cultural chasm separating me from Karimpur's residents—ultimately outweigh the negatives. I do, after all, keep going back.

I can no longer say with surety what led me to India and to Karimpur. Certainly my first trip on the Wisconsin College-Year-in-India program in 1963 was a bit of a lark, although it was also motivated by a desire to see the world and to understand other peoples' lives. There was something of the social activist lurking behind that trip as well: my research project that year focused on the effects of girls' education in a village near Delhi. But I never pursued my activist leanings, instead entering graduate school in anthropology with the intention of returning to India for further study. I still feel strongly the tension between scholarship and activism, but, while pulled toward the latter, I have always chosen the former.

Not long ago, I finished teaching an introductory course on anthropological theory to first-year graduate students here at Syracuse University. We concluded with Margery Wolf's *The Thrice-Told Tale: Feminism, Postmodernism, and Ethnographic Responsibility* (1992). It was an apt ending to this particular semester, for I have never taught a class in which students were so personal in their engagement with the materials of anthropology. As I reflect on their discussions and papers and on my training in graduate school almost thirty years ago, I can only marvel at the differences. Since I first began to work in Karimpur, anthropology has moved from a distant third-person construction to a first-person "I"; from an all-inclusive "the villagers" or "they" to a disaggregated "the women" or "the rich women" or even to individual names; from a lack of historical sense and the dominance of an ahistorical "tradition" to a recognition of multiple histories and spurious traditions; from a strong censure of activist involvement to the current concern with anthropological praxis.[4]

It has always been difficult to know what the relationship between the anthropologist and those studied is or should be. I remember being uncomfortable with the legacy of giving medical help that I inherited from the Wisers, along with Bashir and Bajreng's family. In 1984 that legacy was often a real burden, because I could and did spend hours a day providing quinine pills or putting ointments on cuts or getting bloated babies to a doctor. Several years ago I spent a week in Karimpur and had allocated one day to updating the census of the Cultivator section of the village. The day started when I was called to photograph a Brahman woman who had unexpectedly passed away the evening before. Later my friend and assistant, Umesh Pandey, and I were asked to help a woman in the final stages of tuberculosis: she had not eaten in a week. An hour later we were in a house where both father, about fifty years old, and son, aged twenty-five or so, were also ill with TB. The father asked me to please help them, as they had spent thousands of rupees and still were sick. "But more important," he said, "help my son. I am old, so it is not so bad if I die. But my son is still young." Tearfully, I had to say that I couldn't do anything, that I was leaving the next day. Later I turned to Umesh and said that only a king's treasury could do what needed to be done in Karimpur. And that might not even be enough, even if I did believe in the value of a wholesale infusion of outsider medicines, clothes, fuel, and so on.

I tell this story because my connections with Karimpur and its residents are complex and multifaceted and have been made more so by twenty-five years of world and local history since I first went there. When I hear discussions of anthropology as a form of colonial power, and of the power of the anthropologist, and I remember the young woman that I was—dressed wrongly and hardly able to make myself understood, often ill and yet determined to make some sense out of the rules that must be lurking there, if only I could understand—I don't think of power. I certainly didn't feel powerful. Even when I returned to Karimpur with the status of a full-fledged faculty member, India always seemed to remain the ruler: I never felt I was in a position to alter peoples' lives in any significant way. But another legacy from the Wisers and the British colonial rulers was the dominance of the white man. I could seldom meet the expectations that would suddenly arise among people who remembered the Wisers, their car, and their instant entrée with British officials. Further, aside from helping people who were ill, which I have tried to do, allowing children to stay in school by providing books or tuition, which I have done numerous times, providing hard cash for some endeavor, which I have almost never done, or getting men jobs, which I was asked to but couldn't do, I wasn't permitted to interfere in people's lives, then or now. I couldn't participate in the real work of living: arranging marriages, negotiating honor with one's male kin, finding a sharecropper (or a landlord). As the impure foreigner, I couldn't even help in the house by cooking or washing dishes!

In the pages that follow, I have attempted to make central the stories that Karimpur villagers tell about their lives and their world. These stories take a variety of forms, ranging from personal narratives to folktale and folk song. Some of the stories are folktales and myths in the standard senses implied by those terms. Sometimes they were told to explain concepts and terms I didn't understand. Some were told because I was interested in any tales or myths and would gladly tape whatever was volunteered. Others were told as part of ritual celebrations or to entertain friends. The storytellers assumed my familiarity with local nuance and allusion, despite my obvious ignorance at times. Many of these stories were in fact not told to me, despite my presence and my tape recorder, but to friends gathered around to share in an event. While some of the storytelling events were instigated by me, most of the songs presented here were performed spontaneously in culturally situated events.

Although I have spent literally months sitting and talking to people, most of the material quoted in this book is the result of tape-recorded interviews conducted during 1983–84. These interviews took place in courtyards, in the fields as we watched water flow from tube wells, while perched in trees to scare birds away, in a spot of shade to escape the brutal sun of summer, squatting on verandahs, or sitting in our rooms in Mainpuri. Everyone knew that they were being taped—"so that we can tell people in America how you live and how the village has changed," as I or Bruce would explain. I did most of the women's interviews, occasionally using an interpreter (who would translate either into standard Hindi or into English), and my capable research assistant, Monisha Behal, did a survey of women's attitudes on a variety of topics, as well as some life history interviews. I also occasionally interviewed close male friends. Bruce worked only with men, with the help of two assistants, both from the village. One, Umesh Pandey, is a Brahman; the other, Nanhe Khan, is Muslim. Nanhe, whose *jāti* ranked far down in the Karimpur hierarchy, helped interview poor and lower-status individuals, while Umesh worked with educated and higher-ranked men.[5] People knew of my long involvement in Karimpur and my "passable" Hindi (I can swear but not argue well in it) and spoke to me primarily as a well-informed outsider, who still didn't know *their* story. Bruce's Hindi was less fluent, and many men's responses were accordingly directed in large part at his assistants, who were insiders. Thus, these narratives and explanations are aimed at either an insider or an informed outsider who certainly knew the grosser patterns of Karimpur life, if not the more minute details.[6] As such, I believe that they capture the spirit and flavor of Karimpur life and Karimpur discourse.

The original intention to collect systematic life histories proved to be a largely unfeasible goal in a society where lives are not constructed around linear time, birthdays, and a constant concern with the definition of individual self. But Karimpur residents could and did tell us a lot about themselves and their lives once we let them structure the narrative. Much of what I relate in the following pages focuses, then, on what my friends believed to be important. I have learned to listen to them.[7] In Karimpur, *jāti* relationships are history, as are illnesses, debts, disputes about honor, marriages (those of others—rarely one's own), and household unity and separation. The events of childhood (except in talk among schoolboys), jobs, work, and agriculture are not history. Agriculture and work are discussed regularly, but not as "story" or "gossip" or incident. Childhood is dismissed by the phrases "from when I began to understand" or "when I became knowledgeable," usually implying an age greater than ten. Sexuality was joked about by women but was never mentioned among men, unless they were extremely intimate friends. Sexuality was never something to tell stories about except when it involved someone's public dishonor or affected intercaste relationships—at which point it became vitally important.[8]

There is one additional consideration. When we as participants present accounts of why we do what we do, our accounts may distort our motives, based as they are on our personal, limited knowledge and our political stance. For example, Mohan, the Brahman landlord who serves as one of the guides to Karimpur life, states very clearly that the Brahmans have always kept their servant *jātis* happy and fed. While he may believe this, I, and the serving *jātis*, know it is untrue. Hence it is also important for the reader to be aware of the political and cultural stance of the teller and the implications of that stance for the interpretation of the story or event. I attempt to contextualize the statements of my Karimpur friends, although these are my understandings alone. Stories told to members of the same culture carry different meanings for teller and hearer, depending upon each individual's personal history; those told across cultures, as in this book, present even greater problems of interpretation.[9] My interpretations of the narratives presented here have been formed in a time and place vastly different from the circumstances under which the narratives were originally told. As such, these translations and interpretations are mine alone and are only one possible reading of what was told me.

I recognize that I bear the responsibility of speaking for this community and its inhabitants, as the Wisers did before me, in a way that no one there is yet able to do. Moreover, the twenty-five years of history—my history vis-à-vis the village as well as the history of anthropology and the world—have fomented moral and ethical dilemmas of an unusual sort. Although anthropologists have written about long-term field research, none have discussed the ethical dilemmas of sustained contact with a community. New ways of writing ethnography complicate that ethical dilemma.

Umesh Pandey, one of Bajreng's grandsons and my "nephew," has been teaching a course on Karimpur at Trinity College in Connecticut for the past two years. Recently, he wrote a letter published in the American Anthropological Association Newsletter (May 1992) accusing the four people who have written about Karimpur (William and Charlotte Wiser, Bruce Derr, and myself), but primarily me, of trading money for information and of destroying the honor of his family for generations to come because of what we have written. Umesh's letter highlights that unexamined ethical dilemma. What is our relationship to people with whom we have lived, with whom we have shared tears and laughter, and whom we have come to regard as a second family, yet continue to write about? Does the fact that the people about whom we wrote now teach those writings change what we do? And what of the Queen Sahab who comes and goes, apparently by whim, involving herself in their lives for a while and then disappearing, only to reappear at some unknown future time? Also involved are cultural questions—of the meaning of family in the United States and India, of what binds people together, of the long-term solidarity that marks relationships in peasant society versus the short-term relationships so common in industrialized society. Ultimately we must ask whether it is possible to do truly ethical research. Or do our friendships mask our exploitation and betrayal of our "friends"?[10]

The current debate about the right of anthropologists to write about others is part of this puzzle.[11] But it is that long-term sustained contact that makes more problematic my writing about Karimpur and my friends there. As anthropologists and other social scientists attempt to create new forms of ethnographic writing, ones that capture more clearly the cacophony of the voices of those whom we study, it becomes harder and harder to preserve the anonymity of the friends who aid us by telling of their lives. Following the Wisers' practice of using pseudonyms, I have retained the names they used and have also added many. But I question my own use of pseudonyms, since they are intended primarily to protect community residents from one another—and yet these are the very people who can most easily read through them. So I realize that my friends in Karimpur will often recognize themselves and probably their neighbors. Moreover, while the interpretations of life and history are those of individuals, the events discussed are public knowledge. But in any community marked by power differences, by gender and caste, by owning land or not, the "events" are always interpreted and related in multiple ways. My aim in this book is to point to those multiple readings of Karimpur's recent history. But by doing so, I am bringing into public view—a view that now includes members of the Karimpur community—the everyday voices of politics and interpretation. There is a difference, for example, between simply being powerful, even if those whom you control complain and gossip, and having that power challenged through the emergence of the gossip in print. Recognizing the potential betrayals on my part, I have nevertheless chosen to examine the multiple interpretations of events in Karimpur. Whether my goal of demonstrating power relationships and the various interpretations (including resistance) of them in an effort to present the subaltern and female voices justifies a possible betrayal is a judgment that others must also make. I have tried to spare my friends in Karimpur any pain from the writing of this book. I have probably not fully succeeded. So I apologize in advance if I have failed.

◆

Numerous organizations contributed to the research and writing that have resulted in this book. My first research in Karimpur was supported by the National Science Foundation (Doctoral Dissertation Research Improvement Grant) and the University of Chicago. A Faculty Research Grant from the U.S. Department of Education and a Smithsonian Fellowship supported the 1983–84 trip. Other funding for research in India, in 1974–75 and again in 1989, came from the American Institute of Indian Studies. A generous grant from the Joint Committee on South Asia of the Social Science Research Council and the American Council of Learned Societies gave me a semester off, a semester spent reading and reconceptualizing what had gone before. It was an invaluable aid to the completion of this work.

In addition, many people assisted in the production of this book. None are more important than the many residents of Karimpur, who shared their lives with myself and my family over the years since 1967 and with the Wisers before me. Their graciousness and openness in letting us probe into their lives cannot be reciprocated. To name everyone would require a list of the three-hundred-plus households of the village. But special thanks are owed to Bashir Khan, for caring for me and my family for several years; to Jageshwar Dube, my first guide in Karimpur; to Raghubar, my dear friend and favorite storyteller; to Jagdish's wife; to Caci, wife of Paras Ram; to Maden Sen and his brothers; to the women of Asha Ram's house; and to Parsadi and his wife. Most of all, I acknowledge the many members of my Karimpur family in the house of Bajreng Prasad Pandey, who have shared their home and friendship with me for the past twenty-five years. Umesh and his sister Rajani aided over the years in various research tasks and in transcribing endless tapes. Umesh's caring and warm hospitality have made the recent field trips a pleasure. Other research assistants from the village included Ant Ram Batham, Nanhe Khan, and the daughters of Daya Shankar, Paras Ram, and Masterin. Monisha Behal joined me from Delhi in 1984 for three months and provided valuable aid and insight. My partner at the time, Bruce Derr, participated in the 1983–84 fieldwork and in the initial analysis of these data. The results of his research in Karimpur in 1974–75 have also been immensely useful in comprehending change in this community, and I appreciate his allowing me to use all of these materials.

My other major debt is to Charlotte Wiser and her family. Charlotte opened her village house to me in 1967, shared her knowledge of the village, and made my initial trip manageable in a variety of critical ways. Right up until her death, she supported my work, read what I wrote, and gave encouragement. Since then her family, especially her son Edward, has continued to encourage my attempts to further understand Karimpur. I appreciate this concern.

Portions of this manuscript were read by Umesh Pandey, L. A. Babb, Michael Freedman, Michael Moffat, McKim Marriott, Ann Gold, Gloria Goodwin Raheja, Sylvia Vatuk, Ron Herring, Judy Pugh, Roger and Patricia Jeffery, Priti Ramamurthy, several anonymous readers for the University of California Press, and students at Cornell, Syracuse, and the University of Minnesota. Pamela MacFarland Holway edited my final draft with great care and insight: her vision and clarity have contributed immensely to the end result.

My daughters Shona and Laura made the 1983–84 trip a joy, as they absorbed the India that I had worked so hard to learn. Their cow-dung cakes made from play dough, their enactments of rituals, and their gaiety and cheerfulness were a constant source of delight. That they share my love for Karimpur gladdens my heart. In the past years, they have impatiently put up with my writing of "the book." More recently, Rick Olanoff has provided the support necessary for the final stages of this project and will be immensely relieved that it is finally off my desk! I thank him and all my family profusely. Finally, I owe an enormous debt to the compassion, expertise, and strength of Hal and Bill, who aided me in the personal quest that eventually made this book happen.

"Tell Them to Listen with Their Ears Open"

The Story of Knowledge and Evil Knowledge

There was a king named Raja Vaidh. He had two daughters. They were named by the god Brahma. Each girl received two names. One was named Vidya (Knowledge) and the other was named Kuvidya (Evil Knowledge). The first was also called Lakshmi (Prosperity) and the other Kulakshani (Misfortuned).[1] When the older matured, a boy was sought for her. When the great astrologers and priests were asked, they said, "Your daughter will marry the god Lord Vishnu."

So the king went to Vishnu and said, "O Lord, my daughter is of marriageable age, so you must marry her."

But Vishnu said, "Look elsewhere for a boy."

"Oh no," said the king. "No, she must marry only you." Vishnu then replied that he knew that and finally agreed to marry the girl. So the engagement [*tīkā*] ceremony was held and the king returned home.

When the king's wife heard that Vishnu was the son-in-law, she worried. When should the younger one marry? She had to marry someone of the same status as Vishnu. So the queen suggested to the king that he ask Vishnu to marry the younger one also.

The king went and spoke to Vishnu about marrying the younger one also. Vishnu cried, "Oh my god! I cannot even support one. What have I gotten into?" But the king caught hold of Vishnu's feet and didn't let go. Ultimately, Vishnu agreed to marry the younger girl, too. So he married the two sisters. But before that he asked about their names. The king replied that one was Lakshmi and the other was Kuvidya or Kulakshani. On hearing this, Vishnu said that he couldn't possibly marry Kulakshani. But the king explained that she wasn't like that. So Vishnu agreed to marry both the girls.

Lord Vishnu went in a marriage procession to King Vaidh's kingdom. Both girls were brought in one palanquin. When they reached Vishnu's kingdom, he said that if they stayed together they would surely fight. So he told them that he would have two palaces made for them. Vishnu asked Lakshmi what she wanted and where she would like to live. Lakshmi replied that she wanted to stay in a beautiful house. There should be a *tulsī* [basil] plant in it [to worship daily]. She said that the women of the house should rise at 4 A.M., bathe, and then do *pūjā* [worship]. There should be no involvement with money transactions like loans or interest in the house, and of course no alcohol. Fish and meat were to be banned.

Then Kulakshani was asked what she wanted and she said that women should wake at 9 A.M. and there should be no place of worship and no *tulsī* plant. The women could go around with their hair undone. There should be transactions like loans, rent, and interest allowed in the house. Alcohol, fish, and meat should be freely available. If all of these things were not done, she said, she wouldn't be able to live.

Lord Vishnu gave them their wishes. Then Lakshmi asked Vishnu where he would stay, and he replied that he would stay with her because when women are good, the house will always prosper. If the house is kept dirty, not enough bread is found there, only misfortune. Now, you [the anthropologist] have seen America and India. And you have to know that if women don't bathe and cleanse themselves, if they don't make their hair into braids, they will be like Kulakshani. First, you must fix your hair and worship. You will live happily. So this is the story of Vishnu and Lakshmi. Go and tell the women of America about this story and tell them to listen with their ears open.

This story was told to me in December 1983 by Saroj, a Brahman widow from the village of Karimpur. Saroj, like many Karimpur residents, loves to tell stories about herself, about others, and about the gods and goddesses who share her world. In these stories, Karimpur's residents tell about what it is they do and why it is important. These texts reflect, and sometimes contradict, prevailing ideals, while the discourses of which they form a part support everyday practice.[2] Saroj's story, for example, supports discourses on women's cleanliness, eating habits, religious practices, and financial activities. The story builds upon Hindu conceptions of order and disorder; of coherent action and chaotic action; of *dharma*, doing one's prescribed duty, and *adharma*, going against the proper order of things; of control, subjugation, and oppression; and ultimately of *karma*, one's destiny, which, through one's actions, is constantly being made.[3] It is these basic conceptions of the ways in which the world works, though, that Saroj and others from Karimpur find most threatened in the latter part of the twentieth century.

INCREASING DISORDER

This book describes how Karimpur villagers perceive their world to have changed over time, from the 1920s—when those now elderly were young and India was under British colonial rule—to 1984, almost four decades after independence from Britain. Changes in agriculture, labor relations, political structures, education, and family and gender relations have made the traditional cultural blueprints, based on the authority of those with knowledge and might, unworkable. Only the authority of the gods and goddesses remains, fostering, with the aid of greater prosperity, an outpouring of religious fervor in what Karimpur villagers see as an increasingly chaotic, uncaring world.

Authority in Hindu India is culturally constructed using a model of innate (although, as indicated below, always mutable) qualities in which superiors use reason and might to provide order and protection for those beneath them. This basic paradigm is manifested in the Purusha hymn, in which Brahmans (priests) emerge from the head of the primordial cosmic man, the Kshatriyas (kings, warriors) from his arms, the Vaishyas (merchants, traders) from his thighs, and the Shudras (workers) from his feet. The paradigm is again manifested in the underlying model for the worship of deities: here the worshiper trades service to the deity and faith in his or her powers for the boons and mercy of that deity, which thereby bring order to the worshiper's life. It is seen, too, in rituals to remove inauspiciousness, where troubles are transferred from an afflicted person to someone (usually of lower status) able to "digest" the inauspiciousness or to live with the disorder created by it. We find the paradigm again in the organization of Hindu kingdoms, where high-ranking kings have the most rigidly defined codes of conduct and those lower have relatively loosely defined codes and less autonomy, less power to define order. This paradigm also underlies conceptions of both male and female: males are thought by their very nature to be self-controlled and thus "ordered," whereas the energy-filled female is often thought to lack self-control and hence to be disordered. It also provides a basis for Hindu concepts of the ideal family, which rest on the authority of the male head.[4]

These variations on the basic paradigm of power (whether mental, material, or physical) used by superiors to maintain order for inferiors are all known in Karimpur, although the three most salient ones are those relating to constructions of gender, the family, and the worship of deities. As Karimpur underwent the massive social changes of the 1970s and

1980s, it was the paradigm of the family, which underlies *jajmānī* (traditional patron-client) relationships and hence the village order itself, that was most severely threatened. As the dominant groups of Karimpur saw themselves losing political and economic control of the village and as the poor saw their ties to the old *jajmānī* order eroding, both sought to maintain firm control of their households, a task made difficult by advances in women's education and new definitions of kinship roles emanating from India's urban middle class via cinema and television. It is these manifold visions of disorder that are described in the pages to follow. This increasing disorder, rooted in changing conceptions of authority, threatens the very nature of Karimpur society.

The literature dealing with hierarchy in India focuses almost exclusively on caste, ignoring the social hierarchy of gender and largely denying a material, nonritual basis to the caste hierarchy.[5] In contrast, the literature on gender downplays class and caste differences while highlighting the universal subordination of women in a notably patriarchal society.[6] In fact, gender and class are interconnected systems of hierarchy, with poor women being doubly subordinated.[7] The politics of gender concern the power relationships that exist between the two sexes, whereas the politics of class are concerned with power relationships between rich and poor, landed and landless, high and low caste. Both systems, however, provide power to superiors while demanding obedience from inferiors. Both are also reciprocal: in return for obedience the inferior receives care and protection, benefiting from the order created by the superior. Furthermore, class itself is fundamentally gendered, and the maintenance of social classes is built upon distinctive household roles for lower- and upper-caste women and men.[8] Finally, gender and class politics are interconnected in their responses to change. Hence, one goal of this book is to examine the politics of gender and of class in a time of rapid social change in North India.

Both systems of hierarchy are based on the denial of access to economic resources and political power to those defined as lower. But aside from an analytic demand for a dual emphasis on caste/class and gender and their interconnections, there is also a critical cultural unity to consider, for Karimpur's residents frame their interpretations of the subordination of both low and female in the same terms: both lack understanding and knowledge, and thus, by their very nature, both should be controlled by their superiors. Any one individual participates in both systems, moreover, so that concepts of hierarchy and authority are transferred between the two. I see neither gender nor class/caste systems as causal. Rather, they act simultaneously and in concert to produce the structures of a particular social order.

The challenge to the class order is much more direct than the challenge to the gender order. Strikes by the villager workers against the landlords, demands by the poor for recognition in a variety of everyday ways, and conflicts at the annual village Holi festival all mark the refusal of the low to accept the existing hierarchy of class/caste. The low are particularly articulate in citing the "all are equal" slogans of democracy and in their ensuing demands for that equality.

Within the family, sons are challenging parental authority, whereas women's demands for equality are muted. Women are neither asking to govern nor declaring the family an irrelevant institution. But as disorder increases, gender control becomes the focus of greater attention. Control of women becomes the symbolic focus of male control and control in the community. Yet this inward turning to control within the family is itself challenged by women's education and demands to ease purdah restrictions.

The challenge to older patterns of authority takes many forms, including the ideology of democracy, education for women and the poor, and economic changes such as the green revolution and new labor relations. Men and women, rich and poor in Karimpur have shared cultural assumptions for generations, although interpretations of these shared assumptions often differed significantly. Now, new assumptions are casting doubt on the old orders of class/caste and of gender, calling into question whether the poor and the female really do lack "understanding." This book is about these challenges, about the intersections between old and new, rich and poor, male and female.

MAKING THEIR OWN DESTINY

It is through narratives, songs, and personal histories that we learn of the world of Karimpur's residents, and of their everyday life. In writing this book, I have used whenever possible the words, the stories, and the comments of my friends in Karimpur to illuminate their world. For example, caste (*jāti*) is indeed relevant in Karimpur, a village dominated by one *jāti* group, the Brahmans. Rather than define "caste"—originally a Portuguese word that now comes wrapped in English connotations—in standard anthropological terms, however, I focus on *jāti* as a category that defines actions and activities in Karimpur.[9] The words I use to discuss and describe it are those of the people of Karimpur themselves—for *jāti* is one of the many shared understandings of Karimpur social life that are critical to comprehending Karimpur residents' discourses about their lives.

By making the voices of Karimpur residents central, I am not creating an ethnographic monograph in the classic style. Instead, my aim is to understand how culture as a system of meaningful symbols becomes articulated as people make sense of their lives. In the light of performance studies in folklore and ritual, I contend that cultural symbols are made truly meaningful to the participant in a given society through performances: that, rather than merely existing as part of some abstract cognitive scheme, meanings are most effective when they arise in the context of social events.[10] One way in which cultural symbols are brought into social space, given social and emotional as well as cognitive meaning, is through the stories we tell of ourselves and our neighbors—as we create and recreate our own histories.

I am establishing an intentional interplay between two key areas of data. The first is songs and stories—of gods and goddesses, of kings, of village barbers and rich men—and discourses on religion, politics, the family (and many other topics) that present key cultural symbols in a rather impersonal way. The second is the deeply personal stories told by my friends in Karimpur about real incidents in their own lives. In approaching the more general materials, I am purposely analytical, searching out and explicating the categories and concepts used in creating the world of the Karimpur villager, conscious nevertheless of the disparate views of male and female, rich and poor. In life stories, individuals use the same key cultural symbols to make sense of their personal histories. Here culture is given social as well as cognitive shape. People become actors, not merely fixtures in a social and cultural landscape.

To understand what culture is we must look closely at how people apply, create, modify, manipulate, sanction, and renounce it. Personal narratives allow us to see the ways in which culture as a set of performative blueprints is translated into action. Here the paradigms defined by culture, by cosmologies and classificatory systems, by myth, legend, and traditional narrative, are lived and recreated as meaningful to individual persons seeking to understand their own life paths. These personal narratives have the advantage, too, of being richly textured and contextualized; as concrete examples of human beings struggling with their own cultural blueprints, they allow the reader his or her own interpretations while being denser and more complex than the blueprints they allude to. These personal narratives, richly patterned and open to multiple interpretations, are presented between the analytical chapters.

Fundamental to both the cultural blueprints and interpretations of individual actions in Karimpur is the notion of *karma*. Originally this book was titled *Victims of Destiny*—until an Indian friend pointed out the stagnant, fatalistic quality of that designation, at which point I realized that I had once again fallen into the Western interpretation of *karma* as fixed and determinate. The Western interpretation is rooted in both the English language, where "to be" is the dominant verb, and in our notions of the self as fixed in one's core, hidden inside and waiting only to be unpacked, but set genetically for all time.[11]

The Hindu view of *karma* is based instead on the idea that individuals are in constant flux, as each action creates them anew. And they are constantly acting to change what they are—to eat the right foods, to rub themselves with the correct oils, to perform a ritual or go on a pilgrimage to achieve a transformation of their self or their life situation. *Karnā*, "to do, to make," is arguably the key verb in the Hindu worldview, and both *karnā* and *karma* derive from the same root, *kar*. The Hindu body is an open vessel, defined by Hindus by what it contains at any given moment rather than by some deep-seated genetic core. Hence, whereas the American would say, "I am weak," the Hindu comments, "Weakness is in my body" (*kamzorī śarīr men hai*), not attributing it to a personal and thus perhaps long-lasting quality, but acknowledging it as something from outside that happens to be there, however temporarily. And where we state, "I am a laborer," the Karimpur resident says, "I do laboring" (*main mazdūrī kartā hūn*), the Hindi emphasizing the action rather than the state of being. Numerous examples abound, as in "I am hungry" versus the Hindi "Hunger is attached to me" (*mujhe bhūkh lagtī hai*), or "I speak English" versus "English comes to me" (*mujhe angrezī ātī hai*).[12] Thus my title captures, I hope, the duality of living in a world of *karma*, of actions that determine one's destiny, while never accepting that destiny as fully determinate. One Washerwoman summed up the duality of both having destiny and creating it. At one point she said, rather resignedly, "Poverty is in my destiny [*karam*]." And yet she also fought a court case to legally leave a marriage with a rather well-off man in order to marry a destitute laborer, saying "That marriage was not in my destiny [*karam*]"—despite her active role in ridding herself of it.

Karimpur villagers are not merely commenting upon history but are also fundamentally its creators. The system within which Karimpur's several thousand inhabitants operate often seems to present few options and to appear highly deterministic. Yet as Karimpur residents live their lives, like people everywhere they create them, responding to and sometimes rebelling against the structures in which they are embedded.[13] Some are pleased with the transformations that have occurred in their lives; others desperately wish for the old ways. Because, moreover, history is a type of knowledge that is based on individual interpretations, the "facts" of history derive their importance from how they are interpreted. The facts of Karimpur history are seen differently by men and women, rich and poor, high and low, young and old. "History" is too often the result of reducing these multifarious voices and interpretations to their most common denominator and is almost always the story of dominant males. My aim, instead, is to keep these disparate voices separate so that the several interpretations of recent Karimpur history current in the village can be heard and appreciated.[14]

I focus on four men and women: Raghunath, a poor male sharecropper; Santoshi, a poverty-stricken woman whose husband is the village herdsman; Saroj, the widow of a landowner; and Mohan, a rich Brahman male. Their stories not only provide a narrative thread that runs throughout the book but also capture the voices of rich and poor, male and female. These four individuals represent the four primary views of history that I aim to present. Further, by explicating the lives and circumstances of particular individuals, I can clarify the political and cultural stance of each and the resultant implications of that stance for his or her interpretation of a given story or event.

KARIMPUR AND ITS ENVIRONS, 1925–1984

Karimpur is located in the Hindi-speaking North Indian state of Uttar Pradesh. The largest of India's states, Uttar Pradesh had a population of about 115 million in 1981. Straddling the Gangetic-Jamuna *doāb* and stretching to the foothills of the Himalayas, Uttar Pradesh, with its fertile river basins, has been at the center of North Indian kingdoms for several thousand years. The state also has both the highest infant mortality rate in India and the lowest female life expectancy. While not the poorest of India's states, Uttar Pradesh lacks much basic infrastructure (electricity, clean water, adequate health care), although the western portion of the state, where Karimpur is located, is better off than the eastern portion.

Karimpur is in Mainpuri District, about 80 miles east of Agra and 150 miles southeast of Delhi (see map 1). It is most easily reached by a bus from Delhi down the Grand Trunk Road, a nine-hour trip. Mainpuri has the lowest level of urbanization (11.2 percent) of any district in western

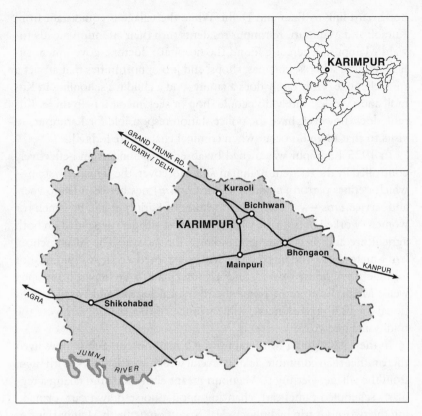

Map 1.   The location of Karimpur in Mainpuri District and India

Uttar Pradesh, although its urban growth rate from 1971 to 1981 was above average for the state.[15] This district also had one of the lowest population growth rates in the same period, no doubt owing to excess migration. Although best known for its dacoits, Mainpuri District exports rice, wheat, and mustard oil.[16] The only notable industries are a few glass factories in the town of Shikohabad, between Agra and the city of Mainpuri. District headquarters since 1801, Mainpuri city was a small service town until recently.[17] Its population was 19,000 in 1901, a figure that did not rise above 23,000 until 1961, when it reached 33,610 inhabitants. By 1981 the city had more than 58,000 residents.

Karimpur lies thirteen kilometers to the north of Mainpuri and fourteen kilometers to the south of Kuraoli, a small service town on the Grand Trunk Road of some 11,000 people in 1981. The road linking Mainpuri and Kuraoli through Karimpur was paved prior to 1910 and is the direct northward link to Etah and Delhi. While the village is equidistant from Kuraoli and Mainpuri, Karimpur residents turn their attention mostly toward Mainpuri. There are found the hospitals, doctors, government offices, courts, schools, cinemas, shops, and job opportunities that attract a rural clientele. Only rarely does a family send a child for schooling in Kuraoli and even less rarely do people shop or seek medical help there. Kuraoli does, however, have the police station responsible for Karimpur, so visits to that town do occur when criminal charges are lodged.

In 1925 Karimpur was owned by absentee zamindars and effectively controlled by the resident Brahman *jāti*. Moreover, the *jajmānī* system—which defines patron (*jajmān*)–client (*kamīn*) ties between landowners and service *jātis*—was a significant feature of Karimpur life. Few men (or women) worked outside the village, and most villagers depended on both agriculture and their Brahman landlords for survival. The village school had a mere thirty students, no one had ever earned a college diploma, not a single brick house existed, and all water had to be drawn from open wells. Medical care came primarily from local *hakīm*s and *vaidy*s (traditional medical practitioners), while women of the *dhānuk jāti* were the traditional midwives.

In the 1920s going to Mainpuri was a major event. Schoolboys lived there rather than commute, taking several weeks' worth of food with them from the village. Getting to Mainpuri meant either walking, taking a regularly scheduled camel cart, chancing upon a horse-drawn cart, or making the two-hour trip by bullock cart. Now, contact with Mainpuri is frequent, and many families have at least one male who visits the town every day. By the mid 1970s bus service from Kuraoli to Mainpuri was regular and reliable, with private buses picking up the passengers unable to fit into state-owned transport. Horse-drawn carts are now regularly found at the Karimpur bus stop, two owned by residents of the village itself. Some cycle rickshaws also go the distance, primarily in the morning or evening. The majority of households have at least one bicycle, used by schoolboys or their brothers and fathers. Only the poor regularly walk to town.

Mainpuri is the market town for this district of almost two million people. Higher crop yields, resulting from the green revolution, demand a wholesale market for the surplus, and larger incomes are expended on greater quantities of consumer goods. Hence, the quantity of goods moving through the district markets from the fields and into the hands of rural consumers through commerce has grown immensely. It is this commercial throughput that is now providing jobs to Karimpur men. They are not industrial jobs but rather those of carrying and storing vast quantities of goods, including the grains funneled into the grain market and the potatoes stored in cold storage plants. With the development of a market for labor and a transportation system that makes Mainpuri a viable work locale, Karimpur men are rapidly shifting from agricultural labor to day labor in the marketplace.

This contact with Mainpuri is male-dominated. Work for women is all but nonexistent in the marketplace of this North Indian town, and rarely do Karimpur women shop there. Karimpur women mostly visit Mainpuri while passing through on trips to their natal or affinal homes or to take a sick child to a doctor. Many women, especially the poor, claimed to go no more than once or twice a year. Certainly they did not go for recreation, as the majority of Karimpur women have never seen a film. Their primary recreation is a visit to the district fair held on the northern fringe of Mainpuri every April.

One approaches the village by road from Mainpuri or Kuraoli. The first visible sign of Karimpur, as one rides down the narrow one-lane country road past fields of wheat, corn, millet, and vegetables, is the high hill with its white shrine that marks the *kheṛā*, a ruined fort to the west of the village settlements. According to the British, Karimpur was once the site of a large town of thousands of people and an active bazaar. After its destruction during the Mughal period, Mainpuri became the preeminent center in the area. Some 250 years ago the father of Karimpur's dominant Brahman lineage received rights to the village from the legendary Muslim leader Khan Bahadur, whose shrine is found atop the *kheṛā*. To this day, Khan Bahadur remains the protector of the village, and women, both Hindu and Muslim, worship him every Thursday when a crisis hits them, their family, or their village.

Approaching the village, cars and buses must slow down on curves at the settlement area. A large banyan tree near one lane into the village became the bus stop, and small tea and bicycle repair shops have opened there, as well as a mill for grinding grain. Nowadays tongas are often found waiting for passengers. A few houses and the boy's primary school surround the bus stop. Nearby is a large settlement of Cultivators who moved out of the main village settlement to alleviate housing congestion there. Further down the road is a small settlement of Leatherworkers (see map 2).

Several dirt cart tracks lead across fields from the road into the main settlement area. Even today, the windowless mud and brick exteriors of the village houses appear unwelcoming to the visitor, as the village remains literally "behind mud walls." The adobe houses are built close to-

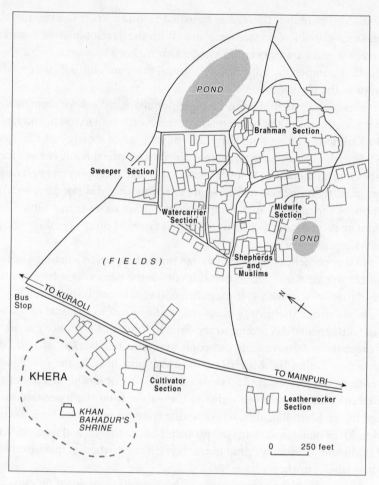

Map 2.   The village of Karimpur in about 1984

gether, frequently sharing a common wall—a feature appreciated by the women, who often visit by going over walls and roofs, and hence can avoid the public lanes. A few major lanes wander through the village, with minor paths leading the unsuspecting visitor into a maze of houses and cattle yards.

The homes of rich and poor follow the same basic design, although those of the rich are considerably larger and now often made of brick. A typical house has a verandah on the lane or path running in front, with a room, usually used by the men, opening off it. Passing through this room, you enter the courtyard, the realm of the women. In one corner is the *cūlhā*, the cooking hearth. These days a hand pump is often found in another corner. One or more rooms open off the courtyard, depending on the family's wealth. These inner rooms are for storage and sleeping during the rains or cold weather. Family goods seem to be stored at random, with no "private" space allocated to any individual. Both men and women keep their belongings locked in tin trunks: seldom does any person need more than one.

While the courtyards tell about the lives of the women, the lanes give insight into the occupations of the men. A large pit in the center of the village is the kiln of the Potter; nearby are the stoves of the Grain Parcher, a favorite village meeting place. Near the pond are the forges of the Carpenters; in front of another house the Tailor sits sewing. On one edge of the village are the presses for sugarcane; down another lane the Sweepers sit weaving wooden baskets. Cows, bullocks, and water buffalo line the village lanes, making it difficult for people to pass; passersby are further hampered by the open drains running down each lane.

In addition to the boy's primary school by the bus stop, a junior school and girls' primary school are found on the opposite side of the village. In 1925 the village school had only first and second grades, and no girls attended. Brahman and Accountant boys and an occasional lower *jāti* boy then attended school in a nearby village for three years, after which they went to Mainpuri, never going past tenth grade. Now after completing eighth grade in the village, the minority of boys and handful of girls who continue in school attend high school and intercollege in Mainpuri, Kuraoli, or another nearby village. Several men have M.A.s, and one young girl is finishing her B.A.

Although a few families in Karimpur live reasonably comfortably, the village as a whole is not well-off. Many families barely meet subsistence needs. Using the village calculation of 0.6 acre as minimal subsistence per person, a family of five receiving all income from land would need three acres for subsistence, and fewer than one quarter of Karimpur families meet that standard. A day laborer earning four hundred rupees per month with a family of four dependents is at the poverty line.[18] In 1984, 44.6 percent of Karimpur households were below the poverty line.

Government programs of several sorts have effected some improvements in Karimpur. Better crops and increased irrigation are important to this general rise in prosperity. By 1984 five houses and the Cooperative Bank and Seed Store had electrical connections. One villager owned a truck, another a tractor, and a third a motorcycle. There were many bicycles and watches, a few radios, two tape recorders, and one gramophone (but no television or video as yet: the first television set arrived in the village in 1988). Still, indebtedness afflicted all but a few large landowners, and the increasingly larger amounts demanded for the dowries of daughters affected all sections of the community proportionally.

Meanwhile, Karimpur's population almost tripled, going from 754 inhabitants living in 161 family units in 1925 to 2,047 inhabitants in 327 families in 1984. Much of this population increase was the result of decreased child mortality, which declined from 458 per thousand in the period from 1932 to 1951 to 250 per thousand in the period from 1972 to 1984. This decline is due largely to better health care, particularly protection against tetanus and the eradication of smallpox prior to 1975. At the same time, fertility was high and increasing: the crude birthrate for 1925–30 was 35.8 per thousand; for 1969–74 it was 41.8 per thousand, increasing to 47.5 per thousand for 1976–83. Further, this population increase was not evenly spread among village social groups, the population of the poor increasing at a rate half again as high as the that of the rich (see table 1).

Along with this population increase has come a shift in the sex ratio, from 866 adult females per thousand males in 1925 to 814 in 1984. The shift in the juvenile sex ratio (under age fifteen) has been even more dramatic, dropping from 900 females per thousand males in 1925 to 790 in 1984. Deaths of female children often come about from those illnesses that are most attributable to neglect, particularly forms of malnutrition, including kwashiorkor and pellagra. More girls than boys also die of fever, diarrhea, and chicken pox (and formerly smallpox), suggesting a lack of medical attention for sick daughters.

In 1925 the village population was composed of twenty-four *jāti* groups: by 1968 the families of one, the Barbers, had moved to a nearby village while another, the Dancing Girl, had died out. By 1984 the Goldsmith families had all moved to Mainpuri, while a local untrained doctor, belonging to a traditional landowning *jāti* (a Thakur) had moved his family into the village. One family belonging to a *jāti* traditionally composed of acrobats had also moved to Karimpur. As we shall see in chapters 5 and 6, there was considerable change in occupational structures over time and a gradual lessening of the connections between traditional occupations and real livelihoods. Further, although their share of the total lands of the village declined, the Brahmans remained the primary landowners and through 1984 were the politically dominant group in the village.

Order and cooperation are key components of the basic paradigm

TABLE 1   POPULATION AND FAMILIES IN KARIMPUR,
GROUPED BY *JĀTI*

Jāti	Total Population			Total Families		
	1925	1968	1984	1925	1968	1984
HIGHEST						
Brahman (priest)	188	332	443	41	43	62
MID TO HIGH						
Bard (*rāy*)	15	14	16	2	2	2
Accountant (*kāyasth*)	6	31	25	1	2	3
Goldsmith (*sūnar*)	11	8		2	2	
Cultivator (*kāchī*)	152	284	415	26	46	59
Rice Cultivator (*lodhī*)	6	17	14	1	3	2
MID						
Carpenter (*barhāī*)	42	57	76	8	8	11
Shepherd (*garariyā*)	26	78	107	6	17	20
Grain Parcher (*bhurjī*)	10	18	29	1	4	4
Watercarrier (*kahār*)	83	191	236	19	35	45
Flower Grower (*mālī*)	17	19	20	1	3	3
Shopkeeper (*banyā*)	14	19	38	3	2	5
Barber (*nāī*)	2			1		
Thakur (landlord)			6			1
LOW						
Potter (*kumhār*)	9	10	10	3	3	3
Washerperson (*dhobī*)	6	15	9	1	3	3
Tailor (*darjī*)	21	15	28	5	3	4
Bangle Seller[a] (*manihār*)	10	12	24	2	3	5
Oil Presser (*telī*)	10	39	55	4	6	11
LOWEST						
Midwife (*dhānuk*)	28	105	167	7	17	30
Cotton Carder[a] (*dhunā*)	9	25	38	1	5	5
Faqir[a] (beggar)	22	46	71	8	12	13
Acrobat (*nat*)			7			1
Dancing Girl (*tawaif*)	3			2		
Leatherworker (*camār*)	29	80	96	8	13	16
Sweeper (*bhangī*)	35	89	118	8	14	19
TOTAL	754	1,504	2,048	161	246	327

[a]*Jāti*s understood and identified in Karimpur as Muslim.

through which Karimpur villagers have interpreted their lives, at least in this century. The value placed on control imposed by superiors was, however, being challenged in numerous ways by the 1980s. To understand these challenges we must first examine the multiple interpretive constructions, as found in narratives, stories, and songs, that are used in Karimpur to articulate ideas of order and control. These constructions all share a common theme: the lack of understanding or knowledge of those in subordinate positions and the consequent right of their superiors to make decisions for them. The first three analytical chapters focus on the assumptions and patterns of Karimpur life from the 1960s and early 1970s, many of which date back to the 1920s. The major challenges mounted against them, and their relationships to wider social processes, are addressed in the final two chapters.

It is within this framework of change that Raghunath, Santoshi, Saroj, and Mohan have been living. Their lives, like those of their neighbors, have been affected in varying ways by the changes in Karimpur since the 1920s, and particularly since the late 1960s, when the pace of change accelerated.

❦

Four Lives

RAGHUNATH, A CULTIVATOR

Dressed in his usual gray-white dhoti and white shirt, Raghunath sat uncomfortably in the unfamiliar chair in our room in Mainpuri. As usual, his pock-marked face was cheery, his betel-stained teeth gleaming in his wide smile. He liked to visit us in our rooms, often showing up in early morning, ready to talk about whatever we wanted. On this September day Bruce asked Raghunath, who was about forty years old, to tell about his life. We had known Raghunath for years, first as a well-known storyteller and singer and later as a friend. We thus knew much of the outline, and some details, of his life story from snippets that one or the other of us had heard over the years. Now it was time to ask him for his own version. On this day near the end of the annual monsoon, he lit a *bīḍī*, clasped his hands around his bony knees as he rocked back in his chair, and said:

> I will tell my life from when I was able to understand. When I was eight, I was a little knowledgeable [literally, had "understanding," *samajhnā*]. At eight poxes erupted all over me. Very bad poxes. After I became ill with smallpox, my mother died. My father and uncle were still there. And also my aunt—the first one. And my grandmother. One day all of these people thought that I had died. For one night I lay in the house. Then I began to breathe. After I began to breathe and after much treatment, I got a little better. Then I had big boils [or ulcers]. When the boils appeared, everyone kept me lying down. When they lifted me, there was pain. They said, "Oh, don't speak of this." Eventually I got better. After a year I was better. Then I was nine. But from then on, I couldn't do much. I didn't have a mother,

17

1. Raghunath, a Cultivator in his early forties

only my aunt. When it was time to eat, she fed me. My arms couldn't reach to my mouth. Then Bhagvan [God] thought a bit and he had my uncle and other people rub my arms with lots of oil. Gradually my arms began to move. Then I could reach my mouth.

By then I was ten or twelve. Then I started thinking about how I should pass my life. What should I do? We are farmers, and there is nothing else. But my father was very smart: he said, "My son will study in school." So I went to school. I went to school for one year. Then I passed a second year. When I was in third grade, my father died: then I had no one. And my aunt, the first one, also died. [Q: How?] She was sick. My grandmother also died. After I became better, then. At home there was no one, just my uncle and me. Then my uncle married again. And he started working. Very slowly our stomachs started to be filled. My aunt had a son and he died. Then she had a second: he died. Then the third also died. Then a fourth was born and died. She had four sons and all died. By then I was fifteen or sixteen. When Chandrabhan [Raghunath's cousin] was born, I took care of him. But no one would marry me because of my arms. When Chandrabhan was one year old, my marriage was arranged. I married a girl with bad eyes—since my arms were also bad. In this way I married. My *bahū* did some work, and I did some.[1] Those people would beat us. My aunt and uncle beat my wife a lot. They said, "She can't work; she isn't able to work." Many worries befell me. There were so many that I thought about taking my life. But I always kept Bhagvan's name. A son was born, but after six months he died. There was a daughter. After a year, she also died. Then I said, "What can I do?"

My aunt began to harass my wife. My wife was with me twelve years. Then, when there were many troubles, she took her own life. She poured kerosene oil on herself. We people were cutting the harvest. After pouring the kerosene, she locked herself inside and burned herself. She sat and sat and sat until she was completely on fire. When we arrived at the house, the door was closed. What was going on? She was still breathing and was not dead. She set herself afire, but her pain became enormous and she began to roll around. Then I asked, "Now, what should I do?" I was really worried because all the villagers said that we would be taken to jail. But I told my soul [*ātmā*] that no one can send me to jail since it was not my fault. It was my aunt's fault. If my wife had told me that there was so much trouble, then we would have separated [from my uncle's household]. But she didn't tell me and just took her life. We took her to Mainpuri. We treated her at the hospital. We borrowed three hundred rupees.[2] I cleaned up her urine and stool every day, but on the eighth day she died. After she died, we had her funeral. My in-laws came and said that they would put my uncle and aunt in jail. But I said, "No. It is written [in her fate]: what was written for her has also affected my fortune [*bhāgy*]. Whatever else is written in my fortune, I will live with that, but don't interfere with them." Then my in-laws said, "Okay. It doesn't matter since she is dead." That work was finished.

My aunt had four sons. The daughter was born after my *bahū*'s death. There were four sons before that. But there was no daughter. When my wife died, Chandrabhan was married. The first time. He was married, but he hadn't had his *gaunā* when my *bahū* died.[3] Then they did the *gaunā*. I lived with them because who else would cook my food? Therefore I thought that whatever troubles there were would be okay; and I decided to stay with them for my life, until I died.

Two years later, Chandrabhan's *bahū* was at her mother's house. She had a fight with her father. She left there and went to a canal where she fell in.

She died. The news came telling what had happened. We all went there immediately. But she had died. Now they had many troubles. My *bahū* killed herself and then this *bahū* killed herself. Bhagvan had punished my aunt.

So we arranged Chandrabhan's second marriage. Perhaps you were here when the *gaunā* took place. It has been about twelve years since he was married. After doing his second marriage, we thought that we should repay all of our loans. First, there is that one, Shankar.[4] I worked for him for two years. I collected cow dung [for compost pits], ploughed his field. I did lots of hard work so that the young children could be fed. Then I came to Mainpuri and I worked in Mainpuri for two years as a coolie. I earned twenty or twenty-five rupees per day. Thus I filled their stomachs and repaid the debt. Because I was owner of half of the land. Those people were four in half the land.[5] And I was alone in half. Therefore I worked hard. Later I quit working in Mainpuri and came home. Then I worked for two years as a laborer for Bhim Sen and repaid his loan. My work filled our stomachs. Then I farmed our own fields. I got two water buffalo and began to farm. Then we got an "engine."[6] But I didn't think about my own marriage because there were these four boys. They would get married and I would pass my life with them. Therefore I didn't plan for my own marriage. But I could get married since I had 1.2 acres of land.[7] But now it is like this—I have arranged their marriages and also that of my small sister.[8] And I worked very hard. But I still have so many sorrows. The Creator [*vidhātā*, a name for God] gave me so much sorrow. There is a fight every day. Someone runs away; someone does something; some keep their earnings in their pocket. So sometimes there is no grain in the house; sometimes there are no vegetables in the evening. Sometimes we get bread, sometimes not. Before there were a few troubles; now there are more. There are many men in our village like this. Dying of sorrow. Only Bhagvan knows the future.

[Q: The 1.2 acres are in your name?] I have 1.2 acres and my uncle has 1.2 acres. [Q: The land is separate now?] The land is together. But there is that matter that I told you about: I got a tube-well engine*.[9] It is worth five thousand rupees. We will lose our lands [to pay off the loan] because of this. This year we won't grow anything so we can't pay anything. But whatever Bhagvan will do, so be it. But if we grew something we could give five thousand rupees. We could give five thousand rupees right away. I say call a panchayat: whatever they say, we will do.[10] Half the land is mine. If you [speaking to Bruce] were to give me five thousand rupees, I'd give you the land on mortgage. I am saying this: I'll have your money, and when you have recovered the loan, then I'll get my land back. In the meantime I'll work as a servant; I'll work for you and fill my stomach. At least the land will be saved: it won't be sold. Because once it is sold, it will stay like that. When I become weak and can't work anymore, then who will feed me? No child, no wife, no one at all. I have many troubles. Now they say, "Sell the land, sell the land." So I live with many troubles. My land will be fragmented and the loan will also be divided. So whatever the amount, I'll give it. So you take our land. If I save a thousand rupees or fifteen hundred rupees or eight hundred each year, you keep it and after two or three or four years the loan will be paid back. In this way, I'll pass my life in a better way. Whatever Bhagvan will do, it will be. Now I rely on him. I say this, "Bhagvan now take me across [give me salvation]." Because there are no children, no wife, no one else.

Bhagvan gave me all these sorrows. Listen, Sahab, the first sorrow is that my mother died when I was very small: I didn't know my mother. A mother is always compassionate. No one else can give the sort of sympathy that a mother gives to her son. Then after my mother, my father died. I didn't know his happiness either. Then my arms and body became bad. The Creator gave me these sorrows. And after that I got my *bahū*. If man becomes weak, then his *bahū* should be able to feed him. Then they can pass their life. And if the woman has any defect, if there is any weakness in her body, then her husband can aid her to pass her life. Marriages should be like this. But my *bahū* is not with me. She has also gone. So the Creator gave me every sorrow. Now what should I do? Now I say that Bhagvan will give me justice.

The boys who were in school with me are now teachers. Some are in the police. And some are in the military. That one Balai, who was in the army, used to study with me. And some are in service or are peons. Then there are those who were Third Division and below me;[11] they didn't know anything and I knew it all. But they are now big men. And I am in the same place. Bhagvan didn't give me prestigious work.

I have four brothers. I worked for them, fed them, brought them up, got them married. Now if one of them realized how much I had done for them, they might look after me. But they don't realize this. They say, "You don't listen to us." When I tell them to get the plough, they say, "You get it. We are going to work as laborers. Nothing comes of ploughing. As laborers, we earn ten or twelve rupees." They keep ten rupees in their pockets and eat there for two rupees. And come home. So I am going to separate [the house and property] very soon. I am going to dump these sorrows that Bhagvan gave me. My aunt fights a lot with her *bahū*s. And with her sons. And with me. One son has already separated. The others will also go, all of them. Then I will have to earn some money. I will earn and feed us. The buffalo is giving milk. About fifteen days ago the buffalo gave birth. I was trying to sell it yesterday so that I can pay our debts. And that male buffalo that pulls the plough, I'll also sell it. And I'll also use that money to repay the loan. If any debt is still left, I'll mortgage a little land. Then I'll think of something. We have to return the money to those from whom we borrowed. It is our life.

I know this much: that Bhagvan knows how it will be. I don't understand this: from birth I haven't known any happiness. I have spent my whole life in sorrow. So now what should I do? Now what should I tell? My life story, it is finished.

Raghunath is a *kāchī*, a *jāti* whose traditional occupation is farming. As do most Cultivators in this village, his family owns a small plot of land and supplements their income with sharecropping and doing labor for

2. Santoshi, the Midwife, with her youngest son

rich landlords. Raghunath was born about 1943, a few years prior to India's Independence. But, as his account shows, the crucial markers in his
life are not world events but points in a continual cycle of sorrows: his illness, which left his arms partially crippled; his father's death, which ended
his schooling and deprived him of any natal family; and his wife's death,
which tied him more firmly to his uncle's family and ended all hope of fa-
therhood. As of 1984, Raghunath was about forty. His small piece of land
has become increasingly important to him as he ages, for without a wife
and offspring he lacks old age security and must hope that his cousins will

give him food and shelter, thereby repaying him for the years during which he fed them.

Raghunath lives in a two-room house of mud bricks and thatch tucked into a small enclave of Cultivators in the center of the village.[12] His close neighbors include Brahmans, Potters, Grain Parchers, and Watercarriers. A few of these families are worse off than his, but most are more prosperous, having more land or more reliable jobs. Sometimes his family has water buffalo—either females for milk or males for ploughing. But animals die easily in North India and are often too expensive for his family to replace.

In 1984 Raghunath's household included his uncle, a prematurely elderly man of fifty-six suffering from asthma and with a limited ability to work; his aunt, about forty-six, a sharp-tongued, strong woman who, aside from her gray hair and toothless grin, appears little worn by her endless childbearing; his three married cousins and their wives and two children; and one unmarried cousin who is studying in grade eleven. His youngest cousin, a girl, had married a year earlier and now, at age thirteen, was usually at her in-laws. In the spring of 1984 the oldest cousin took his family to Ganganagar in Rajasthan, an area needing additional farm labor to work the expanded agricultural lands created by the recent opening of the Indira Gandhi Canal.

Raghunath's belief in the will of Bhagvan is strong, and he is actively involved in village religious affairs. He is a devotee of Basuk Dev, the snake king, who regularly possesses him in a ritual known as *dānk*.[13] Raghunath's skills in becoming possessed by Basuk Dev are known throughout the region, and he is often called to other villages when advice and cures from Basuk Dev are felt appropriate. Raghunath is also a renowned storyteller and singer, and he is an active participant in many men's song fests.

SANTOSHI, THE MIDWIFE

Santoshi and I talked late one afternoon early in 1984 in the shade of the verandah of my house in Karimpur. Since it was the dry season, she had been in the fields most of the day, making dried fuel cakes from the dung of the animals herded by her husband. Usually when she came to visit she was accompanied by the youngest of her four daughters, but today we had planned to talk and she came alone. She wore her usual faded sari, as she had no other to change into. I had only known Santoshi for a few months but admired her spirit and cheerful demeanor in the face of great adversity. She was also very articulate and a good storyteller. Most important, we had become friends. She told her life story on February 27, 1984, at our second formal interview, which followed many casual conversations.

My life? My parents sent me to school to study, so I studied for four or five years. But during my childhood, we lived in poverty, so my studies were stopped. I quit school. Then they arranged my marriage. As soon as I was fourteen years old, they immediately had me married.

After they got me married, they did my *gaunā*. Then they sent me here. There was poverty here. My father-in-law herded animals. They didn't even have enough money for food. Then there is my husband: he is not educated. I am educated. He is not able to get any other work. So, just like his father, he began to herd animals.

Previously, during the period of support [under the *jajmānī* system], we were given some grain and things. But now we have nothing. Now we don't even have a livelihood. They give two rupees for one buffalo [for one month for herding].[14] With two rupees you can buy one kilogram of grain or flour. Now there are more people. Now there is poverty. As there was, so there is now. My life, it is passing in poverty.

Santoshi's rendering of her story in this brief fashion probably reflects both her gender and her poverty. There isn't, for her, much to tell. She has always been poor. But she also clearly resents having had her education curtailed and used to insist on writing things for me to prove her literacy. She also resents her parents' having married her to a man with no education and no skills. Further, no matter how hard she works, she remains poor. This brief story is packed with meaning.

Santoshi is a tiny woman with a cheerful grin showing in her pox-marked face. She is in her late thirties and has had nine children, six of whom are living—two sons and four daughters, ranging in age from one year to seventeen. The other three children—two girls and a boy—died in infancy. Her oldest son lives with his maternal grandmother in another village and attends school there. Santoshi hopes his high school education will get him a good job, although her educated brothers remain unemployed. A second son attends middle school in Karimpur. One of her daughters was badly malnourished and, at four years of age, was unable to walk until we provided dietary supplements. In 1984 Santoshi was pregnant again, but that son died at birth. (She later bore two more sons, one of whom lived past the age of one month and is seen with her in figure 2.)

Her husband, Ramesh, herds cattle for the village farmers, earning up to Rs. 150 per month. Santoshi earns an additional hundred rupees or so by making and selling cow dung cakes, which are used locally as fuel. This is a hot, brutal task much of the year, performed under the blazing sun on the barren lands where the cattle graze. This additional income terminates during the rains, when it is impossible to dry the dung cakes. Her younger son sometimes skips school to work as an agricultural laborer, and her husband will leave the animals in her care if he can get other jobs.

Santoshi and Ramesh lived in a one-room mud hut in an enclave of their *jāti* mates, the Midwives (*dhānuk*), whose traditional occupations were midwifery and making leaf plates. Their one room collapsed in the rains in late 1983 and for months they camped in a neighbor's house, not having the requisite funds to rebuild. They carry the burden of a two-thousand-rupee loan, incurred years ago for a brother's wedding, before the family separated at the death of Ramesh's father. Food, clothing, and shelter are all problematic, as parents and children alike wear gifts and castoffs from others. Hunger is an everyday fact of life. For Santoshi, religion provides little solace, as she seldom has the energy for festivities. Furthermore, as she astutely points out, most women's rituals require preparations that are beyond her financial means.

SAROJ, A BRAHMAN WIDOW

Saroj is a tiny, garrulous woman, toothless and gray at age fifty-nine, but with sparkling eyes and an expressive face. I had known her slightly in 1967, when her older daughters were in school and she was encumbered by small children. One day in October 1983 she followed me into the lane in front of her house and said, "You should do something for women so that they have some work to fill their own stomachs." I became intrigued, especially after learning that she was called "the village Indira." I liked her penetrating comments, her outspoken and sometimes radical views on village women—and on youth generally—and her self-assurance. By early winter, she had become a new friend. She sat at the head of a cot in her large courtyard in the center of the Brahman section of Karimpur. As usual, she had been working when I arrived, but was hospitable and seemingly glad of a respite. She assured me that she could tell her life story because "I am the cleverest woman in the village." On two days in December 1983 she gave this version:

> I was in trouble from the beginning. We were four: one brother and three sisters. My father got one sister married, the oldest. When he died, she had not had her *gaunā*. We lived in misery, in much hardship. My mother married me at age nine to this house. We had many hard times here. But after I came, getting enough to eat became easier; things got more comfortable. In

3. Saroj, the widow of a Brahman landowner

my youth we had few comforts. My first children all died: seven died in a
row. Then seven lived and there was some comfort. But even in comfort,
sorrow again came. Panditji [Saroj's husband] died. Seven years have passed
since his death. Since then I have faced many miseries and hardships.

My older son separated from me two years ago. One son and one daughter still live with me: those two remain a burden on my head. I am barely
able to feed them. The boy doesn't study. The girl demands to study, so I

send her to school. She is good at reading, so I told her to study. He is just sitting!

[A few weeks later, same setting.] The old house was my husband's maternal grandfather's and was made of clay. When I was married, we had land, but there was no one to work it. I was married very young. I was nine years old at my wedding and my *gaunā* was a year later. [Q: After one year? You were very young.] Yes. When I came here, we were very poor. [Q: Why? There was land.] Land there was, but there were no workers and there were no sharecroppers. It was on rent. When the rent came, we paid the tax and the money that was left had to last for a whole year. When I came, there was nothing here. My father had died when I was one year old. My mother had nothing to give to marry me into a good house, so she married me into a poor one. My dowry was one rupee. So I was sorrowful. Upon coming here, there was nothing. My mother's house [*māykā*] isn't far away, so my mother came after a month and asked if I was getting enough to eat. I lied. I couldn't say that I was sorrowful. Why didn't I say that I was sad? If she heard of my sorrow, then she would be more unhappy. So I didn't tell my mother anything about living here.

After I came, the house fell down, the old one. Only one beam and a wall remained. So in the rainy season, we did like this: I used to cook the breads on the hearth while the room filled with water. Those two [mother-in-law and husband] sat on a cot. Then I fed them.[15] Later I ate. As I grew older, I never told my mother that I was unhappy. My mother-in-law was young. It has been fifty years since I married. Then I was young.

We—my husband and I—agreed to work. We would work day and night. There were rewards. A lot. First we got a buffalo for working the fields. It had no tail. Then the house wall was broken. We repaired the ceiling. We cut fodder by hand. [Q: You had no children?] I was young, so there were no children. I was twenty when I first had a child: that son died. Our first seven children died. After the seven died, seven lived.

We sold the buffalo and bought bullocks. They do better work than buffalo. [Q: How much did they cost?] One was six rupees and the other seven. Then we got a female buffalo. [Q: How old were you at this time?] At that time, I was twenty years old. Since we had bullocks and a buffalo, we could churn milk and eat butter. We could work hard. We didn't take from anyone; no one gave anything.

Then the outer room collapsed. It was made of mud bricks. We were earning. Then the children started to come. A girl of seven years died, then this room collapsed. But we were earning a lot. Everyone said to make a brick room. So for four thousand rupees we got two *lakh*s [200,000] of bricks. A men's sitting room was built and a place to cook.

Then the girls matured and we arranged the marriage of the oldest. Her maternal grandmother from Nanamu paid for that marriage, we didn't. Her grandmother had no one else, so she said, "Give me one girl; the *kanyādān* [gift of a virgin] will be made in my courtyard." So she did it. We paid for the younger daughter's wedding. We spent a lot on her marriage. Her house is prosperous, but from the day that we married her, our food has gone bad.

There was one kilogram of gold in our house. I am telling the truth. Now it is gone. [Q: How many years after the marriage did the separation take place?] My oldest son and I separated two years ago. Since then I have been alone. I worried a lot about my youngest son's marriage, so I am doing it. Then I will do my daughter's. Then I will sing the praises of Bhagvan. I never stole anything. I made offerings. My soul [ātmā] is at peace. You must live in your own place, in poverty or in wealth. You can't do anything. I have neither known poverty nor have I lived with wealth. To me, a cot and a sock are alike. The earth has not become bad. What we walk on, it is the Mother of the World. We should touch its feet. Do its honor [ijjat].

Saroj clearly sees herself as having had more impact on her life circumstances than Santoshi does. Despite the early poverty due to the lack of adult males in both her natal and affinal households, her families were always landowners. Hence Saroj saw her and her husband's hard work begin to pay off as they became adults and Panditji could farm his own land.

As a proper Brahman widow, Saroj wears a white cotton sari and one silver bangle. Her glass bangles and toe rings, both local symbols of marriage, were broken and removed upon her husband's death. During her husband's lifetime the family owned ten acres and prospered. Saroj and Ram, her husband, were both liberal in outlook and their daughters were the first in the village to complete eighth grade. They even owned a tractor, the first in the village, at the time of Ram's death in 1976. Of her seven living children, there are two boys and five girls. Only two girls and the elder son were married before Ram's death, so Saroj was left with four marriages to arrange. She sold the tractor to cover the wedding expenses of one. The younger son was married in March of 1984, leaving just the marriage of the youngest daughter, now studying in high school in Mainpuri, to be completed.

When Saroj came to Karimpur in the early 1930s, life was indeed hard: her husband's father was dead, her husband was only thirteen, and they lived alone with her widowed mother-in-law. Only when Ram reached adulthood and could begin to farm did the family begin to prosper. The land was always there, and once they had a team of buffalo for plowing they could begin the climb out of poverty.

Today Saroj lives in the large brick house that she and her husband built themselves, often working at night to save labor costs. Her younger son's land is given for sharecropping, but with only three people in the house to feed, it provides adequate food and money for their needs. Rajani, the daughter, often buys vegetables in town after school; tea is frequently served, and they live well by village standards.

Her older son separated his family from her two years ago, for several reasons. First, there were two marriages left—his younger brother and sister—and both would be costly. He would not have to share in those costs if he separated. Further, both his wife and mother are articulate, strong-willed women, and they battled frequently. After twelve years of marriage he has only a four-year-old daughter. This fact often leads Saroj to curse her daughter-in-law for her infertility.

Saroj is also known throughout Karimpur as "the village Indira" because of her recent involvement in Congress party politics and community development programs. After Ram's death, she was chosen by the village level worker, a minor official in charge of the village's community development programs, to head the women's division of the Charcha Mandal, a group formed to teach nutrition, child care, sewing, and the like. Later, she became active in district politics and traveled to Congress party rallies in Delhi and Lucknow (where she once met the real Indira).[16] Some villagers approve of her atypical behavior, but most find it unacceptable for a Brahman widow. Her local nickname, sometimes uttered in an approving tone of voice but accompanied by a sneer at other times, reflects this ambivalence.

MOHAN, AN ELDERLY BRAHMAN

Mohan was led by his grandson across the open square, around the tethered cattle, and over to the cot in the shade. As he gathered his dhoti, kicked off his dilapidated plastic shoes, and settled himself on the cot, he glanced around and eventually said to the tree trunk, "Well, Sahab, what do you want to learn today?" Mohan may be blind now, but his effervescence has not dimmed a bit, and he hardly ever seems nonplussed, as his quick recovery from his error showed: smiling his wide, toothless grin, he asked if there was time for a cigarette before he began. In his self-assured manner, Mohan took a certain pride in telling Bruce the story of his life.

> I was born in 1916, December 15th or December 16th.[17] For my whole life, meaning for as long as I can remember [literally, since he had "understanding," *samajhnā*] I have lived well. Mostly, I would eat butter, would drink milk, would eat ghee, would eat bread. Nothing was scarce. Whatever I wanted, I had. I ate very well and played with other children. When I was six, I went to school. I learned to read and write, but in school I kept thinking a lot about playing. I was always playing games.
>
> Later we were robbed. [Q: In what year was the robbery?] I think the robbery was sixty or sixty-two years ago, in '24. August 16, 1924. At this

4. Mohan, an elderly Brahman landowner, with his grandson

time I was eight or ten years old. [Q: Was it the first robbery?] Yes, but then I was not knowledgeable; I was not wise. At that time I had my own clothes and jewelry. I asked my father, "Where have my ornaments gone?" He said that they had been stolen. That was a sad time.

Time passed and Sahab [Mr. Wiser] came. Then I would play with Arthur and Alfred [the Wiser's children] in the garden and I would study. I didn't have any household responsibilities. If I wanted, I could help milk the cow or buffalo or carry food to the fields. Only this work. I did not have any responsibility. [Q: You were taught by Raghubar, weren't you?] He didn't teach me, but I started to go to school. You must know this, Raghubar loved people wholeheartedly. But if someone was making a noise in the house, my mother used to say, "I'll call Raghubar" [meaning that he used to beat the students] and then the boys stopped making noise.

So when Sahab came, he saw that I loved playing, and so he said to me, "You tell me about playing." He paid me three annas for each game [that I told him about].[18] I used to explain two or five or seven or eight games, for as long as he had time. He typed himself while I told him. [Q: Which games?] Like *lavo-dara*, *dukā-michonī*, *kathā*, *kabaddī*. The games we played in those days. Most of the boys used to work the fields, used to be busy in the fields. I explained these games to him. For each game, I received three annas. So I earned eighteen annas, twenty annas at one time. I used to get that much.

After finishing the village school, we went to Bicchwan, for third and fourth grade.[19] When I went to Bicchwan, Madan Lal, an Accountant, and Parbat, a Cultivator, studied with me. When I went to Bicchwan, there was an incident. The boys who were my friends didn't know how to swim, but I could swim a little. One day I was eating. I was sitting on a bridge, and it was winter; the wind was blowing from the west. I had a coat of heavy quilted cotton. I took it off and put it beside me on the bridge. While I was eating my food, a gust of wind came from the west and blew the coat off so that it fell in the water. There were boys who were good at swimming—one was from Jaili, called Dayaram. I said to him, "My coat has fallen." I was afraid my family would be angry at me for losing it. They would say, "Where is your coat?" So I asked him, "Can you swim?" None of them were willing. I jumped from the bridge into the canal. There was a gate through which the water comes. Near the gate is a post. Then the water flows back. I fell just before the gate and I did not flow with the water. I wasn't moving. The water was taking me back. If I had jumped to the east between the gates, then the water could wash me through. I could go five to ten hands ahead. I was trying to go to the east and the water was pulling me to the west. Water was churning around: I was in a lot of trouble. I said to the boys, "I am drowning, save me!" None of the boys were ready to do this. The boys said, "Don't fool us." None of the boys were ready. There was a big stone on the east side of the bridge. I dove down, I found the stone, I held on to it. While I held the stone, my hips were caught in the current, and I was tired. I didn't have enough courage to get my coat, which was about two hundred yards away. It went to the bank of the canal. When I was in the canal, I didn't swim to the coat. I came out of the water; then I went and got the coat. I brought that coat, but that's nothing. This story is finished.

After finishing at Bicchwan, I went to Mainpuri to study. [Q: Which grade did you study in at Bicchwan?] Up to fourth. Now when I reached Mainpuri, I stayed there for a couple of days as a boarder. I ate mess food. Next I lived with Seth Dharamdass; there I cooked for myself. I was living in the house of Seth Dharamdass. [Q: Was he a very big man?] A very important man. I knew him because he was a friend of my father and his nephew was studying with my older brother. In that way we knew him well. He had many houses. He gave us a small house. I lived in that house. We cooked food and studied.

At that time I was very fond of field hockey. Whenever I was not in school, I had a hockey stick in my hand until darkness fell. I played the whole day and didn't come back until dark. Finally, my father was called by the board superintendent. He said that I would not pass. "He plays the whole day. Take him home, uncle. He will not pass; he doesn't study a single minute." After he spoke to my father, I came home. In the evening my mother asked me, "Why have you come back?" I told her the whole story. What I would do in the future was yet to be seen. Then it was time to pay the examination fees. She gave me thirty-two rupees and also tied flour and lentils and ghee into a bundle and said, "Go back to school. If there is any trouble [namely, if father says anything], I will take care of it." So I went back to playing hockey as I did before, but there wasn't much time left before the exams—only two or three months. But I kept thinking that I should study more, so I started to study. I thought there would be trouble because I came back without asking my father. If I should fail, it would be very bad.

I remember—after eating my dinner, I used to go to sleep. And at ten o'clock, when all the other boys stopped studying, then I got up and I studied from 11 P.M. to 5 A.M. Of my own will I studied seriously until four or five o'clock. At four o'clock the other students woke when the bell rang. The boys started to study and I would sleep. When the examination fees are paid and papers are filed, after completing the application card, there is no question of sending the boy away. Until they fill out the forms, the boys obey the teachers, but not afterwards. The boys don't care for the teachers. The teachers also do not ask, "Why aren't you studying?" A teacher only asks if he cares for a boy. I got up late and went to school after eating breakfast and bathing. But at 4 P.M. I was again playing hockey. But I changed my system of studying. Finally, my examination was held at the Government School, on March 18, 1930.

When I went for the examination, the teacher used to ask the other students, "What have you done? What have you written?" When my number came, he said, "Get out, go away. Children of pigs don't study—you have not written anything." I was angry and didn't say anything. The day of the math exam he said, "You probably have not done anything on this paper." Then I was angry, and my answer was wrong. He said, "Your score will be an egg [zero]. Nothing. When the results come, there will be nothing."

That same year I married.[20] When the results came, I had a Second Division pass. In math and geometry, I got distinction. If I had two or four more points, I would have been First Division. I had distinction in math and geometry. When I went to see the results, the teacher who used to teach me was there. I touched his feet. He said to me, "Now tell." I was wearing a yellow shirt. I was recently married and was wearing this yellow shirt [a sign of marriage] when I went to school. He asked me, "Why are you wearing this yellow shirt?"

I told him, "When this yellow shirt is worn, I am married."

"Married?" he asked.

"Yes," I said. Again, I said, "I am here to get my results. I have heard that the results have come."

The teacher asked, "The results have come: what is your exam identification number?"

I answered, "400."

He said with disbelief, "400 is pass."

I replied, "So what is unusual? I have passed."

The teacher said, "Have you told me the wrong number?"

I replied, "No, sir, I haven't lied." I was feeling courageous. "400 is my correct exam number." Sahab, I saw the result, and I was Second Division pass. I touched his feet.

He rubbed my back and became very happy. At that time there was no question of cheating. Nobody could cheat. He said, "I don't understand how you passed. I can't understand it. How did you pass? What happened?"

[Some weeks later.] I think that farming is better than service. But now, when it is beyond my control [physical ability], my sons keep male buffalo. I never kept male buffalo during my lifetime. From the day that I quit school, right from that day I have felt that my health must be better than the whole village and I must produce more than all the village and my bullocks must be better than all the village. Above all, every single thing must be better than the rest of the village.

Since I have retired, I cannot go outside. I can only do a little work in the fields. Now I think that I must not speak ill of anyone, nor must I visit bad places. I must sing the praises of Bhagvan. That's all. It is right.

Mohan is a rich Brahman landlord whose father owned over sixty-five acres of land. His family has been one of the most important in the village for most of this century. It is clear from his memories of his early life that he didn't share in the poverty of Raghunath, Santoshi, and Saroj. In contrast to them, he ate well, played a lot, and attended school with all the perquisites of a rich man's son.

Mohan and his brothers all had tenth-grade educations at a time when only 22 percent of Karimpur males had any education at all. He tried to get training as an accountant, but he was too young. From 1930 until 1952 he was a farmer. Then for more than twenty years he worked as a panchayat secretary in a number of different villages in the area. In 1972 he retired from government service at the age of fifty-eight. Just before his retirement, his position was made a regular government position, but he was declared ineligible for a pension.

When he was young, his family had two full-time servants to do agricultural work, each receiving two annas per day plus breakfast. There was a minimum of four bullocks and two buffalo (for milk), but there were often more. His father was also a moneylender. Mohan said that often in June, after the harvest when loans were due, those who couldn't pay would give their bullocks instead, so that the number of bullocks his father owned might increase to ten or fifteen. He thinks that his father regularly had Rs. 20,000 out on loan to others.

Mohan was married in 1930 to a girl then ten years of age. The *gaunā* was some three years later. His first child was a son, who was born after six years and died at ten months of age. Then there were five or six daughters who died. The first son to survive was born in 1950, when Mohan was thirty-four and his wife twenty-eight. A second, and last, surviving son was born in 1962. In addition, Mohan has four daughters, all now married. He is lucky, because his ten acres of land will be split only two ways and his sons, at least, will be able to feed themselves easily.

Mohan is now an old man, blind from cataracts and often led around the village by his grandchildren. He separated from the families of his five brothers only eight years ago and is very proud of having maintained a joint family for some forty years after his parents' death. His family compound is the largest structure in the village, enclosing an open courtyard about one hundred by fifty feet. This house was built in the 1940s. Originally constructed of mud, it has been expanded through the addition of several brick rooms over the years. The courtyard is surrounded by rooms for living and storage and is filled with noisy children, crying babies, and the wives and daughters-in-law of the six brothers. The roofs on the rooms surrounding the courtyard provide additional storage space and serve as passageways to friends' houses, thereby allowing the women to visit without emerging from their seclusion.

The square of open space before the house is filled with large bullocks and numerous buffalo tethered under a massive shade tree. The family's large verandah is the site of most major cultural events in Karimpur: government-sponsored shows, Ram Lila performances, or religious readings. For these events, Mohan's son and a friend control the crowds of men and boys who squat on the ground or huddle on the platforms under nearby trees, while the women and girls cluster together on a side verandah.

Mohan's younger brother was the elected village headman (*pradhān*) in the 1970s. His older brother had been the informal headman (*mukhiyā*) earlier in the century. The family's real power has derived not so much from these occasional public positions as it has from its unity, the number of people in it, and the economic resources it controls, including jobs for laborers and servants as well as through money lending. Family members are slowly expanding outward into new enterprises: some recently bought a flour mill on the nearby road. Mohan is indeed a privileged man in this community.

CHAPTER TWO

"There Should Be Control"

One of the most fundamental divisions in Hindu ideology and social thought is that between order and disorder, between coherent action and chaotic action, between merit and sin, wisdom and stupidity, and ultimately between *dharma* (rightful duty) and *adharma* (nonduty). Mohan, the elderly Brahman landlord, once quoted a proverb: "Without control [*āṅkuś*] one lives like an animal; with control, one lives in settlements." Order is achieved through control. Those who maintain control of themselves and who control others are superior; those who must be controlled are inferior. Basic to control of oneself and of others is one's knowledge or "understanding." Those who possess understanding have the fundamental right to control those who do not. Hence order and control are fundamental to the hierarchical relations, whether of gender, family, or class, in villages like Karimpur. Equally important is the cooperation that is believed to derive from control. Only then, as Mohan notes, can humans live in settlements. The cooperation cum unity implied by living in settlements gives power to the inhabitants, with the result that cooperative styles of life are the most valued.[1] This paradigm is explored in this chapter, first through constructions of gender—as the most basic division in human society—and then as seen in the ordering of the ideal family and of the village community itself.

KNOWLEDGE, CONTROL, AND GENDER

"There is a difference between men and women in intelligence," Mohan told us. "A woman cannot think as much as a man." But, he continued, "The woman is [more] powerful [*śaktiśālī*]. . . . If you become angry because of a bit of pepper [in your food], then you could die at once. If she becomes determined to really harm you, a woman may take the form of Candi, may become Kalika [the goddess of destruction]." He later added, "So the meaning is this: there is kindness [*dāyā*] as well as brutality in women. If darkness comes, she can take life. . . . She is the goddess [*devī*]; she is the first power [*ādiśakti*]." With these words, Mohan captured some of the key components of gender differences as understood in Karimpur. His construction, though, is only one of the ways in which gender—the female gender in particular—is interpreted in Karimpur. As we will see, the meaning of femaleness is complex and contested in various ways.[2]

According to Mohan and many others, especially Brahman males and those most influenced by Sanskrit texts and elite interpretations, women must be controlled because they lack wisdom, yet they are all powerful.[3] As Mohan, himself a Brahman, noted, "The woman is the workshop of man. All are begotten by women." Our interchange continued:

Q: If the woman is more powerful [*śaktiśālī*], how does the man control* her?

MOHAN: Control*. They don't have much knowledge [*gyān*]. How is the lion locked in a cage? It lacks reason [*vivek*]. Man protects her from everything.

Q: If a woman progresses, then she would be knowledgeable. Then how can you shut her in a cage?

MOHAN: I say that if the sun begins to rise in the west, then what? It is a law of nature [*kudrat kā niyam*].

As Mohan commented on another occasion, a woman is born with eight demerits, which are always present. He named seven: daring (*sahās*), uselessness (*anarth*), fickleness (*capaltā*), guile (*māyā*), fear (*bhay*), lack of reason (*avivek*), and cruelty (*adāyā*). For a woman, even a small wrong leads to a major demerit, whereas if a man has some character fault or errs in his actions, the demerit is minor. Mohan gave an example: Suppose an untouchable Sweeper comes to someone's house for a feast. If that person touches the Sweeper's hand while giving him sweets, the person, man or woman, won't become a Sweeper. But a woman will be more strongly polluted by the touch of the Sweeper. She is more affected by human transactions.

The viewpoint expressed by the Brahman widow Saroj was, at times, similar to Mohan's. She discussed women in the course of talking about her own situation:

> The woman is inferior [*chotī*, literally "small"]. A woman can only work according to the regulations [*kāydā*, "customs"]. She can never leave the regulations. If our women go out in the world or my daughters wander in the world, I may be the target of defamation, as well as my dead husband. So it is against my dignity. For this reason, she is inferior. But even though she is small, women have given birth to great persons like Prahlad and Dhurt. In this she becomes major: because she has given birth to all the great saints, she becomes major. Man can't do it. Actually speaking, men could never produce women. But what can I do? I am a woman. A woman can do only what she is entitled to do. Therefore my girls can never meet a stranger: they must stay within all the regulations. If I had not guided them in the regulations, how could they live with the regulations? As the mother does, so the girl.

I asked her how she would feel if she were a man. Her answer:

> I would feel good because if I were a man I could go whenever and wherever I wanted. Now, being a woman, I live in domination [*śāsan*] and work according to the regulations. Even though my husband is dead, I live under his domination.

So a woman must be controlled. But whether that control should come from her husband (or father or brother), as normative statements claim, or from her own sense of right is debatable. Folktales often emphasize the importance of a woman's inner nature and hence provide an alternative vision to those of Mohan and Saroj. The following story of the slovenly wife was told to the Wisers by a village Carpenter in the 1920s. The story contrasts two women, one who has wisdom and one who doesn't: the one with wisdom rules the household, while her husband obeys her instructions.

> In a village lived a Muslim named Akbar. He was very poor. He bought wood, sold it in the bazaar, and bought grain, which his wife would grind. Then he ate. Daily he did his work this way. One day when he was bringing his load of wood, a king named Akbar passed by and asked him, "Who are you and what is your name? Tell me."
> So he answered, "I am a Muslim and my name is Akbar."
> Hearing this the king became very angry and returned to his palace. In the evening he said to his wife, "Look, my name is Akbar and I rule a kingdom. But I met a woodcutter and his name is also Akbar, but he lives by selling wood. What is the meaning of this?"
> His wife replied, "His wife is slovenly [*phūhar*]. Because of this he has many troubles."

Then the king responded, "I am going to send you to his house: you are not slovenly."

His wife responded, "Whatever you say, I will do."

In the morning the king again went to the jungle and, seeing the woodcutter, called to him to come close and said, "Come with me. I will give you my wife and I will take your wife." The woodcutter was afraid, but he went with the king. When they arrived at the palace, the king said to his wife, "Go to his house."

The king's wife got ready and went with the woodcutter. When she arrived, she saw what the problem was. The house was very dirty and broken down everywhere. Immediately she began cleaning, while the woodcutter went for wood. She cleaned until he returned. When he brought the grain, she ground it fine and cooked it. He was able to eat happily and she also ate, keeping some aside. She thought, "In the morning he can go quickly to cut wood. He can take his breakfast and hence bring a bit more wood."

In the morning when he went to cut wood, she gave him the food. He questioned her: "Didn't you eat?"

She replied, "I did eat, but a little food was left over, so I put it aside." Because he had eaten, the woodcutter cut a quarter more wood than before. Selling it in the bazaar, he got half again as much money. He bought grain with the money. Cooking it, his wife fed him and he got stronger from eating so well. He cut more wood, until he cut twice as much per day than before. After many days, his wife had saved a few rupees and said, "Buy a buffalo and put two bundles on it. You carry one bundle."

So he bought a buffalo for three or four rupees and took it with him every day. Eventually he saved twenty or twenty-five rupees, so he bought a bullock cart and again doubled his daily income. Then wood-selling in the market stopped. He said to his wife, "Now that wood-selling has ended, what should I do?"

His wife said, "Make a pile of wood and when someone needs it, you can give it." When he had gathered several piles, an enemy set fire to the wood. From the wood came a great pile of gold. Seeing this, his wife said, "Look at how much gold we now have. Go to the king and ask him to give us land somewhere and build a house there."

So he went to the king and asked him, "Sir, give us a place where we may make a house." The king gave the necessary order and the woodcutter made a fine brick house. One day his wife said, "Today invite the king."

So he went to the king and said, "Here is an invitation to our house."

The king said, "I will come with all my subjects. If you can feed everyone, then I will accept your invitation. Otherwise not."

The woodcutter replied, "I will feed all the people."

The king thought, "Where will he get enough food to feed everyone?" But he accepted the woodcutter's invitation. That evening everyone came. The woodcutter fed them all.

Then the king himself came to eat and his wife said, "Tell me, was that other woman slovenly or not?"

The king said, "Yes, that woman was very slovenly. Since she came, I have lost thousands of rupees." Then he added, "If the woman of the house is slovenly, even the food becomes bad. If the woman of the house is Lakshmi, there is no lack."[4]

This story, like all texts, can be interpreted in multiple ways, by various listeners in various social circumstances. One clear message in this story is that the woman who is ordered is Lakshmi, the goddess of wealth and prosperity. She who is slovenly, *phūhar*, ignores *dharma*, right action, and is thus Alakshmi, nonprosperity. The woman is the decision maker in the woodcutter's house. All his actions depend upon her suggestions and her intelligence. This story, told by a man from a lower *jāti*, contradicts Mohan's statements that women by nature are not intelligent. Further, it is clear that the woman who acts according to her own understanding and intelligence (the king's wife) is not the woman who passively obeys. Hence, the good woman, one who follows the moral codes prescribing correct action, is all-powerful. By the same token, the woman who is improper brings ruin. Saroj's story about Lakshmi and Kulakshani, with which chapter 1 opened, is based on a similar tension between the powerful woman who can bring ruin and the powerful woman who can bring prosperity. Femaleness is both. Moreover, the truly dutiful wife who does not use her own wits and cunning is not necessarily the one most honored. In the popular oral epic *Dhola*, for example, the hero, Raja Nal, has two wives. The first, Motini, has extraordinary powers as the daughter of a demon who taught her magic. When Raja Nal's parents are jailed by a rival king, Motini devises the plan that frees them (and she is the lead figure in that escape). Even after she leaves earth to abide in heaven, she returns to aid Raja Nal whenever he gets into trouble. The second, Damayanti, is the passive, dutiful wife who follows Raja Nal into exile. Both the male singers of the epic and women from Karimpur say that Motini is the more admirable woman and the "better" wife.

The contradictory nature of femaleness—that a woman, although subordinate, holds the family's fate in her hands—emerges again in this song, which was performed by a young Brahman man:

> When a husband acts wrongly, his wife rescues him:
> > when a wife is shameless, who will rescue her?
> Who will rescue her? Who will rescue her?
> The wife offers her husband righteous behavior—
> The meaning of *pativrat* is devotion to one's husband.
> When a cloth is stained, soap can cleanse it;
> > when the mirror is tarnished, who can polish it?
> When a family's honor [*ijjat*] is tarnished,
> > who can polish it?[5]

In this song, as in the stories of the woodcutter and Lakshmi, a family's honor and prosperity are totally dependent upon its women. She is the mirror for her husband, and she can aid him. But the mirror itself cannot be polished by another.

WOMEN'S POWER AND SEXUALITY

Female power is allied to female sexuality. Two themes emerge here: first, that there is a relationship between digestion/eating and sexuality, and second, that women have greater sexual power than men—they can "digest" (*hazam karnā*) twice as much as men. Although many of the comments made by village residents focus on men lusting after women and women seeking to escape, the greater digestive capacities attributed to women are markers of phenomenal female sexuality and female powers more generally. Furthermore, the digestive powers of females—the ability to digest both food and sex—link these two key areas of Karimpur life.

Brijpal, an elderly male Accountant (*kāyasth*) had this to say in response to a question as to whether females are stronger than men:

> You must know that a woman has eighteenfold strength [*atharah guni tākat*]. And [addressing the thirty-year-old research assistant] you are still a boy. And man has ninefold [strength]. But if she is a woman, she can digest eighteen times more. But man can only digest nine times as much. I am telling this important fact to you.

Brijpal added that a woman has so much power (*śakti*) that she can digest more. He then told this story:

> A brother was taking his sister to her husband's house. But on the way evil thoughts entered his mind. She came to know of it. She said, "You are my brother and I am your sister. What is the fault [*dos*]? Satisfy your soul [*apnī ātmā paripūrn*]." As they traveled, they came to a well. They decided to rest there. Sitting down, she said, "Bring a pot of water." At that time people traveled with swords. Nobody traveled without a sword. She took out the sword. Returning with the pot of water, her brother was afraid. She said, "Brother, don't be afraid. What you want will be realized." She filled the sheath with water and it held the water. Then she put half a pot of water on the sword and it spilled off. She said, "Brother, you are a sword and I am a sheath. We can digest it. But the job of a sword is not to digest. My water remains, but yours is gone. You have got ninefold strength, but I have got eighteenfold. I can digest eighteen times as much, so what is nine times?" She said, "You are my brother and I am your sister." And then he said, "I won't go." She said, "No, you must come with me. Nothing has happened." This is an example of that time* [an earlier, more moral time]. Man should try to digest his own ninefold strength. He should not go to a woman always.

This story has multiple readings. One relates to a basic tenet of Hindu thought about sexuality: men have more to lose through sexual intercourse because the loss of semen diminishes their physical and moral strength. The sister demonstrates this with the water pot: a woman can retain her energy, but a man cannot. Another interpretation suggests that even though the female has greater potential sexuality, males are the primary transgressors, for women can control and contain their sexual powers. At the same time, women must be contained to protect them from men. And perhaps the sister protects herself by demonstrating her greater powers, thus actually becoming the threat that men imagine women to be. Finally, the ability to digest inauspiciousness is necessary in order for the Hindu world to function properly: women (and the low) are able to digest more, and more varied, substances than are the high and are also thought better able to deal with any undigested remnants that might lead to disorder.[6]

The same man told a story related to him by his father. His father had gone with a group of seven others to bathe in the Ganges. A Landlord's wife was in one cart; the seven men in another. The young men desired to see the wife's face. So the Landlord asked his wife to raise the curtain on her cart and show her face. When they reached the Ganges, beds were lain with her on one side, then the Landlord, then the young men. After they bathed, the Landlord asked one young man to show her around the fair, and the young man thought that he had become a servant without pay. Now this was very improper, for a woman shouldn't associate with someone not in her family, unless a servant. Then the Landlord said, "Brother, in your soul [*ātmā*] you wanted to see my wife's face. So look. Show her around the fair. You have come to bathe in the Ganges [a most auspicious act]. In the future don't have such thoughts." My friend concluded, "What a deep example my father gave. And he didn't say a word. Now people have bad thoughts even for their maidservants."

Here, the young man's desire to see the face of the Landlord's wife of course constitutes a gross violation of sexual propriety. Indeed, so obvious is the moral of the story that Brijpal's father felt no need for further comment; his silence ("he didn't say a word") indicates that the Landlord's criticism is entirely justified. At the same time, there is nothing in this story explicitly suggestive of women's powers, for the wife is totally passive. The focus is instead on men's inappropriate gazing. For Hindus, seeing is an extrusive process, an outward reach that actually engages the object seen.[7] Hence, even by gaze alone, a woman is assaulted.

Men must be more controlled than women. Brijpal also claimed, however, that a woman whose husband did not come to her after three men-
strual periods could leave him, citing a story about the birth of Sita, wife
of the god Ram, the hero of the epic *Ramayana*. While Brijpal told this
folk version of a portion of the *Ramayana* to illustrate the rights of a
woman denied sex by her husband, the story also raises questions of in-
cest, here between father (Ravan) and daughter (Sita), and ultimately the
issues of sexuality latent in the epic more generally. Sita, Brijpal explained,
was born of the blood of saints and sages killed by the demon-king of
Lanka, Ravan. Ravan had put the blood in a pitcher and had told no one
to touch it, since it was poison. Brijpal went on:

> Now for three months Ravan did not go to his wife Mandodari, so she
> searched for another husband but could not find one equally wise (*vidvān*).
> Since she could not find another husband, she wished to die. So she drank
> the poisonous contents of the pitcher. She didn't understand. She became
> pregnant. Her stomach began to grow. She worried: "My husband didn't
> come near me, but I am pregnant. What should I do?" Then one day she
> got a stone, put it on her stomach, and gave birth. She called the guard and
> said, "Tie this up and take it away." It was a daughter. That was Sita. She
> reached Janakpuri, floating. The king Janak found her in a furrow and ac-
> cepted her.

Sita later marries Ram, joins him on his banishment to the forest, and is
abducted by Ravan, who lusts after her. Brijpal goes on to comment on
the inappropriateness of Ravan's desire for Sita, as she is in some way his
own daughter.

Indeed, the man who improperly lusts after a woman is thought to be
severely punished. In one tale, Basuk Dev, king of the snakes, is said to
have immediately become a leper because of ill-feelings in his heart for his
own daughter, while one of the village Washermen claimed that if you stare
at someone else's daughter, you go to hell. Yet the most charged pairing
is that of brother and sister. Supposedly there is safety in this relationship,
so that women who are abducted will ask to "live as your sister for twelve
years" or invoke the brother-sister relationship when improperly approached.[8] In the popular epic *Dhola*, the hero Raja Nal is tossed over-
board by his step-uncles, who wish to claim his lovely wife Motini. Motini
repels them by saying that she is their sister and they shouldn't treat her so.
A song from the 1920s also comments on the brother-sister pairing:

> May your country be burnt away
> When your brother becomes a lover,
> O daughter-in-law.

5.   A young girl worshiping her brother on Brother's Second (*bhaiyā dūj*)

While the incestuous relationship of brother-sister is forbidden, its charged occurrence in folklore suggests a point of significant tension. The brother-sister bond is supposed to be one of loving friendship, whereas the father-daughter bond is much more distant. Folklore tends to speak the unspeakable, though, and it is not surprising that one of the most common invectives is "sister-fucker," which targets this emotionally charged relationship.

If the brother-sister bond theoretically forbids sexual attraction, the bond between a woman and her husband's younger brother (*bhābhī-devar*) permits it. Here playful joking is allowed, something that would be unthinkable between a brother and sister. Moreover, among those groups that allow widow remarriage (including, in Karimpur, all but Brahman, Bard, and Accountant), marriage to the *devar* is a distinct possibility. The other accepted flirtatious relationship is between *sālā* and *sālī*, between an older sister's husband and his wife's younger sister. Here again, potential marriage partners are matched but are currently unavailable. I have seen teenage girls flirt outrageously with their sister's husbands, being much more open (in the safety of their own homes) than *bhābhī-devar* ever are.

Abstinence from both food and sex is also valued in Karimpur, as in Hindu traditions more broadly. According to the ascetic tradition, ideally the Hindu should not eat at all, since eating, or indulging in any physical appetite, is destructive. Fasting is thus a major component of most rituals, marking the denial of physical appetite and hence the accruing of internal powers that have not been subverted into digestion. Once again, too, a link between sexuality and eating is visible: sexual abstinence is required before many rituals, marking another sublimation of digestive powers to internal powers. The sadhu, the ascetic, who retains his semen altogether accrues the most powers.

Food in India is often used for ordering relationships and creating internal order in one's body.[9] In the *bhakti* traditions, especially those of the Braj region near Karimpur, food as *bhog*, offerings, marks devotion, while food as *prasād*, the god's leftovers, marks the god's spiritual nourishment of his devotee.[10] Hence, food signifies relationships, especially those involving giving and taking, whether between god and devotee, landlord and tenant, mother and child, or husband and wife. Food also signifies the emotions found in those relationships. Sexual relationships and caring, in particular, are marked by food exchanges. It is not surprising, then, that food transactions also mark subordination, whether of females or the low or even of children.

Jāti ranks in a village are manifested through eating patterns—who can take what from whom.[11] Raw fruits and grain are the most freely exchanged. Foods fried in ghee (*pakkā* foods) are more acceptable than foods cooked in water (*kaccā* foods). Except in the case of *prasād*, leftovers, contaminated by the touch of the eater, are least acceptable. Foods,

6. A woman making the design for Pitcher Fourth (*karva cauth*), when women worship their husbands

like anything touched, are affected by and transmit the level of purity of the one who touches them. The products of the cow have the power to purify and hence can reduce contamination from a person's (or object's) touch.[12] Foods cooked in ghee are thus less easily contaminated by touch and more acceptable to a wider group of individuals. Brahmans will not accept food cooked in water from any other *jāti*, while Sweepers accept food cooked in water from almost all other *jāti*s. (See also chapter 6.) Moreover, the meat and liquor that are allowed as part of the diet of many non-Brahmans are believed to heighten the passions and add to the uncontrolled nature of the low.

In Brahman families, a visiting son-in-law of higher status than his wife's family owing to a hypergamous marriage should be served only fried foods. Likewise, a new wife is fully accepted into her husband's household only with her serving of *besan-bhāt*, a meal of a milk curry and rice, basically a *kaccā* meal, marking that it is acceptable for her to serve his family this easily contaminated food. In some families, *besan-bhāt* is the first meal served every time a daughter-in-law returns after a visit to her natal family, reaffirming the marriage bond and her membership in her affinal home. It is also the meal served on the annual festival called Pitcher Fourth (*karva cauth*), when women worship their husbands.[13]

Rank and status within the household are also marked by eating: men eat before women, older women eat before younger. No communal mealtime exists in Karimpur. Rather, individual men eat when ready, often sitting separately in various corners of the courtyard or near the cooking area, with one or two children sharing their meal. A woman eats only after her husband and male elders have eaten, with a wife sometimes waiting into the night for a tardy male to return so that she may have her meal.

"Wifeliness," although it involves procreation, usually does not involve overt sexuality. The sexual, flirtatious woman is inappropriate in the household.[14] Stories told by Karimpur residents include many adventures of wives seeking to gain the love of their husbands. In these tales the connection between sexuality and eating is made clear: the husband signals his refusal of his wife by refusing her food. Further, in order to attract their husbands with their sexuality, the wife must leave the role of wife. The story of the Trader and the Brahman's daughter, written for the Wisers by a Brahman male but told by his sister-in-law, plays out this theme.

> In some city there lived a rich Trader. In that same city lived a Brahman who had a beautiful daughter. The Trader's son was entranced by her and desired to marry her. He said to his advisors, "If I marry, then I will marry the Brahman's daughter. I will not marry in my *varṇa*."[15]

His advisors said, "What is this? Well, we shall arrange his marriage with her." In the evening they called the Brahman and said, "You have to marry your daughter to this Trader's son." On hearing this, the Brahman was very confused and upon returning home laid down quietly.

When his wife saw him, she asked what was worrying him. He said, "The Trader's son has demanded that we marry our daughter to him. If we don't, I will hang."

Then his wife said, "Let us leave for a foreign country using the pretext of bathing in the Ganges." So they began the preparations.

But the daughter said, "You are both of the right age for going on a pilgrimage, but I am very young. At this time, I am unable to go on a pilgrimage."

When they heard this defiance, her parents said, "Now we know that our daughter is agreeing to the marriage, so why leave? Let us put her in a palanquin." So they got a palanquin [to send her to the Trader's house].

One day after the girl had reached the Trader's house, he said, "Come, let us play." Going into a room, the Brahman's daughter fed him food that made him have to piss very badly. He said, "I have to piss."

She replied, "Piss on this Mahadev [a statue of the god Shiva]."

He responded, "This is our god; I cannot do that."

Then the girl said, "Then how can you do this? You are lower than I: I belong to the highest *jāti*. But you want to marry me. If you will piss on Mahadev, then I will marry you." The Trader's son stopped the marriage and sent the girl back to her house. With this wisdom, she was saved.

Then her father arranged her marriage with a Brahman. Later the husband learned that the girl had lived in a Trader's house. Hence he stopped eating bread from her hand and would not look at her face, tying a bandage over his eyes when he came in the house. When the girl realized these things, she called her father and went to her home. She told the whole story. Those people had said, "We cannot eat the breads of a twice-married woman."

Now the Trader's son came to hear of this and he was very upset. He said, "This sin [*pāp*] is mine: I did that and now there is scandal about this poor girl." He wanted to make a plan by which the sin would be removed. He said to the Brahman's daughter, "Think of a way by which you will be made faultless."

The girl replied, "I have an idea, but no money."

So he said, "I'll see that you have whatever money you need."

Then she took a lot of money and paid for four courtesans for four days. She opened a show a short distance from her father-in-law's village.[16] The men of the village came to see the show. On the second day, the girl, who had made herself the Ustadin [master] of the courtesans, asked, "Does any Brahmacari [abstinent young man] live here?"

The people said, "Sure, one lives here." Then she said that whoever brought him to the show would receive five hundred rupees. Greedy for five hundred rupees, the men brought the Brahmacari. When the Brahmacari saw the beauty of the Ustadin, he became very enamored of her and began to live with her and eat her food.

Then the Ustadin said, "Now, as a symbol of your love, give me your ring." He gave it. The Brahmacari was happily living with the Ustadin when in his own house he would not see her face and would not eat her food! After four days, she returned to her village. Then she left her mother's house and went to her father-in-law's house. There she cooked. Her husband was very angry at not finding the Ustadin. The girl said to her mother-in-law, "You leave. I'll feed him today." Her mother-in-law left.

When the Brahmacari came in with his bandaged eyes, he asked, "Whose bread is this?"

She said, "It is mine." So the Brahmacari rose to leave. Then she said, "If you find the Ustadin, will you eat her bread?" Then she told him the whole story from the beginning. Then they began to live with great affection and he loved her and ate her food.[17]

In addition to affirming the link between food and sex, this story makes clear the connection between extramarital enticement and marital servitude. Only by taking her sexuality out of the house and into the semi-wildness of the groves in the role of a courtesan can the woman regain her husband using her charm and femininity. As a wife, these are barred. Note also that, despite men's denial that women possess intelligence, the Brahman's daughter solves both dilemmas—how to rid herself of an inappropriate husband and how to win back the one she desires—through her wisdom and wits.

While the dominant theme is that the wife should not be sexual, women's oral traditions regularly acknowledge female sexuality. As this verse, sung by the village courtesan in the 1920s, indicates, women often have sexual thoughts:

> The mother-in-law worships the son;
> The daughter-in-law worships the penis.

In fact, women's songs in Karimpur frequently speak of an intimate loving relationship between man and woman. Women enjoy singing these songs—which are, in part, a form of resistance against the ideology of male hegemony. This excerpt from a childbirth song (*jaccā*), sung by a group of Muslim women in December 1983, shows that love is indeed on women's minds:

> I have fallen in love with a stranger,
> And as a token of his affection,
> he has given me a child.

Yet another song, which I heard from some teenage Brahman girls in December 1990, goes:

My whole being is filled with pleasure,
The strings in my heart are beginning to tremble,
O my love, my dear love, bring me a precious necklace.

In another song, sung by a group of Brahman and Accountant girls in November 1983, the woman outlines the obstacles in her husband's household standing in the way of a trip to the movies with her partner:

We both will go to the movies.
Your mother, my mother-in-law,
She is the ashes of the stove.
We will both clean pots [with her].[18]
We both will go to the movies.
Your brother's wife [*bhābhī*] is my sister-in-law [*jethānī*],
She is the rice pestle.
We will both beat rice with her.
We both will go to the movies.
Your sister, my sister-in-law [*nand*],
She is the sting of a scorpion.
We will both bite her.
We will both go to the movies.

In many songs, such as this one, women do see themselves both as lovers of their mates and as allies with their mates against his family. Other songs tell of secret meetings, of women awaiting their lovers "with a bed spread with flowers," and of the agony of "the too young" husband, the one unable to be a lover and the father of children. (In the "too young husband" song, the wife's knowledge of sexual practice is contrasted with her mother-in-law's, for the latter visits a shaman to get charms so that her daughter-in-law will become pregnant, not recognizing her own son's lack.) Hence, through their songs, women counter narratives and other discourses that mute love between husband and wife and a woman's sexuality.[19]

Nevertheless, women should eat, whether of food or sex, albeit only as appropriate (although they can, of course, digest more than men as long as there is no excess). Women's fasting in rituals benefits their male kin and family group more than themselves; the power not diverted to food goes for family welfare. And the woman should digest sex in order to provide offspring for the family. Thus, for example, one Karimpur woman, a Washerwoman whose story we will hear below, can rightly seek another husband in order to put her procreative powers to work.

Women who indulge in their physical appetites beyond what is necessary, however, are portrayed as overeating, stuffing themselves, eating more than they can digest. In one story a woman makes sixteen kinds of sweets and gobbles them down as soon as her husband has supposedly gone to the market. (In fact, he is watching her from the roof.) When she falls into a daze from overeating, his relatives call in an exorcist to cure her of the spirits they believe are inhabiting her body. Only when her husband lists the sixteen kinds of sweets does she respond.

Karimpur folktales are replete with images of women who eat or indulge in sexual relations behind their husbands' backs. In one tale, a sage, seeking to discover the true nature of women, encounters a series of women cheating on their husbands. Other tales tell of women who secretly meet men at night or steal away to a sadhu's ashram.[20] Moreover, some wives who married into Karimpur have actually run off with other men. The women are invariably blamed, not the men—although, as we saw in the stories of the brother and sister and the Trader who desired the Brahman's daughter, at least in folklore the men are often the instigators. Moreover, in interviews both men and women constantly repeated the moral injunction that men should not gaze at women. The overt message is that women should be veiled so that men will not sin by gazing at them, that women should be controlled to protect men from themselves. The covert message appears to be that women's appetites are overwhelming and will dominate a woman's actions: not only can women digest more than men, but they also seek to digest more.

It is difficult to know how to interpret these messages. It would appear that women hold power over men as embodiments of sexual attraction, and it is this power to which male discourses are responding. Moreover, women's powers in these depictions disrupt the carefully constructed social hierarchy: disorderliness is power. The tradition of female disorder thus apparently represents a cultural recognition, whether conscious or unconscious, that women harbor an element of potential resistance to the structures of patriarchal society, and hence their resistance is condemned before it can be expressed. Furthermore, the emphasis on female powers through disorder gives women the illusion of power while denying them the real thing.

The image of women as sexually voracious and "disordered" to some extent finds an analogue in class. As elsewhere in India, residents of Karimpur from the lower-ranked *jātis* have fewer constraints on their sexuality than do Brahmans and other higher-ranked *jāti* groups. They have to observe fewer ritual rules prohibiting or controlling sexuality and often, because they are more likely to be living in nuclear families, they enjoy less interference in their sexual activities from their elders. In this regard, they, like women, are thought to lack control of their appetites, which in turn provides further justification of their need for control. Moreover, higher-class men are afraid of the disordered lowly male, a source of resentment and anger, just as they fear the disordered woman. Hence, the sexual and other "disorderly" powers (including the ability to digest many and varied substances) awarded to the socially disenfranchised can appropriately be seen as fostering the same kind of illusion of power as that given to women.

An ironic twist on this theme can be seen in a motif that occurs in a number of tales as well as in the epic *Dhola*. For some reason (a king without offspring, an epidemic of smallpox or other devastating disease), the community must find someone who has fasted that day in order to save their king or themselves. The only person to be found who has not eaten, and hence can perform whatever ritual is necessary, is a Sweeper woman who is too poor and too busy to have had a meal. But her unintended fast saves all.[21] A female Sweeper, in Karimpur the lowest-ranking of human life forms, thus proves able to provide salvation for her community.

This story leads us once again into the connections between social rank and food transactions, the forms of subordination common to both gender and class/caste. The lowly, like women, have appetites that they cannot control without help from their superiors. They eat a wider range of foods, including meat and liquor, than do their higher-ranked neighbors. They practice widow remarriage, not abstinence, and they are less likely to practice rituals that demand abstinence. They also have the right and obligation to digest the leavings of their superiors, demonstrating their greater digestive powers or the acceptability of behaviors associated with the inability to digest. That the lower *jāti*s and women are often conceptually linked in Karimpur is not surprising.

CONTROL THROUGH CONTAINMENT

The primary way by which women are controlled involves containing them physically, using the custom of purdah. In Karimpur, as in much of rural North India, purdah demands that married women, both Hindu and Muslim, of families that seek high status or good reputations remain secluded in their courtyards and houses, usually going out only for the early morning latrine stop in the fields or to leave the village for a visit to relatives, a doctor, or the district fair. Women should be not seen by strange men, nor should they talk to them. Unmarried teenage girls are also restricted in their mobility, perhaps visiting the village shop for some spices or supplies for a festival, but always accompanied by other children. When a daughter-in-law of the village does leave her house, she is enveloped in a shawl, with her sari pulled down to cover her face. Even in her court-yard, the end of her sari covers her face, and she speaks in a whisper in the presence of her husband and any males senior to him. She will also veil herself to show respect when other women are present or on ritual occasions.[22]

Saroj explained purdah in this way:

> But I never went out. Girls can go out to see the cattle, if they are grazing in the fields. I never went to the threshing floor. I also never went beyond the door to give my husband food, as long as he lived. When I used to go in the lanes for a women's ceremony, I used to cover my face with this big shawl. My husband's younger brother [fictive kinship] used to tease me and say, "See, the newly married daughter-in-law has come." When I used to go out of the house for the ceremonies, they used to say that she was the newly married *bahū*. Nowadays the *bahū*s go about the village with uncovered heads. I never lived without regulation. I never went in the lane or out of the gate without a shawl. I still cover myself with a shawl.

> . . .

> The veil [*ghūnghat*] is purdah [*pardā*, literally "curtain"] for women. This kind of purdah is only for Brahmans: they keep it. Not others. As this eyelid is the curtain for the eye. If there is no eyelid, it will remain open, even when you sleep. How could it close? Only this eyelid covers it. This eyelid is the curtain. If dust comes, suddenly the eyelid covers the eye. In the same way, the regulations of veiling are purdah. Women must keep the regulations of purdah. I am telling you the main* thing. Regulations are the ornament for women. Those uncovered women who visit the fair—there are also men there! If you are uncovered or naked, will the men not split their eyes? Will they not see you?[23] Everything is seen with the eyes. If you are covered from all sides, it is difficult to see even your finger. Then what will they see of you? They will not see anything. The veil is an ornament for women. The face of a woman should always be covered. If the women are from a respected house, from a reputable [*khāndāni*] house, it will be difficult to see anything. She can talk to every person, even her father-in-law or husband's older brother. But she should talk according to the regulations. Otherwise it is not good. To live according to the regulations, that is our rightful duty [*dharma*]. We should keep this *dharma* with us. If a woman does not keep her *dharma* with her, she is nothing. She will be called impious [*adharma*]. Yes, people will say that the woman is impious and wicked [*badmās*].

These restrictions ease with age, so that the youngest daughters-in-law in the village are the most heavily veiled. Women of lower-ranking *jāti*s also seldom keep purdah. After all, purdah requires the financial resources to build the structures behind which women hide, as well as to permit the family to hire laborers to replace women in the fields and to provide for them in their courtyards. A Sweeper must be hired to clean the household latrine of those denied even the morning trip to the fields; before the advent of hand pumps, a Watercarrier was necessary to bring water from the publicly located well; a Washerwoman had to take clothes to the pond to cleanse them, and so on. Not surprisingly, a newly rich family will often seek to put its women in purdah, for the ability to maintain purdah is itself a sign of wealth and status. Here, too, we find one source of women's submission to rigid rules of containment: they and their families gain in honor and status if purdah is maintained.

Thus women's roles become constitutive of class. Whereas the norms for "wife" often appear to be class-neutral, they are in fact constituents of ideologies that obscure class differences while at the same time reproducing them.[24] Saroj recognized the class elements when she stated:

> [It is necessary to keep purdah] because these Brahmans, they are Brahma. It is the top *jāti*. If Brahmans act even a little properly according to their fate [*karam*], if they do good work, they are gods [*devatā*]. We say Brahman *devatā*.[25]

Furthermore, according to Saroj, the system perpetuates itself, because "like mother, like daughter." Hence the daughter of a women who has not been modest (because she is poor, forced to work, or whatever) will also be immodest:

> [Purdah] is a matter of virtue [*lajjā*]. The eyes of the woman should be behind the curtain. Virtue [*laj*] is in the eyes. This is one of the greatest rules [*gahānā*] for women. The woman who is devoid of virtue may not be called a woman. Yes, the eyes of the woman must always be screened. If I talk with you, I must keep my eyes hidden. It is the main rule. And the woman who does not keep it is called a foolish woman, and people say her mother is not good, so she acts in such a way. If the mother is good, the girl will be good. Look at the mother: whatever the mother's nature [*śīl*], the girl will be like that. The influence of the mother will surely be on the girl. [She] can never escape.

But while the natal family provides the early training, the husband is the ultimate guardian of a woman. A few lines from a song in a story told by Raghunath captures the imagery of containment, the role of parents, and the husband's dilemma when the boundary surrounding the woman is destroyed, her virtue lost:

O my queen, the garden was planted by the parents,
And I made the boundary myself.
O my queen, I shall not take its fruits
Someone has destroyed the boundary.

While not subject to rules as restrictive as the rules governing women, those of low rank also find their mobility constrained. The regulations here are varied. Some, like strictures on housing, prohibit the low from living near the high and rich, as a result of which members of the lowest *jātis*, those considered untouchables, end up clustered on the edge of the village. Another set of rules concerning the use of space deals with seating arrangements, so that at public meetings, or even in casual conversations, the low are found squatting on the ground or on the edge of verandahs or courtyards, while the rich sit on cots, the oldest and most senior at the head of the cot and others arranged by rank next to him or on nearby cots. As is also the case with women, one result of such regulations is that the lowly are removed from centers of power, from those arenas where decisions regarding their community are made.

Unlike women, however, the lower-ranked male is able to move about the village. The strictures on males are fewer than those on females, with the result that high-ranking females are the most constrained, low-ranking females less so, and low-ranked males the least. As we shall see in chapter 6, rights to space became crucial battlegrounds as the low sought to change the rules of interactions governing Karimpur life.

CONTROL THROUGH SILENCING

Aside from veiling and physical restrictions, women, and low-ranked men as well, are further constrained through "silencing." Saroj mentioned that a woman must talk "according to the regulations," referring to norms for conduct that mandate that a woman speak in whispers (if at all) to older male affines, that she not speak in public, that she show respect to her mother-in-law while speaking, and so on.[26] The ability to speak is one of the most powerful tools available to humans. To bar use of that tool—to deny women a voice or to limit their voices in certain settings—is as potent a constraint as mandating veiling and seclusion or denying people a seat near the powerful.

Women's silence is markedly different from the silence of high-status men. For men, especially gurus and sadhus, the right to silence is a sign of power, whereas women's silence is considered comely behavior, a sign of deference.[27] Men can be silent; women must be. The belief in the necessity of women's silence stands, moreover, in marked contrast to the perceived power of women's speech: it is women whose curse is feared (as also that of the silent swami). A woman's curse is the means of her empowerment, as Mohan implied above when he noted that a person could die from a woman's curse if he complained about such things as pepper in the soup. Men's curses, aside from those of holy men, carry little weight and never appear as major themes in Karimpur folklore. But Karimpur folklore repeatedly tells of the power of a woman's curse, reflecting Karimpur beliefs in women's inherent power—and making it all the more necessary to silence her.[28]

In addition to cultural norms that deny women the opportunity to speak, married women in rural North India are depersonalized or deindividualized through "non-naming." In her husband's village, a woman's given name (such as Saroj or Santoshi) is never used. Rather, she is called *bahū* (daughter-in-law/wife) by all of those senior to her in age (outweighing even *jāti* considerations), while those junior to her address her by the appropriate kin term: *ammā* or *mātā*, "mother"; *bhābhī*, "brother's wife"; *dādī*, "grandmother"; and so on). Through such non-naming, a woman's individual personality is denied. She becomes a series of kinship roles, in contrast to the men, boys, and unmarried girls around her, whose given names are used regularly.[29]

The disregard for the personhood of the individual married woman is reflected, too, in women's rituals. Unmarried girls frequently perform rituals to obtain a good husband or for the sake of their personal welfare. Married women's rituals, however, focus on the welfare of their male kin and family, and thus only by extension on their own welfare. Thus a married woman will worship the goddess Savitri in the Hindu month of Jeth (May–June) in order to gain a long life for her husband, in remembrance and honor of Savitri's outwitting of the god of death, Yama, in order to gain her husband's life. Or during the fall festival cycle, she will join with the women from her lineage at dawn on the first day of the second half of Kartik (October–November) to worship Siyao Mata ("Lampblack Mother") in order to procure sons. Or she will join with other women in preparing the cow-dung enclosure known as Gobardhan ("cow-dung wealth") and worship Krishna to bring prosperity to her family and household. These rituals acknowledge female power, since men cannot perform them. Nevertheless, they also acknowledge that auspicious female power depends upon a woman's link to a man, whether husband, son, or brother. Certainly having a husband who lives long or having sons benefits a woman, but the ritual gain is indeed secondhand.[30]

The one ritual that females inevitably perform as both daughters and daughters-in-law is Brother's Second (*bhaiyā dūj*), which takes place on the second day of the bright half of Kartik. Through this ritual, the brother himself is worshiped, his enemies are destroyed, and he marks his regard for and shelter of his sister through gifts. The ritual returns us to the sexually charged brother-sister relationship. For example, in some versions of the story told on this day, the sister must sleep with her brother and his new wife on their wedding night in order to prevent his death. Moreover, although a brother's long life is one goal of the ritual, women's needs are also more personalized and immediate: the sister benefits directly, when given gifts, from the promised shelter of the brother. A male kinsman is still involved, but he is a natal kinsman and the female gains directly. The contrast to the focus on others in married women's rituals is marked.

In addition, Brother's Second is a ritual that must be performed—for the brother's sake, as well as the sister's. Hence it marks the need for a daughter in the family, for if there were no sister, there could be no ritual. Likewise, a daughter is desired so that parents can obtain merit through *kanyādān*, the gifting of a daughter in marriage. Raghunath, whose uncle had numerous sons but no daughter until very late in life, spoke with pleasure of his cousin and her importance to him and his brothers.

The Karimpur daughter, as well as her brothers, is raised to learn to think of her wishes in relation to others.[31] The girl is married young, certainly by the age of fourteen until the 1960s and by sixteen in all but the two or three wealthiest *jāti*s even today. As a young bride, she is the person of lowest status in her in-laws' household. The feminine role thus marks a woman's embeddedness in familial relationships. (Of course, men are also embedded in familial relationships, but they have many more opportunities to develop friendships outside the family than do women.) In early adolescence, instead of gaining a sense of individual identity, the girl is conforming to the prescriptions of those around her: no rebellion is allowed. At age fourteen to sixteen, more than ever, she must be the perfect daughter/daughter-in-law, veiled and silent, allowed perhaps to vent her frustrations only in her natal home or through song and story.[32]

Picture the young bride, dressed in finery sent by her new husband's family, carried wailing by her maternal uncle from her parents' house to a waiting vehicle (whether bullock cart, truck, bus, tractor, or car) filled with strange men. She has just endured a long marriage ceremony in which she is a mere puppet following directions, heavily veiled no matter what the weather. Hours later, after sitting mute and cloaked while these strange men take her to an unknown place, she is lifted out by a new female relative. Once again ritually tied to her groom, she enters her new home. Neighborhood women crowd around as she sits, veiled, with her eyes downcast, on a mat in the courtyard. Each woman lifts the bride's veil and loudly proclaims her judgment on the girl's appearance, while slipping the silent bride a token payment for the right to view her.[33] The self-control, the suppression of self and feeling, must be immense. Indeed, no woman could or would describe her memories of this event to me; all said that they were too young, too "unknowledgeable," to remember it.

This image of the young bride must be contrasted, however, to the behavior of her female kin during the wedding. As the groom's party arrives at the bride's house and during their stay there, they are regularly abused by the women with lewd songs known as *gālī*. Here women are given a voice: they are allowed to speak and sing bawdy invectives against those men who are taking off their daughter. Moreover, as we saw earlier, women in stories are often the primary actors, working to right wrongs and giving orders to their husbands and male kin. Women are not uniformly silent and under male control, and many, like Saroj, develop leadership skills, despite the overt injunction for "proper speaking."

At the same time, Saroj, as a minor female political activist, is condemned by most Karimpur residents, male and female, for "acting like a man," going wherever she wishes and speaking publicly. One day she told me that "if a widow keeps her tongue quiet, she gets fed. If she moves her lips, she is told 'get out.' " Yet Saroj continues to speak out, even relishing her nickname of Indira, explaining that *she* knows she isn't misbehaving. Thus Saroj, who regularly articulates the dominant silencing rules, is herself a primary transgressor of them, referring to other role models such as Raja Nal's wife Motini or Indira Gandhi herself as support for her position. She also denies Mohan's claims about women, accepting her own intelligence as something to be cherished and proclaimed. Saroj once accounted for her nickname this way: "I myself arranged the marriages and functions according to my own ideas. I never ask others for help and advice. So they call me 'Indira.' Generally people make a comparison between the intelligence of Indira Gandhi and me." In appropriate contexts, then, women should not be silenced.

Gender differences, based on the female sex's supposed lack of wisdom combined with her physical appetites and digestive powers, thus provide an ideological foundation for the hegemonic mandate of control of women by male kin.[34] Saroj captured the ambivalence regarding women with the statement, "If she becomes their [the in-laws'] slave, then she is called queen of the house." Women are to be controlled by containing and silencing them—and the woman who refuses to be contained and silenced is the most dangerous, as are some goddesses and spirits who have, respectively, no male control or home. Women's behavior also becomes, in a less overt manner, one element in maintaining class differences within Karimpur. As we shall see in chapter 3, there are comparable male concerns regarding honor that work to maintain the social order of class, while further reinforcing the control of women.

Low-ranked men, too, are often silenced in various ways: frequently they are not allowed to speak in public meetings and must imply subordination in tone and word when they do speak. Indeed, tone of voice is a powerful indicator of status, and the appropriate tone for asking or begging is easily recognized. Moreover, as we will see in chapter 4, these men, like women, have forms of speech that go against the norms imposed by high-ranking men. Finally, as one of Karimpur's Washermen once commented, "To take a loan from someone is to become the woman of that man." For Karimpur residents, the link between female subordination and the subordination of low-ranking men is clear.

"ONE STRAW FROM A BROOM CANNOT SWEEP"

While the distinction between men-as-controllers and women-as-controlled lies at the core of Hindu ideology and social organization in Karimpur, the paradigm most frequently used to regulate social life is that of the ordered family. Ultimately, the village is seen as one family, with fictive kin ties linking all its members and reinforcing that vision. The ideal family is one that cooperates and accepts the rule of an authoritarian male figure.[35]

Mohan talked about the need for cooperation:

> Where there is cooperation [sangthan], there are various kinds of wealth and property. And where there is no cooperation, there is a shortage of each and every thing or there is an atmosphere of want.
>
> Where there is cooperation there is no need [of the ambition] to pile up wealth. "The minor streams or rivers go into the ocean, but they do not have the ambition [to be big]." So, in the same way, property and comfort accrue without being sought after when there is cooperation; property comes to the properly regulated [kāydā] man.

A young Brahman man used the imagery of a broom to explain the need for a large, cooperating family: "Say there is a broom. If you have one straw separate, it can't sweep. But when all are together, it can sweep."

If the family stays together, its power increases. As Mohan says, take the example of a family with four sons. All have different habits. But the family's power would increase if all four were under the control of one person.

> I am telling what I understand. A family must have one thing. That is, a family is strong when all remain in the control of one [person]. Whatever is said, they must accept that. In other words, having accepted the words of Brahma [the deity], they have become firm and constant in that, whether it is right or wrong. But the family must be controlled by one, whether or not he has money. Unless there is selfishness [on the part of the leader], the power [of the family] will endure.

On another day, he added, "If the family goes every which way, then the whole house is ruined." Saroj also sees the united and controlled family as honorable. Discussing the arrival of a daughter-in-law, she commented: "So the arrival of a new bride shows that either she belongs to an honorable family or to a bad one."

The unified, cooperating joint family—for it is father and sons living together that is the ideal in Karimpur—demands both a trustworthy leader and the respect of the sons. Mohan's family achieved the ideal more successfully than any other Karimpur family: he and his four brothers, as well as his dead brother's widow, their wives, children, and grandchildren lived together for over twenty years after the death of his parents. He attributes this to the character of his older brother: "We understood that he is wise, older, more sensible, would do every kind of good work, but would not do bad work." Mohan describes the brother who currently heads the largest portion of the now separated family as thinking ahead, having understanding, and seeking peace.

One day, Shankar, a Brahman and the village headman, added an insight into the joint family by discussing self-control, particularly sexual self-control. Several aspects of joint family living relate to his remarks. First, as he notes, no one has their own room or even space in the traditional household. In fact, in most joint families in the 1960s, the mother would assign sleeping places on a nightly basis; this gave her immense control over the sexuality of her sons and daughters-in-law. If she felt it appropriate that they have a place where they could meet at night, she would arrange it. A young man, newly married, once complained that he and his wife were being forbidden to sleep together because he had had a bad cold for some time and his grandmother thought they should remain apart for the good of his health. This raises a second point: male health is threatened by too much sex, for a man loses vital energy through his semen. Hence, controlling male sexuality is especially important.[36] On these issues, the headman remarked:

> But if the society lives together [*samāj ikhaṭṭhe*], your self-control [*sanyam āpkā*] is maintained. If you live separately, you lose your self-control. You get a separate room. You get a separate cot. You have separate food. Everything becomes separate. This affects your health [*tandurustī*]. But when you live together—you have your mother at one place, sister at another, *bhābhī* [older brother's wife] somewhere else, or a servant at some place—then self-control is not difficult. You don't have any place to indulge yourself. This is the greatest factor in good health. That is why it is essential for the family to live together. Now it is important to understand that all this is a gift of nature [*kudarat*]. If it is not in me, then how can we blame others? This tendency to live separate is very dangerous. They say that if a young daughter is alone in a room, then even her father should not go into that room. She is the girl whom you have produced out of your own seed, out of your own body, and she is young. So you should not go into that room. So when our family lives together, then we get less time, and we get more opportunities to work. We would not even be able to think about it [sex]. That is why our health used to be good.

Equality among all the members within the family and unchallenged decisions by the head are necessary to the smooth functioning of the united family. I learned these lessons soon after beginning fieldwork in 1967. I was living in a family that included four married sons, along with their wives and children. Whenever I brought sweets or fruits for treats, I was required to give them to the grandmother, who would distribute them amongst her sons, daughters-in-law, and grandchildren. Her decision as to who got what amount carried weight: mine did not (although I find that twenty years later, I am allowed to make distributions myself). Further, if I bought saris for the women, they had to be identical, apart from color, for the women at each tier: my brothers' wives all should get one kind, my sisters should get one kind; the daughters of the family all one kind, and so on. Likewise, frocks for the girls or sweaters for the boys could differ in color only, unless I wanted to instigate fights and high levels of tension among the women. So I learned the appropriate buying patterns, those used by heads of households. Thus it is easy at holidays or at more public events like the district fair to identify family groupings because of the clusters of girls in identical dresses or boys in matching shirts.

Mohan once told his (somewhat idealized) version of the rule within his family:

> In the United States, when people get married, a man becomes master for himself and feels that his duty is to his wife and children. But here in India,

whenever there is a guardian and we make the bread in one place, we cannot say, "My wife does not have bread. Bring some for her." Or that, "She has no blouse." Whether she has no clothes or she changes into a new sari every day, I do not have the right [to give clothes her or to complain]. . . . We are either oppressed by the older people or we have respect for them. There is another thing: we cannot say that she does not have a sari so why don't you bring one for her. And I cannot bring one either. The time never came when I had to think about whether she had clothes or not. No one [namely, his wife] ever said to me, "I have no clothes or other things." No one ever told me any problem. If she had, what could I have done? That rule has been in my mind till now. But for the past five or six years we have become separate. Now I do all of this that the family wants—saris and clothes for the children. Before my brother was master of the family and I was always behind. I never was concerned whether my children were in trouble or were happy. I never worried about this.

The unity of the joint family depends, too, on the wife's first duty being to her parents-in-law, not her husband. As one young man, a Watercarrier, explained:

First of all she should think about the family. Then me. . . . First of all she should take care to feed them. My mother is old, so she should massage my mother. It is her duty to eat the food after my mother, my older brother's wife, and sister. If my parents want her to clean the pots, she must clean them. Even if she feels that she is a new *bahū* and she need not clean the pots now, her duty is to clean the pots.

Mohan said that the women must also see to equality, not giving bread rubbed with ghee to one person and plain bread to another. Above all, the good daughter-in-law is one who serves and obeys her father-in-law/mother-in-law (*sās-sāsur*). As a poor Cultivator said, "She should accept what the father-in-law and mother-in-law say. She should accept what the household people say, whether they are right or wrong." The authority of the parents-in-law is key, because if a woman seeks favoritism through her husband, the unity of the family is threatened. I vividly remember a young man in his twenties telling us that his mother and aunt (his father's sister) used to like his wife very much, but that he hadn't liked her. Now he loved her, so they no longer liked her. Without his affection, the unity of the family was secured and the power structures unchallenged. Once his affection was attained, the power structures that allow for the ideal unity and cooperation were threatened.

Behavior within the family marks the hierarchies. Respect for those senior is demanded: sons respect fathers and older brothers and obey their mothers, with whom a more affectionate relationship exists. Sons cannot smoke, play with their children, or talk with their wives in the presence of their fathers. The Flower Grower's wife says that sensible (literally, "un-derstanding," *samajhdār*) boys show respect to their fathers, but some, like one of her sons, refuse to listen to the advice of their parents. Women must also show respect within the household. A *bahū* asks her mother-in-law what to cook, how much spice to add, whether she can go to the fields, and so on, even when she is forty and the mother-in-law sixty or more. *Bahūs* also show respect through veiling, by touching the feet of senior women on ritual occasions, and through their eating patterns.

The rule of those senior is not always benign, however, and decisions are regularly enforced with physical punishment. The household head (or more senior person) has "understanding" that the others lack. If they do not accept that understanding, that wisdom regarding right and wrong, the message can be reinforced through physical punishment. Husbands can beat wives; fathers can beat sons (and more rarely daughters). The Flower Grower's son, a young man in his early twenties with an eighth-grade education who does construction work in Delhi, explained the roles of husbands and wives thus: If a wife erred but did so in public (sitting with her friends, for example), she should not be corrected, for that would be an insult. But in private, a husband could say something or beat her. "In other words, you should scold her, if she makes an error. You must make her understand that she must not do so." A Sweeper woman said, resignedly, "If we don't work well, we're bound to get a beating." The young man from the Watercarrier *jāti* told of one occasion on which he hit his wife:

> At that time I was studying in high school. It was 1978. One day the food wasn't cooked. On that day, I said nothing. On the following day, I was also made late because the food wasn't cooked. Again I didn't speak to her. On the third day again I was made late. In this way, I was late each day. On the fourth day, I went again. Then it was summer. I sat on the roof in the air. Then after eating, I hit her four or five times.

So a husband's duty is to make his wife understand things through phys-ical coercion if necessary. A wife can also correct her husband: if he drinks or gambles, she should try to forbid him. But she cannot beat him, although everyone knew of wives who did in fact hit their husbands when angry.

Children should be physically corrected as well. The Flower Grower said, "If he [a son] does some wrong work, beating is a duty." Alok, a Brahman man in his thirties, claimed that "if the father tries to make the boy understand [*samajhānā*] and if he does not accept [that understanding], you should beat him." A poor Cultivator concurred, saying "[if a son doesn't obey] so beat. You beat and I beat. The good man should beat. We must press them." Teachers also have the right to use physical punishment. Mohan talked of his mother threatening to call one of the village teachers when he had misbehaved, because the boys feared the teacher. Raghunath added this:

> The child is beaten when he doesn't go to school or studies but knows nothing. And second, when the child is mischievous or doesn't work, then he is beaten. All children are beaten. Everyone hits their children till they are ten or twelve. It is to bring them on the right path. There may be two or four who are not beaten. But I hit my brother [actually his cousin] a lot because he wouldn't study.

The goal is to teach through fear. Mohan captured the essence of control as understood in Karimpur: physical punishment and verbal abuse are used to instill fear.

> A child who fears that when the parents come, they will shout at me, [that child] won't play in the dirt, won't use foul language, won't fight with anybody. But if he has no fear, he will play in dirt the whole day. Because he has no fear, he will use bad language toward others. So there should be control—for every man and every woman.

Without fear, according to Karimpur residents, there can be no control and the elders in one's family have the right and duty to "cause understanding." Similarly, those who are senior in the village can beat "understanding" into those of lower status.

In many ways, the village is perceived as one large family. The fictive kin ties that link everyone are one mark of this "family writ large" conception, although there are other ways in which the fictive kinship of one large family is marked. When someone dies, the whole village shares in the grieving by canceling music events or other celebrations. In 1968 a Leatherworker named Horilal died on Holi, the popular spring festival characterized by the throwing of colored powder, raucous play, and role reversals.[37] Within minutes of news of his death, all Holi celebrations throughout the village came to a sudden end.

An annual event that is part of the Holi celebrations also demonstrates village unity. *Holī milānā*, to give the greetings of Holi, takes place on the first day of Holi. Everyone dresses in their best finery, often in new clothes purchased for the festival. With hair slicked down, the men of the village circulate in long streams greeting the residents of each house, stopping at the larger landlords' homes for cigarettes, *bīḍīs*, betel leaves (*pān*), or a cooling drink.[38] A truly united village would have every man visiting every house in the community, but in fact the Brahmans did not visit the houses of many lower-ranked *jāti*s until recently. As we shall see in chapter 6, this symbol of village unity also becomes a point of major contestation when the lower-ranked *jāti*s seek to demonstrate higher status.

The village also marks its unity in the ritual of *khappar*, literally, "pot." *Khappar* takes place just as the rains begin in late June and is performed to rid the village of illness and disease. Throughout the day and evening, men, mostly from lower-ranked *jāti* groups, become possessed by Devi, the goddess who lives in a shrine by the bus stop. Then, toward midnight, a man dressed as the goddess circulates through each house in the village carrying a pot (*khappar*) symbolic of the goddess, in which he collects all the disease infesting the village. The ritual is concluded when the pot is dumped into the fields of an adjoining village, thus ridding the village of the collected disease and thereby providing protection for humans and animals in the dangerous rainy-season months ahead.

The perceived unity of the village was further articulated when a fire swept though the Brahman section of Karimpur in April 1984. People claimed that the fire was caused by the accumulated sins of the village as a whole, but especially by its Brahman leaders. Just as the sons of a family are ultimately the responsibility of the head, so too the sins of the village are the responsibility of its dominant *jāti*, in this case the Brahman landlords.[39] Here again individuality is muted. Whereas an individual can sin and hence affect his own life course by altering his destiny (*karma*), he also alters that of his family, lineage, *jāti*, and village, for an individual is not a unique entity but shares substance and moral codes with all of those to whom he or she is related, in ever larger circles. All those belonging to the nation of India also share in the same way.

If a family should be united, so too should the dominant group. A retired Accountant attributed the power of Karimpur's Brahman landlords to their unity:

> These people [speaking of Thakurs, commonly landlords throughout northern India] used to understand that they were landlords. Also those [Brahmans] because they were wealthy. Above all, there was unity [*sangthan*] among them, whereas elsewhere there was no unity. Everything depends on unity.

By the 1980s that spirit of cooperation was felt to be missing and hence Brahman domination had lessened. (See also chapter 6.) Further, as we shall see in chapter 3, concerns for family honor (*ijjat*) lead to one-upmanship amongst the Brahman families.

The hierarchy of *jāti* groups and Brahman domination are dependent upon the same cultural constructs that enable men to control and suppress women or fathers to control sons. The lower *jāti* groups lack understanding. Raghunath explained the relationship between knowledge and physical power in this way: "See, these arms are the Chattri [Kshatriya]. Because only these can do everything. Brahman lives in the brain. Brahman leads with his brain. So Brahmans were kept on top, then Chattri." The Accountant claimed, "Actually speaking, the lower *jāti* people were not knowledgeable [*samajhdār*], whereas they [Brahmans] were knowledgeable because they were educated men." Raghunath used the model of the family to explain how different *jāti* came into being:

> There were no Sweepers [*bhangī*]. There were four brothers. Of the four brothers, the oldest one was thought bigger because he was older. Whatever the oldest ordered, they did. He became Brahman. And the one in the middle, he said, "We cannot disobey when he speaks. If he will order me to beat someone I will beat him." Okay, then the [third] one said, "He obeys the older one and fights. I am the middle one so I must do something. I must do some peaceful work. I must do some work from which all are in peace. To live in peace is best." He began work from which peace comes. He began peaceful work. And the one who was lowest [*nīce*], he was youngest [*chote*]. They said, "Go and bring tobacco. Do this work, then we will do ours." And they began to give orders. So he became a slave, the youngest one. Those who did the work, they became Shudra. There was no Sweeper [*bhangī*], no Leatherworker [*jatav*]. They were born later. They [the other *jāti*s] did this kind of account: "You are Leatherworker, you are Washerman [*dhobī*], you are Sweeper, and you are Potter [*kumhār*]." So the *jāti*s were created this way.

According to this model, the higher-ranked *jāti*s have the right to dominate because they are older and wiser. Moreover, village society has the family as its basic paradigm. The village is a family, and, as in a family, those older and wiser must control those lower.

As these discussionions of gender, family, and *jāti* demonstrate, "understanding" or knowledge is the primary attribute of those who are dominant, while those who are oppressed lack knowledge and understanding. The word most commonly used to describe this knowledge is *samajhnā*, "to know, to understand, to comprehend." A child lacks understanding, as we saw in Raghunath's life story when he said,"I will tell my life from when I was able to understand [*samajhnā*]. When I was eight, I was a little knowledgeable [*samajhdār*]." Mohan began his life story similarly: "For my whole life, since I had understanding [*samajhdār*] . . . " Children, women, and the lower *jāti*s do not have understanding to the same degree as do Brahmans or higher-ranked males. Everyone is believed to gain in understanding as they age, but an individual's potential to understand is based on his or her birth as male or female, low or high. That "understanding" is fundamental to Karimpur conceptions of the control of women, families, and the lower *jātis* makes the inroads of modernization especially threatening, because education becomes the route by which this dominance is most directly challenged. But before looking at issues of change in Karimpur, let us first hear from the village headman and from an impoverished Brahman. After that, we can look more closely at Brahman dominance and lifestyles and also at the meaning of poverty in Karimpur. Throughout these discussions, the model of the family will reappear, as will a concern for wisdom, knowledge, and "understanding."

Shankar, the Village Headman, and Sudhir, a Poor Brahman

Shankar is in his early seventies, a strong, gray-haired farmer, always dressed in a dhoti, eschewing even the pajama-style pants worn by so many Karimpur men. We usually talked with him at his house, a large brick structure in the Brahman section of the village. His was the first brick house in the village and remains one of the largest homes. Connected to his sitting room is the room that houses his tractor, one of two in the village. He uses his tractor for ploughing, as the engine for a tube well, and to convey humans and goods from place to place. During the summer wedding season, he frequently rents it out to carry wedding parties.

It wasn't always easy to find Shankar, for his duties as headman of the village panchayat and as a Brahman leader often took him out of the village. But we found him a willing helper in our attempts to comprehend social change in Karimpur. On several occasions he told us stories about his life and his opinions on a range of topics. Like Mohan, he was a student and a sportsman, although he seemed more resentful of the opportunities that he missed than Mohan was. I have arranged excerpts from his stories into a kind of narrative. As it derives from a number of interviews, it should not be read as a systematic life story, such as those of Raghunath, Santoshi, Saroj, and Mohan. Rather this and the subsequent narrative sections of the book present incidents or stories in which Karimpur residents try to make sense of their lives.

Like Mohan, Shankar had much to say about his days at school in Mainpuri and about his successes as a sportsman.

When I was a child, I studied in primary school. At that time, I didn't have a sound mind; I didn't know what I was and what I was not. From seventh grade on, I studied in Mainpuri. Even then my mind wasn't developed. Then I went to the Mission College. My health also wasn't good.

I belonged to a very poor family. When I was studying in seventh or eighth grade, my father was unable to pay my fees. Once he had to pay fees, but there was no money. My father was passing through a lane: there he found a purse. There were twenty-five or thirty rupees in it. He said, "I knew that you would ask for fees, and I didn't have them. You are lucky that I found the bag with this money in it. Now you can pay your fees." He found something good. It was his teaching: although you are poor, when you go to bed, it should be comfortable. First class*. It should be first class* if it is cold. There should be a mattress. It shouldn't be expensive, but it should be comfortable. He taught me in this way. While I was in school, he used to say that you must always wear simple clothes, never expensive ones. Whatever he meant by expensive then. But you must keep one set of expensive clothes. If a Collector's son has good clothes, on special occasions your dress should be better than his. But you should wear simple clothes daily. Nowadays boys like to wear expensive clothes.

There was a group of wrestlers. I felt that if I lived with the group, I would become like them, have their qualities whether good or bad. So I made contact [with them]. I did physical exercise and reading. Up to sixth and seventh grade, I was nothing. Then my health improved. I began to run races of six kilometers. Because I was with them, I used to exercise. And I used to defeat the famous wrestlers of the time. Jugnu and Mata Din were the wrestlers in Mainpuri. I used to defeat them. So they began to accept me as a guru. Those two wrestlers were famous in the district, yet they began to call me guru. . . . Then my health became very good. I continued playing sports through tenth grade. I was captain of every team. . . . There were only two schools in Mainpuri—the Mission College and the Government School. No one in either was my equal. My health was the best in both schools.

Yet I was from a poor family. People say that "milk forms health; ghee forms health." No. Health is formed by good conduct. . . . People in Mainpuri were proud of my health. In other words, no matter what street I walked down, the people used to look at me with admiration. My health was so good. My body was strong and my mustache still had not grown. I used to wear a neat dhoti and shirt and had books tucked under my arm. So wherever I went, I was honored.

. . .

There was an Anglo-Indian team that played football from Soran: the center for playing was in Aliganj. So a team from Mainpuri District went there: I went also. Here I kept my honor. There was also an Anglo-Indian team from Etah. First they made a goal. I was playing at the end. There was a Captain Chaturvedi, and he said, "Now we are down by one goal. So why are you playing back? Go ahead." So I began to play forward: my speed was well known. So those at Aliganj began to praise me, saying, "This boy is an airplane." When I used to run, people used to say, "His heel does not touch the ground." I ran very fast. So as soon as I took the ball, people began to shout, "Bravo, Bravo." So I made four goals and beat the Anglo-Indians.

When I was reading in seventh and eighth grade, when I had passed middle school, then I was married. Even though I was almost twenty, I didn't know what is woman and what is man. [In other words, his conduct had been so good that he hadn't known women.]

Slowly my influence [in Mainpuri] increased. But because of misfortune I couldn't go on. Unfortunately, I didn't have any contacts. My friends who entered the army have already retired with the rank of superintendent*. If I were in service* I would have prospered. But service was not written in my fortune [bhāgy]. This is destiny [karam].

My father was ignorant in everything. Because of him, I could not do anything. If somebody had given me even a bit of help, if there had been anybody to push me ahead, then I would have succeeded. But there was nobody in the house to push me. My father, even though poor, was very fond of educating me. It was his only hobby. But he gave no thought to service*. He was not aware that he could push me ahead in service*.

At that time service* jobs were not common in our village. I was the first person to get a job outside of the village.[1] I don't think anyone else had had a job outside. . . . So when I saw a whole village made of pakkā [brick] houses, I also felt like building a pakkā house. After all, when you see something, you are affected by it.

After bewailing his father's inability to get him a proper job, Shankar went on to discuss the effects of modernization on farmers.

[Farmers] had a better time then. They did not have to pay anything for what they got. Now everything goes toward filling up the engine [buying fuel]. In procuring fertilizer. If you ask me, in reality men are more unhappy today. They don't get any profit from sharecropping. Before, a man used his own strength to get a harvest. We could get a good harvest by using our pond water free. Of course, we produced less than we do now. We didn't use fertilizers, didn't irrigate the fields four times, and hence the harvest was smaller. But from a comparative perspective there were more benefits then.

The wheat harvest was 160 pounds for one-fifth of an acre. And that was with free water. Those who did not cultivate their fields properly could produce about 80 pounds. But it was a very hard work. We used to plough each field twenty times with a wooden plough. Now we plough it three times with an iron plough. Except for one well, there was no water anywhere. So we could only irrigate an acre by working continuously for sixteen days. But then we would get only five bundles of wheat from that acre.

Sharecropping was practiced, but mostly we used to cultivate our fields ourselves. It was easier then to find laborers. Today we have to dig potatoes and we need three men for it. Where will we find three men? We cannot find laborers and the crop cannot be reaped on time. A bonded laborer is not even available. Now the laborers have land of their own and they cultivate their own fields. Who will till our land now? We are hard-pressed to cultivate our own land.

Another problem is sterilization. When I was first approached about sterilization, I did not know what its impact would be. If I had, I would have married again and would have had more children. With more children we would have prospered. Our land would not have come under land-ceiling laws then.[2] Vasectomy [*nasbandī*] has hurt us a lot.

Like most of Karimpur's Brahman landlords, Shankar regretted the changes that freed the poor from many of the bonds they had had with the landlords of the village and the intrusion of the government into village life.

Now there is not much sincerity and love between people. [The low] are not in my control but are standing freely themselves. The truth is that Bhagvan has given us less power and we can no longer help them. They are better than us now.

I tell you that earlier we knew how to be dependent upon ourselves. Now we are dependent upon others. Our condition has worsened. Neither the tube well nor anything else has benefited us. If we had built our own tube well, it would have been profitable. This government tube well has been broken for two years. All the crops have dried up. Had it been ours, we would have had it repaired or would have done something about it. If we had four or six tube wells of our own in the village, then we would have prospered.

[Shankar explained that he had wanted his son to get a service job.] In fact, I wanted to dispose of all my land. But if fate [*bhāgy*] doesn't support you, nothing happens. I tried a lot—as I said—and you can consider it my fault, my boy's fault, or fate's fault. I think that it is important to have a job. When I was employed, there was a collector at Dhanehara who gave a speech in which he said that however well may you be eating or drinking, however high may be your *jāti*, you cannot progress unless you have a second source of income. If you buy bullocks, you should rent them out; you may work in a shop; you may lend money. Money should flow into the house from outside. If you are totally dependent on agriculture, then you can never progress. I guarantee that. . . . You may have a small business. You may buy bullocks with its earnings. If you then sell them, you can get a profit of two, three, or four hundred rupees. You can buy bullocks again. Then you can progress. You can use your profits to put fertilizers on your fields or for some other purpose. But if you are a family of ten, and all of you are dependent upon agriculture, then you cannot progress.

In a revealing discussion of purdah from a man's viewpoint, Shankar told this story of the "unknown guest." It also points to concerns that he had about the potential for sexual relations with women of the house.

Today a guest came to my house. The wife of my brother-in-law's boy. I saw her as soon as I went inside. She touched my feet. I said, "Who is this woman?" Now neither she nor my daughter-in-law spoke. I was hungry, so I drank milk and sat there. Earlier I had had three breads rubbed with ghee.

Now what must I do? None of my granddaughters were around. So I could not ask [a granddaughter] who this woman was, the one sitting there in my house. Neither she nor my daughter-in-law could say. So I sat there silently. What to do? To go inside would have been an offense. [Q: What did you feel?] The thing is, a man's mind is always changing. Today I am ready to serve you. But the time might come when I am ready to shoot you. Today I understand that she is my daughter-in-law. I must see her all day, every day. Men are always captivated by seeing. Men are not such great ascetics. They become distracted upon seeing a woman. So I must not look. Whoever wears the veil does not speak. But what should I call her? That is the trouble. If my wife had been there, I could have asked her, "Who is this woman?" I could say anything to my wife, whether with laughter or with anger. But I can't speak to my daughter-in-law. Suppose I spoke with laughter, corruption might grow in me as well as in her. What purpose do I have with her? Whatever you do, you get its fruits.

Shankar was very proud of his married daughters and the successes achieved by their husbands, who all had good jobs as professionals. He spoke of his grief when his younger daughter's husband died.

My greatest sorrow came one day when I was lying on this roof. A friend, the senior engineer of my son-in-law, called to me. I don't know what name he called. His truck was on the road and he was standing below. It was a gloomy night, maybe it was two or three o'clock. My wife and son and I and maybe others were sleeping on the roof. He said [in English], "Dixitji has expired."

Now I asked, "What [man named] Dixit has died?" Perhaps he thought that I did not understand English.

So he responded, "I have come to bring you the news."

"What are you saying?" I replied. So my greatest sorrow came when I heard that my son-in-law had died from heart failure. . . . Then I came down and asked him what happened. There was weeping and crying. This was my greatest sorrow. The property, the land, the money are nothing.

I had great affection for that son-in-law. Well, he was the younger one. But I loved him because he used to accept my advice. He was very gentle. After the marriage, he didn't ask anything. Yet I helped him a lot.

It is terrible when one's offspring have troubles. Have I, the father, done anything to cause this? Is there some want in my songs to god [*bhajan*]? Is there some lack in my reaching to Bhagvan? What bad deeds have I done, that this happens to me?[3]

Otherwise, I was happy. A man isn't happy because of money. But if his sons, daughters, grandsons are happy, then he is happy.

. . . I have just come from my morning duties and have eaten. Today I don't have any other work. I have sung the songs of god. Now there is no more work for me. So I go on like that. In the world, man goes onward by fate [*karam*]. So now my fate is this. To do the service of you people.

Shankar lived with his wife and two sons. His older son was handicapped and unmarried, while the younger, at age thirty, had five children, three daughters, and two sons, ranging in age from newborn to nine. With only two capable men to work the family's land, both Shankar and his son worked hard. His older brother lived in a house nearby, with his one son. They had split some years back in a stormy separation, one perhaps best compared with a contentious divorce. Indeed, in Karimpur families the break between two brothers is much more serious than that between a husband and wife. Shankar and his brother had a particularly difficult separation.

Unlike Mohan, Shankar's family was neither large nor particularly powerful in preceding generations. Yet Shankar is currently in his second stint as headman, having been elected the first headman of the village in the early 1950s. His influence is great, and there were no major complaints about the decisions that he made or about corruption.

One of Shankar's neighbors is Sudhir, a Brahman man now in his early thirties, whom I had first known as a young teenager. Sudhir's grandfather had been the *mukhiyā*, or traditional leader, of the village, as well as a priest for the dominant Brahman lineage in Karimpur. Sudhir's lineage was related to the main lineage in the village through an affinal tie several generations earlier. His grandfather had several sons who shared in their father's land, and Sudhir's father was one of five brothers, all of whom had a right to equal shares of the family inheritance. His father's share was less than two acres, barely enough to support a family of five children. Then, about 1966, Sudhir's mother died of tuberculosis. Mrs. Wiser provided drugs to the children for the following year to prevent them from also getting TB. But after his mother's death the family never prospered. Sudhir's story begins not long after his mother's death.

My mother died shortly before I took my eighth-grade examinations. I went to Kuraoli for my examination. In order to obtain food, I borrowed flour from one house, lentils, salt and pepper from someone else. I made arrangements to eat by borrowing. Other students used to bring yoghurt and eat breads fried in ghee. Often I went in the morning without even eating and took my exams. I would return about 1 P.M. and then eat. Even so, I got a Second Division pass.

Next I began to study in ninth grade in Mainpuri. I also had problems then. My father took a mortgage on my bicycle [which Mrs. Wiser had given him to attend school]. So for several days I would get to Mainpuri [about seven miles away] by sitting on the back of a friend's cycle. Sometimes I would walk. Finally, I asked my father, "Where is the bicycle?" He told me that it was in Mainpuri and he would bring it in two days. So I said that I would walk. But months passed. Still I didn't have a bicycle. Later when I heard that he had mortgaged it, I was filled with sorrow. It had been given to me: it wasn't even ours, yet he had still mortgaged it.

Finally, I said to my father, "Unless you bring the cycle, I will not go to school." I walked for maybe six months. Sometimes I got a ride on someone's cycle. Then I stopped. When my father heard that I had not gone to school, he rushed toward me to beat me and told me to walk. I said that I would not walk seven miles each way every day. So he would beat me for not going to school and I would run away from the house. Sometimes I had no food for two or four days, sometimes even six days. Sahab, when the stomach is filled, people say "Eat, come and eat here." But nobody asks the hungry to eat.

I would go to a sugarcane field and steal canes to eat. Or I would eat peas in the pea field. One time that man caught me: I ran toward the pond. Then I thought, "Why should I run? I haven't eaten in eight days." So he caught me and snatched the sugarcane and swatted me a few times. I thought that the whole world troubled me. Slowly the days passed. Sometimes I would work at harvesting wheat or sugarcane. I ate at various people's houses.

Then one day, Mohan's brother said to me, "Sudhir, come work for me. I'll give you thirty rupees a month and feed you." So I worked for him for several years.

Then later, that Shopkeeper said to me, "Sudhir, why are you just sitting around? Come, I'll make your life better."

I asked him, "How?"

He said, "You work for me at the electric mill. You'll make things better for yourself." He gave me forty rupees and two pounds of flour a month. He even gave me cigarettes to smoke. I worked for him for one month.

Then Mohan's brother asked me, "Why are you working for that Shopkeeper? Work for me." So I began to work at his mill for sixty rupees a month. I worked there two or three years. Then our relationship was broken off. I kept on falling ill. Nobody even asked if I needed food. So if I was sick, I would just remain lying on my cot. Once I got well, I began to work for him again.

One year I went to a town near Delhi for six or eight months. I came back here when my sister was married. She was married in June. My uncle asked me to stay at home. I stayed a year, then he forced me to run away again.

I got married. I brought my bride from Bengal. My father left me when I was very young, after my mother died. My brothers and sisters were little. They used to eat at Mohan's house. Once I lived in Rajasthan for a year and earned two hundred rupees a month, including food. I did farm work there. For a while I cooked food for ten to twenty men, but I didn't do well. It was twenty-four-hour duty, cooking for that many men.

Sudhir's wife is from Bengal, a marriage that he arranged himself but through contacts made by his uncle. Sudhir would not have been able to marry a Brahman girl from the Mainpuri area, as his family had lost too much, in both land and honor. Moreover, Karimpur's Brahmans were dismayed by his marriage to the Bengali girl, for no one knew for sure what *jāti* she belonged to. She certainly wasn't a Kanya Kubja Brahman. The financial arrangements in this marriage are unclear, but certainly her family paid no dowry. Sudhir described the reaction in the village to his marriage thus:

After I married and came back here, the villagers objected: "She's unknown. What *jāti* is she?" I was thrown out of my *jāti*. I was boycotted [could not attend any Brahman functions, nor would a Brahman attend any at his home]. I said that it didn't matter. And my wife accepted it. Even my uncle's wife [with whom they shared a house] wouldn't speak to us or even feed us. Then I was away for two days working as a laborer. My uncle's wife told my wife not to take any flour nor use the pots nor go near the hearth. One day I forcefully entered her cooking area and ate some breads. The next day my aunt came into my room and threw out our clothes, our cot, everything. She said that we could not eat with her or share her house. I had not thought to live separately. Yet she said that we couldn't live with her. So the next day I went to the market and bought three utensils: a tray [used as a plate], a water pot, and a small bowl. That's all. I got three pots. And spices like salt and pepper. Then I said to my wife, "Now we are separate. You must do all the cooking." She said that she would and ever since I have been living and eating comfortably.

[Q: When you first brought your wife here, did she speak Hindi?] I tell you this. In Bengal, they talk half Hindi. If you speak Hindi, there is some understanding. I used to understand her. But if you talked fast, then she could not understand. But if you spoke very, very slowly, then she understood. She wasn't troubled by the village women. She would just sit silently. And now I have eaten in every Brahman house.

The customs in Bengal are different. I stayed there twenty-five days at the time of the marriage. The marriage took three or four days. Then the boy should stay at the girl's house for fifteen or twenty days. Then they can go. [Q: Why?] The custom there is that they must see how the boy is. Does he talk to the girl? Is he nice to her? Then the parents ask their daughter, "Is it all right or not?" If she says yes, then it is good, and on the following day they let them sleep together. If she says no, there is trouble.

I got married three years ago. Last year, I took her back to visit for twenty days or so. The reality is that Bengal is a very poor country. People's fate doesn't even include clothes like you and I wear. So when we reached there, my father-in-law and mother-in-law embraced us and wept. I had sent a letter saying we would come for the festival. But the truth is that most girls who marry [people from far away] don't go back. So they think that their daughter will never be seen again. So when we went there, my father-in-law was overjoyed. Everyone gathered around. I would like to go again, but I don't have enough money.

.   .   .

Of my grandfather's land, only half an acre remains. All I have are my hands and my feet. My whole life has been troubled.

Sudhir saw his troubles starting after his mother died. His father drank and gambled and eventually sold the remaining land. His brother now works as a cook in the Punjab, leaving only Sudhir in the village. Sometimes one of his father's brothers visits or brings his wife for short time. Sudhir's father was missing. When asked about his family's downfall, Sudhir responded:

Previously, the family was all together. Everyone used to earn a lot. But now there is no unity. One person goes here, another goes there. No one accepts any advice from another. Say there is a broom. If you have one straw separate, it can't sweep. But when all are together, it can sweep. But now everything is separate. The land is separate. If someone has a minor problem, all they do is sell a piece of land. Or drink liquor. But they don't meet their expenses by working. Now I earn one hundred rupees. My uncle earns four hundred, but he gambles. If I gambled, where would I end up? I am thinking about the future. If I don't work hard, I won't progress.

Sudhir and his wife hoped for a child. One son was born and died. Meanwhile, this small family continued to struggle, but at least Sudhir's hard work was keeping them afloat. Moreover, when an extremely poor Muslim widow from the village, a woman who fed her family by begging, had a daughter who was of marriageable age, Sudhir was a leader in organizing village support so that the girl could be married in a respectable fashion. He used the only inheritance he had, his hands and his feet, for his family and for others also. Sudhir's ancestors were amongst the most respected and wealthiest in the village. But one's behavior in this life does indeed affect one's fortunes, so Sudhir can hope that his hard work will regain some of the status and respect that his family lost as a result of the behavior of his father and uncles.

"Power Comes through Money"

Being rich and powerful in Karimpur is almost synonymous with being a Brahman. But not all Brahmans are rich; in fact, one-twelfth of the Brahman families (five of sixty-two families) are barely able to meet subsistence needs. Moreover, some non-Brahmans are rich: one Shopkeeper's family and one Accountant's family are very well-off, while many others manage to build brick houses, educate their sons, and feed themselves with no worry. But there is no other group in Karimpur that can equal the Brahmans in political and economic clout, as much a fact today as it was in the past.

This chapter focuses on the Brahmans—on their lifestyles, worldview, and aspirations. I am concerned, too, with how wealth translates into power and respect. In addition, the Brahmans are subject to the onus of special burdens that are not faced by non-Brahmans: concerns about honor, demands for patronage, and pressures to conform to the social standards defined as worthy of their status as leaders of the community.

BRAHMAN BY BIRTH

Mohan is clear about what constitutes being a Brahman:

> Brahmans? They have become Ishvar [god]. Brahman is a separate thing. They are eternal [*anant*], are not even born of Ishvar. Even Bhagvan has touched the feet of Brahmans. Has a Brahman ever touched the feet of Bhagvan? Look in the *Ramayana*.[1]

. . .

There is an artificial diamond and a genuine diamond. However much the genuine diamond is pressed and cut, it remains genuine. And the artificial will remain artificial.

. . .

The Brahmans have come from there [heaven?] to discover the truth. Having discovered the truth [they] will go there again. He [a Brahman] knows each and every thing about Bhagvan.

The Karimpur Brahmans believe, then, that to be Brahman is to be unique, to be a true diamond and stand in a special relationship to Bhagvan. Brahmans are by nature at the top of the Hindu hierarchy: this is their birthright. They alone emerged from the head of the first man, Purusha, and they alone have the gift of knowledge.

Mohan's brother said this:

It has been told in the scriptures that Garuda asked a saint, "Tell me this: what is the best life form [*joanj*, literally, 'shape']?" Then he said, "I have feeling for all, but I have more love for humans. And among humans I have more love for Brahmans. I have much love for Brahmans, who are knowledgeable."

However, other *jāti*s can reach knowledge of Bhagvan. As Mohan added:

Each must perform his own profession [*tarīkā*]. Take us. If we hear the roar of a bullet, then we would immediately have the shits. But a Kshatriya would give his life; he would not run. . . . I am saying that all are able to reach Bhagvan by acting [righteously].

He went on to explain the Vaishya, or Trader *varṇa*, as having this nature:

What we eat goes in the stomach, so it is Vaishya. [It stores food.] It comes together in one place. They [Vaishyas] are known as the sons of Lakshmi. People of other *jāti*s cannot hope to accrue as much wealth as stays with them. The Chattri [Kshatriya] never gets wealth. . . . See, these arms are the Chattri. Only these can do everything. And the Brahman lives in the brain. So Brahmans were kept on top, then Chattri.

These comments reinforce the importance of knowledge and understanding as critical to rank, a point discussed in previous chapters.

One becomes a Brahman, or a member of any other *jāti*, at birth as a result of deeds in one's previous lives. Mohan offered this explanation:

7. Brahman men gathered near Mohan's house

According to the deeds [*kām*, "work"] that you did in your previous birth, you will get [your] nature [*prakriti*].

. . .

[It is] because of actions in a previous birth [*karam ke sanskār*] that you found a birth in a Brahman family. You are now consuming your earnings from the previous birth. Penance, sacrifice, pilgrimage, wealth, money, whatever there is—descendants, offspring—all is due to the earnings from your previous birth. You are consuming them in this birth.

In Karimpur, then, to be born a Brahman is to be chosen on the basis of previous worthiness. They are people with special rights, special knowledge, and a special relationship with Bhagvan. Based on prior actions, these rights are given at birth. The prior actions define the person's nature (body and soul) as an intertwined element, an intertwining that produces the physical and moral being called a Brahman.

The Karimpur Brahmans are Kanya Kubja Brahmans, one of the many Brahman *jāti*s found throughout India. They marry only other Kanya Kubja Brahmans, who themselves are internally subdivided into named ranks. Ideally one should marry one's daughters into families from higher-ranked subdivisions, while wives should come from lower-ranked subdivisions.

Within the *jāti* hierarchy of Karimpur, the Brahmans are ranked highest both because of their special role as priests and because of their economic power. Even today, comprising only 21.6 percent of the population, they own 58.1 percent of the agricultural lands of the village.[2] Their high status is continually reaffirmed in food and service transactions. The Brahmans only rarely eat food not cooked by other Brahmans, whereas people of the other *jāti*s willingly accept food cooked by Brahmans. Further, members of most other *jāti*s provide at least some ritual service to the Brahman houses. These landowning Brahmans actually consider priesthood a lesser occupation than farming. Hence only four Brahman men frequently perform priestly duties in the village, although all Brahman men are addressed as *panditjī* (literally, "honorable priest").

Yet people from other *jāti*s sometimes dispute the Brahman's claim to be so extraordinarily special. In discussing *varṇa*, the fourfold division of Hindu society that encompasses the myriad *jāti* distinctions, Raghunath said:

> *Varṇa/jāti* means nothing to Bhagvan. Just like Shudra and Vaishya and just like Brahman and Kshatriya: Bhagvan himself understands them all to be one. "All are my offspring." . . . When the earth was created, there were four people, perhaps: they made these *varṇa*s. I understood this. There is not any true [*pakkā*] report.

Raghunath's story about the four brothers who created the *jāti*s (see chapter 2) puts forth a view of the origins of *jāti* that allows for oneness, for equality, at the same time that it explains separateness and discrimination. He later added, "There are two groups: Hindu and Muslim. There are many different *jāti*s among Hindus. But now it is not like this. All want to be one." Here Raghunath is presenting a view of *jāti* and *jāti*-ranking that is relatively new in Karimpur and is related to the propaganda about democracy espoused by the government. This view will be examined further in chapter 6.

Raghunath has a special story for his own *jāti*, the Cultivators, whose traditional occupation is farming:

Kshatriyas are of the Surya Bansi [the royal lineage of the Sun, the lineage of the Lord Ram]. It means this. I am born from Lav, son of Ram. And those who are Lodhi [a closely related *jāti*], they are born by Kush [Lav's twin], just as Valmiki [author of the Sanskrit rendition of the *Ramayana*] made them. Lav was born of Ram Chandraji, and Kush was also. So they call themselves Kushva. Well, I am born from [Lav]. Four boys were born to him. But all four were not alike. The father thought, "Now what should I do: there are four boys, they must become educated." So they began their studies. [One] became an Accountant. And there are Grain Parchers. They lived in dirty conditions and started doing their work. "We must learn to parch." So at that time they started doing their work. They became Grain Parchers. Well, there were also the Cultivators. The Cultivators worked very hard in the fields. They began to be called Mahatiya.[3]

Raghunath agrees with Mohan that *jāti* is determined by "the account of one's past actions" (*karam ke hisāb se*). But while he and other people from lower-ranked *jāti*s have explanations that allow a hierarchical system of social rank based on birth, these explanations contain subtle and important differences from the Brahman point of view. To the lower *jāti*s, all men were once the same: of the same mother or of the same lineage. But at some point, because of age, ability, or even sin, these men became different and the *jāti*s developed. Humans must, after all, be able to live with dignity and a sense of positive self, but the Brahman explanation of *jāti* does not permit this for all Karimpur residents. The Brahman view emphasizes the distinctiveness and separateness of the Brahman, whereas the other *jāti*s emphasize original sameness; they focus on the essential oneness of all *jāti*s, but particularly the unity of those ranked lower. This perceived unity was continually reaffirmed in Karimpur discourse: most non-Brahmans talked about "those people" [*voi log*] or the "big people" [*bare log*], usually with an accompanying glance in the direction of the Brahman neighborhood. At the same time, everyone talked of the *chotī jāti*s, the "small castes." In Karimpur, the *bare log* are made up of just one *jāti*, the Brahmans, while the *chotī jāti*s include everyone else, sometimes united politically against the *bare log*, but always united in poverty and powerlessness.[4]

BRAHMANS AS PATRONS

The land owned by the families of Saroj and Mohan only came under their full control in the 1950s, when the newly independent Indian state instituted land reforms that abolished large estates. (See chapter 5.) In the

8.   The house of a wealthy Brahman family

1920s Karimpur revenue rights were held by two absentee landlords, but
the Brahmans were the primary tenants, those who effectively owned the
land and claimed its produce. After Independence, absentee landlords
were abolished, however, and the primary tenants became owners of the
land.[5] Karimpur Brahmans continue to own the majority of the lands, although in recent years there has been an increase in land transactions,
with considerable amounts of land changing hands and some of it being
sold to non-Brahmans. Mohan's father was the primary tenant to sixty-
five acres in the 1920s, while Mohan's share is a mere ten acres, since his
father's land was distributed among the six sons. As Mohan noted, his father was wealthy even then, being a major moneylender and patron of
others. Saroj's husband had primary tenancy rights in ten acres, but since
there was no adult male in her husband's family, their initial financial situation was precarious.

The political power of Brahman families evolved from their ability to
control others economically: other *jāti*s were largely dependent upon the
Brahman landlords for survival. Many were tenant farmers, renting land
or sharecropping. Others were bound to Brahman households through
the *jajmānī* system, the hereditary system tying patron families to families of lower *jāti*s who provided necessary economic and ritual services.
The patron is the *jajmān*; the client is a *kām karnewālā*, or *kamīn*, literally, "worker."

Mohan described the duties of each of the service *jāti*s under the *jajmānī* system. His view is that of the patron, always providing and caring for his workers, and is representative of the view of Brahman men, especially those who remember the system as it was prior to the mid-1960s. His comments also include his assessment of the current situation regarding the *jajmānī* system, and he details the roles retained and lost by the *kamīns* over time.

Watercarriers: Previously, Watercarriers [*kahār*] worked for us. They used to bring water; they used to take food. During a wedding ceremony, they used to work as laborers and they got food [as compensation]. And they took what we gave in faith. We made them happy. If a boy got married, they carried the palanquin. Six people used to go with the palanquin. For the whole marriage each of them used to get fifty *paise*.[6] Sometimes they got more. We used to feed them when our children were born, at marriages, and at the time of death. We also called them for carrying invitations. They used to call people to come to feasts.

In those days there were no hand pumps or wells in our houses. There was only a well before the Flower Grower's house [down the lane]. All the Cotton Carders and Shepherds used to draw the water from the same well. Our *bahū*s and girls—they did not draw the water. The Watercarrier drew the water and was given food as pay. Now that there is a well in the house and also a hand pump, our women draw their own water.

Leatherworkers: Leatherworkers [*jatav*, also known as *camār*] brought yellow clay for plastering at the time of festivals.[7] And they also replastered [with mud] the housefront and washed the walls for the two big festivals—Holi and Divali.[8] When they had plastered and whitewashed and we thought that they had worked as hard as six or eight men, then we paid them. We didn't want laborers to be short [of pay]. We gave them lentils, mustard oil, vegetables, wheat. I mean, whatever they were lacking for the festival, we gave them, so that they could also celebrate their festival with joy and laughter. If they asked for clothes, we gave them clothes. They also used to get one bundle of barley and one bundle of wheat from the fields.[9] If they worked in a field, then they got to glean it. They got whatever grain fell in the fields. Now they don't do any plastering or whitewashing, so they don't get bundles of grain and the gleaned heads of grain. Their work has finished.

Barbers: The Barber [*nāī*] works for you. Whatever you grow in your fields you must give to him. You must give a little bit of everything. A minimum of eleven pounds of sweet potatoes,[10] one bundle of barley, one bundle of wheat. As much sweet potato as he needs, he'll take. He will take rice. If he has a buffalo, he will also take one or two days' worth of fodder. If he has to stay for a long time when he comes to cut hair, then you have to feed him. The Barber is from another village. He does his duty. There is no major change in the Barber's work. When the Barber was from our village, he used to come in the evening, sit on the cot, and begin to massage you. When someone from inside called you for dinner, he would go with you to eat. He also filled the water pipe with tobacco. It was the custom.

Midwives: The Midwife [*dhānuk*] men made the leaf plates used at the time of marriages or deaths. Whenever they worked, they were given food. We used to make them happy [with gifts] at the time of marriages, but nothing was given at death ceremonies. If a boy was born, we paid the midwife thirty pounds of grain. And if a girl was born, we gave twenty-three pounds. The midwife will massage the *bahū* with oil as long as she must stay inside [usually ten days].

Carpenters: First Nekram was my Carpenter [*baṛhāī*]. Either you pay forty-six pounds of grain to him for each plow, or a bundle of barley and a bundle of wheat with stalks. He'll take whatever you give him from your field. If you don't give anything from the fields, then you have to pay forty-six pounds of grain per plow. Plows are made only once a year, in the month of Kuar [September–October]. If a farmer needs small parts of a plow periodically, that is no problem. We did not use the plow daily.

Blacksmiths: The work of the Blacksmith was to sharpen the plow's blade, and to make cutting and scraping tools: the reaping hooks and also the sickle. Whoever works with iron is the blacksmith. [A Carpenter did blacksmith work in Karimpur. Mohan's Carpenter and Blacksmith were not the same person until recently, when most Carpenters stopped doing *jajmānī* work.]

Washermen: The Washerman [*dhobī*] will take the clothes one day and bring them back the next, when he receives cooked breads.[11] When he washes the clothes from a birth, he will demand thirty pounds of grain. He washes clothes, and he gets bread. For washing clothes he takes what you grow in your fields, like sugarcane juice, jaggery, sweet potatoes, wheat, and so on. If he has cattle he will take fodder for one day.

Potters: We have four major festivals. For each festival, they [*kumhārs*] provide whatever people need—two pitchers, four pitchers. If we need other kinds of pots, they also provide those. The Potter gives pots [to each house] four times a year [at major festivals]. But because the festival of Saluno takes place during the monsoon when they can't make pots, they make pots in three batches. They used to take a bundle of barley, a bundle of wheat, a bundle of lentils, sweet potatoes, rice, carrots, radishes, vegetables, fodder. The Potter's lamps are very critical at Divali. People will give him puffed rice and wheat then. We make them happy. At the festival of Pitcher Fourth [*karva cauth*], he brings the pitcher. Then he gets sweets.[12]

Now they don't make pots like they used to. It has changed. They used to collect cow-dung cakes from the forest [to fire the kiln]. Now they buy that fuel. In the village, cow-dung cakes are expensive—five or six rupees for a hundred cakes. Fuel is costly, and they can't get enough. Yet they make a few pots for festivals. Now they do their own work. They'll make a pot if you need it. But you have to pay ten pounds of grain.

Sweepers: The Sweeper [*bhangī*] does what she did before.[13] She will clean the bathroom and will get bread daily, and she will also take food from the fields as others do. . . . They work every day. We try to keep them happy. And we also give food to them at the harvest.

9. An Oil Presser in the 1960s with the old-style press

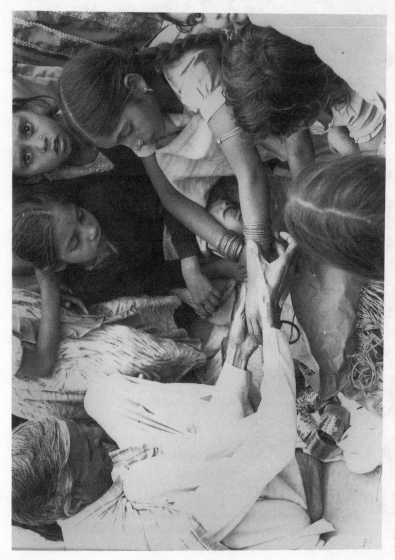

10. A Bangle Seller selling at the door of a Brahman house

Oil Pressers: The Oil Presser [*telī*] used to take twenty-three pounds of mustard seeds and return ten and a half pounds of oil. They took mustard from the house, returned the oil, and kept the oil cake [which could be sold as cattle food]. They were *kamīn*s. If we had a feast, we used to call them and feed them and give them sweets. They also took food from the fields.

[Q: If Oil Pressers were good, why did they stop doing this work?] Because of the old oil press [*kolu*] and machines. At first the Oil Pressers used to give an extra half pound, but they stopped. They said, "We cannot give that much more." People objected, "You were giving that much earlier, so you should give that much now." Also, the machine age came. Slowly the Oil Pressers stopped pressing oil, and we started to carry our mustard seed to mechanical mills.

Flower Growers: They [*mālī*s] used to provide flowers and leaves, and they used to eat at the marriage feasts. They also used to get money at weddings. Four or five rupees. He brings the crowns for the bride and groom and gets paid. Now, they take ten rupees and they are not happy. Even now I give them one rupee and something from the fields [at every harvest].

Shepherds: In the olden days there were no flour mills. They [*garariyā*s] used to grind the grain at the time of weddings and funerals. They provided the *kankan* [a bracelet of hair tied on bride and groom] at weddings. At a birth, they brought milk from their houses for the baby.

[Q: What did you use to give them?] For milk, we paid one rupee and a cheap sari. We gave them whatever was possible. [Q: Did they stop their work or do they still do it?] They still provide the *kankan*. But in the olden times, the women used to grind five pounds and would get two pounds of grain. Now grinding is quick, and for five *paise* ten pounds are ground. So because of the electric flour mills, they are able to rest, and we are also comfortable. But machines can't give *kankan*s, so they give those.

Grain Parchers: They [*bhurjī*s] used to eat at weddings and receive *bainā* [a ritual offering made only to certain service *jāti*s]. We used to give them food from our fields, too. They used to carry the grain for parching from our home, and after it was parched, they returned it to our homes. In return for their labor they used to get grain. They were working as *kamīn*s. Now they have some objections.[14] So their customs have changed a little bit.

Cotton Carders:[15] We used to give them [*dhunā*s] cotton to card. They were paid by how much cotton they carded. For carding one pound of cotton, their payment was one pound of grain. They also got food at weddings. We also gave them sugarcane juice and jaggery. When they gave us the cotton [for wicks] at the time of Divali, they got grain. When they gave us cotton for jackets, they got two pounds of grain. They also used to get produce from the fields as other *kamīn*s did, because they too were *kamīn*s. It was like this—even if we gave them only a little, it was sure to make them happy.

Bangle Sellers: The Bangle Seller [*manihār*] used to come to the house to sell glass bangles to the women. [Brahman women were secluded and thus unable to visit shops; moreover, bangles must be put on by the Bangle Seller as they fit very tightly and only he can fit them properly. So it was necessary for him to visit each household.] They used to get grain [*akhat*]. We gave them four pounds plus whatever amount they asked for the bangles. They also used to get produce from the fields. And ate the same way as others did at weddings, deaths, and so on.

Faqirs: The Faqirs [a Muslim *jāti* of beggars] were also *kamīns*. They came to weddings [where they were musicians]. Now we have English bands and they don't come, but earlier they used to play very well. We paid half a rupee for each instrument. For two it was one rupee. A drum was half a rupee. They ate like all the others.

Bards: The Bards [*rāy*] used to carry invitations at times of happiness or sadness. We used to take their advice on invitations: how and when we should send the invitations. It was also their work to make the *sona* and *sani* [ritual designs] in the month of Savan [July–August].

We gave them food and also offerings [*dān-daksinā*].[16] They were not given grain from the fields. They used to get this *pad*. [When people die, at the time of the funeral feast, family members bring clothes and pots called *pad*, which are inauspicious offerings received by someone lower, in this instance the Bards.] We also gave gladly to them at marriages.

Dancing Girls: She used to profit from *jajmānī*. If your daughter had a wedding, she went there and sang a few songs and received two or four rupees. She also got produce from the fields. While she was able to sing and dance, she earned this way.

Tailors: They [*darjīs*] sewed the clothes and charged five pounds of grain, whether the garment was big or small. In the old days, there were no machines. The work was done by hand. On the sixth day after a baby was born, he used to bring clothes for the baby and received grain. They got food from the fields as well. He also charged separately for every piece he sewed.

Cultivators: We didn't think that the Cultivators [*kāchīs*] were *kāmwāle* [workers]. They had one duty: after a death, the Cultivators sang *anrayā*. [During the Holi festival, Cultivators used to sing songs called *anrayā* at the gate of the family of a man who had died during the year to remove the *gamī*, the grief, from the house.] This was their work. We used to give them a tray of sweets at the funeral. There was no special Cultivator [that is, no hereditary or fixed relationship between families]. They used to come to sing together. *Anrayā* is not just one man's work. Someone plays the drums, someone else the cymbals. *Anrayā* was sung at Holi.

Brahmans: The people [*brāhmans*] who were pandits did work such as sacred thread ceremonies, marriages, birth rituals, and funerals. They used to set the [auspicious] time for a wedding or for some worship, and they also told the time and date of festivals. They gave new sacred threads at the festivals, too.

Mohan adds that Goldsmiths (*sūnar*); Rice Cultivators (*lodhī*, a Rajput farming *jāti*), Accountants (*kāyasth*), and Shopkeepers (*banyā*) were not *kamīns*, or workers, for Brahman patrons.

Most important, however, are his thoughts on the relationship between *jajmān* and *kamīn* that had been present in his childhood and was largely in place through the 1960s.

We did not keep them [workers] as slaves [*gulām*]. We had love for them. Even if you are my brother or grandson, you cannot quarrel with my *kamīn*. We will give our life for him. There was no unjust force used against them. If you don't have a *kamīn*, then you can ask my *kamīn* if he will work. But I will not let him be pressured into working [for others].

. . .

We always used to feel that our *kamīn*s should not have any sorrows. If they do not have grain in the middle of the night, we will give them some. If no food, [we'll give them] food. If police and other people try to trouble them, we do not let them. If he steals your sugarcane, I will not give you permission to beat him. I will beat him myself. I will say, "You can take of my field in exchange for what he took." *If my kamīn is insulted it means that I am insulted* [emphasis added]. Once we had a lot of lentils and this cattle yard was full of the dry stalks. There were very few lentils elsewhere in the village or nearby. It was time to make thatch roofs. So Partap asked me to give him ten bundles of stalks to make the thatch roof. We refused. The Cultivators came who were working for our family. . . . My great-grandfather gave them one bundle each. Om's great-grandfather was sitting here at my gate and Chaubeji was also here. Chaube asked, "Where did you get those bundles?" They told him the name of my great-grandfather. He asked my great-grandfather, "Why did you refuse Partap but give to those people?" My great-grandfather replied, "Will you do the work that they do for me? Will you? You can buy [what you need]; you are a rich man. They have such faith in us."

Mohan's retrospective view of *jajmānī* contains a nostalgic feeling of "the good old days" when Brahmans were seen as giving full expression to their noblesse oblige. For Mohan, the ritualized give-and-take of *jajmānī* epitomized the special position Brahmans perceived themselves as holding. A younger Brahman from a family once nearly as powerful and respected as Mohan's, however, took a slightly different perspective. Om, now in his thirties, has seldom in his adult life felt the full obligations of *jajmānī* or experienced the level of respect of a *jajmān* interacting with his *kamīn*s that his grandfather did. Yet on major points, his view coincides with Mohan's.

In the British period, when *jajmānī* was working well, and also before the British period, the relation between *jajmān* and *kamīn* was like father and son. When only the zamindars ruled, the people were very troubled. Where kings [*bare log*, literally, "big people"] ruled, the people were happy.

*Jajmān*s were dependent on *kamīn*s; *kamīn*s were dependent on *jajmān*s. In the presence of each, life was half [that is, together they made a whole].[17] The *kamīn* always wanted the well-being of his *jajmān*. He used to pray to Bhagvan for their wealth. He helped a lot at the time of marriages. If the *jajmān*'s household was big, then he would also be wealthy. And he would get more goods and more work. He would get a better reputation in his society [namely, his *jāti*] because he was the *kamīn* for a big house. When the *jajmān* was powerful [*śaktiśālī*], then the *kamīn* too would be powerful. Therefore, when the *jajmān* was in trouble, the *kamīn* used to help as much as he could. So he used to help at the time of marriages. Even if the master was short of money, he told the people coming to arrange a marriage that they [the *jajmān*'s family] were very well off. The *kamīn* knew that if there were no more children in the family, then *jajmānī* would be over. And their troubles would increase. So the *kamīn* used to help his master in any way that he could.

In the same way, the *jajmān* used to keep his *kamīn* in mind. If the *kamīn*s were hungry or naked, if there was a wedding in their family, or if someone died, he used to help in every possible way. The *jajmān* used to feel insulted [*veījjatī*] if his *kamīn* went to another *jajmān* for a loan, or if the *kamīn* felt the need of money and the master was unable to help. It would mean that the *jajmān* is also dying of hunger and cannot support his workers. In such cases it would mean that the *jajmān* did not have honor [*ijjat*].

If there was no food in the house of the *kamīn* and no food in the house of the *jajmān*, and the *kamīn* came to the *jajmān*, either the *jajmān* gave from his home or borrowed from somewhere, but the *jajmān* had to give to his *kamīn*. Even if the *jajmān* was hungry he *had* to take care of his *kamīn*. If the *kamīn* went to another *jajmān*, he was dishonored [*veījjatī*] because his *jāti* people would insult [*upmān*] him by saying, "He's dying from hunger." But if he received [what he needed] from his own *jajmān*, no one used to say anything because he was bringing from his own house.

But if some *jajmān* was angry and wanted to change his *kamīn*, he could not. He could not leave him. Because of their union, no other *kamīn* would come to serve that *jajmān* until their society* gave permission*. But they could change the worker. If *kamīn*'s wife was away, then her husband could send a woman from another house. If there was no man in the house, then the chief [of the *jāti*, the *mukhiyā*] would arrange [for a worker]. If someone wanted to change a worker, there was a panchayat [literally, "a council of five," but generally a meeting of the leaders of the *jāti* or village]. The panchayat used to favor the *kamīn*. The *kamīn* could not be changed. Although the *panch* [council] was mostly Brahmans, the quarrels were always because the *kamīn* was given less than he used to receive. If there was trouble, the *jajmān* still had to give. The *kamīn* is dependent on the master, and it was the obligation of the master that the *kamīn* not be in sorrow [*dukhi*]. At the time of marriage of a boy or girl, if the *kamīn* had any trouble with such things as money, clothes, or a bullock cart, then the *jajmān* used to help.

Basically, the Brahmans had a union, too. Other *jajmāns* did not give to another's *kamīns* if their own *jajmān* was not giving. First, the second *jajmān* would ask the *kamīn*'s own *jajmān*, "Should I give to him or not?" Therefore, in every way it was like the relationship of father and son. Brahmans were like kings, and the *kamīns* were ruled.

Mohan's and Om's accounts of Brahman attitudes toward their workers parallel that presented by William Wiser in his classic description, *The Hindu Jajmani System*, originally published in 1936. In the 1920s, eighty of Karimpur's 161 families were *kamīns* (excluding those of Brahmans, Cultivators, Goldsmiths, Shopkeepers, and Accountants). Thirty-two of these families derived the bulk of their income from *jajmānī* ties.[18] Other families were used as *kamīns* for some services, and every family in eighteen of the twenty-four *jātis* was practicing the traditional occupation at least part of the time. However, whether all these *kamīns* were happy, as Mohan states, is questionable. Wiser had a prosperous Brahman man rate the economic standing of every family actively involved as a *kamīn* in *jajmānī* relationships: sixteen of the eighty *kamīn* families enjoyed a "good" economic status, eleven had a "fair" economic status, and fifty-one had a "poor" economic status.[19]

Jajmānī involved more than a mere exchange of goods and services. As Wiser states, "The strength of the system depends . . . not on the actual payments made but on the concessions granted to the different occupational groups."[20] Most of the concessions he lists consist of economic benefits: food, fodder, clothing. Others suggest additional forms of patronage: a free residence site, credit facilities, opportunities for additional employment, casual leave, and aid in litigation. Brahman patronage thus extended beyond purely material benefits. As Mohan said, if the police troubled a worker, the *jajmān* would help. Moreover, a family was more likely to obtain credit from a *jajmān* than from elsewhere, and on better terms. He could also count on employment at harvest and planting times.

Even today, Brahman patronage extends well beyond the lingering payments for services rendered. In the 1920s education was almost exclusively limited to Brahmans. With education came the knowledge and ability to manipulate the bureaucracies that tied Karimpur to the colonial government of the British and the tax collectors of the zamindars. Education is more widespread in the 1980s, but few non-Brahman men have been educated beyond the eighth grade, and the number completing a B.A. is minute. Educated Brahman men, still tied to specific *kamīn* families through old ties of solidarity if not of actual employment, are called upon to take their *kamīn*s to the government hospital or to a local doctor, to find a lawyer, to arrange a tractor to convey a marriage party to the bride's house, to accompany a man to the law court, and so on. With the spread of local government agencies, cooperative banks and seed stores, development offices, and new medical facilities have come greater demands for help in dealing with these agencies.

Thus, for example, the forty-five-year-old head of a Carpenter family, who no longer even worked as Carpenters but were still attached to one particular Brahman family, insisted that the son of that Brahman family, aged only thirty-two but with wide experience in the district town and beyond, accompany him to Agra, eighty miles away, to see a heart specialist about the palpitations that he had been having. He was able to enter into the world of modern medicine, itself remarkable, but only with the support of his better-connected Brahman patron and friend.

As we have seen, patronage means giving food and payments for services, but it also includes serving as an intermediary in dealings with bureaucracies or giving loans. Brahman patrons continue to provide these services. During the heyday of the *jajmānī* system, moreover, Brahmans were able to control their *kamīn*s because they held the dual power of knowledge and wealth. Thus, when one younger Brahman man questioned an elder, "So the reason for *jajmānī* was illiteracy and poverty?" the answer was, "What else?"

POWER IN KARIMPUR

Mohan's family has had considerable wealth for several generations. Wealth, both as land, which enables a person to hire others, and as cash for lending, is the basic source of power in Karimpur. Alok, the oldest son of a formerly powerful Brahman family that is now experiencing some financial difficulty, described the importance of wealth from his perspective:

> All is dependent on money and on power. If I have money, then I can forcefully make someone obey. Man always needs money. The poor want money. Someone doesn't want to greet me respectfully: what do I do? We think that somehow we should get him to the point where he will yield to us. We must somehow get him degraded—get him caught by the police or call him a thief or dacoit. Then he will be weak from lack of money. When he is weak from lack of money, he will come to us to beg cash. I will give him money on interest, and, after taking my money, he will always greet me, "Panditji, namaste." This is the method of domination.

Prasad, a Grain Parcher who was once very poor, concurred in this assessment of the role of power. As he remarked during a discussion of insults, "He who is filled with power [*śakti jabardast*] is able to bring litigation. I am a weak man [and therefore don't bring cases against others]." He added, "In these ignorant times, whoever is strong [*jorāvar*] presses upon those without strength [*nibal*], and whoever is without strength keeps on sinking."

Both Om and Mohan agreed on one point. Om said:

And power is always worshiped [*aur śakti pūjā hameśa hotī hai*]. In our religion, power is also worshiped. Krishna was very powerful [*śaktiśālī*] and he is known as Bhagvan. Ram was very strong [*tākatkar*] and he is known as Bhagvan. So power is worshiped everywhere in the world. Whoever is powerful [*śaktiśālī*], they are always asked [for things]. And with power, one gets money. So what could be more powerful than that?

Mohan commented:

Of course we worship power. There has been power since the beginning. If the gods and goddesses had no power, then who would worship them? Why do people go to Jaykayan [a local god]? He has some power from Shivaji. That is why you and I accept him.

In Karimpur, the gods are powerful and thus are worshiped, as are wealthy human beings, who must be greeted respectfully.[21] Power in forms other than money is also respected, and ultimately worshiped. Om talked about a poor Shepherd man, highly regarded in Karimpur for his kindness to others and his ability to use traditional cures: "But first and foremost was the fact that he had physical power [*phiji kalvavar*]."

Physical power, including health, and money are linked. As Om went on to say:

Power [*śakti*] comes from money. This is the most important thing. Money is power. Now if I am sitting, silently suffering from fever, and a thousand rupees come into my pocket, then I won't have fever. My mind will become well because there is money in my pocket for expenses.

Here Om clearly associates internal, physical well-being with the power of money, which creates societal well-being. In most Hindu thought, the internal self and social self are interrelated.[22] In Om's example, the social health achieved through cash in the pocket contributes to the physical health of the person. A third form of power is mental power, such as that used by a healer who knows the necessary ritual sayings, a "scientist," as in the example below, or even that of an educated man who can mediate for others in the outer world.

A man's powers, whether physical or monetary, must be used wisely. Om elaborated on this point:

> But there are many men, who even if they have money in their pockets, are perhaps misers. If there is a small river filled with water, how much can it overflow? But a big river filled with water can overflow all over. Money power is like this. If money is combined with physical power, then that man may be lost in pride. He becomes very proud and arrogant. And when there is pride, there will surely be sin [*pāp*]. Man makes progress until and unless he does not become proud.

. . .

> If a man is beautiful, he becomes proud because of his beauty. There was Nakul in the Mahabharata. . . . When Nakul died, he was the most beautiful of his brothers. Dharmaraj Yudhisthir was king. When Nakul was dying, he asked, "Brothers, why am I going to die now?" And they said, "Because you take much pride in your beauty. As long as you are proud, you cannot reach Ishvar [god]. He who is without pride, he can know Ishvar and always lives happily."
>   Now the interpretation is that pride destroys power. If we have power and we are proud of that power, then we will use it. And the use will cause pain to the whole world. It will cause pain to society. So then all the people of the village together will try to suppress it, and for this they can do whatever they like. The whole village might act together or might seek assistance from another village. . . . So in this way the proud man will be all alone, and to control him, all will fight him together. Though they are small, when they gather together they increase in number. Consequently, they will have greater power. . . . But when somebody gets the opportunity, nobody loses it; power is always worshiped. It is true, whether it is the power of money [*paise kī śakti*], physical power [*sarīrik śakti*], or mental power [*mansik śakti*]. There is also mental power. And when all these three powers* are together in one person, then it is very difficult to beat it. What did Ravan have?[23] Ravan had money, he was also a scientist*, and he had much mental power. So everyone used to be afraid of him. All feared him. And when he gave trouble to everyone, all the kings united as one. And all fought against him, while Ravan fought alone. Thus all killed him because he had become proud.

The overly proud man can lose power, as indeed some Brahmans have. At the same time, several non-Brahmans have been able to gain power within Karimpur by becoming wealthy and using their wealth carefully. One such instance involves Bhim Sen, a Shopkeeper, who was very poor in the 1920s but is now quite wealthy. As a poor Cotton Carder put it, "Now there is Bhim Sen. If the police inspector comes, he stops at his place; if the deputy comes, he stops at his place. He has money, and money presses on everyone [including the police]. Therefore he has honor [*ijjat*]."

Maintaining one's power while avoiding the pitfalls of pride is not easy. Many Brahman families have lost power and prestige recently. This is often due to profligate sons, to the overextension of family resources through easily obtained government loans for capital investments in farming, or simply by having too large a family. While Brahmans firmly believe that a large family is a strong family, distributing a fixed amount of land among many sons typically leads to a weakened family of small landholders. Too many daughters can also impoverish a family, as daughters require exorbitant expenditures on dowries, which can necessitate taking out loans at interest rates of 100 percent per year and the mortgaging or sale of family fields.

Families that have gained power recently were generally similar to Saroj's family in the past—families with underutilized economic resources. They were in that position primarily because there were no adult men to farm and supervise their land. These families managed to retain their resources during these manpower shortages and have lately reaped the benefits of having both resources and the needed men. Outside employment, like Mohan's job as a panchayat secretary, is another major factor in having the income necessary to be powerful in Karimpur. These jobs also provide new channels of influence and outside contacts, which can further contribute to the family's ability to act as a patron.

Education is another critical source of power. As Mohan's account of his early life indicates, money enabled him to get an education, whereas Raghunath left school as soon as his father died and his family could no longer afford fees, books, and clothes. Even today, a boy has little chance of passing tenth- or twelfth-grade examinations without special arrangements for studying and tutors, so that the costs of education are beyond most families. But education is an absolute necessity if a boy is to obtain any employment other than manual labor outside the village. There are advantages to having an educated daughter now as well, because her marriage may be arranged with an urban and/or elite family, thereby establishing powerful affines. In this context, education does offer further possibilities for gaining and maintaining power, whether for boys or girls.

The ultimate key to gaining and maintaining power, however, is wealth. It is wealth that leads to physical power through health and to mental power through education. And wealth is the key that opens the door to honor.

GAINING AND MAINTAINING HONOR

All villagers, but especially Brahmans like Mohan and Saroj, pay constant attention to gaining and maintaining honor (*ijjat*). A man strives constantly to build up honor for himself if he lacks it, or to maintain or increase his honor if he has it. The honor of a person is visible in the respect shown by others. Being a Brahman, in the hierarchical system of *jāti*-ranking, should, at least in theory, guarantee some respect. Having power, especially that derived from money, also generally enables a person to gain honor. Proper behavior, being concerned for others, and having virtuous women are also necessary in order for a person to be respected, whereas insults challenge a person's claim to honor, especially if made publicly. Moreover, honor belongs not just to a person, but extends to his or her family, lineage, *jāti*, and community.

Honor is, first of all, a matter of money and power. Om was asked about honorable men one day and replied:

> Right now among the men [of Karimpur], people think most highly of the elected headman [*pradhān*], Shankar, because he is headman of the village and he has lots of land. He doesn't have any physical strength [Shankar is old], but he has the power of money. Second, he has the power of domination [*śāsan kī śakti*], and he has the power of administration [*praśāsanik kī śakti*] because he is *pradhān*. Moreover, he doesn't have quarrels with others. Quarreling decreases power [*jhagaṛa śakti ko kam kartā hai*].

Indeed, Shankar, the current *pradhān*, is thought by most to be a man of considerable honor. The honor of other Brahmans is, however, more questionable. Raghunath, the Cultivator who was crippled as a child, discussed several Brahmans one day while sitting in our rooms in Mainpuri, his comments focusing on the actions that lead to, and detract from, honor:

> Among the Brahmans, Krishna, Ashok, Tej, Prithvi and others are characterless because they were blemished for one reason or another. They have lots of money and property, but because of their boys and girls they have lost prestige. Raju's son, Ganesh, possesses honor, but because of his brother's character, he is thought not to have honor. The members of Indar's family bought their wives from outside. So they don't have honor. Triloki's house has boys who steal, and others have wives who live with others. So when people learn this, they do not have honor. Like Sunil: he has no honor. Even though he is wealthy, his character is bad. Ganga's son is like a Sweeper [thought by the elite to eat foul foods and generally to be of bad character]. So nobody calls him [for feasts, a matter of honor]. He eats everyone's food like he is a Muslim or something.

Here it is clear that honor indeed involves more than wealth. Further, a person's honor is dependent upon those in his or her family.[24] Raghunath listed his criteria: "Honor comes in every way. Honor comes from wealth; honor comes from land; honor comes from your daughters and daughters-in-law living inside the house and not speaking to others. A person who never steals is also honorable." This latter point is crucial to Raghunath, who was later asked whether there were any men of his *jāti* who had honor. He replied, "Yes, many, for we don't steal." Where honor cannot be based on wealth, as it usually is for the Brahmans, other aspects become more critical. Yet, even if not all Brahmans are viewed as honorable, when we inquired about honorable men in the village, no one ever spontaneously listed a non-Brahman. Hence although honor, like rules for women's proper behavior, is ideally available to be pursued by all, the distribution of honor in fact functions to maintain the class structure of Karimpur.

Several Brahmans felt that one earns honor by showing concern for the welfare of others and by keeping one's promises. Mohan, as usual, was clear and forthright:

Now honor [*ijjat*] is also like this: if a man comes to you, he must not return from your house dissatisfied. Suppose I come here to your place and ask for five hundred rupees. But you have no money. So you say, "Grandfather, I am helpless. I have no money at present, otherwise I would never refuse you. But I am helpless." Peace enters my heart because [I know] you have no money. So I am satisfied with you. But if you say, "Go! I will not give anything to you," my soul will be troubled because you didn't give. . . . But all these things are based on the foundation of wealth. He who has money should give all men every possible kind of help. There should be either money or wisdom. There should be peace and contentment in the heart. He should be pleased. I mean, to cause distress for the soul of any man is wrong. There is no honor in this. Honor is like this: a man should leave you satisfied. . . . So whether he is poor or rich, he must not speak ill to others. And he should not steal another's daughters-in-law and daughters or fields. To live without giving offense is honor. It is doing whatever you can to help others.

Om concurred with Mohan about the importance of consideration for others by emphasizing the lack of honor shown a miser:

The man who acts miserly never has respect [*sāmmān*] in the world because the miser himself doesn't even eat. And he collects money. He must give expenses for the good works, but he doesn't pay for those. That is why the men look askance at him. . . . He is watched with lowered eyes because where he must spend on good works, he cannot. But if he doesn't spend on others, he must spend for himself, he must feed himself, he must wear good clothes, he must spend on his own family. If he doesn't spend, he will not find honor [*ijjat*], he will not get respect [*sāmmān*], he will not be part of the society, he will not be part of the village.

But the man who opens his heart, who possesses money and does not do for himself but is for the poor, doesn't even have good clothes. But he is always ready to help others. He is always ready to make others happy. Therefore, those in his society always honor and respect him.

A twenty-eight-year-old man and aspiring politician of Raghunath's *jāti* who had been to school and was friendly with local government officials also acknowledged the honor attained by serving others. As he put it, "This free service gives me honor from the village. And it makes me part of good society in the village. . . . It is called leadership."

As Saroj and other women know, honor is heavily dependent upon the women of a family. "If the woman runs away, the nose of the whole family is cut," said one poor man, meaning that the honor of the entire family would be lost. In telling one of his folktales, Raghunath said, "If you have a son, he will kill you; and if you have a daughter, she will reduce your honor." Raghunath elaborated on the behavior necessary in order for a woman, and hence her family, to have honor:

> The woman who has honor lives inside the house. Suppose I go to someone's house and from outside I call, "Anyone here?" The one who has honor comes quietly, face hidden by a veil, and answers softly. We say she keeps much honor [*ijjat rakhtī hai*]. On the contrary, suppose I come from outside and call out and the woman comes quickly to the door and asks unashamedly and without hesitation, "Who is it?" and then says, "He is not here, he is coming. Come in and sit down." She speaks unnecessarily and too much. She is not a woman of honor. The woman who doesn't have the inclination to speak and doesn't talk and remains veiled has honor. For example, suppose my sister Shona is carrying breakfast to me in the fields. On the way, there are two boys. And the boys say, "Oh girl, where are you going?" We tell her that she must reply only this much: "I am taking food to my brother." [We say] that if the boys ask you more questions, you should not speak anything more to them, you should go straight [to the field]. You should not speak to those people any more because they can do or say bad things. Then she has honor. But if she speaks or goes somewhere, then she doesn't have honor. Girls who talk with boys are not honorable. So you keep your own honor: honor is in your own hands, whether [you are] a boy or a girl or a *bahū*. . . . Whether [you are] a man or a woman, honor is made by your own hands. Sometimes there is a very honorable man who is rich, and everyone knows him. But others live in his house who destroy honor. That Brahman has four sons, but when I was a child, he purchased his wife. Similarly, the Potter purchased his wife. So they didn't keep any honor. The

son's wife of that family eloped, and this is not the work of an honorable person.

There is a story (*kahānī*) told in Karimpur that emphasizes the importance of female behavior while also playing on the patron-client, rich-poor dichotomy. In this story, a Barber goes to another village into which both he and his landowning patron, here a Thakur, have recently married. While there, the Barber is to check on the two wives, whom neither husband has yet seen, for they have not had their *gaunā*. So he goes to see the two women. He finds his wife standing in the doorway buying greens. That day, he is fed spinach at his wife's house. Then he goes to see the Thakur's wife. As soon as she sees a strange man in the lane, she turns around and hides in the house. And at her place he is fed *pūrī*s and *kacaurī*s, both fried foods that indicate respect to those who receive them. The Barber is very irritated that his wife has not kept strict seclusion and has fed him a lowly food, while his Thakur's wife was most proper. So in his report to the Thakur he reverses the situation and says, "Listen, Thakur, my woman is good and at my in-law's house I was fed *pūrī*s and *kacaurī*s, while your woman is bad and there I was fed spinach." The story continues with the Thakur rejecting his wife, who must then earn his love by seducing him under the guise of a dancing girl.[25]

A male gains honor, then, by having land and wealth, by being kind to others, by keeping his word, and by having virtuous women who maintain purdah. Families can lose honor through their women by buying brides (such a bride is by definition not a proper woman) or by having daughters or daughters-in-law who elope, become pregnant prior to marriage, or are seen outside too often. Men may bring dishonor to a household by stealing, gambling, drinking, and eating taboo foods, and by being unkind or miserly.

Non-Brahman families also have honor, but to a much lesser degree, and in Karimpur it is Brahman honor that is always on the line. If a given family's honor declines because a son gambles or a daughter has affairs, then other families stand to gain. Hence Brahman men are constantly involved in intrigues of honor, which work against the Brahman unity that is felt to underlie their dominant role. Sunil, who Raghunath said had a dishonest character and hence little honor, assisted the daughter-in-law of a wealthy and previously respected Brahman family in running off with her lover. Sunil thereby gained in the game of honor. The family with the errant *bahū* tried to find a new wife for their son so that they could cut the tie with the "bad" wife, who had been caught and returned to her parents. But a second marriage for their son could not be arranged, which meant that they had to face even more dishonor by bringing the *bahū* back. Sunil gloated.

The game of honor is played out by manipulating the opposed actions of showing respect (*sāmmān denā*) and giving insults (*upmān karnā*). Showing respect acknowledges that the other person has honor. Giving an insult, or being disrespectful, challenges the other's right to honor. As a Watercarrier explained, "Honor and respect are like this: Sahab has come and I give him a place to sit. This is a matter of honor. If I do not say to Sahab, 'Please sit' and he remains standing, it means that I am insulting his honor." Showing respect means, first of all, greeting a person properly—by saying "Ram, Ram" or "Panditji namaste" or "I touch your feet" (*āp ke paun chue*), a common greeting expressed by Brahman men to their elders. It may also mean offering a chair, a place on a cot, or standing in another's presence, all critical issues between Brahmans and other *jāti*s, as we shall see in detail in chapter 5.

Women must also show respect to their elders. They should cover their faces before elders and touch the feet and massage the lower legs of women senior to them. Women who are in purdah seldom leave their courtyards, but the eldest wife in each house and the daughters of the village do pay visits, both for ceremonies to which a number of women may be invited or to see a friend or relative in another house. If a daughter returns from her husband's house, women from the village will visit her and she will visit them, often taking other women from her father's house with her. For these visits the women visiting will dress in good saris, put on their jewelry, and generally try to make the best possible impression. When a number of women have been called for a ceremony, such as the celebration of the birth of a boy or functions connected with marriages, the younger wives of the household must touch the feet and massage the legs of the senior women, whether visitors or members of her own household. Women are ranked by their husband's place in village genealogies. (Fictive kinship is maintained among all residents of Karimpur, so two men of the same chronological age might be generationally regarded as grandfather and grandson, as, for example, was the case with Om and his best boyhood friend, who was officially his "grandfather.") The woman married to the genealogically "junior-most" man must touch the feet of all women senior to her, including all daughters of her *jāti*, who are from birth considered to have higher status because when they marry, they will marry into families of higher status. Women's visiting thus turns into an endless display of rank and respect, as veiled *bahū*s move from woman to woman touching and pressing their feet and legs.

These actions, whether they lead to honor or dishonor (*veījjatī*), are motivated by modesty (*śaram*). Modesty is a matter of conscience and leads to right and wrong behavior. It is learned from parents and peers and also upon experiencing insult. Om said, "When insulted, you learn modesty. Because of modesty, a man knows that because of this matter, modesty has come to me." The well-behaved person has modesty. Our Grain Parcher friend said, "Those women who are respectable, they feel modesty." The person without modesty (*beśaram*) acts crazily and dishonorably. As our friend added, "The woman who is immodest says whatever comes to her mind—she acts in an upside-down way." So if you should show respect or act in ways that gain honor, but you don't, you are acting immodestly. A woman is immodest, for example, if she gives birth in her parents' house, for it is a matter of modesty that a woman not exhibit her sexuality before her parents. She should also not sleep with her husband in her natal home. A woman is immodest if she does not veil herself before her elders. A man is immodest if he insults another purposefully, or drinks or gambles or behaves badly. Smoking before one's father is an insult, as is not greeting another person properly. Having modesty is necessary to gaining honor, for without it one acts wrongly. And if one lacks modesty, the result, dishonor, affects the whole family, the lineage, or even the village. Some people even say that Karimpur men have trouble finding brides because all the Brahman men lack honor and hence the village has no honor.

An insult (*veījjatī*), in contrast, is something done to you that clearly shows that others think you have no honor. Not being greeted respectfully is an insult, and Brahmans thus get very angry when men of lower *jātī*s do not pay them the proper respect. (Alok's example, given above, of the power of money leading to a court case because a man did not say "Panditji namaste" is a prime example of this concern.) But there are other ways of insulting people: not calling them to participate in a ceremony or to accompany a groom in his marriage procession or not inviting the men of a given family to attend a feast given for a marriage or death. Recently, Mohan's family had a *bulūā* (a gathering where women sing celebratory songs) to mark the birth of Alok's son, the first great-grandson in the family. Mohan purposely did not invite the women of his brother's family to attend as they were currently feuding. In another instance, Sunil, the Brahman who helped his neighbor's daughter-in-law to elope, managed a subtle but piercing insult to Mohan's family. Sunil's son was being married, and he invited Mohan's family to send a man to participate in the marriage procession, as was appropriate because they are rather close kin. So

Mohan's son prepared his clothes and bedroll, for the members of the wedding procession would stay overnight. He then waited and waited. No one came to call him. Sunil should have sent a servant (usually a Watercarrier or Leatherworker) to bring the bedding and call the young man when it was time to leave. But no one ever came. It was a notable insult.

The goal, then, is to have honor, and honor is established when others show respect to a person and do not devise insults. Although wealth is essential for great honor, even among wealthy families the behavior of disreputable sons or women can lead to insults and bring dishonor upon the household, the lineage, or even the whole village. Inasmuch as it is recognized through social actions, then, honor is ultimately dependent upon society.

BRAHMAN LIFESTYLES

The honor and power of individuals, families, and *jātis* are derived from social actions and the recognition of those actions by others. Those who hold honor and power must not remain passive, however, but should avail themselves of every opportunity to further enhance their reputation. Opportunities are provided in the course of daily life and in the celebration of special occasions. The Brahmans of Karimpur, as the primary possessors of power and honor, have provided the majority of examples over the years of how to incorporate such enhancements into the daily routine. In fact, many of these actions have become so synonymous with power and honor that they are frequently emulated by other *jāti* groups in what has been termed the process of "Sanskritization."[26]

One of the most prominent features of Brahman everyday life is the imposition of purdah on their women. All Brahman houses are built with an inner courtyard, which is universally recognized as the domain of women. Most of these houses are spacious, and nowadays most are at least partly made of brick. Wells or hand pumps are becoming more commonplace in the courtyards. Ostensibly installed to ease women's labor, they further lessen the need for women to venture outside the house. (The decline of *jajmānī* relationships with Watercarriers has meant that women must draw water themselves, which entails leaving the house if they have no private pump.) Among the women inside the house, chores are divided by age and social role, with the mother-in-law or her daughters doing any outside work, such as making cow-dung cakes or feeding the animals, while daughters-in-law grind grain, cook the meals, and clean inside the house. Vendors do come to the door with items for women, and various service castes provide other supports for women, but these are all carried out within the proper rules of etiquette demanded by purdah. Men must perform certain activities that support the purdah restrictions of their women as well, doing most of the shopping in the bazaars, accompanying women when they do go out, hiring additional laborers rather than utilizing women's labor, and so on.

Brahman men and women dress well, the young men in Western-style clothing, their elders in dhotis or *kurtā-pajamā*. The women have gold earrings and rings, saris made of synthetic fabrics, and warm shawls. Nowadays most young wives use *sindūr*, a red line in their hair parting, and *bindī*s, the red dot worn by Hindu women on their forehead. Their children have ribbons, plastic bangles, and other minor "luxuries."

Brahmans also eat better than others in Karimpur. Tea is slowly becoming a custom in the mornings and can be offered to visitors. The men regularly bring vegetables from the market to supplement home-grown lentils and grains. Some families even have fruits on a regular basis, while almost all drink buffalo or cow's milk. In surveying women's food habits surrounding childbirth, we asked about concepts of proper diet during and after pregnancy. Brahman women had very clear ideas about what was acceptable (primarily food classified as "cold," to counter the internal "heat" caused by pregnancy) and claimed to give fruits and milk to pregnant women. The poor, in contrast, tended to laugh at the question, before responding, "We eat whatever we have." Brahman women also claimed to give special foods to those who had been ill, especially if this had been suggested by a doctor, whereas the poor found even requests for milk impossible to meet.

Brahmans are also healthier, not only because they eat better but because they receive better medical care. They respond more quickly in treating severe illnesses, especially those of men and male children. They prefer the hospitals and clinics in the district town over either the traditional healers in the village or the two self-proclaimed doctors residing there. Their child mortality rate is significantly lower than that of the poor, and the average ages of both men and women is high for the village as a whole.

Another aspect of everyday life that has come to be increasingly associated with honor and power over the past few decades is education. Brahmans educate all of their sons and daughters, at least through fifth grade. Most boys complete eighth grade, while a few even have B.A.s and M.A.s. None, however, have gone to schools outside the local region nor are any professionals. Most families hope that at least one son will get a job in "service" (namely, a regular, nonmanual position) while another son will remain in Karimpur to manage the lands. Education further enhances the marriage possibilities for boys and girls alike. A well-educated young man can demand a higher dowry, while a well-educated young bride can possibly provide her family with good connections. In either case, the ability to keep a child in school is a further display of a family's wealth.

Brahmans also have critical connections to government officials and other urbanites, either through schooling, jobs, or marriages. Hence they can get loans for such projects as a cow-dung gas plant—and the cement allotment for the gas plant can then be used to build a second story on their house. They can prod brick kiln owners into giving them bricks when there are shortages. Since all village headmen have been Brahmans, they have ready access to government development schemes and opportunities. The ability to take advantage of opportunities in the wider arena of district affairs is another facet of being a Brahman in Karimpur.

These everyday aspects of life reflect the power and wealth of certain villagers in relatively subtle ways. There are times, however, when the power and wealth of certain families is quite ostentatiously displayed. These times are most often life-crisis rituals such as weddings and birth celebrations, although occasionally some other ceremony may provide an opportunity for such display. Weddings are the occasions on which the most overt expression is given to differences in wealth, or at least to differences in borrowing power, among the Brahmans. There is keen competition among villagers to hold the largest feast, or to have one's son receive a more generous dowry than anyone before, or to have one's daughter marry into a richer family than any girl from Karimpur has in the past. These status-markers do not come easily, however, and a family will often find themselves deeply in debt for many years following such an occasion. The easy availability of low-interest loans for agricultural development has spurred the competition for ostentatious display in recent years. Many of the wealthy landowning Brahmans of Karimpur have taken out loans from banks and cooperatives, amassing large amounts of monies originally intended for other purposes and then using them for wedding expenses. While this scheme provides a source of ready money for weddings, problems arise when it comes time to repay the loans, problems that often result in the mortgaging or outright sale of land. Even so, losing land to pay for weddings, especially ones so lavish and memorable, is more acceptable than losing it for other reasons. Furthermore, the respect and honor garnered through the staging of a lavish and ostentatious display greatly outweigh the inconvenience of mortgaging some land.

While by any urban standard, the richest Karimpur Brahmans are poor, within Karimpur their lifestyle bespeaks a high level of relative wealth. They can afford to keep women in purdah and to educate their young; they dress well, eat more nutritious foods, and take advantage of medical facilities. Moreover, they are in the best position to manipulate the local governmental systems in order to maintain their advantages.

Everyday Brahman behavior is thus oriented in large part by concerns for (1) *jāti* status, in which Brahmans feel a clear superiority; (2) patronage, as both a right and a privilege, but through which the Brahman's ability "to take care of" others is also demonstrated; (3) sustaining one's power, whether material, mental, or physical, which ensures that others will "worship" one and hence become one's clients; and (4) the search for honor, to be found in the respect paid by others, a respect earned primarily by a person's ability to control the sources of power and be a patron. But the Brahmans of Karimpur are no longer secure in their superiority of *jāti*, patronage, power, and honor. Changes in agriculture, labor, and education have led the poor to question Brahman dominance. Before we examine these changes in relationships between the rich and the poor, let us examine the life of someone more like Raghunath or Santoshi, someone who is poor and whose life is guided by a different set of issues.

Sheila, the Washerwoman

Sheila, a Washerwoman by *jāti*, lives with her husband, Sonu, and two children, a boy almost two years old and a girl about four, in a one-room house on the edge of the village. Sonu's family migrated to Karimpur when he was a child, after the village near the Ganges where they lived was swept away in a flood. At that time the Karimpur Washerman was old and feeble and welcomed the new family. By the time I knew them, though, two other Washermen had primary rights to most of Karimpur's families. Sonu's siblings had all moved away, and his mother lived mostly with his sister. Sheila and Sonu were thus left with irregular jobs washing clothes in Karimpur and nearby villages, and Sonu attempted to find work as a day laborer or cycle rickshaw driver in Mainpuri. During the harvest season (April to June), he was employed at the village seed store collecting grain brought by farmers, and his earnings from that period saw them through the rainy season (July to September).

Several times I met Sheila and Sonu as a couple. Their cheerful caring for each other was perhaps unusual and hence appealing to my Western eyes. I also relished the ease with which we could communicate: when Sheila came to our house, we often chatted, and I soon learned that her Hindi was more accessible to me than the obscure dialects spoken by some village women. I later realized that this was due to her five years of schooling and her upbringing in Mainpuri, where more standard Hindi was current.

I first saw Sheila moving about the village as she went from house to house collecting clothes. Eventually I saw their house, tucked behind a large Brahman complex near the pond where Sheila washed clothes. Bits and pieces of her story emerged, and I wanted to talk to her further. However, Sheila didn't want to talk in the village, fearful of repercussions from her Brahman landlord and possibly the jealousy of others. So she came with her small son to Mainpuri and met me in my room there. We talked several times, and some of her reflections on her life are given below. I have reordered our conversations into a coherent narrative but have marked individual sections as units.

When I was a child, I went to school up to fifth grade. After fifth grade, I got married. My parents used to work hard and that's why they stopped my schooling. We had to work washing clothes. My brother used to work and study also. Two of my brothers went to school; two of them worked with donkeys [carrying bricks or dung cakes]. They worked at the brick kiln. And my mother, father, my little sister, and I washed clothes.

. . .

I used to wash clothes even while in school. When the cock crowed in the morning and it was still dark, I used to go and wash clothes. My brother used to go too, and my mother. We would finish washing lots of clothes before sunrise. Then we would go home and eat. I used to fix my hair, dress, and go to school. Then I would come home. I would eat at home and when the bell rang at noon, I would go back to school. After school, I used to help my mother and father gather the dried clothes, tie them, and put the bundles on our heads and on the donkeys to take home. I would go twice a day to school and twice to the river bank. I didn't return to school after passing fifth grade. I can write letters even now. I can write and also read. I didn't study English.

Sheila and her family worked for the family of the raja of Mainpuri, a Rajput, heir to a family that had been in the district for several centuries. The raja's family owns the fort that dominates the town of Mainpuri, and the family retains certain other privileges, such as running the district fair every April. The raja's daughter, whom Sheila calls Beti Sahab (literally, "daughter," plus an honorific), is the only heir.

I used to wash Raja Sahab's clothes. We used to wash Rani Sahab and Raja Sahab's clothes. When their son was born, they gave us ankle bracelets; they gave five sets of clothes to my mother, five sets to my father, and clothes to all the children. They also gave five utensils and ankle bracelets made of silver. Then the Raja Sahab's son died. The Rani Sahab died too. Afterwards Raja Sahab died. Now Beti Sahab is around and comes once in a while. She stays for a short while just like you do in the village. Yes, she comes and then goes off to her place. She comes to the temple for one hour to worship. Now she will come and organize the fair [at the Devi temple].

One year it wasn't held because she said not to. No shops were set up and none of the grounds were prepared.

On another occasion, Sheila spoke about her marriage. She had been married previously. Her first husband ended that marriage by not bringing her to his house. For a while she succeeded in forcing him to accept her, but the arrangement didn't last, as is related below. It is possible that her infertility led to the break.

[Sheila was married at ten or eleven.] I was very happy. My elder sister told me that this is a good marriage because it's a marriage of young ones. Then I said it was really a marriage of children. My husband had asked for a watch. He was really a young bridegroom. I had dolls made of cloth. We hardly used to talk. We hardly understood anything. Not a thing. I tried to tell him that just as there is a pair of dolls, we too are bride and bridegroom. When I had my *gaunā*, my sister-in-law and my husband's brother's daughter stole my doll so I gave one of them a slap. My husband in turn hit me with a stick. He hit me with a small stick. I caught hold of it and broke it. So we started a fight and they said, "Look, even at this young age they have started fighting." He didn't realize that he's a man and that I am a woman. He didn't realize that he is a bridegroom and I am a *bahū*. Children nowadays know this much. He didn't know that he is not supposed to fight or hit. Ultimately, I got my doll back. I used to play in my in-laws' house. If they asked me to dance, I used to dance. If they asked me to sing, I would sing, too. At that time, I didn't know: I didn't have modesty [*śaram*]. I didn't understand [*samajhtī*] then.

After my *gaunā*, I understood. I got my period three months after my *gaunā*. I was this small when I had my periods [pointing to a thirteen year old]. My mother-in-law used to say, "She can't do anything—throw her out." I was small: where could I go? At that time my breasts were just developing. But my mother-in-law said that girls should get married and produce a child after only one year. Nowadays kids are married, go in a wedding procession, and one year later they have a child in their lap. . . . I used to make love with my first husband, sometimes once a month or once in one and a half months. Sometimes only two weeks passed. Mostly after a month or a month and a half.

I fought a court case [when my husband tried to leave me]. He said he was leaving me. I told him he couldn't do so. "If you leave me, I will still stay in the house and make bread and lentils." I fought the case, even though he didn't want to. I fought the case for one year, and I won. After I won [the right to maintenance, presumably] he called me and said he would not give me food and clothing, but he would take me to his house. That we would live with much love. Then I conceded. My mother and father sent me to him again. I lived well for eight or nine months, and I stayed well. My parents gave him jewelry. While I was doing well, my sister got married. That very year. He told me that he would take the jewelry [to my parents], but I didn't want him to take the jewelry. But then I thought that we are doing well together, so let's take it. He took off all of my jewelry. He took it all. All of it [and never gave it to her parents]. Then he sent me to my parents with my uncle [mother's brother]. He said, "Go with your uncle." He sent me away by lying and cheating. He said, "Go, I'll call you again." But I didn't hear from him. For eight or nine months he didn't send me any news [of himself or call her back to his home]. I sent him a letter, but still he didn't come. Then his aunt next door died [his father's older brother's wife]. Then his grandmother died. On her death I myself came with my brother. I stayed on for two or four, maybe six, months, and then I went away again accompanied by my husband's younger brother. I went way after being told to go and honor my brother at the Brother's Second [*bhaiyā dūj*] ceremony.[1] I took along five dried coconuts and many homemade sweets.[2]

I was going to be sent alone. But my husband's brother accompanied me as far as the bus stand. I was clever. I said that if I am sent alone my parents would think I have run away. That's why my husband's brother was sent with me. He claimed that he didn't have the bus fare, but I said I would pay his way. I had brought some money secretly. Since I am from Mainpuri I know everything. I had told him that I would pay for the fare. Otherwise people would think that I had run away. Among the lower [*choṭī*] *jāti*s there's always a lot of gossip. Had I come alone I would have been accused of running away. So you should travel with somebody, even if it happens to be a small child. Then no one can talk.

Then I went again [to my husband's house] with my younger brother. Without any modesty [*beśaram*]. Because men are superior [*baṛā*]. He's a man. I said, "Let's go." A woman is a woman. So I said, "He's a man, I'm a woman." It didn't matter if we were to break up, but I had to go there. But he doesn't think of me. He came to visit in Baisakh (April–May) after five years.

Sheila then told of meeting Sonu. Sonu had had a job printing cloth in a factory in a nearby town, but he had lost that job and was working as a rickshaw driver in Mainpuri when Sheila met him. Her parents and brother did not accept this second marriage and have not spoken to her since.

Sheila also talked about her sometimes difficult relations with Sonu's mother, who doesn't live in Karimpur, preferring the better accommodations available in her daughter's home. As a result, Sheila had no adult woman around when she gave birth. She tells of Sonu's doing the cooking when she gave birth and of the celebrations for her son's birth.

[Sheila married her current husband through a court marriage, that is, without a religious ceremony and without family permission.] I have already told you that whatever is written in your fate [*kismat*] will happen.[3] Now you live in America: your country is very far. But it was written that you would come to Mainpuri and to this village. Definitely you have come. And others didn't come. Whatever is written in your fate is bound to happen. My father and mother could arrange a marriage for me anywhere. But whoever is my partner is in my fate: I will live my life with him. But a marriage could not have been arranged with anybody else, never mind how handsome he is, never mind how much friendship one makes. . . . When you are young and your mother and father choose a boy for you, it is good. It is honorable to get married that way. One's honor [*ijjat*] cannot be lost when one's mother and father arrange a marriage at a young age. . . . When my mother and father got me married, I didn't get along with him. So I arranged my own. It was my choice. It was written in my fate. I became friendly with him gradually. He was related to me like a brother. He used to drive a cycle rickshaw and wash clothes. He used to wash clothes and park his rickshaw while drying the clothes. I used to go there to wash clothes, too. I used to wonder what this rickshaw driver was up to near the clothes. I was drying the clothes and he was there. I thought he had come to steal the clothes. If I went off somewhere, he might just steal two or four pieces. So I told him to go away. But he replied, "Sister, I won't steal clothes. I am resting. I drive the rickshaw at night and rest in the day. I won't take your clothes." I felt better after he had explained all that.

· · ·

[Sheila's brother sells cloth in Delhi near her first husband, who has a job that pays seven to eight hundred rupees per month.] I don't communicate with him because I came to Karimpur of my own choice. My brother yelled at me and said he would see me only when I was dead. My natal family told him that I married on my own. It would be something else had I told my parents about it. But I married without saying anything to them. That's why my brother warned me that I shouldn't come before him. He is sorrowful that I can't see him because if I do, he might say something to me. I also have sorrow because they are my parents, my brother. That's why I don't go near them. If they are in the bazaar, I don't go near them. Their house is near the Rani Mandir—toward the Rani Fort.

I had one sister younger than me. She studied up to the eighth grade. Eighth or tenth. And when she was a little older, around eleven years old, she was married. She was this big [lifting her hand]. Got married around eleven years old. The *gaunā* took place three years later. She was fifteen when her *gaunā* took place. After that she went to her in-laws in *ronā* [literally, "crying," a term used to refer to the time a girl goes permanently to her in-laws' home after the marriage ceremony]. There she found much sorrow. I mean her husband's younger brother used to beat her. He used to ask her to bring food and water immediately. No matter how fast she brought it, he would complain. He used to beat her up without any reason. She stayed there two or four years, and after that went somewhere else. At the second place she stayed two years. She had no food or clothing there. There was too much work and struggle. We can't struggle that much.

That's why I myself came to Karimpur. I stayed here for a year and again there was trouble with my mother-in-law and husband's sister. When there was fighting, my mother-in-law went off to her younger daughter's place. There she was given food. A fight started because we didn't give money to my husband's sister. If there is a fight, someone has to leave. There are no qualms about that, but by then I was pregnant.

My husband went to get me [after the fight]. Only then I did come. He went and stayed [with his sister] for ten days, and after that he left again because I had pains in my stomach. He left and came back after eight days. Then the boy was born.

[At the time Sheila's son was born] this young niece [aged twelve or thirteen] was here. Then my niece's older sister came also. I called her. She cooked the food and washed the utensils. And he [Sheila's husband] used to make food and then go off for work. My young niece used to carry and bring water. Then her father came and took her away. After he took her away, I started washing clothes on my own.

I had a child ten years after my marriage [meaning her first marriage]. Eight or ten years later. Nowadays girls of sixteen get children. Nowadays they want children immediately. My child was born eight years later. In the tenth year this one was born.

[This older one is] four years. And this one is one and a half years. He will be two in July. After July is complete. He [her first husband] left me because I had no children. I explained that some get children late and some early. We don't know if we will have them later. When our time* has come. I tried to explain, "There is still time*."

. . .

When the girl was born, I was given an injection and I lay down. Then the girl came out very fast. And when the boy was born, I was lying down in pain. Shanti [the government midwife] came; Kedar's wife came and Laltu's mother—both the mother and the daughter-in-law came [these latter two are untrained midwives of the *dhānuk jāti*]. Then Radhe Shyam's wife [also a *dhānuk* by *jāti*] came. All four came and didn't leave me. One caught my hands, the other my legs. I was made to sit once and the baby came out and afterwards I lay down. And after I was lying down, he made *harīrā* for me.[4] [Q: Who?] Your brother [namely, Sonu: here Sheila uses village fictive kinship to identify her husband as my brother]; he made *harīrā* real quick. He started grinding the stuff and asked how it is made. He ground fennel, cumin, and caraway, along with currants. He cooked all of it together and put it in the bowl and gave it to me. [Q: Then did anyone came?] Yes, we invited people, and the *caruvā* was held and *satiyā* made.[5] [Q: Which husband's sister came?] No one. The other Washerman's wife is related as a sister to me. She did the *satiyā*. Shanti's mother-in-law [*sās*] did the *caruvā*.[6] When my mother-in-law is not here, she is related to me like a mother-in-law. I look up to her just like my own mother-in-law. I gave her one rupee. She did the *caruvā*. And when I invited her, I gave her *batāsā*s [puffed sugar candies, used as honorific offerings in rituals]. She blessed me profusely. After that, *batāsā*s were distributed and the drum was played.

I also asked Sheila about how they managed to survive on their meagre income. She explained:

[To eat for] one day, for one meal I need two or so pounds of flour. Four or six pounds are needed for two meals.[7] A minimum of four or six pounds are needed for one day. . . . Sometimes we feel less hungry, so we require less food. Sometimes five pounds are enough. Sometimes four pounds are enough because we eat less. . . . We can eat more vegetables. We consume two pounds at one meal and also a half pound of lentils. A half pound of lentils costs Rs. 1.25 or 1.50. Good lentils cost Rs. 2.50. I haven't bought any for a long time. Once he [Sonu] asked for good lentils and I said I hadn't made any, nor any vegetable. But potatoes are very cheap, but we don't eat them a lot because in the heat they give us trouble.

When it's hot, rice, chick-peas or *besan* [chick-pea flour] are okay. Cold foods are eaten then.[8] Carrots are eaten with *besan*. Carrots are cold. And now green vegetables are popular, like jackfruit and okra. [We also use] a quarter cup of oil in a day. A quarter cup costs 75 *paise*. We also need two-tenths of a pound of spice daily, or one-tenth of a pound one time and one-tenth of a pound the second time. Sometimes we don't use it at all. Sometimes you can't even afford a tiny bit. Sometimes we have none. So we make the vegetables plain [with no spices or salt]. Whenever the proper time comes, we eat. Now there's no one there to tell him [Sonu, when he is driving his rickshaw in Mainpuri][9] when to eat and when not to eat or where to get food. When I go to wash clothes, I dry them after the washing, and then we come back to eat. In town, one can get leftovers, fermented. The workers get that. Leftovers are given to them. The laborers are satisfied with that because they like to save what they earn with such toil. Sometimes if I work for ten or fifty houses, I get enough to eat. Five people can eat off ten houses [because the Washerwoman is given cooked breads at each house when she returns the clean clothes]. And sometimes we get a pajama or a shirt; sometimes smaller clothes are given, which don't fit. But we can't eat or drink clothes! We have to save the money that we earn through our toil. That's why one has to be satisfied. It doesn't happen in the village. The poor stay poor. When she [my assistant, Monisha Behal, from Delhi] was here, she asked how much a Sweeper gets. In one month she gets one and a half or two rupees [from each house]. That's not good. It's nothing. Sure she gets a bread daily and the money, but that's nothing. Now, she goes to clean other people's shit and garbage, and that's what she gets for a month. There's no benefit for her. How can she raise her children? And if her husband isn't working, how can they get along on three rupees a month? Then they get thirteen pounds of grain [at the harvest]. Each village house gives thirteen pounds. How many days will last with that? Does it last six months? No one can eat for six months [on so little]. [Thirteen pounds is] enough for just three or four days. They work for six months and [from each house] they only get enough for four days.

Most of the poor in Karimpur have to borrow from a wealthy landowner at some point. But the poor also help one another, as in this

incident, where Sheila describes a loan that she gave to an equally poor
Watercarrier family.

> [Sheila loaned money to Murli, the Watercarrier] because it was the
> Asharhi *pūjā* [a festival in late June]. There would be a lot of work plastering
> the houses. That's why he asked for money, in case I had any. I used to put
> twenty-five or fifty *paise* in a tin, which had totaled up to ten rupees. I kept
> two rupees for my expenses and gave him eight. So I told him to spend the
> money, but to return it quickly. If I had to spend my own money for some
> reason, I would need the loan back soon. Now Murli says he doesn't have
> any money. Then that Muslim family had a baby girl. I worked there and
> got twenty-two pounds of grain: I gave Murli six pounds and kept sixteen
> pounds for our house. We ate all that. And now Murli says he'll repay me
> only when he gets some money. He won't give. I said that it's okay, and
> ever since I have stopped asking for my money. Now he's going to Bewar [a
> nearby town where the men can get coolie jobs] if he gets the bus fare. Peo-
> ple are saying that he should give me some money, but he responds "How
> can I give? I'm not a millionaire. Now that I don't have money, how can I
> give you any?" When he gets there, he'll give me [the money]. [Sheila's hus-
> band] goes there, and there's always a fight about the money.
> [Sheila gave money to Murli because] if I need money, I go to them and
> get it. Now they wanted money, so I gave it to them. The *bahū* doesn't
> come here, but the mother-in-law does.

Sheila went on to describe the respective roles of a mother-in-law and
daughter-in-law when it comes to activities outside of the house. Her narrative differs from Saroj's, given earlier, because the poor have to leave
their houses to work. Nevertheless, the presence of a mother-in-law permits greater restrictions on movement.

> I work, so I go out. If my mother-in-law were here, I wouldn't be able to
> go out. The mother-in-law does the outside work, and the *bahū* does the in-
> side housework. Murli's wife has an older daughter who grazes the goats
> and brings grass for them. That's why Murli's wife doesn't go out. Only
> when there is someone to help in the house can you go outside.

Sheila has also been threatened by her Brahman neighbors, as in this
incident.

> [Five years ago Sheila was beaten by Triloki, the Brahman landlord
> nearby.] My niece went to get *bainā* [ritual offerings given to *kamīn*s for
> the Holi festival]. We were working at the time of the festival and therefore
> went to get *bainā*. Ashok, another Brahman man, saved me, because he and
> Triloki began to fight. They fought because he was trying to save me. He
> hid me in his house. Then he took me out of the house and I ran to the
> Midwife's house and I hid there and this rascal Triloki came looking for me,
> but he had hurt his foot. I was saved. Okay, he beat me, but it doesn't mat-

ter because I am from a lower *jāti* and he didn't spoil my honor [*ijjat*]. But the Ahir folks [a cattle-herding *jāti*] came from a nearby village for a fight and went to his house. Kids of this size beat him up so much. He beat me because he thinks that I am poor. I was beaten because we are poor. And in this he cursed me. . . . He will be killed one day. But I can't say anything because I eat their bread. And when they give good bread, I eat it.

Sheila, like many women in Karimpur, was afraid of the one option available for birth control, a tubal ligation. She also told me once that you shouldn't interfere with your body, because Bhagvan gave it to you and its condition and your childbearing were part of your fate (*bhāgy*). If you didn't have the children allotted to you by your fate in this lifetime, you might be worse off in your next life; you might even be widowed.

I'm scared of the operation. I get scared, as I feel there is no life in my body. My body gets weak. I don't know what an operation does. Whether it does good or bad to one's life or finishes it. That's why. With an operation you get nothing but weakness. But [the government] gives money for food. People desire the operation because the children can eat. But instead of buying ghee for my health, I would go and buy more grain for the whole family. I think of that and that's why I feel weak. Because of fear that I would buy grain and not ghee. We once had a buffalo, which gave milk. I used to drink milk. Women who get milk from the house can be operated on. They have milk and ghee. You need to have milk or money. Then you can get fruits and other things. You won't feel weak then, no matter how hard you work [because the food will give you strength]. Poor people—they are given money and therefore they get the operation. They think they can buy grain with that money.

. . . .

[Q: As you understand it, how can Indian women make their lives better? What should happen to make their lives better?]
A woman's life would be fine if she ran the house well and if the man has a service job [*naukarī*, a regularly paid, permanent job]. It's good if the children eat properly and the husband eats well. These make one's life good. Because if a person gets a service job, they are well paid. Some women also work in the house and that's why life is good. For instance, some Water-carrier women work at cleaning utensils or washing clothes. Their husbands also work—do service. . . . Yes, you must work at some job that pays. If you work hard without getting money, it is useless. It's no use struggling if there is no caring.
[Q: What hopes do you have for this daughter?] The hope I have for this girl is that she will study as much as she can. This way her life will be good. If she goes to school, she can get a good marriage. She'll be happy, and we will be happy too. And if she is sorrowful, we will be sorrowful because our daughter is in sorrow. That's why she must study and get good jobs. Then her life will be good for her and me.

11.   Sheila, the Washerwoman, with her young son

[Q: Why do you think you have sorrow?]
In my life it has been written in my fate [*kismat*] that I will have sorrow.
Bhagvan must have written that I should do labor, beg, struggle. Bhagvan
has written the way that my life will be made. Now if I get grain, Bhagvan is
writing that they are getting grain.

Throughout the interviews that I had with Sheila, she was always trying to justify her life to herself and to me. Why was she poor? Why did
her marriage fail? Like Raghunath, she found her answers in the actions

of Bhagvan and in her fate, written at birth. Yet she did not passively accept her fate: she waged a court case over her first marriage and lost her natal family when she chose to marry Sonu. And, while she saw little hope for a more secure financial future for herself, she had hopes that her young daughter would fare better. To her, education was the answer, or at least part of it.

Sheila's husband Sonu had similar thoughts, saying once that the gods make a person rich or poor. He also recognized that if you could break out of the cycles of oppression, litigation, illness, and the resulting continual debt, you could advance. After he paid the rent on the cycle rickshaw that he drove, he earned six or eight rupees a day. Grain alone cost four or five rupees a day, leaving little, if anything, for vegetables, oil, or spices. He did work every day when he was not sick, yet he could never get ahead. During the year that we knew him, his rickshaw was hit by a car; he was injured and couldn't work for more than a month. Then Sheila got hepatitis and was ill, unable to wash the clothes of her patrons. The debts mounted. Daily work for the next year might just have gotten them out of debt—if there were no further illnesses or emergencies to eat into their minimal earnings. As Sonu also said, the Brahmans of Karimpur didn't want them to succeed, wouldn't let them rise up and advance their status. So despite their struggles, Sonu and Sheila find themselves all too often caught by their fates.

CHAPTER FOUR

"Poverty Is Written in My Destiny"

Many Karimpur villagers share in the poverty of Sheila, or of Raghunath and Santoshi. The levels of poverty vary, so that some, like Santoshi's family, have only one set of clothes and no house, while others, like Raghunath's family, have several rooms in their house, a courtyard, and even a buffalo to provide milk, some of which is sold. Sorrows, such as those that Raghunath highlighted in telling his life story, are common—parents die, illness strikes, filling children's stomachs is a constant problem, debts pile up, dowries must be found. Moreover, poverty affects males and females differently: poverty, too, is gendered. Women who are poor have different opportunities for work and fewer purdah restrictions than richer women. Some, like Sheila, contribute to household incomes, while at the same time being subject to male power and even physical abuse in the household and threats of personal injury from wealthy men. Others can only watch as husbands attempt to feed their families, for they have no traditional women's jobs that would allow them to make their own contributions. Hence the relations between poor men and women differ from those between rich men and women. Likewise, the relations of poor men to rich men (or women) are not the same as those of poor women to rich women.

Added to the crushing poverty is the devastation caused by India's brutal climate, which leads to cholera (and, previously, smallpox) in the hot season, floods that wipe out crops and provide breeding places for malaria-carrying mosquitoes during the monsoon rains, and pneumonia and hunger during the short days of the cold season. Death is a frequent occurrence, and those families without adult males suffer most.

A family that starts poor and has few resources finds it immensely difficult to become prosperous. Illness, marriages, deaths, flooding, and drought recur with a daunting frequency in the life cycle of most poor villagers. The cyclical nature of poverty itself, continually striking with a new catastrophe just as a former one is alleviated, makes poverty truly a matter of destiny. Thus, in Sheila's words, "Poverty is written in my destiny" (*hamārī kismat men garībī likhī hai*). Yet Karimpur's poor daily voice their resistance, whether through songs and stories that ridicule rich landlords, malicious gossip about the hated Brahman moneylender, heroic ballads that laud the district's famous dacoits, or slow work, poorly washed clothes, or surly greetings in the village lanes. Only rarely, however, as we shall see in chapter 6, do these covert forms of resistance become public confrontations that seek change within the system itself. Most of those born poor remain poor, unable to escape the fate that gave them such a birth.

LIVING ONE'S DESTINY

Fate, sorrow, and the actions of Bhagvan are all interlinked in the lives of Karimpur villagers. Sometimes Bhagvan is kind, and through his mercy a person's life improves. If an individual has a truly good fate, he is born a rich Brahman and will never suffer. But if a person's fate is based on a heavy load of accumulated sins, he or she will suffer by being born into a low *jāti* and will be poor throughout this life.

Karma, fate, is derived from the verbal root *kar*, to do, and is first of all a matter of action. Since a person is always active, he or she is continually accruing the fruits of these actions. Thus *karma* is a process. That process results in a change in bodily substance, because one's sins or merit adhere to the body. As one villager commented, "He sinned previously: he is riddled with is sin" (literally, "sin adheres to him," *binne pāp kiyā pahle to usko pāp lag gāī*). Once sin or merit is in your body, you obtain its concomitant rewards or punishment.

The concept of fate, *karma*, is comprehended on two levels. First, as a key component of the Hindu belief in transmigration, it defines what a person is at birth and, in broad terms, the outlines of his or her life: material circumstances, sons, riches, happiness or sorrow. Second, a person's fate is also dependent upon how she or he acts in this life, for sins and merit are constantly accruing and changing a person's standing with the

12.   A house in a poorer section of Karimpur

gods. Thus the gods may feel that a given individual has been meritorious enough in this current life to wipe out a bad fate based on past lives.
Or the gods may arrange immediate retaliation for sins just committed.

Most critically, what a person is at birth—their *jāti*—is dependent upon
fate. First, the gods decide into which family that individual will be born.
Then, on the sixth day after birth, the goddess of fate, Behmata, tallies up
the sins and merit from that person's previous lives and writes their fate,
in lines on their forehead, for this life. As Raghunath says, what you are
in this life is due to your previous lives. If you are born into a landed Brahman family such as Mohan's, your fate is good. If born into a poor family like Santoshi's, your fate is bad.

In explaining his malformed arms, Raghunath put it this way:

At the beginning I was a child. In this life, I hadn't done any actions
[*karam*]. But in my previous life, I did such actions. . . . [Q: So you have
the fruits of those actions?] Yes, those very fruits [that caused this physical
defect].

So, on one level, fate explains one's birth—one's *jāti* and relative material circumstances. Nevertheless, one's future remains unknown. A song
sung by the courtesan living in Karimpur in the 1920s goes:

> It was not the fault of Kaikeyi,
> No one knows the consequences of previous actions.
> Raja Dashrath had four sons:
> Two were exiled,
> Yet two were left to rule the country.
>
> Again misfortune fell upon Raja Nal,
> He drove the bullocks of the Oil Presser.
> No one knows the consequences of previous actions.[1]

The references here are to heroes well known to all in Karimpur: Raja
Dashrath, father of Ram, hero of the *Ramayana*, which is often enacted
in Karimpur during the fall Dashahra festival, and Raja Nal, hero of the
popular oral epic *Dhola*, frequently sung at marriages and other festivities. Because of an earlier promise to one of his wives, Kaikeya, Raja
Dashrath was forced to banish Ram, his oldest son and heir, to the forest
for fourteen years, an exile on which Ram's brother Lakshman accompanied him. Dashrath himself died of sorrow for what he had done. Raja
Nal angered the god Indra, who brought devastation to his kingdom. Nal
was banished, to become a leper and finally to work as a slave for an Oil
Presser, an ignominy unsuitable for a raja by birth. The courtesan's song
continues to lament the misfortunes of other mythological heroes and
heroines: Raja Harishchand, who was sold into slavery; Draupadi, whose
clothing was ripped off when her five husbands lost a dice game with their
enemies; and Raja Moradhvaj, whose son was sawed in half by his own father. If these heroes have no control over and knowledge of the consequences of actions in their previous incarnations, ordinary humans surely
have none either.

A similar idea is repeated in this song popular in Karimpur in the 1980s,
in which one's birth is seen as the cause of the sorrows of this life:

> What is fated [*karma jāti*] cannot be postponed or hidden,
> Raja Dashrath was born under inauspicious stars,
> Sita was abducted, Dashrath died,
> In the forest were troubles.[2]

Here again the reference is to the Raja Dashrath, father of the god-hero
Ram, and to Ram's wife, Sita, who was abducted by the demon-king of
Lanka, Ravan.

On another level, however, the consequences of merit and demerit are
evident immediately, in this lifetime. Here Karimpur villagers see karmic

theory as more than a theory of transmigration. In this view, people know the consequences of their actions and must assume personal moral responsibility for their destiny. A song collected by the Wisers in the 1920s contains the line, "Don't milk the cow into a sieve and then blame fortune."[3] In explaining a fire in Karimpur in 1984, villagers attributed it and the resulting deaths to greed, drinking, adultery, gambling, mistreating the poor, and other visible sins. Those who suffered in the fire saw the fruits of their actions in this lifetime.[4]

One's actions are measured as demerit (*pāp*) or merit (*punya*). Demerits are most widely defined as actions that cause sorrow to others (*kisī ko dukh denā to pāp hai*, "If [you] give sorrow to others, then it is evil"). Meritorious actions are those that follow *dharma*, duty, namely, that which supports merit. *Dharma* is doing proper work—digging a well, feeding the poor, building a *dharmaśālā*. It is also *punya*, merit. To steal, to look at another woman, or to refuse to feed a beggar is *adharma* or *pāp*. One does *dharma* or *adharma*, as defined by one's own principles or tradition, and thus one performs acts of merit or sin. A person should do his or her own *dharma*. As one man stated, "Each [man or woman] should do his or her respective works, which are *dharma*." *Dharma* is something that a person has and does; it defines actions (*karma*) as good or bad, giving a person *punya* or *pāp* as the fruits of those actions. A proverb commonly found in Karimpur discourse says, "The root of merit is always green," that is, merit always brings rewards. This proverb was always used in reference to reaping the rewards of merit in this life. In one story, a father is banished from his kingdom by his son. The father behaves righteously, serving god and helping others, whereas the son errs continuously. Ultimately, the father regains his kingdom, while the erring son is banished.

So the concept of *karma* is operative on two levels: it is called upon to account for one's initial life situation and to explain the results of one's actions in this life.[5] Most of the time, one does not know whether one's fate is the consequence of actions in this life or a previous one. Sometimes, though, it is clear that a man has sinned and has received the fruits of his action. The poor tell of a rich Brahman landlord and moneylender, who was the village headman prior to Independence. People say that when he came near, the poor were as frightened as when the wind (a spirit) attacks a child. This landlord liked it, they say, when someone's bullock died, for then he could benefit by giving a loan. But the landlord died a horrible death, with maggots eating away at his body. Raghunath claims that the moneylender died this way because he was eating the earnings of his sins; the fruits of his sins were an agonizing death. But at other times, the evidence is less clear. When Saroj's house was spared in the fire, people said that maybe she was more faithful to god than they realized, for how can one tell what is inside a person? Only god knows that. Finally, if there is no obvious sin or merit in this life, then clearly one's fate is the result of actions in a past life.

But whether the result of past or recent actions, fate is used by rich and poor alike to account for the basic facts of their lives. The wife of the Flower Grower stated, "Daughter, whatever sorrows are in one's fate [karam], those you suffer. It is written [in the lines of fate on one's forehead]—sorrow and happiness." The village Accountant's wife attributed her children to fate: "I am happy. If there were no children, I would have been unhappy. God is good. Whatever is in our fate [karam] will happen." A Carpenter, discussing how much education children should have, said, "And if more schooling is written in his fortune [bhāgy], then he will study more." Saroj, the Brahman widow, also sees offspring, in this case her son's children, as a result of fate, but she is highly equivocal about whether this fate was determined by actions in this life or a past one:

> If I were good, then my fate [karam] would have been good. Then my son's wife might not be barren.[6] Whatever fault [dos] there is, it is our own. [Q: How do you know your fortune (bhāgy) is bad?] What! Is my fortune [bhāgy] not bad? Grandfather [her husband] has died. My son has separated [his family from hers]. And these two remain unmarried. Whether I do theft or forgery, somehow I have to get them both married. So how can I say that my fortune is good? It is not good, it is horrible!

Even Shankar, the village headman and one of the richest men in Karimpur, blamed fate for the fact that he did not get a good job as a young man:

> Slowly my influence [in the district town] increased. But because of misfortune [bhāgy hīn], I couldn't go onward. Unfortunately, I had no source [for a job]. Those who were admitted into the army have already retired with the rank of superintendent*. If I were in service*, I would have prospered. But service was not written in my fortune [bhāgy], so what to do? This is destiny [karam].

From these statements, we see the ramifications of fate, as Karimpur residents attempt to make sense of their own personal histories. Sons, poverty, widowhood, grandchildren, jobs, happiness and sorrow are indeed a matter of fate, but that fate is based on actions in this life, as well as in previous lives. As Saroj said, "Whatever fault there is, it is our own."

SORROW

Raghunath saw his life as filled with sorrow, as organized around a series of sorrows, in fact—his mother's death, his illness, his wife's death. Many others as well, especially the poor, frequently used sorrow to explain their life circumstances. As a concept, sorrow is closely linked to fate.

There is a genre of stories in Karimpur called *kathā*, which are religious tales most often told in conjunction with rituals. *Kathā*s explain how a person can reap the rewards of ritual behavior, providing service to the gods, having faith in them, and singing their praises. In the *kathā* for Tuesday, for example, a poor, childless woman fasts weekly and worships Hanuman, the monkey god heralded in the *Ramayana*. One week she has no offering for the god, so she continues her fast for seven days; by the following Tuesday she is so weak that she faints. Hanuman, pleased by her great love and faith, rewards her with a son. The *kathā* ends, "So from the kindness of Hanumanji, all sorrows are removed and there are many happy gains."

In the Karimpur symbolic system, sorrow is opposed to simple distress. Sorrow, *dukh*, emphasizes individual mental well-being and general material conditions. Sorrow further implies some lack or wrong action on the part of the one who is sorrowful. It is long-lasting, enduring. Sorrow is also a result of one's actions, one's *karma*. Sorrow can be removed by the actions of a deity such as Hanuman, who can recognize meritorious actions and give one a son where none had been written into one's fate at birth.

Sorrow is best understood when contrasted to *kast*, distress, and *musībat*, trouble. Distress implies that the physical well-being of the individual is endangered. This physical danger is usually caused by an external agent, not oneself. And distress is brief, immediate, not enduring. *Musībat*, trouble, refers to periods of distress that sometimes are given by god in response to one's actions. Yet these are not necessarily enduring sorrows that can be removed only with the help of some deity. The gods are never said to "make troubles [*musībat*] go far away" nor do humans talk about their lives as defined by *musībat*. Only sorrow, *dukh*, is appropriate in these two contexts.[7]

Further, sorrow—along with sins and merit—is shared amongst one family (*gharwāle*, those who share a house), lineage (*khāndān*, calculated patrilineally), and village (*gānv*). Hence the proper actions of one person may counter the sins of another. When Alok's house did not burn down in the fire, people commented that the merits of his grandfather had countered the sins of his father and uncles. When another house was saved, Raghunath said that there must have been a *satī* [a wife who sacrificed herself on her husband's funeral pyre] in that lineage (*khāndān*) who had erased its sins for generations to come. Further, there is an implicit belief that even if you are sinned against, those sins are deserved—that Yama, the god who tallies the scores, matches up individuals. If you are fated to have no sons, your daughters are comparably fated to have no brothers. If a man is fated to die young, his wife is fated to be a widow. But this does not deny the possibility of acting; in the religious tale that justifies worship to Shiva on Mondays, Shiva first gives a childless man a son destined to live for only twelve years and then saves that son from death at age twelve because of the faith and service that the man and his son have shown to Shiva.

Hence Raghunath's use of sorrow as the basic organizing principle of his life story is by extension a karmic explanation. Sorrows are part of one's fate, determined either at birth or as the result of actions in this life. They are enduring and can be removed only by the actions of powerful gods and goddesses, themselves responding to meritorious human actions. Indeed, much ritual action in Karimpur is aimed at removing sorrow and hence altering one's fate, as did the father and son who worshiped Shiva and thus gained a life of more than twelve years for the boy.[8]

The Grain Parcher summed up these connections one day while discussing his own life and his shift from extreme poverty to relative prosperity:

> I was happy while a young man. I earned a lot. God gave it. And I married off my sons. So the time of happiness continued. So now, through the mercy of Bhagvan, I am not sad. I have been happy thus far. What is sorrow? Sorrow and happiness come according to how we act. They come according to duty [that is, following one's *dharma*].

In this worldview, shared by rich and poor alike, poverty is indeed a matter of destiny, but that destiny rests indubitably upon one's actions, whether in this life or a previous one, as well as on the gods who interpret and respond to those actions. If you act properly, with faith, and some god is merciful, you will indeed get happiness or a son, a job or a good marriage for your daughter.

BEING POOR

To be poor (*garībī*) is a result of fate and is a major facet of being sorrowful. The features of poverty, which are well known, are featured in song, story, and everyday discussions. Raghunath sang the following song one day in 1974. The signature line attributes the song to the legendary poet Kabir. The focus here is on the mental anguish and loss of knowledge that accompanies hunger and poverty:

> When poverty [*kangālī*] comes,
> All wisdom [*caturāī*] is forgotten,
> Immediately all knowledge is gone, when it comes.
> Oh, when poverty comes,
> A shadow falls on the head,
> And all the villagers shout "Foolish,"
> And the wife says "Stupid,"
> When poverty comes.
> When poverty comes,
> All wisdom is forgotten.
>
> Immediately all knowledge is gone, when it comes.
> When poverty comes,
> All wisdom is forgotten,
> Torn clothes, torn dhoti.
> The poor can do nothing,
> Not even get a loan.
> In the house, a broken dish;
> Selling it, he ate beans.
> The whole world laughs when poverty comes.
>
> Torn clothes, torn dhoti,
> The poor can do nothing.
> Kabir says, "Listen brother, be a sadhu,
> Sell grass and eat, when poverty comes."
> When poverty comes,
> All wisdom is forgotten.

The eighteen-year-old son of the Flower Grower defined poverty this way:

The features of poverty are these: bread, clothes, house. [Q: Why house?] Those without homes are the poorest. Even the bird makes a nest to live in. You and I are human. Animals can fill their stomachs too [but even they need a house].[9]

But poverty does bring a type of inhumanness, for some human beings, like Santoshi, do not have houses. A song sung by a Muslim girl in 1974 captures the essence of poverty in Karimpur:

> There is a blister constantly in my heart,
> In this inhuman [*bedardī*] fashion I must live.

In the house no wood, in the house no sticks.
Only a few cow-dung cakes in the corner.
In this inhuman fashion I must live.
There is a blister constantly in my heart.

In the house no wheat, in the house no grain.
Only a little rice in the corner.
In this inhuman fashion I must live.
There is a blister constantly in my heart.

In the house no girl, in the house no boy.
Only a few puppies in a corner.
In this inhuman fashion I must live.
There is a blister constantly in my heart.

Poverty is no fuel, no food, and no children. Another song, a *kīrtan* sung
at a wedding in 1984 by a teenage Cultivator girl, describes misfortune
as no wealth, no home, no husband, and no sons:

O Bhagvan, what troubles [*musībat*] have come to me.
O Bhagvan, what have you done.
You took all my wealth, my home.
My husband is also gone.
And now my son is dead.

If one is poor, the ability to work to feed oneself is crucial to surviving. The Flower Grower's wife said that her "hands and feet can still do
work, so I am okay."[10] Jiji, whose husband beat her regularly and gambled away his earnings, said, "I did not know the love of my husband. All
I knew was that Bhagvan had given me two hands and I had to work with
them to earn a living." Santoshi put it more forcefully. She says that the
poor eat only what their hands can give, implying that they can earn a living only if they work and that they have no material resources to work
with. Her husband herds cattle; she makes cow-dung cakes; one day their
house collapsed. As she repeated several times, "No one has as much
poverty as I have."

Santoshi also claimed that the poor have no friends:

[Q: Who is your friend in your *jāti*?] Sahab [speaking to me], my friend in
poverty? Nobody is my friend. Sahab, when someone must eat [that is, when
someone is forced into begging], only then do they become friends. Since
my brothers-in-law separated [their houses from the joint family], then who
is there to be a friend?

Several songs reiterate this idea. A verse found in many episodes of the
popular epic *Dhola* goes:

Oh, in distress comes misfortune, in adversity comes calamity.
In distress, the bullocks don't lend a shoulder,
Then brothers and relatives don't speak to you,
And descendants turn their backs.

When destruction comes to man,
First lightening falls on the brain.
One's own mother is like a lion,
And father seems like Yamraj.[11]

Another song heard in 1984 focuses on the idea that when one is in trouble there is no one. After lines relating the travails of Raja Harishchand, whose son dies, who himself is sold to an untouchable, and whose wife becomes a prostitute, the song concludes:

The truth is that in periods of trouble [*musībat*],
there is no one. . . .
Whatever is destined must happen.[12]

Clearly, being poor in Karimpur is not an enviable position. Thought to be stupid and foolish, because if one were wise one would not have been born poor, lacking friends, and having only one's hands and feet with which to survive, the poor do indeed live in a close to inhuman fashion. Their agony is increased by Karimpur's brutal climate, bringing with it death and disease that disproportionately affect Karimpur's poor.

THE CYCLE OF SEASONS

The seasons and months of the Hindu calendar provide organizing principles for many aspects of Karimpur life. In a genre of songs called the "songs of the twelve months" (*bārahmāsī*), each month is conceptualized as having a distinct ethos and tone, focusing on ritual, social, or climatic events. Hence some months are associated primarily with a major ritual; some take note of social events such as the return of daughters to visit their parents or the marriage season; and yet others are noted for climatic conditions of heat, rain, or cold. Each of the seasons has a different impact on the lives of Karimpur residents, and while all people are affected, the poor are least insulated from the force of Karimpur's harsh climate.

The two cycles of rainfall and temperature are especially important. Some 90 percent of the rainfall in northern India occurs between late June and mid-September, with floods still possible into October. A few showers fall during the winter months (December and January), but otherwise dryness prevails the rest of the year. The temperature cycle is more consistent, moving slowly between extremes of hot and cold, ranging from a daily high of 120° F or more in May and June, prior to the monsoon, to nighttime lows of 40° F in December and January. With few man-made devices to buffer the extremes of hot and cold, temperature is a critical feature in the yearly seasonal cycle.

Given these patterns of rainfall and temperature, the north Indian recognizes three seasons of approximately four months each: the hot season (*garmī*); the rainy or wet season (*barsāt*, or even more commonly, *chaumāsī*, literally, the "four months") and the cold season (*sardī* or *jāṛā*).[13] The hot season runs from March through June; the rainy season from July through October; and the cold season from November through February. Three cropping seasons are associated with these: *kharīf*, the rainy season crops of rice and corn, harvested in October and November; *rabī*, the winter crops of wheat and barley, harvested in March and April; and the hot season crops of melons and cucumbers, harvested in May and June.

Two periods are most often identified as times of hunger: the middle period of the rains, about late August and early September, and the cold season months of December and January. These months also find men without employment, as some laboring jobs (notably brick making) are curtailed because of the rains, while others are limited in the cold season because, as one middle-aged man put it, "The days are short and they [employers] don't get enough labor for their money." Moreover, January and February are also a slow time for farmers, with the crops planted and the harvest still far off. There is little or no demand for agricultural labor at this time.

The spring harvest of wheat and barley is the main income-producing crop for the village and the time when loans taken out for the past year are repaid. (As Mohan told us earlier, farmers often repaid their loans to his father, a major moneylender, by giving him their bullocks, so that the whole square in front of his house would be filled with animals.) The hot-season month falling in May, after the harvest, is the most auspicious time for weddings, for farmers are finally freed of their chores and the harvest can cover some wedding costs. It is important, though, to realize that *gaunā*, the consummation ceremony, is not calendrically tied to this month and may not take place for several years.

For the poor, the rains bring a variety of difficulties. Raghunath sang a portion of a song known as the "Twelve Months of the Farmer" that laments the troubles of farmers during the monsoon:[14]

> Oh excellent, you obtained a share of land.
> And how is your peace, my husband?
> I do not find any happiness.

At the beginning of the month of Asharh [June–July],
The rains begin to fall heavily,
And the earth gives up *kājal*.[15]
In their minds the farmers are pleased,
The ropes of the bullock do not stop.
But our year is desolate,
Seeing this, my heart is breaking.
Oh yes indeed, you obtained a piece of land,
But our bullocks, buffalo, and wealth
Were given to the headman.[16]
The government tax is not yet paid,
And how is your peace, my husband?
I do not have any happiness.

The month of Savan [July–August] begins,
The girls are singing their songs,
And today is the festival of Green Third [*hariyālī tīj*].[17]
But my daughters are bereft,
No salt, oil, or flour in the house.
Neighbor, something is due daily,
There is nothing for expenses.
There's a court case for the big field,
The headman demands a hundred,
But the recordkeeper wants even more,
The landlord, too, demanded a bribe,
And how is your peace, my husband?
I do not have any happiness.

Friend, Bhadon [August–September] is a stream of water,
The sky has been torn open,
The grindstone and oven are ruined,
Our portion of poverty has come.
The river has become flooded,
The crop is destroyed,
The cattle have died from hunger.
My sister-in-law's corn is submerged,
My sister-in-law's rice and
My father-in-law's mustard are damaged.
Millet, lentils, and corn are ruined.
And how is your peace, my husband?
I do not have any happiness.

This song captures much of the anguish of the poor farmer, who is constantly at the mercy both of the climate and of powerful figures such as the headman and the village recordkeeper. In tropical climates like Karimpur's, the wet season brings food shortages, illness (especially diarrhea, malaria and its complications, and various kinds of boils and skin diseases), and a high mortality rate among animals and humans, both infants and adults. In this season the poor and weak, especially women and the young, are particularly vulnerable.[18]

But the rains also bring the water that is necessary for this farming community to survive. And they are cooling after the brutal heat of June. When the rains come, the brown landscape turns green and everyone rejoices. Married women often return to their parent's homes for the rainy season festivals, where they hang swings in the trees and joyfully swing high in the cool, damp breezes. Women's songs celebrate this season, as in this excerpt from a song sung by Tailor girls:

> *Hariyālī tīj*, oh my sister, color is everywhere.
> *Hariyālī tīj*, oh my sister, color is everywhere.
>
> Oh sister, who had my shawl dyed?
> Oh sister, who had my shawl dyed?
> Oh listen someone, who, oh who, had a necklace made for me?
> Oh my brother, who took me to meet my dearest friends?
> *Hariyālī tīj*, oh my sister, color is everywhere.
>
> Oh sister, my mother had my shawl dyed,
> Oh listen someone, my father, oh my father, had a necklace made for me.
> Oh my brother took me to meet my dearest friends.
> *Hariyālī tīj*, oh my sister, color is everywhere.
>
> Oh my mother, when, oh when, will my shawl be worn?
> Oh listen someone, when, oh when, oh when will my necklace be worn?
> When, oh when, my brother, will I meet my dearest friends?
> Oh on *tīj*, I'll wear my shawl, child,
> Oh listen someone, on Snake's Fifth, oh on Snake's Fifth,[19] I'll wear my
>   necklace, and at Savan, my brother, I will meet my dearest friends.
> *Hariyālī tīj*, oh my sister, color is everywhere.

BIRTH

Aside from the more blatant illnesses associated with the monsoon, there is a hidden toll as well, and one that especially affects women. Karimpur births are unevenly distributed throughout the year: the culturally appropriate time for resuming lovemaking after the heat of the summer and rains is the festival season of Divali (October–November), which creates a peak in the birth curve in September, a time of heavy rains, high humidity, and temperatures in the nineties (see figure 13). In fact, 41.2 percent of all births occur during the four months of the rains. Moreover, a disproportionate share of newborns die during the rains: some 50.2 percent of all children born in the monsoon season die by the age of one

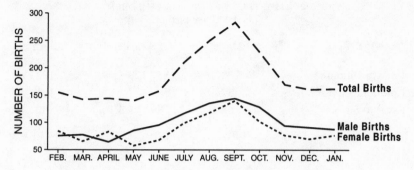

13.   The curve of births by month in Karimpur

month. The high infant death rates associated with the monsoon have a cyclical effect on mothers, leading to more frequent pregnancies, greater malnutrition, and overall ill health, for mothers whose infants die are likely to become pregnant in the following cold season, giving them little respite from the malnutrition and anemia associated with pregnancy in rural India. Frequent pregnancies are a detriment to women's health. These factors in turn lead to less viable infants, more deaths, and thus again to repeated pregnancies.

The poor Midwife Santoshi's birth history is typical. In 1965, when she was sixteen or seventeen, her first daughter was born in July during the monsoon: the child died within a day. Two years later during the monsoon she had a son, who lived. She nursed this boy for three years and had her next son after four years, also during the monsoon. He is now fourteen or fifteen and in eighth grade. Her fourth child, a daughter, was born during the hot season two and a half years later: she lived. Another daughter born just two years later also lived. Her next daughter died at the age of two and a half from tetanus and probably malnutrition, as did another daughter born one and a half years later. A girl born in 1978 lived, as did another born three years later, but she suffers from severe malnutrition and cannot walk at the age of three. A boy born during the monsoon in 1983, her ninth child in eighteen years of childbearing, died from tetanus when he was two days old. Another born during the rains in 1984 died at a week old. Her eleventh child, a son, born during the rains two years later, lives. Perhaps not surprisingly, Santoshi now complains of weakness and ill health.

Santoshi's birth history has some notable characteristics. Her first child came several years after her marriage was consummated when she was about fourteen years old. While that first child died, the second, a son,

TABLE 2   MORTALITY RATES FOR CHILDREN, 1984
(per 1000 live births)

Age	Males	Females	Both
1 day to 1 month	138	125	132
1 month to 1 year	87	143	101
1 year to 5 years	68.6	93.5	80

was cherished and nursed for a long period. After the third child, the birth intervals began to narrow and she had six daughters, four still living, in a ten-year span. Seven of her eleven children were born during the rains: four of these seven died as infants. Santoshi's pregnancy record thus reveals both the recurring patterns of monsoon births and of the resulting deaths.

Saroj, although a Brahman, was poor in her youth. Her children also died often and young: she had fourteen pregnancies, with eleven births during the rains. Three of those born during the monsoon died when they were only five or six days old. Two others died between the age of one and two from malnutrition, one during the hot season and one during the rains. Another died of smallpox during the heats of May, which was the smallpox season in northern India, and a seventh died of pneumonia during the cold season. Saroj's childbearing years began about age eighteen and lasted until she was forty-four.

DEATH

Two facets of death are critical to residents of Karimpur, especially the poor: the high level of child mortality and the deaths of adult males. In the period from 1975 to 1984, the overall Karimpur mortality rate was 132 per one thousand live births for infants under one month, a high figure that was even higher twenty years ago (see table 2).[20] Child mortality in Karimpur is sex-specific, with more female children dying than male children. Data on Karimpur births and childhood deaths show that 32.5 percent of all children born die by the age of five, including 36.1 percent of all female children and 29.5 percent of all male children.[21] Males are most likely to die of tetanus while very young or of pneumonia while toddlers. Females, whose neonatal death rate is lower than that of males, died more frequently after the age of one month of malnutrition, fevers, diar-

TABLE 3   REPORTED CAUSES OF DEATH FOR CHILDREN
UNDER AGE 5, 1984

Cause of Death	Total	Male Deaths	Female Deaths	Mortality Rate (deaths per 1000)
Tetanus	136	87	49	58.5
Pneumonia	89	51	37	38.3[a]
Malnutrition	85	30	54	36.5
Fever	73	27	46	31.4
Diarrhea	61	22	39	26.2
Evil spirits	40	21	19	17.2
Childbirth	39	19	20	16.8
Cholera	36	16	20	15.5
Smallpox	31	10	21	13.3
Accident	9	7	2	3.8
Measles	8	3	5	3.4
Premature birth	8	4	4	3.4
Skin disease	7	4	3	3.0
Swelling[b]	6	1	5	2.6
Boils	6	2	4	2.6
Deformity	4	2	2	1.7
Other[c]	20	10	10	16.8

[a]Includes death of one child of unspecified sex.
[b]Probably kwashiorkor.
[c]Causes mentioned include polio, murder, tuberculosis, injections, malaria, eye disease, mouth disease, pain, and vomiting.

rhea, and (earlier) smallpox (see table 3).

Karimpur residents are blatant in their discrimination against female children. A toddler about to topple off of a cot onto a brick courtyard is not prevented from falling, as the grandmother comments, "Let her, she's only a girl." In one instance, a young mother of three daughters induced a late-term abortion, almost killing herself, convinced that the fetus was yet another girl. Births of daughters are not celebrated, unless it is the first child born to that woman, and sometimes not even then. Moreover, none of the birth songs honor the birth of a daughter, and, as Mohan noted (see chapter 3), midwives are paid less when a girl is born than when a boy is born. A baby girl's placenta is commonly thrown on the compost pile, rather than being buried in a room of the house, with no concern for a spirit that might get at the placenta and through it the newborn. The auspicious head-shaving ritual called *mundan* is often eliminated for daughters, especially in poorer families. Daughters are breast-fed for shorter periods, which contributes to the malnutrition noted above, as the mother shortens the interval between pregnancies in an effort to get the desired son. In 1984 several three- and four-year-old girls (including, as we saw, one of Santoshi's daughters) were so malnourished that they were unable to walk. In the one case of male and female twins that survived infancy, at the age of one the boy was fat and glowing with health, while his sister was scrawny, with yellowed hair. She later died.

One of the most frequently mentioned sorrows was the death of parents. Certainly Raghunath saw his parents' deaths as two of the most influential events in his life. A Grain Parcher now in his seventies remembered his parents' deaths in a similar way, for at age eleven or twelve he was in charge of the family. That was a time of sorrow, for they didn't eat. The death of parents, especially that of fathers, puts already poor families in a precarious position, for houses without adult men have few opportunities for earning a living. For a farming family, even one adult male is insufficient. Raghunath spoke of his uncle only slowly being able to earn enough to take care of the family and of the importance of his own contributions. The Flower Grower's son spoke of the difficulties his family faced in his childhood because his father "was only one pair of hands" and there were five children to feed. Now, with he and his brothers all grown and in a joint family with only one daughter-in-law and one grandchild, the family is relatively prosperous. The fact that so many in Karimpur listed parental deaths as a major sorrow reflects the importance of parents, but especially adult males, in alleviating poverty.

Women die more frequently than men before the age of forty, most commonly in childbirth or of related complications. In 1984 there were forty-two widowers in the village, thirteen under the age of forty-four. Most widowers remarry, since raising children alone is difficult. Ram Chandra, however, a Carpenter whose wife died in 1984, leaving him with four sons aged twelve, eight, five, and three, did not remarry. Because he had small children, he seldom worked outside the village and took out loans in order to eat, for his fields yielded only enough for two months a year and food was a constant problem. Yet for him, the idea of a wife and potentially more children was more problematic than raising his children alone.

As we have noted, families, whether those of landlords or landless laborers, left without any adult males are particularly vulnerable. Opportunities for women to earn money are rare in Karimpur. Although women of the lower *jāti*s do field labor, the only acceptable field work is with male kin—husband, father, or brother. Hence the only women hired as field laborers were widows. Women have a few other earning opportunities. They can make cow-dung cakes and sell them, at fifty *paise* (less than five cents) for one hundred cakes. If they can manage the initial investment, they can raise a milk-animal (goat, cow, or buffalo), getting fodder by scraping grass from the roadside or persuading a rich farmer to let them weed his fields, and then sell the milk. Women whose family *jajmānī* occupation included female services (Watercarriers, Washerwomen, Midwives, Barbers, Sweepers) can seek to expand their clientele and earn something through their traditional occupation. Before the advent of electric flour mills, widows would grind grain for the richer families.

One option for the poor widow is to remarry. In 1984 there were sixty-nine widows living in Karimpur. Twenty-three belonged to wealthy Brahman, Bard, or Accountant families where widow remarriage is prohibited. Eighteen belonged to minor landowning families where remarriage is allowed, while the remainder belonged to poor, usually landless, families, where remarriage is also allowed. In addition, there were eleven remarried widows, nine from very poor families. Three women had contracted second marriages with their husband's younger brother (the practice of levirate), a common choice in landowning families to ensure that any land that might be claimed is kept within the family.[22]

Widows without grown sons faced the most difficulty. In the absence of aid from her husband's lineage, one Cultivator wife with a daughter of about ten moved in with her neighbors. Her husband had owed them a considerable sum, so in exchange for his remaining land, they care for the woman and have arranged her daughter's marriage. With the land gone, though, she is now totally dependent upon her neighbors' generosity. A Muslim widow, who has two young daughters, survives by begging. Two or three times a week she makes the rounds of Karimpur and nearby hamlets, getting enough handfuls here and there to feed her small family for the next few days. This household lacks a cot to sleep on or a quilt for the winter cold. When her older daughter was married in 1984, twenty or so Hindu villagers contributed food and goods for the ceremony and the necessary (but in this case small) feast. This family survives, but barely.

A Carpenter whose father died when he was about nine years old described his mother's attempts to provide for the family:

> Your house [speaking to our Brahman research assistant] and others gave her whatever work there was. She used to do work in the house. She used to carry water and cook food. Our land was covered with water, so there was no harvest. There was no livelihood. She had me study through the seventh grade. Then she also died.

His maternal uncle subsequently arranged his marriage, since he was the only son and he was alone. Until his *gaunā* several years later, he wandered about, after which he settled in Karimpur and learned carpentry.

Women widowed in their teens or early twenties, aside from those belonging to higher-ranked *jāti*s who cannot remarry, almost invariably remarry, with their parents usually arranging the second marriage. The greater access that the rich have to health care is seen in the fact that Karimpur has no Brahman widows under the age of forty-five, which implies that there have been no recent deaths of young Brahman males, whereas the poor had several women in their teens and early twenties widowed in 1984 alone.

ILLNESS

The illness of men, women, or children puts an immense burden on the poor. Preventive medicine is almost unknown in Karimpur. Tuberculosis and polio, both preventable, are rampant, with almost a dozen children crippled by the latter. Tetanus, the primary cause of neonatal deaths due to unsterile birthing practices, has not decreased in frequency since the 1950s, although tetanus injections are available in the village and are sometimes given to newborn males. A few pregnant mothers also received tetanus inoculations, thus protecting the newborn as well. Immunizations for mumps, measles, diphtheria, and rubella are rare.

Much illness goes untreated. Women have less access to medical care than do men, needing permission from husbands and/or mothers-in-law to seek care, a companion for the bus trip to Mainpuri, and money to pay the bills. One day I agreed to take a woman suffering from a serious vaginal discharge to the "lady doctor" in Mainpuri. Within minutes, I had a car full of women, all with gynecological problems needing treatment. When a poor family decides to give medical care to a woman or child, it often means losing a day's wages and the husband's place in the job queue he was in, in addition to which it costs a minimum of a day's wages in bus fares, doctor's fees, and medicines. It easily takes a week or more for the family to recoup its losses. One young man who had lost two daughters to gastroenteritis (probably due to dehydration) at about age one, both when he was away, finally had to give his family an order: if his third daughter got sick and his wife felt she needed treatment, his family was to send her to the doctor immediately. Only by stating the priorities prior to a crisis could he hope to prevent a third death from delayed care.

Afraid of the government hospital, where care—if there is any—is minimal and often performed brusquely, people shift among private practitioners of varying quality. Resident in Karimpur itself are several *vaidy*s practicing Ayurvedic cures, shamans (*bhagat*), and a self-trained "doctor" (who learned his skills compounding medicines for a better-trained "doctor" in a nearby town). Given that a wide array of drugs (both prescription and nonprescription) is freely available in the Mainpuri chemists' shops, the primary requisite for setting up a medical practice is enough chutzpah to convince prospective clients of one's abilities. Several local men were also given one month of government training to teach them how to deal with minor ailments and are kept on a small government stipend, providing nonprescription drugs periodically to treat their families and neighbors. Their knowledge is meagre, however, as we learned the day Mohan's grandson asked us how to use "talcum dusting powder" to treat diarrhea, confusing the English word "dusting" with the Hindi *dast*, diarrhea. There is also a government-trained midwife kept on a monthly stipend to help with childbirth, although she is called in only for problem cases as she demands additional payments for her services. A nurse-midwife ostensibly runs a woman's clinic, but after a year I had still not seen her. The women of Karimpur unanimously felt that the main goal of these two women was to get women sterilized, and there was much lament about the lack of pills for controlling pregnancy. Most children were delivered by traditional midwives of the *dhānuk jāti*, who had hereditary ties to given families.

Mainpuri has a government hospital, but it lacks an operating room, it has no generator to cope with the frequent power outages, and it boasts but one oxygen tank, which is shared amongst its patients. Relatives are responsible for most of the care, and drugs, including IV solutions, have to be purchased in the bazaar a mile away. There is also a TB hospital and a women's hospital, where not even cesareans are possible. Serious cases from all three hospitals are sent to Agra, three hours away, if the families can arrange transport. There are also excellent Christian hospitals in Kasganj, two hours north, and Fatehgarh, one hour east. Private doctors included one gynecologist and a variety of male practitioners, some who run "hospitals." Reliability is always an issue: one woman with postpartum fever was thrown out of one such "hospital" on a dark rainy night after she went into shock when administered an injection. Her family came to us for our car to get her to the government hospital.[23]

Even when someone sees a doctor of quality, treatment can be problematic. Injections are preferred, but patients rarely make repeat visits for the required follow-up injections. And when pills are prescribed, only a portion may be purchased. Once the visible signs of illness are gone, the family will stop medication. Finally, frequent shifts in medical practitioners are common, so that a really ill person may see—and receive medications from—several doctors a week, or even in one day.

Ram Chandra, the Carpenter whose wife died leaving him with four small children, described his family's battles with illness:

> My older son was sick three times.
> [Q: What illness did he have?] First, he had diphtheria, in the throat. I had him treated by Sharma [a well-known Mainpuri doctor]. I mortgaged my wife's jewels. When that was not enough, I mortgaged something else. I took a loan of a hundred rupees from Krishna, so I could get him treated.
> [Q: How many rupees were spent?] Four hundred rupees that time. Then he became okay.
> [Q: When did he become ill the second time?] Three years ago. His stomach swelled up and his feet became very thin.
> [Q: What was the illness?] It was *jalandhar* [probably kwashiorkor].
> [Q: Where did you get the treatment?] In Fatehgarh [a town an hour away].
> [Q: Why not in Mainpuri?] First I had him treated by Dr. Sharma. I spent one hundred rupees. Then I got treatment from a *vaidy*. Then as there was no cure, I had him treated in Fatehgarh. I took some wood from nine villages. Satya Pal and I were partners. I got six hundred rupees and used that for treatment.
> [Q: To whom did you take him in Fatehgarh?] To Dr. Singh, private*. He has a hospital*. I spent 375 rupees, and then another 475 rupees.
> [Q: How did you pay the debt?] I did some more work, purchased wood and sold it. I had some grain in my fields and that fed us. I worked. I also sold some ornaments. As the interest kept on increasing, I sold ornaments.
> [Q: You have told of when your child was ill. What about your wife?] Then there is one more child of seven years. He got polio when he was three. I spent two or three hundred rupees on his treatment. I was troubled. I thought, I have a little bit of land. So I will sell it. But how will I feed the children? Then my wife fell ill. There was a mass in her stomach. I took her to Mainpuri, but there was no relief. So I went to Fatehgarh. I sold one silver ornament for five hundred rupees and got her treated. The doctor* said it was her spleen [*tillī*], so I got her spleen treated. I came back. I said, "I can go nowhere. I have no money." I got her treated at Ram Autar's. He gave all kinds of bottles: he made her drink from five kinds of bottles and her stomach became less swollen. But the mass did not go. In the month of Kuar [September–October], she had a fever for five or six days. I got her an

injection from Rajiv: he is a Cultivator. I also got her an injection from the doctor near the Cultivator's. There was a child of three months in her stomach: it aborted. After eight or ten days, she got fever [literally, "a fever came to her"], so I got an injection*. Then one evening she started vomiting. She vomited a lot all night. I sat on the ground: everyone next door was awake. Then she spoke to me: "You should not sit on the ground. Sit on the cot." She touched my feet and said, "My condition is not good. It is coming into the bones of my body." I was awake all night and slept only at dawn. Then she woke me, "Call the doctor*." So I went and called the doctor*. He gave her an injection* and left. Her hands and feet became cool. I said that she had had no relief. . . . Then I went to Anjani [a nearby village] to call another doctor*. He was in the military. I went to call him. Just as I found him, Satya Pal's brother came and said, "Uncle, run fast." I asked what was the matter. The boy finally said that my wife had died [*khatam hui gai*].

In this narrative, we see the toll that medical expenses can take on a family living on less than ten rupees a day. By Ram Chandra's account, he spent about two thousand on these illnesses, close to a year's income for a family that was barely subsisting to start with. And in his wife's final illness, we see Ram Chandra's helpless search for a doctor who could cure her.

CYCLES OF DEBT

Ram Chandra's story illustrates the cyclical affect of debts and poverty on Karimpur's poor. One loan is paid off, and then another calamity strikes. Debt has many causes: illness, floods, drought, marriages. And even as one worry is lifted, the probability is high that another will strike.

Getting out of debt depends on daily wages and household budgets. Until the late 1970s most Karimpur families lived off of agriculture, either farming their own lands, giving land for sharecropping, being a sharecropper, or being an agricultural laborer. Sharecroppers generally worked on a half-share basis, putting in half the seeds, fertilizer, water, and manure, plus all of the labor, and receiving half the harvest. Some men worked on a one-quarter basis, working full time for a landowner and receiving one-quarter of the harvest. In the 1960s laborers received less than five rupees per day and one meal. In the 1970s it was five to eight rupees per day, plus a meal. By the early 1980s wages had risen to eight to twelve rupees per day, but often without a meal. Moreover, by that time farmers had to compete with the demands of the urban labor market, forcing up wages. By 1983, then, farm labor was often the least preferred because it was often necessary to wait months to be paid and to ask repeatedly for one's wages, an act that poor men found demeaning and, with the increased availability of alternative sources of income, could avoid.

Ram Chandra earned eight to ten rupees per day when he worked, which was never more than twenty days a month. He needed six or seven pounds of grain per day to feed his family of six. Given that grain cost a minimum of three-quarters of a rupee per pound, half his income was thus spent on grain alone. Oil, spices, salt, and perhaps some lentils or a vegetable would take at least half of the remainder, leaving him at most two rupees (about fifteen cents) per day beyond food costs to cover the days he did not work, along with other expenses.

Sheila, the Washerman's wife, calculated her expenses this way:

6–7 lbs. of grain/day	Rs. 4.50
lentils (cheap kind)	Rs. 1.50
2 lbs. vegetables	Rs. 1.00 (min.)
2 oz. oil	Rs. 0.75
3 oz. spices	Rs. 1.00
(although she would use	
only 1 oz. if necessary)	
TOTAL	Rs. 8.75

Sheila sometimes got food payments for washing clothes, perhaps enough for one person per week. Her husband earned some six to eight rupees a day driving a cycle rickshaw most of the year, although he earned better wages during the May harvest when he worked at the local seed store hefting bags of grain. But he was in an accident in 1984 and couldn't work for a month, which of course cut into their income. Sheila also gets old clothes from her *jajmān*s, but, as she asked, "Who can eat clothes?"

Raghunath had this to say about daily expenses:

[Q: If one earns ten rupees a day, is it enough to feed a family?] It is and it isn't. If I get ten rupees a day it's not enough because I have a mother, father, wife, and two children. At least nine pounds of wheat will be needed, for six rupees. Vegetables are at least one and a half rupees. Then there is salt, peppers, oil, and so on. Then also there are *bīḍī*s [cheap cigarettes] and other expenses at home. If one is alone or there is a family with only one child, then it is enough. But Bhagvan is such that if someone is earning ten rupees and his expenses are twelve rupees, and his wife and children can't work, then he can take four-fifths of an acre of corn on half-shares and his wife and children can work on it. The father continues to earn ten rupees per day. That is how they manage to survive. If there is no land, the young children work on other's land.

Raghunath's explanation also suggests why the poor of Karimpur have higher fertility rates than the rich. From 1925 to 1975 the population of the poorest *jāti*s increased by 255 percent, while that of the Brahmans grew by only 149 percent. Fertility rates for the last twenty-five years are comparably disproportionate for rich and poor. In the period from 1968 to 1974 the fertility rate for the rich was 35.1 per thousand while that for the poor was 44.8 per thousand. Fertility for both groups increased in the period from 1975 to 1984, when the fertility rate among the poor was 47.8 per thousand and among the rich 40.1 per thousand. For the poor, children—especially male children—imply income.[24] Raghunath himself tells of working for three years in the late 1950s, from the age of fourteen to seventeen, as a laborer, irrigating a rich farmer's fields by swinging large leather bags of water from natural tanks into irrigation channels. By the age of fourteen, he earned more than he ate.

Because of the constant debt, often for food alone, that the poor invariably find themselves in, they are unable to break free of the dominance of the Brahman moneylenders. Krishna, the most hated moneylender in the village, charges 4 percent per month. He is also able to find laborers at critical harvest times because of people's indebtedness to him. Santoshi's teenage son often missed school to work for the Brahman family to whom they owed two thousand rupees taken by her father-in-law as a loan when her husband's brother was married. The loan now falls on her family's head.

In order to understand the cyclical nature of debt as it contributes to poverty, let me examine Raghunath's history in some detail.

> Born about 1943: household contained his father, uncle (still a child), mother, and grandmother. By the early 1950s, they had 6.4 acres of land but no access to water, so they could not grow wheat. Their main crop was corn.
>
> Late 1940s: His mother died. His uncle married for the first time.
>
> Early 1950s: He got smallpox and his arms were injured.
>
> Mid 1950s: He attended first and second grade.
>
> Late 1950s: His father died. He was left with his uncle, aunt, and initially his grandmother. His uncle had no surviving children. There was a loan of Rs. 100 taken out for death feast for father. They could not repay it, so it rose to Rs. 500 after five or six years.
>
> Early 1960s: Married a partially blind woman. Took out a loan of Rs. 300 for wedding costs. Sold his wife's gold and a bullock after two years to pay back Rs. 500. (Two children were born but died.)
>
> Mid 1960s: His first cousin married at age eleven. No debt. Received Rs. 500 as a dowry, which covered wedding costs.
>
> Late 1960s: His wife died. Took out a loan of Rs. 450 for her hospital expenses, plus Rs. 100 for the death feast. Sold a goat to repay part of the loan after one year.

The next year: Took out a loan of Rs. 100 for *gaunā* costs for his cousin's wife. Soon thereafter his cousin's wife died. Took out a loan of Rs. 150 for her burial expenses.

1969–71: Worked for two years for Shankar to pay back loans. Earned Rs. 100 per month or equivalent in food, plus loan payment.

About 1970: Took out a loan of Rs. 350 loan for bribes in land consolidation to ensure good fields in reallotment.

1971: Cousin's second wedding. Dowry of Rs. 50. Took out a loan for Rs. 1,000 for expenses from Bhim Sen Banya. Sold gold to pay back some of the loan. Worked for Bhim Sen for two years to pay back the rest of the accumulated loans.

Late 1970s: Got a government loan of Rs. 5,000 for a pump set ("engine") for a tube well. By 1984 he had repaid Rs. 3,000 but still owed 4,000. His oldest cousin had a son.

1979: Second cousin married. Took out a loan of Rs. 1,400.

1981: Third cousin married. Took out a loan of Rs. 1,100. Received Rs. 500 in dowry, plus ten pots. Spent Rs. 1,000 on clothes for the bride and groom; Rs. 300 on transportation for the groom's party (*barāt*); and Rs. 300 at the wedding itself in miscellaneous expenses.

1983: Wedding of thirteen-year-old female cousin. Took out a loan of Rs. 1,300. Also used the spring harvest to feed the groom's party, leaving no wheat seed for the following year or any to sell for fertilizer. Result was an inadequate wheat crop in 1984. Oldest cousin also had a second son.

1984: Ate potatoes as primary food for the month of February, as nothing else was available. Loans totaled over Rs. 8,000, with interest. Sold two-fifths of an acre of land for Rs. 7,000.

The size of Raghunath's growing family contributed to their woes. Their initial acreage, with water, was adequate for a family of maybe six or eight, but by the late 1970s there were at least twelve people dependent upon it. The family remained joint, with Raghunath sharing the major decisions with his asthmatic uncle and dominating aunt. Raghunath obtained the loans for the many weddings, and so he in turn was responsible for paying them off. It was his two-year stints with large landowners/moneylenders that repaid the loans for his cousins' weddings. As his account of his life story implies, Raghunath considers his cousins as both his siblings and his children. They are all much younger than he is, and his concern for and pride in his "sister" and "brothers" is immense.

Fortunately, the family had an excellent reputation as farmers, so obtaining land to sharecrop was never a problem. Raghunath could also easily obtain work as an agricultural laborer. But in addition to the major crises detailed above, the family had continual problems with draft animals for farming, as a pair of male buffalo or bullocks are necessary to get sharecropping jobs. Several times they had buffalo die, throwing the farming into jeopardy. And every year they would have to borrow several sacks of grain to survive until the next harvest, when the seed store asks one and a half sacks for each one borrowed.

In 1984 his oldest cousin sought a job in Rajasthan, where skilled farmers were needed after the opening of the Indira Gandhi Canal. This cousin's wife and children soon followed, as did a second cousin and his wife, relieving the pressure in the small house in Karimpur. But these cousins did not contribute to the family left behind, as Raghunath had hoped, and, what with the decrease in their labor force, the family's ability to farm declined. Although this book is about the period up until 1984, Raghunath's subsequent history is revealing. He himself worked in Rajasthan for several short periods over the next few years. Then as age (and a serious drinking problem) began to wear on him, he sold all of his land, putting the money in a time deposit account. Unfortunately, a friend convinced him to speculate in the garlic wholesale market in 1989, so he borrowed against his savings and lost his total investment. He will continue to do day labor as long as he is able and then will become dependent upon his cousins for sustenance. Whether they will provide properly for him is unknown.

Raghunath's history of constant debt, of illness, deaths, marriages, the need for draft animals, and food shortages is typical of Karimpur's poor. Even hard workers are unable to beat the odds of low salaries, high interest, and too many children. Sonu, the husband of Sheila the Washerwoman, comments on his inability to prosper this way:

If Bhagvan wills it, then I will be rich. Or Bhagvan could make me poor. . . . If no one should fall ill from anything, if no one was sick, if the children should not be sick, and no trouble [*khokat*] catches me—if that happened and if Bhagvan wanted, then I might begin to eat bread [prosper]. [Q: What is the meaning of trouble?] I mean no unexpected event. No quarrels with anyone. There must be no litigation. By this I mean trouble.

To move out of poverty is difficult indeed, for it requires immense and uncontrollable good fortune.

Some, do, however, break the cycle. One of Raghunath's relatives has begun to prosper. Ravindra has a household containing only his mother, his wife, and one small child. Raghunath described his situation in this way:

Radhe, Manoj, and Dilip split their families four years ago. Ravindra [son of Radhe] had five acres of land. He farmed it. Each of the three had five acres of land. But Bharat and Lakshman [sons of Manoj] must share five acres. But Ravindra is the only son. Bharat and Lakshman were also in debt. . . .

And Ravindra worked hard at farming. Later he opened a shop. He earned a lot. . . . It was only two years ago. He has a buffalo, and the buffalo gives a lot of milk, as much as 130 or 140 rupees a week. The buffalo used to give five hundred rupees a month [more than a day laborer could earn]. His mother takes very good care of it. So Ravindra has become wealthy. His expenses are low.

But while Raghunath recognizes the value of a small family with few expenses, he, like the rest of the poor, advocates large families with many sons. But it may be the minor landowners such as Raghunath and his relatives who will be among the first to feel the pressures of a decreasing ability to support themselves and hence will begin to advocate smaller families. Meanwhile, the small landowner and the landless are caught in an almost inescapable cycle of poverty.

OLD AGE

Raghunath's life also raises the issue of another group of poor in Karimpur, the aged. Mohan, Saroj, and Raghunath all spontaneously brought up the problems of being old in describing their lives. For most families in Karimpur, aging relatives are a concern. Karimpur's population is slowly growing older, as life spans increase and medical care becomes more available. Some 6.5 percent of the population was over fifty-five in 1925, but by 1984 the figure had risen to 9.1 percent. From 1925 to 1984 the average age of widows in Karimpur increased from forty-seven to sixty-seven, while the average age of widowers rose from fifty to sixty-two. Moreover, this elderly population is likely to be widowed and/or living in joint families. While the average age of the head of a nuclear family remained about the same between 1925 and 1984, the average age of the head of a lineal joint family increased from forty-seven to fifty-six. The aged and the widowed are most likely to be living with a son and his family: in 1984 only one old widow lived alone, and no elderly men lived alone.

This elderly population is poor. Despite the fact that they often live in families that are prosperous, they themselves are frequently mistreated and not adequately fed and clothed. Arun, a Brahman landowner, expressed his concern for his elderly grandmother, saying that women should have land in their own names so that they need not beg from their sons, as his grandmother must. She moves between two of her son's houses, and while a certain love and respect are present, she is also the target of verbal abuse and is the last to receive a new quilt or shawl. Her best friend, also from a landowning family, is said to be beaten by her daughter-in-law and not fed properly.

One day I asked Raghunath about the treatment of old people. He spoke of a friend whose father "was about one hundred" and whose son abused him. One of his neighbors is an elderly man who must go begging from house to house, as his nephew often does not feed him. But, as Raghunath mentioned on another occasion, this old man has a "cracked mind" and causes trouble for the nephew. But even though the land is in his name, his nephew controls it, and thus food is sometimes problematic. Raghunath also spoke of the mother of one of his friends:

> Vivek's wife is good, but her conduct is wrong. She does not attach any importance to her mother-in-law. But that one is her mother-in-law. And she is the daughter-in-law. The mother-in-law must give the daughter-in-law knowledge: do this work, do that work. But the daughter-in-law doesn't care if her mother-in-law lives or dies. We should have duty to those older and senior.

Then he spoke of Mohan's crippled brother: no sons in the village were as caring of their fathers as this man's son, who carried his father outdoors every day and fed him with his own hands. He added that in any other house, the old man would have already died.

JOY AND LAUGHTER

Being poor does not mean a life of unalleviated misery. Karimpur residents, poor and rich, female and male, have many joyous moments and many pleasures. Most depend on personal skills, and few require more than a token payment.

One of the most frequent pleasures is enjoyment of children, whether one's own or those of a close relative. In the early morning and evening, men often sit on the verandah or at the edge of a lane playing with the younger children of their family, gently teasing them or taking pride in a child's growing verbal abilities or toddling steps. Or a father or grandfather might take the family's two-year-old along when he fetches cigarettes from one of the village shops. In the cold December and January evenings, a small fire is lit on the verandah or near the lane, and the men and children (and perhaps older women) gather to warm their fingers and toes, gossip, sing, and tell stories. When a male visitor is present, a small-scale competition may develop, as the teenage boys demonstrate their growing skills. If the visitor himself is skilled, he finds an attentive audience.

Oral traditions, whether a kinsman's telling of a well-known tale, a group of men gathering to sing religious songs, women tormenting a male wedding party with obscene songs, or a government- or village-sponsored folk opera, provide the most frequent forms of entertainment in Karimpur. Dependent only upon individual skills, time, and inexpensive instruments, these are available to all. If a landlord or an anthropologist sponsors a professional performance, everyone happily attends. In 1984 a government-sponsored folk troupe came to the village and performed on the wide verandah at Mohan's house. With his son and a friend keeping the peace, the open square in front was packed with over five hundred men and boys, some clinging to tree limbs or sitting on a courtyard wall for a better view. To one side was a cluster of a hundred or more women and squirming children. The ribald jokes of the performers, the dancing girls, and the threats of the villain were greeted with glee and laughter. On another night I sponsored an oral epic singer whose home is in Karimpur. Some two hundred men crowded onto Prakash's verandah, while the women of his house and close neighbors listened from the rooftop.

On the day of Snake's Fifth, a group of lower-ranked men skilled in *ḍānk*, the ritual of snake possession, gather in an open area near Raghunath's house. Here Raghunath, as the devotee of the snake king, Basuk Dev, becomes repeatedly possessed by the snake king, who answers questions of concern from anyone passing by. The possession is induced through song and drumming and is controlled by an exorcist, a man who knows the mantras that can control the snake king when he is present in his human devotee.[25]

Women also find time to play with children and to gossip with neighbors. The Washerwoman, the Watercarrier, and the Sweeper all serve as sources of information about happenings elsewhere in the village and are thus valued visitors. The Washerwoman's visit to a rich landlord's family is usually extended, as the purdah-bound women take the opportunity to catch up on village news. On festival days and at marriages and the births of sons, the women, whether rich or poor, celebrate with song. If a son is born, songs remembering the birth of Krishna are sung. At marriages songs extolling the beauty of the bride or groom, comparing them to Sita and Ram, are performed. Other songs may affirm the bride's reluctance to leave her home or a mother's anxiety over the arrival of a rival for her son's affections.

Karimpur's frequent festivals provide brief breaks throughout the year. Although the celebrations of the poor are anything but lavish, both the respite from work and the drawing together of family and community are

14. Children playing

clearly important. In addition to yearly celebrations, a more affluent *jāti*-mate may sponsor a *kathā*, the telling of a religious story over the course of several days by a renowned pandit or guru, or a *kīrtan*,[26] a song event where men sing continuously for twenty-four hours, or a *jāgin*, an all-night song session in honor of one of the goddesses.

An event enjoyed by most villagers is the annual district fair, held at the Devi temple in Mainpuri. This ten-day event every April draws tens of thousands daily. Packing food for the day, those who have the resources pile onto a tractor, truck, or bullock cart to ride to town. Others walk. The air is filled with the sound of women singing songs honoring the god-dess as the bullock carts slowly wind toward the town. Most people try to spend the night so that they can see the lights or even attend a movie. The women also shop for a variety of household goods and small trinkets, while the children crave a cheap toy.[27] Thus, in a multitude of ways, joy and laughter do enter the lives of poor and rich, women and men.

ESCAPING POVERTY

Karimpur's poor recognize the relationship between wealth and oppres-sion, while at the same time using the cultural category of fate, *karma*, to explain their own personal oppression. A Watercarrier said, the powerful subjugated the poor "because of wealth. Whatever we used to produce, we used to take to their houses, even the grains of the chaff. Only then did we take our share. . . . It was because of poverty: we had nothing and they had everything."

Moreover, the poor saw the relationships between patron and worker as being like those between parent and child. The metaphor of the fam-ily was made explicit in the comments made to Bruce one day by a group of Watercarrier men:

They [Brahmans] say they kept us like *mā-bāp* [mother-father, that is, as if they were our parents], that all we had to do was go to them and we would receive. But to *mā-bāp* one must show respect and humility. We would go with folded hands, and we might receive, if we were properly humble. They helped us in the courts or with officials, to be sure. *They* could read: *they* had time to go to school because *we* were working their fields for them. By keep-ing us illiterate they could keep us unaware of our rights—they could take advantage of us if we went against them because they knew the workings of government, they knew the officials, and they had the money to pay bribes. They were *mā-bāp*, and sometimes they showed the love that *mā-bāp* are supposed to have for their children, but sometimes they beat us, just as *mā-bāp* sometimes beat their children.

Although, as I have shown, Karimpur's poor do indeed believe that their poverty is due, in part at least, to their fate, they refuse to acquiesce completely, and certainly the above statement is a critique of Brahman dominance. They firmly believe that behaving properly in this life will gain them rewards in the next, if not in this one itself. Further, they also believe that those rich men who mistreat them will receive *their* just rewards, either now or in a next birth.

Bruce talked one day to an elderly Muslim Cotton Carder whose family had been among the poorest in the village in 1968, but whose son, educated with help from Charlotte Wiser, had prospered. Karim succinctly stated the position of the poor:

> Now they eat [charge] two annas on a one-anna loan. So now the Brahmans are blind [literally: he means Mohan and his brother]. Now what must be done? If you eat improper behavior, then you shall be born of improper behavior [*harām ko khayyo tau harām ko paidā huyyen*]. There is me. I have fed my children through my labor [*mazdūrī*]. I did nothing immoral [*harām*]. I worked hard. Therefore my offspring are good. If I had fed my descendants by acting immorally, then they would be bad.

Not only does Karim account for his own family's recent prosperity, but he also makes reference to Mohan's blindness, caused, as he and many others believe, by the suffering Mohan's family has given others.

But Karim's discussion of "eating" one's immoral behavior is more than a justification of the notion that righteous labor will yield positive results, in contrast to the negative results earned through unjust moneylending and other wrongs. It is also a form of resistance to the power of the rich, which demeans them behind their backs, and sometimes even to their face, however subtly.[28] Karim continued his discussion:

> My grandfather took a loan on paper for a hundred rupees. Eventually, because of interest, it was tens of thousands of rupees. Yet that wife's brother [*sālā*, a potent obscenity in Hindi; he means Mohan] didn't care.
> [Q: So what now?]
> Now that *sālā* says, "Where am I standing?" "Why?" "Where?" "Who is it?" [Mohan is blind and cannot see who is there.]
> [I say,] "I am Karim."
> [He answers,] "So fix the tobacco" [in a clay pipe, as used by elders in the village].
> Now one [Mohan] is sitting there, and the other [Mohan's blind and paralyzed brother] is sitting here. I myself am smoking. I say, "Take the pipe." That one puts out his hand. The other puts out his hand. Now to whom should I give it? I fold my hands. "Oh, Mohan."
> [He replies,] "What? Where is the pipe?"

[The other says,] "I also don't have the pipe. Oh, Karim!"
[I say,] "What?"
"Have you given the pipe to anyone?"
[I answer,] "To whom should I give it? You are both blind."

Karim then continued:

> One time I was at the bank [a cooperative society located in Karimpur].
> He [Mohan] said, "Karim, let's go; lead me."
> I said, "Let's go." Perhaps I didn't watch carefully. So he stepped in Ar-
> jun's drain [an open ditch through which flows all the refuse from a house,
> muddy, stinky, and black]. His feet were very wet.
> He said, "Karim, where am I?"
> I said, "What?" I added, "I don't see anything." So these are the fruits of
> actions [*phal ke karni*]. I eat what I earn. I have not stolen from anyone
> even now.

Karim, in his somewhat devious way, is able to ridicule his Brahman landlord. And he clearly enjoyed telling of his success. The poor of Karimpur
regularly use gossip to demean their Brahman superiors and hence to re-
sist, psychologically at least, their dominance.

A favorite target of village gossip is Krishna, one of the biggest Brahman landowners and moneylenders in Karimpur. The poor take loans
from him only when desperate, for his accounting is notoriously inaccu-
rate and yet he calculates interest avidly. Krishna, a former wrestler, is the
epitome of the "bad rich"—usurious, lecherous, and constantly demeaning to those who seek favors from him. Young girls are forbidden to walk
past his verandah in order to avoid his gaze and comments, and his "grab-
bing at his crotch." Yet according to the poor his evil ways are already affecting his life: they point to his lame, partially blind son as evidence of
his "eating of his sins."

The fire that swept through the Brahman section of the village in April
1984, a fire that started from the fire used to light Mohan's pipe, provided an opportunity for resentment to be articulated forcefully and, for
a change, overtly. Villagers were united in the opinion that the fire was
caused by the sins of their Brahman leaders, particularly Mohan's family.
Furthermore, there was the curious fact that, although the fire started at
Mohan's house, it did minimal damage there. However, a rocket-like ball
of fire went up that then burned the grain stored by Mohan's family at a
distance of one-quarter mile from the village. No one had any doubts:
God had not succeeded in his punishment at Mohan's house, so he tried
a second tactic, burning the harvest. One man said, "Think of this: the
fire started at Mohan's, and everyone else's harvest was saved. If he was
not a sinner, how did only his harvest burn?" Likewise, a Sweeper argued:

I say this: he destroyed all the houses, he did. Otherwise, how did the fire start there? I say, everyone kept their harvest near the village. His was kept [way out] there. And others were kept here. And all these were saved. Only his caught fire: what is the reason? Is there some defect? Or is there a lack of morality? Or sin? Or some other thing?

Moreover, even the Brahmans believed that the village had accumulated too much sin, that the pot of the village was full of sin. Saroj herself blamed it on women and men who are irreligious, who do not follow *dharma*, do not give to beggars and sadhus, and have not built temples.

Furthermore, the anger of the poor finally spilled over into outright confrontations. To take one example: The fire had stopped just before reaching Arun's house. Arun's brothers were thought to be troublesome, bringing destruction to both the village and their family by selling off their land. Arun's daughter returned to the house a few days after the fire in tears because one of the Sweeper women had commented, "All the other sinner's houses have burned. Now we'll have to burn yours." This kind of open, face-to-face attack is rare in Karimpur, but the enormity of the fire allowed it to surface throughout the village and gave many a chance to vent years of pent-up anger.

If their stomachs could be filled some other way, the poor would avoid working for the Brahmans. A Leatherworker in his late twenties, with a fifth-grade education, discussed the habits of the Brahman landlords.

> I worked as a laborer for that family one day. Then his wife said, "Son, cut the fodder."
>
> I responded, "Grandmother, I have worked during the day. I have no contract to cut fodder at night. I also have a life." When I went for my wages, they had cut them by two rupees.
>
> They said, "We are giving you six rupees. If you'll cut fodder, then we'll give eight."
>
> So I said, "Grandfather, give me six. I won't cut fodder." So Sahab [to Bruce], I feel satisfaction [*santos*] in my soul [*ātmā*] in every way. . . . In the village, people look down upon me. Some [landlords] say that these *sālā*s [an obscenity, here meaning the lowly, or even more specifically the Leatherworkers) don't come and work for us. They don't come to our door [asking for work]. I am truly a Leatherworker by *jāti*. Therefore you [Brahmans] say, "Do the work of making cow-dung cakes. Don't live near us." But if you give enough for me to eat, then I'll work. Now I need five pounds [of grain], and if you give five and a half pounds, for a whole day I'll toss your cow dung [for fertilizer]. Otherwise, how can I raise my children? . . . [When I had children], then I was happy. The heart becomes a little greener when you have children.[29] By working, I can educate them a little. I worry constantly about whether Bhagvan will give enough so that I won't need to take a loan from anyone. I want my stomach to be full.

One form of resistance is the refusal to work, when the need for money is not so pressing as to force the poor to take jobs. For example, few of the younger women of the Midwife *jāti* have learned the skills necessary to pursue this hereditary occupation, refusing to do this unclean work unless the pressure of money is extreme.[30] Moreover, the pay is minimal and even then they often have to wait months and ask repeatedly before receiving their earnings. The elderly Flower Grower's wife said that she used to work (often grinding grain) only in houses "where there was love," suggesting the basis on which conscious choices are made when hereditary ties are not involved. Slow, incomplete, and incorrect work is another form of resistance.[31] Not surprisingly, the Brahman landlords continuously complain about the quality of work.

Oral traditions other than gossip also serve to articulate the protests of the poor. The song of the wife whose family fields are lost in the monsoon, quoted earlier, is one example. Other tales tell of conflicts between different social groups, with the poor sometimes outwitting the rich. No doubt the oral epics and songs so popular in Karimpur that focus on the travails of Harishchand, sold into slavery, or Raja Nal, forced to work as an Oil Presser, reaffirm for Karimpur's poor the potential depths to which the rich and powerful can fall. Other songs tell of modern heroes like the renowned dacoits Chabbe Ram or Phoolan Devi. These robbers of the rich become lauded in the lore of the poor. But dacoits from wealthy families such as Karimpur's Brahmans are strongly condemned.

Many of the poor feel that the Brahman landlords will do everything possible to prevent the rest of the village from prospering. A young Cultivator claimed that several noted Brahman dacoits purposely stole from the poor to prevent their upward progress. He also blamed the failure of an attempt in 1980 to open a twice-weekly market at the Karimpur bus stop on these same Brahman youth. Shopkeepers from Mainpuri had started coming to the market but found themselves so harassed by the Brahman dacoits that ultimately the market closed. He added, "They have land but don't work. So they sell it [to live off its earnings]. We have a little bit of land, and we eat because we work hard." As this statement suggests, much of the personal dignity of the poor derives from their sense of righteousness: they have earned legitimately, whereas those others steal. What they eat—both figuratively, as in the fruits of their actions, and in reality, the food in their mouths—is thus more legitimate.

Yet in this life, changed circumstances are rare. Few families have managed to alter their positions in the economic hierarchy of Karimpur. The *jajmānī* system, linking landlord and poor, defines the poor as beggars, because the payments from the *jajmān*, whether distributed daily to a Sweeper or at harvest times to a Carpenter, are given only when asked for "with folded hands." Remember, also, that Sheila's husband captured the link between being poor and being female, saying that to beg is to make oneself like a woman, namely, powerless.[32] Tied to servitude through traditional *jajmānī* ties, bound to moneylenders because of loans, having few options for employment outside of the village, and facing frequent death and illness and high birthrates, Karimpur's poor are indeed trapped by the destiny of their births. Their life cycle is characterized by a constant series of crises, which often push the adaptive capacities of the poor beyond human limits. Given this circle of poverty, families face chronic frustration. Merely to survive is to struggle; to gain economically is all but impossible.

Even in the 1980s many cannot escape the facts of their initial situation. But some have been able to, and the changes of the past twenty years are continually altering the relative status of rich and poor, along with the political and economic dominance and patronage of the Brahmans that were key facets of the earlier system. In the following chapters, I will focus more specifically on these issues of change, as they affect economic and political relations in the village and as they affect the inner workings of families. As the "understanding" of the poor increases, and likewise that of women, paradigms that have guided Karimpur life at least through most of this century—paradigms built on controlling those who cannot "understand"—are increasingly threatened.

Jiji and Kamla, Two Widows

Women tend to be hurt first in the downward spiral of poverty. And of women, widows, especially those from poor families, are particularly vulnerable. I have chosen the stories of two widows, one recounted by the widow herself and the other told by Raghunath about a relative. Moreover, both these women had difficult times while married—Jiji because her husband was a useless gambler and Kamla as a barren woman, first widowed and then married to her first husband's younger brother.

Jiji (literally, "older sister") is a Watercarrier and is considered by many to be the poorest person in the village. Her story illustrates the difficulties that confront a woman trying to earn a livelihood for herself and her children. Jiji's own mother was widowed young and remarried after five or six years. Jiji lived mostly with her maternal grandparents, where her mother had returned after her first husband died. She was married young—at eleven or twelve—in a simple ceremony, which took place in 1962. Her marriage was consummated a year later, and she had her first child within a few years. Her six pregnancies left her with two living children, a boy who was about ten years old in 1984 and an older, married daughter. She was widowed prior to her daughter's marriage in 1982. When she began doing work in our kitchen and hauling water, we eventually began to talk. Probably with Jiji more than any other woman, I sensed the differences separating us. For one thing, her Hindi was very colloquial: she spoke a dialect that I often had trouble with. Moreover, she was never able to bridge the power difference, always treating me as she would the Brahmans for whom she worked. But she had a touching naïveté, which was probably what endeared her to others in the village, where she was thought an honorable woman, struggling as best she could. Over several days, seated uncomfortably at a table in my room in Karimpur, she told me about her life. I have rearranged her comments into a narrative.

Jiji's story emphasizes the breakup of a joint family, and she dwelled upon the story of the separation of her small household from that of her in-laws.

> I was separated from my mother-in-law within a year of my marriage [she probably means after her *gaunā*]. I had gone to the Ganges to bathe at Dashahra. My husband had asked his father, "Father, I will go bathe." He replied, "Why go alone to bathe at Dashahra? Why don't you take your wife with you?" My mother-in-law had gone to her aunt's near Mainpuri. My father-in-law bought vegetable oil to make *pūrīs* [fried breads] for us to take. I had my neighbor fry the *pūrīs*. We both went to bathe at Dashahra. When I returned, my mother-in-law created problems and forced us to separate. My husband decided to leave the house, picked up my box, and went out. I put on my clothes and was ready to go. Later there was a compromise. We lived with her for three months. Then I went to my mother's for two months. By then this house had been constructed. I have lived separately since then. My *gaunā* was held one year; in the second year we separated.
>
> When my son was born, my mother-in-law was there. She cooked for me. But my son was born after the separation. My son died at fourteen days. . . . Sometimes after I had been at my mother's place, my mother-in-law would have me with her for one or two months. Then she would cause us to separate again. Ever since my husband's brother married, we have been totally separate: I was never with her after his marriage. She gave me the job of cleaning under the cattle and taking the cow dung to the fields. His wife's job was to cook. My job was to grind the grain and clean the dung. So we separated. The old lady did nothing. I cleaned under the cattle and collected dung and helped grind. I also made cow-dung cakes. I used to clean the pots. When she forced us to separate us, I said, "Go to hell. You told me to do this work. You can do this work now. You don't fetch the water and you don't cook."

One day Jiji spoke of the death of her first son. Clearly she believed that her behavior caused his death, not the tetanus bacillus so rampant among Karimpur's newborns, to which some fifty out of every thousand fall victim.

> My son was well. But I didn't know that a mother should not keep her back toward her son on the cot. [Q: Why?] Suppose the baby lies on this side and the mother has her face turned the other way. Without knowing, Jamghantu [a spirit that attacks children, giving them tetanus] can catch the baby. My son was healthy. They were playing music. A birth ceremony had

just been performed. I was watching the musicians. I didn't know. In those days, girls were not so wise. My older sister-in-law came just then. She said, "Why are you standing here watching this show? Keep your son in your lap." I replied, "It doesn't matter. He is on the cot." Just then the music ended. His teeth were tight. [His jaws couldn't move.] My father-in-law came, and my husband's sister. Many people came quickly. But my son could not be cured.

Probably before the separation, Jiji's husband started to gamble, as had his father. Jiji was soon forced to be concerned about feeding her small family. Her husband shared in one acre of land with his father and two brothers, but there was little food from this land and he took whatever household money there was for gambling. He also beat her regularly. As she said, "I did not know the love of my husband. All I knew was that Bhagvan had given me two hands and that I had to work with them to earn a living." When asked how she felt about her husband's death, she replied, "Sister, what can I tell you about my sadness? I had problems from the start." She started making cow-dung cakes to earn enough to feed her children, but her husband would search the house and find the hidden money. Somehow they managed until her husband's death in 1982. Six months prior to his death, their one daughter was married. The family was poor, but they borrowed nine hundred rupees to pay for the wedding. Since her husband died, she has paid back six hundred. Now her daughter lives with her husband in the Punjab, where he does field labor.

Unlike most village women, Jiji had earned trifling sums before her husband's death, as she tried to protect (and feed) her family while he gambled. But even though she had been earning, widowhood forced her into new income-generating activities. She no longer could survive simply by making and selling cow-dung cakes, a routine activity of women that is often expanded to generate additional income. Since her husband died, Jiji has sought other employment of various sorts. Changes in Karimpur have denied her the traditional work of widows fifty years ago. In those days, most grain was ground on large grinding stones in each house, often requiring hours of female labor per day. With the advent of grinding machines, however, most richer families no longer grind their own flour, and poor women are thus denied a source of acceptable employment. For a year Jiji worked in the nearby district town, earning her food and forty to fifty rupees a month washing utensils or storing garlic. But this work was poorly paid, and she didn't have her son with her, so she returned to Karimpur after a year. Now she tries to raise goats, given her by her brother, does field labor during the harvest and planting seasons, and works cleaning pots and carrying water for Brahman families on ritual occasions. For this she earns four to six, sometimes even eight or ten, rupees a day. All together, she works some three to four months a year on a regular basis. Food for herself and her son costs two or three rupees a day (for bread, oil, spices, and a meagre amount of vegetable), so she must stretch her money. Her clothes are filthy and falling apart. Her few cooking pots are worn. Her one-room mud hut has only one cot and a torn quilt for the winter.

Her husband's brothers and father also died about 1982, leaving the three young widows alone. One has since married a distant relative from Karimpur and gone to live in the nearby town; the other returned to her parents. Only Jiji remains in the village, with no affines to aid her. A critical move was her reestablishing of connections with her brother, whom she had not seen in years: her mother is dead, and so this one brother is her only potential source of aid. For a while her son lived with his uncle, but Jiji missed him dreadfully and brought him back to the village, despite the problems of feeding and clothing him, as well as not being able to supervise him while she works. In this next section, Jiji discusses her problems with feeding her family.

Last year I earned two quintals of grain from harvesting. I also cleaned pots for others, worked for daily wages, sold *narī* [a kind of water grass that is eaten], and gleaned grain from the fields. I didn't have vegetables: I had potatoes in my field, so I ate those. I think that I harvested [others' fields] for twenty-six days. Last year people troubled me. It is like this. These people say things without cause: they say she is quarrelsome, she abuses others, she is wealthy. But only I know how I pass my life. I don't abuse them. They tease me. Yes, if you trouble me, I might say things. Now my daughter has come to visit: her child was hungry all day. My daughter couldn't eat. Well, some may say it is wrong. People will say, "She doesn't treat her daughter well; it is too much trouble for her to feed her daughter." But I am laboring outside. Can't she cook for herself and her brother so they can eat?

Yes, people say I have money in a bank. I don't even know how to send a telegram! I sent a cable to my brother. Those men were with me to help. You ask them. I swear by *karam* and *dharm* that I have nothing in the bank. Whatever I earned from selling dung cakes, he [her husband] used to spend gambling.

Once people stole from me. I had a small ornament made when things were cheap. I had it made for 140 rupees. I sold ghee to get the money. Then I went to the market to sell handmade rope [for cots]. I had never been in the market before. I didn't know anything. I made the rope here and went to sell it in Mainpuri. Some cutthroats met me. I didn't know that I would be cheated. Otherwise, I would have cried out that they are cheating me. They took everything.

The family for whom I've been working has promised to give me a sari and blouse at the festival. But the head of the family forgets and is confused. So if he forgets, he may or may not give anything. I can't get clothes for my son. Last year I bought a shirt for him for six rupees [about fifty cents] at Holi. I worked for others and bought underwear, a shirt, and trousers. It took one and a half meters of cloth. So he had one set. My brother also had clothes made for him. I bought one synthetic shirt and one cotton shirt. . . . You [addressing me] gave me this sari. I don't wear it all the time. I wear it when I go somewhere. . . . I have only one broken cot in my house. My daughter and son sleep on the cot: I sleep on the ground. I spread a bag of jute on the ground.

I have three goats right now. I haven't sold them yet. I couldn't sell them. One of them gave birth four days ago. The other one hasn't given birth in three years. . . . I can't take them to the cattle market. If someone comes to the house, I will sell them. I can't carry them to the market. My daughter is here. I have told you: I don't know buying and selling. I have these goats. If someone came to my house and bargained, I would sell them. I can't bargain or sell at the right rate. It is life. It will pass somehow, with sorrow or happiness. I am not so clever. Other people go to the market or the cattle fair. I can't go.

One landlord still owes me seventy rupees for digging potatoes. I borrowed from the shopkeeper for food, for oil and such. My seventy rupees are still with him [the landlord]. He ignores me and says he will pay today or tomorrow. What can I do? There aren't many jobs for women.

[Q: If he pays the seventy rupees today, what will you do?] My daughter is here: I shall send her home. I have to buy vegetable oil, clothes for her. This money is not enough even for clothes. And if he doesn't pay me, I shall bear my troubles.

The visit from Jiji's daughter was very problematic. Since all daughters born into Karimpur families are required to marry into another village, all married daughters live somewhere else. It is expected that they will spend a few weeks each year (more earlier in their marriage and fewer later) visiting their parents and natal village. Jiji's daughter was married to a man working in the Punjab and she resided there most of the time. Then this daughter returned to her husband's village in Mainpuri district, and friends contacted Jiji about having her daughter visit.

My daughter returned from the Punjab [where her husband lived]. Then I got a letter from the sister of the one who sings *Dhola*. "Your daughter has come. Come and see your daughter." Then someone came from there. He complained, "Your daughter asks me everyday to call her mother." I left the mustard half-threshed and went to bring her. I brought her on *tīj* [a festival day]. . . . But I am not happy. She wants her mother to grind and cook and feed her. I wish that my daughter would cook for me so that I could work outside. [Q: Why did you bring your daughter?] She has come after two years. She will stay one or two months. She will go back by herself, if no one comes to take her. She is very eager to return. She says, "I am in too much trouble here."

Jiji then went on to say that people were turning her daughter against her, adding:

> I shall not call her again in my whole life. Also, she will not come. She will not come even if my son gets married or if I am ill. She doesn't get good food here. She is in trouble while here. She doesn't like it. She doesn't even want to see her brother. She has no love for her brother.

Like many others, Jiji, though only in her late thirties, worries about becoming old. She is also concerned about her son: will he grow up to cause trouble for her or will he be a help?

> My biggest worry is how I will pass my old age. My life has been filled with worries. What I have earned today will be finished tomorrow. I will not be able to work. That is the biggest worry for me: what shall I do when I grow old. My health will not help me. This worry is always with me. When I pull a bucket from a well, my heart beats very fast. This is the greatest worry in my life.
>
> Sometimes I feel that however good my son is, his friends will change him. I am afraid that he will become like his father and gamble. The neighbor's son takes him everywhere. He plays those games [like gambling]. I have explained to him again and again that he is not to play. That even if he has no money, he should not play in order to win money from others. That he should not steal from others. The others can steal, but he should not. He went with the boys from our section and picked gram [from a farmer's field] and they were beaten. When I heard, I could not bear it. I also beat him. Other people blamed me for punishing him. I can't accept that reproof. My heart is clean.

Jiji is known throughout the village as being honorable and hard-working, someone who is doing her best. No one laughs at her, since she does work usually done by men. People respect her efforts to feed herself and her son. But it is a hard life, for even though she comes from a *jāti* whose women traditionally worked in others' homes and where purdah restrictions are minimal, she is working harder than almost any woman in the village and at jobs not normally held by women.

❧

Jiji made the decision not to remarry, partially because she had a son and a small amount of land. One day, though, I was talking with Raghunath about widows in the village, and he told this story about a woman belonging to his *jāti*. Kamla was forced into remarriage, in this instance to her deceased husband's younger brother. This decision was made primarily to keep land within the family, as new inheritance laws had given Kamla rights to half her husband's family's land. But since Kamla was older than her brother-in-law, the marriage did not take place immediately.

> Ashish's father had a brother. I don't remember his name. His son is Suri. Now each brother has a half share in the property. My father was the middleman for Suri's marriage. Kamla, his wife, was my maternal uncle's daughter. Suri died three years after marrying. When he died, all the land went into Kamla's name. The reason that the land went into her name was that Suri's father had died. There were only two people in the family, Ashish and this lady. And his mother. They were very poor. The mother used to grind flour in the village. That was before the flour mills. She used to get one pound after she had ground three pounds. She worked for the Brahmans or for houses where there was no woman or where the woman was sick. They called her and she supported herself this way.
>
> Ashish was very young then. And half the land came in Kamla's, the widow's, name. There were seven acres. So Ashish's mother decided to marry her son to the widow and asked the widow about it. The old lady [Ashish's mother] asked my uncle to arrange the marriage of the widow and her son. She said that her son was younger, but it was alright. After three or four years, the marriage took place. Much later, they still had had no children. They were worried. Now Ashish had twelve or fourteen acres of land [his plus the widow's seven acres]. The land was together, although half was still in the name of the widow.
>
> Now they thought about what they should do. They talked a lot to the widow. The old mother came to my father and uncle and suggested, "Let my son be married again to another girl. You advise your sister about this." My uncle explained it to her and said, "You don't have any children, but these people will not trouble you." Ashish also promised that he would not trouble her. So she agreed.

As the next part of the story shows, one concern in the second marriage was the age of the bride. She is some twenty years younger than Ashish, so considerable time must have passed between his first and second marriage. The second, however, was blessed with progeny: Ashish had six sons and one daughter. (Both he and Kamla were in their sixties, while his second wife was only in her mid-forties; his eldest son was twenty-two years old.)

Then they arranged Ashish's second marriage. This bride was old enough and from a very poor family. With the blessings of Bhagvan, they got two sons. After they had two sons, Ashish and his wife began to trouble the first wife. They beat her, too. She used to come to my house from time to time. I was too young to understand. Once they beat her a lot. They beat her with a stick and she came running to us. She stayed two days. The power was in our hands because the land was in her name. They sent her out of the house and she stayed with relatives. Many people came to her. We took his bullocks and buffalo [since they were hers]. Finally, his relative came and touched our feet and asked, "Please keep our respect." So Ashish called her, and she lived happily for a few days. Then they began to trouble her again.

Now the problem is that Kamla does what Ashish convinces her to do. She wrote a bond on her property, saying that it is hers as long as she lives, then it is Ashish's. So now he is completely powerful. They trouble her very much. Ashish had six sons. One has died. Now five are left. When she was troubled again, I refused to help. Her maternal relatives complained, and I replied, "What can I do when she has signed papers giving him possession? When the land was in her name, Ashish had pressure on him. But now there is no point in pressing him." . . . Now she gets a shirt and sari once a year. She doesn't have anything. Now her maternal relatives don't come. She is passing her life somehow.

Kamla, who had virtually no choice in either of her marriages, was widowed once and all but deserted for barrenness a second time. She receives shelter, along with minimal food and clothing, from Ashish's family. If she had not had a legal claim to some land—which came about only because her first husband's father happened to be dead, and so Suri had the land in his name when *he* died—she would most probably have returned to her parents after she was widowed and would have remarried somewhere else. But even then, her barrenness might well have led to similar results: almost inevitably the husbands of barren women take a second wife, and once that wife bears children, the barren woman often begins to be mistreated. Her only recourse is her father's or brother's household, and indeed the few Karimpur women I knew who were barren often returned to their parents' home. One barren Brahman daughter of Karimpur, who had married into another village, initially came to her brother's house only irregularly, but some ten years after her husband's second marriage she was a permanent resident of Karimpur.

While only a few women need to return permanently to their natal homes to live, the refuge and help provided by brothers and their natal families are of critical concern to all Karimpur women. Hence brothers are worshiped in the annual ceremonies of Brother's Second and *rakṣā bandhan* (literally, "the tying on of protection," which takes place on the fourteenth day of the light half of the month of Savan). Brothers provide other kinds of support as well. For example, they are expected to bring gifts for the wedding of a sister's child, and the sister actually returns to her brother's house to demand those gifts (*bhāt*). They must also give gifts when their sister has a child. The importance of a brother is marked symbolically by the toe rings put on a bride during the wedding ceremony. Karimpur women believe that they should always wear a pair of toe rings on each foot, "one for the husband and one for the brother." Brahman women remove all their toe rings when they are widowed, but the lower-*jāti* women continue to wear the ring for the brother as long as they have a brother who is alive. It is not surprising, then, that the brother is one of the key people in a woman's family and that she worships both for his long life and for his protection.

CHAPTER FIVE

"The Domination of Indira"

Although Karimpur's poor felt strongly oppressed by the Brahman land-lords in the period prior to the late 1970s, they began to see some relief from that oppression with the changes of the 1970s and 1980s. Concurrently, the rich have found themselves threatened by recent changes in the economic, political, and social systems in which Karimpur villagers engage, despite increased material prosperity for many among them. As the village headman, a Brahman, put it:

> But the condition of our people was better [in 1925]. Now the village people [meaning the Brahmans] are not so good. . . . But theirs [the situation of other *jātis*] was bad; their condition has improved. Only ours has become worse.

A Shepherd in his forties captured the viewpoint of the poor:

> The domination was carried out by the landlords and the British. The English used to give allotments of land in rural areas. As you became wealthy, you purchased a zamindari. So we were oppressed by the landlords in the past. But now there is the domination of Indira.[1]

The changes that have occurred since the 1920s have entailed an increasingly overt challenge to the dominance of the landlords. Certainly this is the view of both rich and poor in Karimpur, the rich lamenting their loss of dominance and the poor reveling in their ability to challenge "the system." Further, relations among the state, landlord, and laborer have changed over time, most fundamental being a shift in authority from the landlord to the state. These social changes that have come about at the village level are embedded in changes in the larger political economy, changes that include independence for India in 1947; the creation of a democratic state, with local, state, and national elections held regularly; the implementation of government policies regarding the role of agriculture in India's development; the advocacy by the state of education for all; and the establishment of health care policies. As the impact of these wider societal initiatives began to be felt in Karimpur, economic relations and material conditions changed, as did the community's view of itself.

There is a paradox here, however, for while the state is now ostensibly supporting the laborer *jātis*, with programs designed to aid the poor, for example, or to ensure the appointment of untouchables to office, its green revolution policies have in fact encouraged the development of a new capitalist landlord. This paradox has its roots in the agendas of a democratic state that uses populist policies to maintain itself. The dominant elites appeal to the lower *jātis* and classes through an ideology of populism that specifically holds out the promise of support for the low, such as Indira Gandhi's slogan *garībī haṭao*, "Banish Poverty." Yet the primary benefits of many populist policies are grabbed by the landlords.

Since Independence in 1947 the state in India has grown rapidly and has accumulated enormous powers over the economy generally. In the first years after Independence the agricultural sector was largely ignored as the state focused on industrial growth. But an agricultural crisis in the mid-1960s, precipitated by several years of bad harvests but also by the continued exploitation of the agricultural sector by the state, led to a state-initiated green revolution. The state expansion into agriculture included subsidized credit and electricity, the provision of new seeds and fertilizers, and government-set minimum prices for wheat, sugarcane, and some other crops. These measures accelerated market forces that were already beginning to affect traditional patronage systems like *jajmānī*. Likewise, the state has sought to direct programs to the poor, with the obvious desire of maintaining power through that vote bank, and to curtail the power of the richer peasants. While the Congress party, the ruling party for all but three years from Independence through to the mid-1980s, has thus maintained its voting blocks, it has also supported the growth of capitalist agriculture.[2] This chapter focuses on these broader state initiatives and their implications for socioeconomic change in Karimpur, as well as on the villagers' reactions to some of them.

THE INCREASING INTRUSION OF THE STATE
INTO AGRICULTURE

Many factors mark the shift in authority from the zamindar (literally, one with land) and the local Brahman landlords to state institutions. These include new laws regarding land ownership, credit facilities, development schemes, democratically elected governments, health services, and education. These facets of socioeconomic change are interrelated, for the control of land, which is the primary means of production, coincides with other networks of social, economic, and political power. Change in one segment of this network thus yields change elsewhere.[3] The shifts in authority from the owners of land to the state are sketched below in order to provide a context in which village interpretations of change can be understood.

LAND OWNERSHIP

The history of land ownership in Karimpur is complex and can only be outlined here. Most critical are the initial de facto control of the village by the Brahmans and the shift of some land to other *jāti* groups over the past thirty years (see table 4).

Prior to the Mainpuri area being ceded to the British by the nawab of Oudh in 1801, Karimpur Brahmans held tenancy rights granted to them by the legendary Khan Bahadur, who, they say, was the founder of the modern village. Khan Bahadur is said to have taken away the rights of the Ahirs and Thakurs, other farming *jāti*s of the region, and given the village to the ancestor of the dominant Brahman lineage of Karimpur.[4] That lineage traces its roots to this single ancestor thirteen generations back, some 250 years ago.[5] Patrilineal descendants through the male line of this one Brahman ancestor comprise 70 percent of Karimpur's Brahman population today, with the families of daughters whose husbands moved to Karimpur comprising another 20 percent. (The remaining 10 percent of Karimpur's Brahmans are descendants of the zamindar's agent in the village.) Although the dominant lineage itself has many serious factional splits, their common ancestry aids in the united front that they often present to the other Karimpur *jāti*s.

After the area was ceded to the British, Karimpur's Brahmans were not able to meet the new revenue demands and the rights to Karimpur were sold to a Brahman from a nearby district. His son fell into arrears in 1890, whereupon the rights to the village were sold to two merchants (*banyā*s),

TABLE 4   DISTRIBUTION OF LAND IN KARIMPUR, GROUPED
BY *JĀTI*

Jāti	Total Acreage		
	1925	1968	1984
HIGHEST			
Brahman	721.02	572.60	562.90
MID TO HIGH			
Bard	1.72	14.80	10.00
Accountant	3.54	7.40	7.60
Goldsmith	0.00	0.00	
Cultivator	150.26	209.60	167.14
Rice Cultivator	11.75	13.60	10.00
MID			
Carpenter	16.81	13.80	14.00
Shepherd	1.28	19.80	23.10
Grain Parcher	0.00	4.80	5.60
Watercarrier	36.01	45.00	45.92
Flower Grower	4.95	4.20	5.46
Shopkeeper	0.28	5.20	39.90
Barber	0.81		
Thakur			0.00
LOW			
Potter	0.00	0.00	0.50
Washerperson	0.04	0.20	0.00
Tailor	1.09	2.80	3.00
Bangle Seller	0.00	0.40	0.00
Oil Presser	0.30	10.00	10.80
LOWEST			
Midwife	3.79	10.60	43.30
Cotton Carder	0.00	2.00	3.00
Faqir	7.14	2.80	0.12
Acrobat			0.00
Dancing Girl	0.00		
Leatherworker	6.51	12.40	12.80
Sweeper	3.21	1.60	3.40
TOTAL	970.51	953.60	968.54

who divided the village into two equal shares. One of these then sold his portion to the raja of Awa in 1899. Hence, in the late 1920s, when the Wisers were in Karimpur, the village was "owned" by the raja of Awa and a *banyā* merchant.

Rights to land under both the Mughals and the British hinged on the right to collect revenues, a portion of which was due the rulers. In neither period, though, did those with revenue rights have the right to sell the land. A large zamindar would lease his land to permanent tenants, who either farmed it themselves or leased it out to tenant farmers, through sharecropping, mortgage arrangements, or, more rarely, for a rent payment in cash. These absentee landlords seldom saw the lands they controlled, instead leaving daily supervision to their agents. William Wiser reported that in the 1920s the zamindars were seen only at the semiannual harvests to collect rents. Even then, their agents did the actual collecting, with the result that most villagers had never seen the zamindars, whereas all of them knew the agents.[6] The tenant cultivators were further harassed by requests for "contributions" to the agents above the revenue and rent demands. In Karimpur, these additional demands fell mostly on the non-Brahman tenants. No Brahman talked about the pressure of *nazrānās* (additional levies) or *begār* (forced labor), whereas many of the poor did.[7]

In the 1920s, then, the power of Karimpur's Brahmans came from their standing as second-tier tenants cum landlords, for they had permanent tenancy to 74.3 percent of Karimpur's cultivable land.[8] Since they then constituted only 24.9 percent of the population, this was clearly a disproportionate share of the land, providing the basis for their control of the village. The Cultivators controlled another 13.7 percent of the arable lands, putting 88 percent of the village land under the control of two *jāti* groups. These permanent tenants were responsible for paying revenues to the absentee landlords, one of whose agents was a Brahman family that moved to the village and built one of the largest houses there (and some of whose descendants are today hated moneylenders). The Brahmans in turn subleased their lands to other Karimpur residents, most commonly using a sharecropping arrangement called *batāī* (halves), in which the landlord provided the land plus one-half of the seed, fertilizer, and compost, while the sharecropper provided the other half, along with water, labor, animals, tools, and so on. Each received half the crop, with the landlord paying any revenues due.[9]

With Independence in 1947 came laws aimed at land reform. The tenant cultivators became legal owners of their land following the passage of the Uttar Pradesh Zamindari Abolition and Land Reforms Act (1950). The effect in Karimpur was that the Brahmans became the owners of most of the lands to which they had previously had permanent tenancy rights, although some of their lands—those that exceeded the ceiling for individual family holdings set by law—were transferred to other *jāti*s. As a landowner, one now had the right to sell one's land. But there was little buying and selling of land prior to 1968: my 1968 landholding figures, according to which the Brahmans owned 60 percent of the land and the Cultivators 22 percent, mark the shift made at the time of zamindari abolition.

By the mid-1970s, though, the buying and selling of land was becoming common, as families sought to pay dowries or other debts through land sales. One acre of top-quality land sold for as much as Rs. 62,500. By 1984 prices had risen further to Rs. 87,500 per acre. Often lands were sold in default to a moneylender when a loan could not be repaid. Similarly, many of the acres owned by the Shopkeeper were obtained through the purchasing of land initially mortgaged to him. Other sales were negotiated with relatives or friends. To sell land was to be dishonored, however, for it meant that you were unable to care properly for your family. Some men began selling land to support second families (with women other than their legal wives) outside of the village, leaving their legal families to suffer from inadequate holdings. Many Brahmans were involved in this selling of land, and the overall result was a continuing shift in landownership away from the Brahmans, further eroding their dominance of the village. By 1984 the Brahmans owned only 58.1 percent of the village's cultivable lands, and the Cultivators only 17.3 percent. The Shopkeepers were the primary beneficiaries, as they bought land regularly. Some land was also purchased by residents of nearby villages and thus moved out of village hands.

At the same time, land distributions to the poor kept the total acreage owned by Karimpur residents stable, with the government distributing excess village common lands to the landless.[10] In Karimpur, the major distributions were made in the 1970s, when Mohan's brother was headman. The primary benefactors were the Midwife *jāti*, since one of their members was *upprādhan*, assistant headman, for the village: the Midwives gained 34.7 acres of land between 1975 and 1984. This distribution also accounts for a shift away from landlessness between 1975 and 1984 (see table 5). Some of these lands were saline and thus relatively useless, however, with the result that most of the new landowners can get one crop a

TABLE 5   SIZE OF FAMILY LANDHOLDINGS
IN KARIMPUR

Size of Holding (acres)	Number of Families		
	1925 (N = 161)	1968 (N = 246)	1984 (N = 327)
0.0	73 (45%)	99 (40%)	92 (28%)
0.01–4.99	40 (25%)	94 (38%)	173 (53%)
5.00–9.99	15 (9%)	29 (12%)	36 (11%)
10.00 and over	33 (21%)	24 (10%)	26 (8%)

year at best from their allotments. Moreover, as of 1984 many still lacked the official papers giving them ownership of lands that they had been promised and in a few cases had begun farming.

LAND CONSOLIDATION AND IMPROVEMENTS

A second critical factor in the distribution of landholdings was the land consolidation program in Uttar Pradesh, which reached Karimpur in the late 1960s. Under this program, a farmer's fields, often spread among twenty or more minuscule plots, were to be regrouped into a single plot in the case of a small landowner, or two, three, or more plots for a large landowner. Land consolidation, which took place in Karimpur between 1967 and 1970, was a tedious process since the value of each initial plot had to be determined (on the basis of size and quality of land) before new plots of the same total value (though possibly larger or smaller in terms of acreage) could be awarded.[11] Land consolidation also brought government officials into direct contact with villagers and increased the number of court cases fought over land-related issues. Moreover, most families spent a minimum of three hundred rupees in bribes to ensure a proper redistribution during this process—and the elected headman, Bahadur, took the opportunity as an intermediary between villagers and officials to fill his own pockets, ultimately receiving a jail term for the embezzlement of government funds.

Arjun, a blind Cultivator, described to Bruce his troubles at the time of consolidation:

15. A Brahman farmer leveling his fields

Son, I had a lot of troubles come to me during consolidation. I had [only] two-fifths of an acre of land in the dry area [*ūsar*] but was given one acre there in the consolidation. My whole account was ten acres [with his brother and cousins]. For the whole lineage [some ten families], there were fifty acres. I wanted land in a good place, where I had had it before. But not one officer listened to me. I gave a bribe. That, too, wasn't returned. [Q: How much did you give?] I gave three hundred rupees for a bribe. I gave it myself. Raghunath gave a bribe also, using a Brahman intermediary. I didn't get my money back, nor did I get the land. I kept being told that a good plot would be given. I used to beg for one plot in the dry land and one good plot.

Many found themselves in Arjun's position of having given bribes to no avail, whereas others—like Raghunath—were able to use their connections to maintain their current position or even improve it.

Some lands were also improved. Following a severe flood in 1963, in 1964 the state engineers constructed a drainage canal through the fields to the west of the village. One result was that some of the poorest land in the village, previously often too wet to be used in the rainy season, became some of the best quality land in the village. By the early 1970s, then, farmers had a few larger plots rather than many fragments, and one large section of poor land was now drained and highly valued.

IRRIGATION FACILITIES

Prior to 1952 Karimpur farmers were dependent upon their wells, tanks, and rainfall, for none of the branches of the various canals running through Mainpuri District extended near enough to be used for Karimpur's fields. Although I have no specifics on installation, by the late 1960s there were eleven Persian wheels, six owned by Brahmans, three by Cultivators, one by a Leatherworker, and one by a Watercarrier family. These devices consist of a series of cans attached to a large wheel, which is turned by walking bullocks along a path. Each can in turn is filled, brought to the top of the well, and tipped into a canal leading to the fields. Persian wheels were thus demanding of human and animal labor, requiring two men and a team of bullocks or buffalo to operate, and a third man and a second team to allow for rest periods if continuous operation was desirable, as it was during busy seasons. And even then only three- or four-fifths of an acre could be irrigated in an eight-to-twelve hour day. Rental charges for a Persian wheel were minimal. There were also two chain pumps: one shared by two Brahmans and one by two Cultivators. Both chain pumps—which operate on the same principle as the older Persian wheel but are more efficient—were used exclusively by their owners. Villagers with land near tanks often used a leather bag lift-system (*lenṛī*) to move water into irrigation channels, a system demanding much labor for little return. Others who had wells sometimes used a bucket lifted by bullocks (*dhekulī*) to obtain water. The ideal situation, of course, was rain, because then the expenses of irrigation could be cut or perhaps eliminated altogether. Even now, farmers rarely use irrigation for the rainy season crops, always hoping for rain the coming day and reluctant to put out cash unnecessarily.

In 1952, however, an electric tube well was installed with help from the West German government. This well never supplied water to more than about 300 acres (out of 980), although its official command area— the area that an irrigation project is ideally capable of irrigating—was variously given at 719 acres (in 1968) and 618 (in 1975).[12] In 1975 the charge was Rs. 4.50 per hour, for about 175,000 gallons of water, although if either the condition of the pump or the strength of the electrical supply were bad, the yield was less. Further, the water traveled through up to 3.18 miles of lined channels to the farmers' fields, with a resulting water loss due to absorption and evaporation, the severity of which depended upon distance and the condition of the channels. Farmers also had to walk the channels when it was their turn to receive water to prevent diversions by other farmers.

The tube well was controlled by a government appointee, the GTW operator. In 1968 this was a young Brahman man who lived with one of Karimpur's richer Brahman families. At the beginning of the cropping season, farmers who sought to use the well (some seventy to seventy-five farmers a year) were given an identification number. When a farmer needed water, he would contact the GTW operator, who would enter his name in the current rotation list. He would receive water, day or night, when his number came up. Since much of the electrical power is diverted to industrial areas during the day, irrigating at night was common. But even the schedule given the operator by the Mainpuri electrical board was unreliable. A farmer thus had to be ready to listen for the "pip-pip" of the tube-well engine in order to maintain his turn in the rotation.

Moreover, opportunities for fraud were many. First, the command area covered the better fields, owned primarily by Brahmans and Cultivators. And perhaps not surprisingly the richer farmers were somehow able to move up the rotation list rapidly, while poor sharecroppers often waited days for water. Second, the operator could "embezzle" units of electricity: if a farmer forgot to check the reading on the meter before and after receiving his water, he could be falsely charged with more units of electricity than he had actually used and the extra units then sold below the fixed rate to someone else. Third, it was illegal to use the government channels for irrigation from private wells, leaving over one and a half miles lying idle, since the water supplied by the government never reached them. As private tube wells began to be installed after 1968, farmers attempted to use these channels, paying a bribe to the GTW operator if they were caught. By 1984 the pump on the government tube well had broken and although rumors of repair were rife, nothing happened. But by then, private tube wells were dominant.

Beginning around 1968 Karimpur farmers began to invest in privately owned pump sets, with bore holes located near their fields. Three factors led to the expansion of irrigation in the late 1960s. First, the promising new high-yield wheat seeds being introduced at this time required five waterings per season to be productive. Second, land consolidation was almost completed, so that farmers could confidently install pump sets in fields they knew would be theirs in the future. And since their fields were now united into one or a few large plots, at most three bore holes would generally suffice for the irrigation of all of a family's fields. Third, the government set up programs to make low-interest loans to farmers for pump sets. By 1970 ten pump sets had been bought; by 1975 there were fifteen; by 1984 there were thirty-four. Of the fifteen pump sets in 1975, 80 percent were owned by Brahmans, while two of the other three were owned by the Shopkeeper who had begun buying land. But by 1984 eighteen of the thirty-four were owned by non-Brahmans.

One impact of this shift is that Brahmans and non-Brahmans now have equal access to water. Pump sets can be obtained through ten-year government loans—although this scheme, too, is abused, as some sets are quickly resold and the money spent on dowries and other such expenses. Farmers without a pump set may have a bore hole, so that they can rent a pump set when water is needed in their fields. Rental in 1984 cost Rs. 8–10 per hour, plus additional labor and diesel costs. And although farmers complain that diesel fuel is expensive and the electricity erratic, no one is denied access to water.[13] In addition, several Persian wheels are still operating, although both chain pumps are gone. Some still use the leather-bag method to irrigate rice fields from ponds during the monsoon, when water levels are high and the labor expended therefore less.

The disadvantage of the current Karimpur situation is the reliance on diesel engines. Diesel fuel is often not available, and it is indeed expensive. Further, diesel pump sets are stored at home and so must be moved

16. The Brahman widow Saroj installing a two-burner stove as part of the program of the Charcha Mandal

to the fields for each watering, which requires several hours of labor and a bullock cart to convey the heavy engine. If a field takes four hours to water, a whole day might be consumed in getting the engine to the field, setting it up, and hauling it home later. As one young farmer remarked, those with electric engines save time, for they need only turn on a switch. Electricity, however, is almost as erratically available as diesel and more likely to force farmers to irrigate at night, when electrical supplies are switched from urban industries to rural areas.

RURAL DEVELOPMENT SCHEMES

Starting in the 1950s the national government, through its state systems, started a community development program organized around the concept of a block, a group of villages with a central headquarters staffed by specialists (in agronomy, public health, veterinary practice, and so on) and a series of village level workers (VLWs), who were to determine the "felt needs" of the villages under their supervision and serve as multipurpose extension agents in meeting those needs. Each district was divided into a series of blocks of 60,000 to 80,000 people (although by 1984 these averaged some 110,000 persons in Uttar Pradesh). The Block Development Office was to be the primary outlet for the services of veterinarians, agricultural extension workers, training groups, and the village level worker. Based on the ideas of the American architect and town planner Albert Mayer (who also borrowed from the Wisers' experience running a community development program in the village of Marehra in Etah District), the community development model was intended to promote the active participation of all members of the community.[14] The VLW, in particular, was to become a friend and ally of the people, not someone whom they feared.

The VLW is a young man trained to teach farmers the latest agricultural techniques and to aid them in obtaining seed, fertilizers, equipment, and loans. Karimpur's first VLW, a Brahman man who took rooms in a Brahman house, arrived in the mid-1960s. (A later VLW lived with Saroj's family.) In the early years of new seeds and fertilizers, the VLW played a key role in farmers' adoption of the new farming techniques leading to the green revolution. More recently, he has been instrumental in aiding farmers to obtain loans for pump sets, tractors, and threshing machines. Until the late 1970s, though, the VLW was seen as an ally of the rich landlords. Only recently did a shift occur, with the VLW living in quarters rented from a Cultivator family and having greater social ties among the small landowners and tenant farmers than among the rich landlords. This change was largely due to the recruitment of VLWs from the newly educated but lower-ranked *jāti*s, so that kin ties and friendships linked the more recently recruited VLWs with non-Brahmans. Here the state is legitimating the rising aspirations of the lower *jāti*s and classes. The VLW in turn takes on the role of a patron, with his *jāti*-mates as his clients, providing them with information on improved farming techniques and helping them to secure loans, while continuing to provide similar benefits to the dominant groups. In 1983–84 three VLWs (all non-Brahman) were in Karimpur for training, but no regular VLW was resident there that year.

The block program has fostered other initiatives for social change. In the late 1970s, under the Janata government, a Charcha Mandal, a "Discussion Circle," was organized with a male and female section. One of Mohan's nephews ran the men's unit, while Saroj was chosen to head the women's unit. This was the sole development activity directed at women. Although Saroj should have held monthly meetings to instruct members in nutrition and sanitation, these did not occur, at least certainly not in 1984. Rather, once a year some twenty village women were chosen by Saroj to attend a five-day training session at the block headquarters, near Mainpuri, where child care, cooking, nutrition, and sanitation were emphasized. Although the block intended these programs for young mothers, Saroj generally chose older Brahman women, usually with married sons, to attend, no younger women being allowed to go and her social network not including the poor. She told me of being chastised for producing this list of high-class older women, but the list the following year still included a preponderance of Brahman women over forty years of age. A small sum (twenty-five rupees) was paid each woman at the end of the week as an additional motivation for attending.[15]

Another initiative aimed at women was the provision of smokeless cooking hearths. In April 1984 supplies for thirty "smokeless stoves" were sent to the village, to be installed in thirty representative houses by Saroj and several co-workers (each paid a hundred rupees for the task). Including a two-burner stove and a pipe to draw out the smoke, these were desirable, prestigious items. Perhaps not surprisingly, the list of recipients included all the major Brahman households, the assistant headman from the Midwife *jāti*, and other politically important households from a few other *jāti*s. As the lucky recipients soon discovered, however, the new stoves used more fuel than the traditional smokey clay stove. Further, the two-burner stove confused the women—who had never cooked more than one item at a time, were not prepared to watch two pots at once, and did not expect their food steaming hot. Within six months, all had been removed. Despite its good intentions and the expenditure of considerable resources, this government program failed because it was unconnected to the realities of village women's lives and experience.

Tied to the block development scheme are credit unions and programs for the rural poor, as well as initiatives designed to encourage the use of new seeds and fertilizers.

THE COOPERATIVE BANK OF KARIMPUR

A major institution, opened in the late 1950s, is the Cooperative Bank, commonly called the "bank" or "godown," located on the southern edge of the village. Serving twenty-five villages, it has about fifteen hundred members, 132 of whom come from Karimpur. Any individual can become a member by purchasing one or more shares valued at ten rupees each. Each member may then take out a loan of fifty rupees in cash, one hundred kilograms (one quintal) of wheat, and fifty kilograms of fertilizer for each share owned. (Other grains are also available to those who hold more shares.) In addition to loans, the co-op also collects the wheat levy imposed by the government to supply the government-run ration shops and distributes price-controlled cloth and sugar. There were frequent complaints about who had access to cloth and sugar, as there was a clear bias in this distribution toward the wealthier residents of Karimpur.

Despite these complaints, the head of the bank—a Brahman, appointed by the government, who served in Karimpur for eight years in the 1970s and returned again in 1983—is generally felt to be a fair man. Stories of blatant corruption at the bank are rare—although there, as elsewhere, bribes can be effective. Moreover, even though the cooperative is open to all, Brahmans dominate its membership. Most Brahman families are members, some having two or three persons on the membership list, while in 1984 only nineteen Cultivator families were members (see table 6). A Watercarrier man stated his reason for not belonging as this: "In my opinion, there is no possible benefit from membership in the seed store. Because I am an uneducated man, an illiterate villager, the personnel take advantage of my illiteracy." Nevertheless, the bank has broadened its membership since the landless and the poor began to receive allotments of village common lands and since more and more of the poor obtain education.

Although the bank is not the only government institution that gives out loans, a more detailed look at its practices is instructive in pointing

TABLE 6   COOPERATIVE BANK MEMBERSHIP AND
LANDHOLDINGS, 1984

Jāti	Members	Total Acres[a]
Brahman	60	397.56
Cultivator	19	50.10
Midwife	12	37.22
Leatherworker	8	21.60
Watercarrier	6	16.52
Carpenter	6	12.07
Oil Presser	5	6.12
Shepherd	4	10.92
Sweeper	3	9.03
Accountant	2	6.49
Washerperson	2	6.12
Flower Grower	2	1.53
Cotton Carder	1	3.00
Rice Cultivator	1	2.66
Faqir	1	2.10
TOTAL	132	583.04

[a]Refers to the total acreage over which ownership was claimed according to the society's membership records.

up the differences between government and nongovernmental sources of loans. Seed loans must be repaid in kind, at an annual interest rate of 25 percent, or a penalty is imposed. Fertilizer loans are repaid in cash, with 11 percent interest. Cash loans are also subject to 11 percent interest. The seed store stocks both seed grains and food grains. Food-grain loans are dependent upon landholdings: each person who owns one or more acres is allowed four quintals. The landless are not allowed food-grain loans. In 1983–84, some five hundred members sought food-grain loans, for a total of 1,265 quintals. At 25 percent interest, the return at the spring harvest was expected to be 1,581 quintals. Full payment, including interest, is due by May 31 of each year, the end of the main harvest season. If payment is not made by that date, the defaulter has until June 30 to repay, with an additional penalty of 12.5 percent. After that, a court case can be filed, and the defaulter's crop can be seized and auctioned, his land can be auctioned, or he can be jailed.

In years when there is a natural calamity, however, such as a drought or hail when the harvest is standing in the fields, the interest and/or the entire loan may be forgiven. This decision is dependent upon the filing of a report by the village accountant, another government employee. But if the crop fails because the owner neglected to irrigate his fields properly (even if this was due to a shortage of diesel fuel or of electricity to power tube wells), no exemptions are allowed. When asked when he would file a case, the bank director replied, "It depends on our laziness. The law is not weak; only the one who imposes it is weak." He also noted that the amount in default had risen from Rs. 60,000 in 1976 to Rs. 198,000 in 1984. He put some of the blame on his immediate predecessor, who, he claimed, had often made loans in excess of the stipulated amount, giving, for example, a farmer ten quintals of food grains instead of the allotted four. Clearly, the bank director has immense discretion, and small bribes could often force a change of heart. In 1984 the director earned a thousand rupees per month, owned his own truck, and otherwise appeared prosperous.

Aside from bribes, there were also many other ways around the system. Farmers told me of repaying their loans on May 31 and then taking out a new loan on June 1. Hence, they were always in debt to the government for the same number of quintals. And if the land owned by a family was in more than one name, each landowner was eligible for his or her own loan. The rich, too, have their own ways of manipulating the rules, and using government agencies for financial profit was a popular practice.[16] Nevertheless, unlike the village moneylender, the government could and did jail defaulters. Tales of personal woe are not effective with the impersonal institution of a government bank, and despite their enthusiasm for government programs, many villagers got themselves in trouble, as we shall see later.

SEEDS, FERTILIZERS, AND CASH CROPS

A variety of initiatives have transformed the agricultural practices of Karimpur farmers. New seeds and fertilizers have certainly been a major component of this green revolution. Some time after Independence, farmers started using compost on their fields, with chemical fertilizers added in the late 1950s. Compost pits dot the village, to be dug out and their contents put on fields before the dry-season crop is planted each fall. Often a farmer will put thirty or forty cartloads of manure on a single field. But more important in increasing yields and affecting social patterns in the village have been high-yielding varieties of seed, particularly wheat. About 1965 a progressive Brahman farmer experimented with the new wheat seeds, achieving significant increases in yield. Several farmers were trying them in 1968, with notable success. By 1974 almost all farmers were using the new seeds, together with more sophisticated fertilizers.

While farmers continue to apply manure to their fields, chemical fertilizers are necessary to achieve the yields possible with new hybrid seeds. These fertilizers can be purchased either at the seed store or on the open market. But the cash inputs necessary for modern farming are so great that there is little room for profits, especially since the costs of these inputs have gone up substantially. Urea was Rs. 28.25 per fifty kilos in 1968, Rs. 52 in early 1974, Rs. 104 by late 1974, and Rs. 113 in 1984. (The sharp increase in 1974 was due to the 1973 oil embargo, which demonstrates how dramatic an impact the world economy can have on the Karimpur farmer.) To plant one acre of wheat, a farmer needs fertilizer costing Rs. 175, plus at least Rs. 600 for water. His yield might be as high as a thousand kilos, which, selling at the government-controlled rate of Rs. 152 per quintal, would yield a profit of Rs. 745 per acre but without labor costs or the costs of keeping draft animals. By 1984 all farmers were using some chemical fertilizers, though often less than the ideal amount, since they did not have the cash to purchase more. Not surprisingly, poorer farmers were most likely to use less fertilizer than recommended and thus obtain smaller yields, as they faced greater cash shortages than their richer neighbors.

Although the new seeds require more water—and water applied in a timely manner—and fertilizers than the old, the yields are two to three times greater. During the 1920s the average yield per hectare (2.5 acres) of wheat was just over 1,000 kilos; in 1968–69 farmers reported yields of 1,600 kilos per hectare. By 1975 some farmers were reporting yields of 2,500 kilos, and in 1984 yields were in the range of 2,200 kilos.[17] The new wheat seeds, in particular, have had ramifications for all crops. Since wheat had been largely a subsistence crop, farmers could now provide for their families with smaller acreages of wheat. By the 1970s many were using their extra land to plant new cash crops, taking advantage of new marketing facilities and the demand from urban areas, and thereby satisfying their own desires for cash to purchase the consumer goods now available in the market.

For some crops, the shift has been marked, as less profitable crops are replaced by new, more remunerative ones. Barley has almost disappeared from Karimpur fields; peas, planted by most farmers as late as 1968, were gone completely by 1984; sugarcane had decreased markedly over the same time span;[18] the acreage planted in cotton, which accounted for some 9 percent of the rainy-season lands in 1925, was limited to less than an acre by 1975 and had further decreased to one-fifth of an acre in 1984. Corn (maize) became more popular, while millet acreages declined. Meanwhile, potatoes became widespread after a cold-storage plant was opened in Mainpuri in the late 1960s, facilitating their cash-crop potential, and garlic (a crop demanding eight waterings, now possible with the new irrigation facilities), fennel, and mustard became significant dry-season crops. Peanuts were a widespread rainy-season crop in the 1970s, although an infection in the early 1980s wiped out the Karimpur crop.

The importance of cash crops can be seen in this example from Raghunath. In 1975 Raghunath planted a total of 0.9 acres of garlic, 0.6 acres on half-shares and 0.3 acres of his own land. He bought one quintal of seed for Rs. 625. He spent Rs. 90 for fertilizer and Rs. 310 for eight waterings, for a total production cost of Rs. 1,025 (plus labor from his family). He harvested 1,800 kilos, giving him 600 kilos from the sharecropped field and 600 kilos from his own field. He kept one kilo for his family's use, one quintal for seed, and sold the remainder—just under 1,100 kilos. He sold his garlic for Rs. 2.8 per kilo, so he grossed nearly Rs. 3,100, giving him a profit of roughly Rs. 2,000. (Compare this to the profit of Rs. 745 on an acre of wheat, discussed above.) That same year, a Brahman farmer planted two acres of garlic with fennel mixed in. Using stored seed, he spent Rs. 320 on water, Rs. 150 on fertilizer, and Rs. 15 on three days of hired labor for weeding, for production costs of Rs. 485. His yield was 3,000 kilos of garlic and 600 kilos of fennel. Keeping 800 kilos of garlic for seed, he sold the remainder for Rs. 7,375, together with all the fennel, for Rs. 2,250. His profit was thus Rs. 9,140, excluding family labor.[19] Because the supply of water is now reasonably reliable, more farmers are willing to risk planting cash crops, especially since their subsistence needs are met with smaller acreages in wheat.

People in Karimpur say that three acres are needed in order for a family of two adults and three children to live at a subsistence level. Here is an imaginary account of a family growing no cash crops and without any variety in their planting. (In fact, Karimpur farmers always grow a variety of crops and try to include a small portion of a cash crop. Further, no provision is made here for fodder crops for the water buffalo or bullocks necessary for farming.) If this family planted its full acreage for the rainy season in corn and for the dry season in wheat, and used the optimal amounts of fertilizer and water, they might get the following results:

Dry-season wheat yield	3,000 kg.
Save for food (full year)	1,300 kg.
Sell 1,700 kg.	Rs. 2,584
Water/fertilizer/seeds/ hired labor	Rs. 2,400
Profit on wheat crop	Rs. 184
Rainy-season corn yield	2,400 kg.
Sell all	Rs. 3,600
Water/fertilizer/seeds/ hired labor	Rs. 900
Profit on corn crop	Rs. 2,700
Total profit for year	Rs. 2,884
Rs. 4/day for basic oil/spices/lentils	Rs. 1,300
All other expenses	Rs. 1,584

If this family is from a lower *jāti* where women can plant, weed, and thresh, the family will benefit from her labor. They might also choose to keep children out of school to work in the fields. What is clear, though, is that farming three acres really does amount to bare subsistence.[20]

Hence, farming remains problematic. Mohan, the elderly Brahman, said this:

> My sons are willing to farm. We have always had land, and they have been working it. And they have been happy. But now [because they are farmers] nobody comes to arrange marriages; nobody values my sons; nobody gives them any respect, honors them by asking them to sit awhile, so we feel bad. Hence, we are forced to find service jobs for them. People working in a salaried job are happy. Today we cannot survive by farming. Salaried people are at an advantage. In a job, you can get enough money for one family to live nicely. But in agriculture it is not possible. Nowadays agriculture is very costly. The prices of fertilizer and plowing have increased: the government has increased the prices so much that it is costing a farmer ten rupees an hour for his fertilizers, seeds, labor, and irrigation. Every time you irrigate, it's going to cost a lot. Now you must plough four or five times before the land is ready. You must water four or five times, buy fertilizers, seeds—and the cost of the implements! The farmer gets almost nothing in his stomach by being honest. With dishonesty it is different. So the farmers are losing substantially. Farmers don't have any voice. Nobody listens to them. . . . The things that a farmer needs, like cloth, spices, butter, iron, and brass— those things required by the farmers—their cost has increased many times, but wheat sells for only 150 to 160 rupees. Because of the increase in costs,

wheat should be sold at 300 rupees. Only then will the farmer be able to buy other things. But the price of wheat increases only by four or five rupees per quintal each year. By then the prices of other things have increased by twenty-five or thirty rupees. So this is the problem.

Mohan here articulates the many issues facing Karimpur's farmers in the 1980s. Wheat is sold at a government-controlled price, a price that provides a subsidy for the urban dweller. But the cost of farming has increased tremendously, leaving little for the necessities that must be bought, let alone new clothes, household goods, or the much-desired consumer products. Increases in prosperity are due to increased yields, not to the relationship between farming costs and the prices paid for grains. Women, moreover, voice the same concerns. Saroj told of addressing a women's political rally in the state capital of Lucknow, where she spoke about the problems facing farmers:

> When I was called before the mike, I spoke about my concerns. My potatoes are rotting. I said that if you intend to eliminate poverty and make the poor happy, you must do it carefully. No one is listening to the farmers. . . .
> When a farmer goes to a cloth merchant to buy a sari, the cloth merchant asks twenty rupees for it. When he receives twenty, he gives you the cloth. . . .
> But farmers cannot fix the rates of their goods. The government fixes the rates. Farmers are not valued. Everyone, rich or poor, eats the grain grown by farmers. If farmers don't grow grain, what will Indira and others eat?

It is not only the Brahmans who see problems for farming families. Brijpal, the Accountant and owner of several acres, also found fault with the government:

> But the real power [vāstavik śakti] is in their [the government's] hands. You go and cast your vote*. But it is they who open it. They have the power [śakti] in their hands. They have got big capitalists [pūjīpati] in their hands. We say that this is our government. But this is not our government. The government is that of capitalists. You tell me one thing. The farmer labors from morning till evening. He sweats in the fields, and then the whole nation gets to eat. Bread is mostly eaten in Hindustan, and it is we who produce it. He who produces iron, he lives in big hotels. He travels in airplanes. He eats well. But we farmers work from morning till evening and feed the nation, and yet we do not get two square meals a day. At times we eat only with salt. At times we have vegetables, at times we don't. At times we have lentils, at times we don't. It is paradoxical that we should say that we are happier than before.

But perhaps it was the Muslim Cotton Carder Karim who stated the dilemma of the modern farmer most succinctly: "Our production has gone up to ten quintals, but our debts are fifteen quintals."

Karimpur's farmers do not blame others alone for their dilemma, however. Frequently they blamed their own work: they have, they say, become lazy. The Flower Grower's wife said, "Our boys and sons prefer to lie around and eat. They must eat well and dress properly." The headman, Shankar, had this to say:

> Farmers used to get up at four o'clock in the morning. Now they don't get up that early. For example, at four o'clock they would have to feed their cattle. At that time wooden ploughs were used. At night a man used to feed his animals. He would sleep in the daytime if he got a chance, and then he would plough four-fifths of an acre. With the crow of the cock he would reach the fields. Earlier, a man used to work very hard. He used to carry all his equipment and ploughs on his head and he used to walk on his feet. There was no other way. . . . At that time animals were very big. The bullocks were of very good quality. Now we can't find such high quality bullocks. Not anywhere. Even people of other *jāti*s such as the Cultivators—these people also had very good bullocks. . . . Now they just plough their fields in any way they can. Anyway, who ploughs his fields with bullocks now?

Shankar overstates the nonuse of bullocks, as most Karimpur farmers do use them even today, although he himself has a tractor. But his eulogizing of the hard-working farmer echoes a theme frequently heard. Brahmans, in particular, blame their sons for being lazy, especially since many refuse to farm after passing high school or intercollege. Several families have sons who are unemployed, while their lands are given to sharecroppers. At the same time, most would agree that farming is easier now. Before a man could plough only three-fifths of an acre a day with his old-style wooden plough. Now he can get up at sunrise, plough an acre before 7 A.M., and return home. Irrigation is also easier: it used to take a whole day to irrigate one-fifth of an acre of land: now two acres can be irrigated in a single day. So what is defined by some as laziness may in fact be the rewards of modern farming.

THE INTEGRATED RURAL DEVELOPMENT PROGRAM

Government initiatives for development in both urban and rural areas are outlined in the Five-Year Plans drawn up by the central government, to be implemented by the individual states. Over time, the plans moved away from a focus on industrialization toward greater attention to the agricultural sector, and various programs aimed at the rural poor were initiated. But by the time of the sixth Five-Year Plan (1980–85) the Indian government recognized that its previous programs directed at the rural poor (those run by the Small Farmer Development Agency and the Marginal Farmer and Agricultural Labour development programs) had not been not successful in attacking rural poverty, although both were intended to facilitate the extension of new technologies to small farmers and laborers. Hence, a new antipoverty program was instituted with the sixth Five-Year Plan. Unfortunately, the resulting Integrated Rural Development Programme (IRDP) was neither fully integrated nor directed at all the poor. Rather, the program aimed at providing productive assets for the poor, including irrigation facilities, bullocks and farming implements, dairy animals, tools, and training for cottage industries. It was hoped that the provision of these assets would provide self-employment for poor households, allowing them to earn incomes above the poverty level. Landless people could obtain loans with a 50 percent subsidy for livestock and agricultural implements, with an upper limit of Rs. 6,000. Those with less than three acres qualified for a 25 percent subsidy on such loans.[21]

In Karimpur, the poor often found themselves caught between powerful landlords and the government programs. Sonu, the Washerman, ended up in a particularly precarious predicament. His Brahman landlord pressured him into obtaining a buffalo with a loan from the IRDP—the idea being that the buffalo would belong to the landlord, who would repay the loan. Two years later, though, the Brahman had paid back only about Rs. 700 on a loan of Rs. 2,400 (plus an additional subsidy of Rs. 800 from the government), although Rs. 125 were owed per month. Finally, the Brahman told Sonu to take the buffalo himself and repay the loan, plus an additional 150 or 200 rupees to the Brahman. Sonu was thus left with a buffalo that no longer produced milk and a debt of Rs. 1,700. Sonu claimed that the VLW had prepared the papers for the buffalo, knowing that the Brahman was actually to receive the animal. Here the intent of the IRDP was thwarted by a member of the village elite and the government agent, who were able to pressure a poor tenant into abuse of the system. And not only was the government's intent thwarted but Sonu was held responsible for a debt that he had not incurred.

AGRICULTURAL MACHINES

Various programs run through the Block Development Office provide loans to farmers for agricultural machinery. The most important assets acquired through these programs were pump sets for irrigation. Typically, a farmer such as Raghunath would receive a loan of seven to ten thousand rupees to purchase a pump set. He would have ten years in which to repay the loan; if he failed to do so, he would be obliged to forfeit the machine. Here again, abuse of the system was common. Many farmers would sell the pump sets to pay for dowries or bills resulting from illness or death. Others merely squandered the funds. But, in fact, taking out loans was a way of using the system, whether it was the old system of using the moneylender, who often did not receive repayment for years, or the new system of using the government, whom one did not repay until one's very livelihood (fields or crops) was threatened. And as the Indian farmer has learned, democratic elections can even lead to amnesties on repayment of loans or major portions thereof.

Other machines that altered farming practices in Karimpur in the 1970s included tractors (one owned by the headman, one owned and then sold by Saroj's family, and a third owned and later sold by another Brahman landowner). Tractors could also be attached to threshing machines or used to pump water. They were also commonly rented out for ploughing and to carry wedding parties. Two households (that of a rich Brahman and of the Shopkeeper who had prospered through sales and money lending and eventually gained control of considerable land) acquired electrical threshing machines. Other agricultural implements had become standard in many houses by the 1970s, including fodder cutters, ox-drawn mechanical grain threshers, and improved ploughs and cultivators. The acquisition of machinery, however, was not a primary goal of most Karimpur farmers.

It was primarily loans for agricultural machines and the inputs for the green revolution that led Bruce to talk of the "new poor" in Karimpur.[22] The new poor are formerly wealthy landlords who have overextended themselves with loans that they are unable to repay. One example is Devi, a Brahman farmer who owns fourteen acres of land. He works eight acres himself and lets out the remainder on half-shares. Hard-working and not involved with women, gambling, smoking, or liquor, Devi would seem to be the ideal farmer. Yet on January 27, 1984, Devi was jailed for fourteen days at the Tahsil (subdistrict) Office in Mainpuri: his crime was nonpayment of loans. His nephew explained it this way: "The Tahsil keeps people in jail just for insult, or perhaps the farmer will get scared and will pay immediately." In fact, it is possible for the government to seize all of the farmer's crops and sell them at an auction, or even to seize his land. More commonly, the farmer pays an additional penalty, plus the costs associated with his case. Devi was fined an additional two thousand rupees and given three months to pay.

Devi's debt history is as follows:

For the marriage of his oldest daughter in the late 1970s, Devi gave one acre of land on *vapāsī benāmā* to another Brahman for Rs. 15,000.[23] (The marriage costs were at least Rs. 16,000.)

He took out a loan of Rs. 4,000 for fertilizer from the Punjab National Bank. The fertilizer was immediately sold in order to get cash to pay off another loan he had taken out in order to buy some land from his younger brother, who had long ago separated from the family.

He took out a loan of Rs. 2,000 from the Land Development Bank.

He borrowed approximately Rs. 6,000 to Rs. 7,000 per year from the Cooperative Bank and Seed Store in Karimpur for seeds and fertilizer.

About 1978 he took out a loan for Rs. 7,000 in order to buy a diesel engine pump set and portable pipes. This he sold for Rs. 3,500 in 1981 in order to help pay for a second daughter's wedding, having made no payments as yet for the engine.

He has handled these debts in the following ways:

He has repaid Rs. 10,000 of the *vapāsī benāmā*, but the time has expired and the balance is due now. He plans to sell his lentils and potatoes in order to pay the balance. He was helped somewhat by the fact that the holder of the note has said that Devi may withhold payment of Rs. 900 interest until a later date.

The Punjab National Bank is demanding immediate repayment. The bank submitted a complaint to the Tahsil Office, which led to his detention.

The Land Development Bank is demanding immediate repayment of that loan.

Devi claims that his crops were damaged by hail in each of the preceding two years and hence he has been able to repay only Rs. 2,000 to Rs. 3,000 each year on his debt to the Cooperative Bank.

He still owes for the pump set, although there are several years yet to run on the debt before total repayment will be demanded.

Devi later said that he felt that the government should stop giving out loans, should "finish this greediness." He feels that because the loans are available, farmers are taking them and thus learning bad habits. But the loans can never be repaid by the income from farming. Rather, the farmer just takes on additional loans to pay off previous ones. He concluded, "I have made a vow that I will never again take the money of the government."

Unlike the landless and tenant farmers in Karimpur, who borrow primarily to take care of food and illnesses, Devi and some of his landowning friends seek a level of living that is beyond their means. Weddings, for example, now cost up to fifty thousand rupees. Many have educated sons who refuse to farm but have no other jobs. As one former *kamīn* noted,

"They do not do hard work. Those people are used to eating the earnings of our labor." Government credit is readily available, but the government is not as forgiving about the timeliness of repayment as the village moneylender. Many of the poor have thus been more careful in their use of government loans and opportunities. And since few belong to the credit union, that resource is unavailable. One successful small farmer commented:

> The loans have provided a lot of help—I borrowed for an engine [pump set]. I earn four thousand rupees every season and have bought one more. So now I have a daily income of a hundred rupees [from rentals]. . . . We are very happy. There is much progress [and that] progress is because of the loan.

For most, however, the comment of Karim, the Muslim Cotton Carder, is more realistic: "Now all the village is in the grip of government debt."

A final twist to these government programs is that Karimpur residents, increasingly dependent on government bureaucracies, find themselves relying on bribery as a means of achieving their goals. As one of the older Watercarrier men succinctly put it: "Whoever wants to obtain his goal has to give money." Others said, "Money is required everywhere." Families must pay bribes to buy a pump for irrigation, to get a loan for bullocks or buffaloes, or to have their crops and fields properly recorded. It is the village accountant, they say, who profits most, because every farmer must pay him, whether it be five rupees or a canister of sugarcane juice or a bundle of carrots or grain.

THE PANCHAYAT RAJ ACT

After Independence the state government of Uttar Pradesh passed the U.P. Panchayat Raj Act to establish a system of local councils to direct and implement development programs in the villages. The Karimpur panchayat is based on the boundaries of the revenue village established by the British in the nineteenth century, so that Karimpur is the largest unit of nine villages and hamlets that together elect a governing body. All of the elected headmen have been Brahman males from Karimpur. One of the Shepherd men explained the success of the Brahmans:

> According to what I know and understand, the Brahmans have plenty of money to spend on the election. We people have nothing at all. Suppose we have two-fifths of an acre of land and another two acres on shares. This extra land is supplied by them [the Brahmans]. And suppose we don't give them votes—we think that if we don't give them votes, they will never again give their land. So how shall we produce enough food for our family? We have to bring up our children upon the land of Brahmans.

Moreover, the Brahmans say: "Son, my prestige depends on your mercy." And they get us to swear to give them our votes. So we think that they have sworn in the name of their dear sons. So we give them our votes and consequently they emerge victorious in the elections for headman.

Local elections are won through patronage: those who can call on a great many clients are more liable to win. Through the early 1970s elections often split along the lines of *jajmānī* patronage, with each set of *kamīn*s voting for the candidate put forward by the group of Brahmans for whom they worked. Hence it is not surprising that all the headmen have come from one of the factions of the powerful Pandey lineage that first inhabited the village in the time of Khan Bahadur. None of the minor Brahman lineages, those of married daughters whose families moved to the village and those of the zamindar's agent, have ever successfully won an election. State and national elections are more complicated, however, with sections of the village voting for candidates of their *jāti* or most acceptable to their *jāti*, rather than by party. The exception is the lowest *jāti*s, who often voted for one of the Marxist candidates.

The elected panchayat serves primarily as a development agency, while most political and civil disputes are taken to informal *jāti*-based groups for settlement. The role of the panchayat is to maintain, upgrade, and develop public facilities in the village. A major responsibility has been the awarding of excess village land to the landless. Shankar, the current headman, estimates that these allotments awarded 88 plots in 1973, 298 plots in 1975, 113 plots in 1976, and 81 plots in 1979—a total of over a thousand acres for the combined villages governed by the Karimpur panchayat. Clearly, then, the two headmen during the 1970s had many opportunities for graft, as many stories substantiate. Some of the landless paid to have land put in their names; others had land promised to them but never received it. In 1984 Shankar said that three people had recently come to him with titles to the same plot, the ultimate blame falling not on the headman but on the old recordkeeper. Shankar also regrets that only fifty acres are left to be distributed, and they are so far from the village centers that no one wants them, thereby eliminating his opportunity for patronage.

Shankar was the first headman elected after Independence, as well as being the current one. The first election was held as an open meeting, with raised hands to give a vote. A few women attended that meeting, but their votes were not as important as they currently are, when turnouts, especially for village elections, are very high. During his first term, from 1948 to 1953, Shankar claimed to have gotten a road into the village, a bus stop, a post office, culverts on some roads, and the cooperative bank. A later headman got a new junior school and more roads. Shankar has no major plans for his current term: he would like a high school in the village and perhaps some more roads. But it seems clear that the panchayat as an elected body is, in Karimpur at least, largely ineffective as a development agency. The goal of democratic village-directed development has been thwarted by hierarchical structures that permit patronage, albeit in a new form, to flourish.

If the elected panchayats are not effective as development agencies, gatherings of respected men, also called panchayats, serve a more useful function, being commonly used to settle disputes in Karimpur. These informal gatherings often take place on short notice, when a conflict breaks out, possibly between two groups of the same *jāti*, possibly between *jāti*s. No official group exists, nor is there a fixed membership for a panchayat gathering. Rather, those affected by the dispute call together a group of men to act as mediators in the conflict and arrange a settlement. These men should be aware of the complicated social relationships in which the dispute is embedded and should aim at a compromise acceptable to all. Although some incidents result in court cases, the majority of disputes are settled in the village. Panchayats deal with issues such as widow remarriage (allowed for all *jāti*s except Brahman, Bard, and Accountant), marital disputes, household boundaries, separating the households of brothers, and fights between men of different *jāti*s. It is in these gatherings that the everyday conflicts of Karimpur are resolved.[24]

The ideal is that the men chosen as panchayat members will be just (*nyāy*). Mohan says this:

> [The convenor] thinks that I know that Krishna will tell just things [*nyāy kī bāt*]. So I will call Krishna. And if I come to know that Krishna might do wrong, then I won't call him. . . . There is a story.
> There were four brothers who were merchants. They used to live separately. Then the four brothers were advised to purchase cotton. Cotton is a good investment. So together they purchased cotton. They filled the house with the purchased cotton.
> After they had purchased it, though, cotton became cheap. Now what should they do? They felt the loss. One said, "Brother, leave it stored. When the rate rises again, we will sell it." But after fifteen days or a month, since there were cotton seeds in the cotton, rats began to eat it. Now what should be done? So one said, "Bring a cat."
> The four brothers bought a cat. All four used to feed her. And used to protect her. So there was no loss. Then one day, a fire was burning outside since it was winter. The cat came out from the cotton to warm itself at the fire. One of the brothers hit it with a stick, saying that the rats are causing loss in the cotton and here you are warming yourself at the fire.
> So the cat's leg was fractured. She could not walk or move. The three

other brothers said that you have fractured the leg of the cat. So he got it treated. Now she had a bandage tied to her, and she came out to pee. She passed through the fire, and the bandage caught fire. So the cat ran away and entered the room where cotton was stored. Consequently, all the cotton was burnt.

Now the brother was caught: "You sister fucker, give me my money" [his brothers said].

He said, "Why must I give it?"

"You broke the cat's leg; you are the one who did it all." Then a panchayat was called so justice [*nyāy*] could be done.

So he [the accused brother] went to call a Thakur. On the way he met a boy with a plough. He asked him, "Where is the Thakur?"

"Why?"

"There is a panchayat."

"But he is deaf."

But he went on and met a girl [the Thakur's daughter]: "Where is the Thakur?"

"He is blind."

Further, he met the Thakur's wife. He asked [after the Thakur] and she replied that he had died five years ago.

At the same time, the Thakur arrived and said, "Here I am." The brother told him that his wife had said he had died. "For her, I am dead." Then the brother explained that the Thakur's daughter had said that he was blind. "Yes, I am blind for her. Because she is marriageable and I have not seen a boy." And the boys said that he is deaf. "Yes, I am deaf for them. I do not listen to whatever they say." Then the brother thought that the Thakur would be just.[25]

So they went [to the panchayat]. The brothers were asking for four or five hundred rupees. The Thakur asked why. "How did he do everything? How did he burn the cotton? Brothers, he should get five hundred rupees. You three together give him five hundred rupees. The cat had four legs. He has broken the leg of his share. Your legs carried her to the fire. Had the three legs of your share been broken, how could she have reached the fire? You all should give five hundred rupees to him who had broken the leg of the cat." Justice was done. Panchayat was done. Settlement [*phaislā*] was made.

This story can be interpreted either as the ideal version of justice in Karimpur, one in which social relationships are restored via a resolution that all agree to, or as an ironic comment on justice gone astray. Mohan went on to say that the weak party calls the panchayat and obviously tries to gather men who will be fair to him. I found, however, that panchayats were often called by those with greater power, as a way of further denigrating those lower. Hence the Brahmans would call a panchayat when one of their boys was abused by a boy of a lower *jāti*. Or, as in the case of a death discussed just below, the girl's family called a panchayat because they felt that they could win on the merits of their case, but they lost because the boy's family fixed the panchayat's membership. Mohan also added that since Independence the panchayats have had no right to enforce a decision, although the courts did (and that some judges did not take bribes). But a right decision would ultimately be enforced by "nature." Previously, decisions were enforced by society (*sāmājik*), but no longer.

Often the result is not "fair" but instead supports the group able to wield the most power. The death of a Brahman daughter-in-law by burning led to a major panchayat. The young woman was married into a family whose habits were not good (to quote the neighbors), and she was not treated well by her in-laws. One day she locked herself in a room, doused herself with kerosene, and lit it.[26] By the time the family was able to break in, she was badly burned, though still alive. I arrived moments later and volunteered my car to take her to the hospital in Mainpuri. A dispute broke out over who would accompany the badly injured girl, which delayed the departure, and she died before being brought to the car.[27] Within moments the family hitched up a bullock cart, filled it with wood, and immediately took the body to the cremation ground. The goal was to be rid of all evidence before the police arrived. The police did arrest the father-in-law and husband, but both were freed within a day. Meanwhile, the girl's natal family sought some recompense for the loss of their daughter. Her father wanted the dowry returned, as she had been married only a year or so. They asked to have a panchayat held the next day. The in-laws responded by sending for influential relatives from a nearby town. These men arrived in starched white shirts and pants, riding in a jeep with guns prominently displayed. The superiority of the in-laws' contingent led to a resolution that the family would build a temple in the dead girl's honor. Years later, there is still no temple, and the husband is remarried.

HEALTH CARE AND THE STATE

The rather meagre health care services available in Karimpur were discussed in chapter 4. It is important to note, however, that the government is committed to better health care, that trained midwives are sent to the rural areas, and that Karimpur does have a Maternity and Child Health Clinic, although it is open only irregularly and the personnel are more committed to family planning than to pre- and postnatal care.

All in all, health care has improved, resulting in lowered child mortality rates and longer life spans. But preventive health care is still all but absent, with few children receiving tetanus injections and an even smaller proportion being immunized for polio or diphtheria. Mohan's grand-nephew is crippled from polio, as are another half dozen village children. Malaria has been resurgent in recent years, and tuberculosis is rampant, often hitting several members in a single household. Our loyal research assistant in 1983–84, who transcribed interviews for hours each day for nine months, died of TB two years later. The cough that periodically bothered him had never been properly diagnosed, despite our sending him to one of Mainpuri's better doctors.

The government's primary goal in village health care has been family planning and birth control. While abortion is legal, I do not know of a Karimpur woman who sought a medically approved abortion. Some did, however, try other methods of abortion, sometimes risking their lives. One Carpenter woman sought advice from an older Brahman woman one day, for she was pregnant again and had nine living children. "Vinegar," the old woman told her. "Drink lots of vinegar." On another occasion, a young Cultivator wife, mother of three daughters, almost bled to death after an attempted abortion, performed because she was convinced that the child she was carrying was also a girl.

The government programs emphasize the prevention of pregnancies. Several men, all from the lowest *jāti*s, were forced to have vasectomies during the Emergency in the mid-1970s.[28] One male government employee also had a vasectomy to meet his unit's quota. The government nurse-midwife in Karimpur expends more effort on promoting birth control than on helping women with births. Most women who have sought modern forms of family planning have opted for tubal ligations, performed at "camps" in Mainpuri. But horror stories result: women tell of having their clothes removed, of excessive pain after the operation, and of not being able to work. Understandably, these stories tend to deter many women who might otherwise choose to stop expanding their families. One widow in her thirties decided to have the operation because of the money that would be paid her (although the midwife who registered her had to lie about her marital status). But the operation resulted in a serious infection that hospitalized her and cost some six hundred rupees, never repaid by the government. As she is one of the poorest people in the village, her story has a particularly discouraging effect on others.

Nevertheless, some women, especially from landowning families, are seeking some form of birth control. Most wait until they have four or five living children and then have a tubal ligation. Saroj's daughters, however, had declared their families complete with three children, a model that gained increasing favor among Karimpur's landed during the 1980s. But coexisting with the view of the landed that small families are indeed desirable is a view current among the poor that women should not use birth control. As Sheila the Washerwoman explained earlier, a woman's body—along with the number of children she's destined to have—is part of her fate; she should not interfere with it. The probability of Karimpur's poor resorting to family planning in the near future is thus low. In fact, birthrates have been rising. For the poor, children's labor and potential financial contributions, as well as the social security they provide for their parents in old age, outweigh the benefits of smaller families.[29]

People's perceptions of changes in Karimpur's economy have had unexpected affects on health. In the worldview of Karimpur's villagers, what you ingest affects your body and mind. And people no longer ingest the same foods that they did half a century ago. The quality of the new foods, whether grains, potatoes, or oils, is different, a difference that is believed to have negative affects on humans. Mohan spoke about the shift from cooking in ghee to vegetable oil:

> Because they are using vegetable oil, people's thinking has become bad [vegetable oil is hot, so people become hot-tempered]. When we used to have pure ghee, our minds were also pure. Now we don't get pure food, so our minds have also become bad.

Not only do the new foods change thinking, but they cause illness. As Brijpal, the Accountant, explained:

> Disease occurs more frequently because there isn't a single crop today that doesn't have fertilizers in it. You may grow carrots, but you can't do it without fertilizers. If you try to grow sweet potatoes, you must use fertilizers. . . . So fertilizers have entered the body.

Shankar, the Brahman headman, presented a similar position:

> There were very few human diseases then. Now there are more diseases. The reason is that first you put compost on your potato field, then you put fertilizer on it. The seed grown with chemical fertilizer is very harmful to humans. Let me tell you. Grow one seed with chemical and another with compost. Then taste both seeds. The one with chemical fertilizers will be dry and not sweet, while the one grown with compost will be sweet.[30]

He went on to say that polio, which he claimed did not exist earlier, is spread by eating too many potatoes (also uncommon in his youth) and fertilizers. He further added that he met someone once who told him that the Arabs regarded Indian potatoes as the cause of polio!

Both Mohan and Brijpal voiced support for traditional cures as well.

Brijpal said that when a person used to get malaria, "You tied the head, brought some neem leaves [believed to be cooling], and your headache vanished." "Now," he added, "you cannot stop a headache without an injection." Shankar voiced some support for the new medicines, saying that now people are less ill from malaria and there are more medicines. "But," he pointed out, "then medication was based on other practices. Things like neem leaves or cow dung were used, and the fever was asked to leave. These cures were used a lot. And they were quite efficacious."

Not only are the foods and medicines different now than in the 1920s, but some are less available. We were continuously reminded that the new profession of selling milk in the growing Mainpuri market had resulted in less milk for Karimpur's residents. Brijpal commented, "Now who can eat well? You go and ask. Even those people who have buffaloes tied at their door do not get to drink milk. They sell it to buy salt and chilies." Brijpal went on to say that even Bhagvan has changed because where he once demanded ghee for offerings, now he accepts vegetable oil.

In addition to changes in basic diet is an increase in alcohol consumption. In growing numbers, Karimpur men drink too much. Most drink a country liquor made of sugarcane juice, and there is probably a still in Karimpur. Drinking, as Bruce discovered when he was invited to do so by Raghunath and his friends at Holi, involves pouring a tumbler full and chugging it. One complaint about drunken men is the abuse that they give to their families. Injuries do result, either to the one who has been drinking or to his kin. Raghunath was injured when his bicycle was hit by a car on the Mainpuri road after one of his drinking nights; one of the Brahman men seriously injured his son while drunk. A Sweeper woman whose husband works in Calcutta complained that the men gamble and drink, and then come round to her doorstep. Further, she said, if they spent the ten rupees on grain for their children it would be better.

ATTITUDES TOWARD EDUCATION

In the 1920s the one school in Karimpur had two grades. Boys such as Mohan attended primary school in Bicchwan, a town on the Grand Trunk Road about two miles east of Karimpur, and then, if continuing in school, attended classes in Mainpuri, seven miles away. By the 1940s a primary school offering grades one through five existed in Karimpur. Finally, in the mid-1960s a middle school was opened in the village, making grades six through eight available for the first time to girls. In 1968 the eighth-grade class had three girls, one of whom was Saroj's daughter. By the

1960s demand had also led to a second primary school, for girls only. It had no building but used various donated verandahs until a second school building was put up in the early 1970s. By the 1980s this school also had boys in the lower grades, although most boys attended the other primary school for grades three through five. Students attending high school (grades nine and ten) and intercollege (grades eleven and twelve) must choose among schools in Bicchwan, Kuraoli, or Mainpuri, while those attending college may go farther away. Some 49 percent of Karimpur boys between six and ten years old now attend school, although only a handful continue to intercollege or beyond, while 57 percent of girls attend primary school. The dropout rate for girls is much higher than for boys, however, with the sixth through eighth grades having three times as many male as female students (see table 7).

Education, particularly for girls of all ages and for boys past fifth grade, is not evenly spread throughout the village. Overall, 23 percent of Karimpur women are literate, in contrast to 44 percent of men. Among the lowest *jāti* groups, 9.5 percent of women and 28 percent of men are literate. And looking at the poorest families, only 4.1 percent of women and 12 percent of men are literate. Seven *jāti*s have but one or two literate adult women, while another seven have no literate women at all. For the poor, school is still a luxury many cannot afford, not even for sons. While fees may be waived for those belonging to scheduled castes (lower-ranking *jāti*s identified by the government as needing special educational and job opportunities), books and clothes are expensive, on top of which the income derived from a son's labor is lost. Further, it is all but impossible—especially in the sciences—to pass the examinations without private tutoring, adding further expense. The children of the nineteen Karimpur Sweeper families are still forbidden to attend the village schools since they remain very literally "untouchable" to their higher-status neighbors. While legally they have the right to attend, the threatened walkout of all other students has effectively barred them from education. A few Sweepers—one woman and five men—are literate, having gone to school elsewhere, usually in Calcutta while their fathers worked there. And two young boys are now attending school out of the village.

Dropout rates among the poor are also high, especially after fifth and eighth grades. Raghunath quit school after his father died, as did Arjun, another Cultivator, who described his situation as follows:

> I used to study. . . . But when I would play, the master would beat me. Catching both my ears, he would haul me up. So I would run away to the desert areas where I would eat wild berries. There used to be a lot of berries

TABLE 7   PERCENTAGE OF LITERATE MEN AND WOMEN
IN KARIMPUR, GROUPED BY *JĀTI* LEVEL

Jāti Level	1925		1968		1984	
	Males	*Females*	*Males*	*Females*	*Males*	*Females*
Highest	42 (44)ᵃ	20 (17)	79 (169)	30 (44)	76 (166)	49 (109)
Mid to High	22 (104)	0	41 (79)	6 (9)	52 (126)	21 (45)
Mid	12 (12)	1 (1)	19 (37)	2 (4)	36 (106)	16 (33)
Low	28 (4)	0	42 (19)	0	46 (36)	17 (8)
Lowest	8 (6)	1 (1)	11 (18)	1 (2)	28 (76)	9.5 (21)
TOTAL	22 (89)	6 (20)	37 (278)	9 (59)	44 (493)	23 (216)

ᵃFigures in parentheses refer to number literate.

in the desert. I studied till fifth grade. Then my father died. After the death
of my father, I was in sorrow. Then I took care of the cattle, did the farming. My father used to do those things. I was small.

Santoshi, the poor Midwife, sent her oldest son to her father's to be educated there at her father's expense. She also expressed the difficulties
faced by poorer children in school:

The Brahman boys make mischief in school. If my boy does anything, he is
beaten. The teachers beat. They don't teach. They only fill the roll card and
go on sitting uselessly. They don't tell the child what he should know. More
attention is paid to the rich and less is paid to the poor.

At the other end of the educational ladder, Brahman men are increasingly getting B.A. and M.A. degrees. Whereas in 1968 only one man was
working for a B.A., in 1984 fifteen men (ten of them Brahmans) have
B.A.s and five Brahmans have M.A.s. (No non-Brahman has yet obtained
an M.A.) Further, all but ten Brahman men are literate, and more than
half have gone to high school or beyond. Brahman girls, however, only
rarely continue past eighth grade, as families are reluctant to send a girl
by bus or cycle to a school some six to ten miles away. In 1984 two girls
commuted to Mainpuri for intercollege and one (Saroj's daughter) to
high school, while one five-year-old girl went to an English-language
nursery school. Several girls have completed high school courses privately,
and one recently married eighteen-year-old is doing her B.A. privately,
the first B.A. student among the daughters of Karimpur families, although
several wives who married into the village have intercollege degrees.

Despite increased education among females, most Karimpur women feel that girls are educated if they are able "to write a letter home if there is trouble with their in-laws." Parents remain concerned about their daughters' treatment in their husbands' homes, and literacy gives them a way of knowing the circumstances there. Ram Chandra, the Carpenter whose wife died after a long illness, believes that girls should be educated so that they become "sensible" or "understanding" (*samajhdār*), but since they don't get jobs and only remain in the house, fifth grade is enough. The fact is that poor daughters of landless families either do not ever attend school or do so only through second or third grade. As a young woman of the Midwife *jāti* said, "When impoverished, who can send girls to study?" A factor compounding the problems of education for women is that educated girls require larger dowries, since families seek to find comparably educated mates for them and dowry demands increase with the level of the boy's education. Thus, educating a daughter carries with it the risk of demands for a large dowry. Some families, however, desirous of good marriages for their daughters to boys with decent jobs, pursue education for their daughters, knowing that arranging a marriage to a boy with a B.A. or M.A. for a girl who is illiterate—or even one with an eighth-grade education—will be difficult.

Yet few doubt that the need for education has increased. Brijpal, the elderly Accountant, whose family has a long history of well-educated sons and daughters, explained it this way:

> In the olden days, those who had passed seventh grade had done everything. During my father's time, boys who passed second grade immediately got jobs as accountants. In my time, even fourth-grade boys got jobs. Then seventh grade became necessary. So I finished seventh grade and became an accountant. I did one year of training and then was named a *patvārī* [land recordkeeper]. Then high school was necessary. Now intercollege is necessary. . . . Girls need less education because they don't get jobs.

Currently his son, who has a B.A., is irregularly employed in the Home Guard, a paramilitary government force, while his son's wife-to-be has begun training as a police woman. His wife said that girls should be educated "so they can get a good boy, and if Bhagvan gives them misfortune, they can stand on their feet and live their lives well." For a few families, service jobs—any permanent, regularly paid work, whether as a factory worker or schoolteacher or as a peon—are even possible for girls.

Many see education as a way out of poverty. Santoshi has one son who finished intercollege but unfortunately could not find work and now drives a rickshaw. Nevertheless, she fights to keep her second son in high school.

But her daughters have no education, despite her own pride in her ability to read and write. Sheila, the Washerwoman, and her husband both dream of education for their young children, while Raghunath hopes that his youngest cousin, currently in high school, will continue his education and get a good service job.

Brahman families too believe that educating their sons and daughters will somehow lead them to better lives. Yet they recognize drawbacks: educated sons who are unable to find service jobs, for example, may also refuse to work the family lands. Many families thus see sons sitting idle, while sharecroppers take half their crops. As one middle-aged Brahman male put it:

> A man wants a job after finishing his education. He runs everywhere. . . .
> Later, when he cannot get a job, he farms, but he cannot do such hard
> work. He feels that to farm is dishonorable [*veĩjjatĩ*]. He thinks that he is
> too educated to do farming.

But aside from the argument that the government should provide jobs for all educated men, no solutions to this dilemma were ever offered.

As the poor have begun to confront the Brahman landowners, education has remained a key factor. But other factors are also critical. Many poorer families are no longer tied to Brahman moneylenders through loans, as the various government loan programs provide for seeds and fertilizers, pump sets and cattle—although, as we have seen, the very poor find little relief in government programs. Families unable to pay off loans are bound to their moneylender, and even today those who use a village moneylender find themselves called to do agricultural work at peak seasons. The poor Midwife Santoshi, for example, had difficulty keeping her teenage son in school at harvest time because the Brahman to whom they were indebted demanded his labor. But as the landless and tenant farmers leave agriculture for other jobs, their ties to the Karimpur landlords weaken.

THE LANDLORD'S LOSS OF DOMINANCE

As the preceding pages have shown, the social, economic, and political changes, especially those related to the increasing authority of the state, that have taken place in Karimpur over the sixty years since the Wiser's first studied there have led to a serious decline in Brahman dominance. While the Brahmans still control many of the state institutions, such as the Cooperative Bank and Seed Store and the elected panchayat, as well as most informal panchayats, and have significantly higher educational levels than almost all other *jātis*, and remain the primary moneylenders, they are not the kings they once were. Both they and their fellow villagers are well aware of this fact. Thus, while the former *kamīns* have a new sense of self-respect, the Brahmans feel themselves losing power. Despite their own greater material prosperity, they see themselves as worse off than they were "in the time of domination." They also see the government as "pro-poor" and are therefore antagonistic to the many programs set up to aid the poverty-stricken, even though they are the brokers for the state development handouts, either through their control of the panchayat, the VLW and other government agents, the Charcha Mandal, and the Cooperative Bank, or through their greater access to governmental institutions of various kinds.

Mohan summarized the current situation thus:

> Previously, the poor had no means of livelihood. We had everything—wells, gardens, fields, barren lands, desert, goats, buffalo, animals, grass. From every angle they were dependent upon us for money and goods. But now they have their own means. They have fields. They have land. Now they do not want our assistance. They do not need us; therefore they do not want to do our work. This is reality.

In chapter 6, I will examine the ways in which the many changes in Karimpur life since the 1920s have challenged Brahman authority, as well as the authority of the village community and the family. Whether among the rich or the poor, the old forms of control are in decline and increasing chaos marks class and gender relations, both in the village and in the family.

Sunita, the Shepherd's Wife, and Saroj Revisited

Sunita, the wife of a landless Shepherd, was a talkative woman, energetic in spite of the many woes that she related. When I used to walk from where I lived to the other side of the village, she would often be found in the lane near her house chatting with other women or would come bursting into the courtyard of other friends of mine there, anxious to be in on whatever was happening. She was about forty-two years old and had three sons, aged nineteen, seventeen, and ten; one daughter was married, and two other children had died in infancy. Sunita was married at the age of ten to a boy about fifteen years old. Neither had had any education. Her husband works as a laborer, as do her oldest two sons, while she herself does fieldwork during the harvest season. I talked with her at length four times during the winter of 1984 in her house. Here are some of her comments.

It was nice at my mother's house. But I was married in a bad way. My sister and I were married at the same time, in one ceremony. Eight people came from Karimpur, and thirteen from her husband's place. Three bullock carts came from this place, and three from my sister's husband's place. My parents cried a lot. They wondered how they would feed two wedding parties. My mother's brother gave some help in the marriage. He told my father not to cry because so many people had come.

My marriage took place in poverty. I am telling you truthfully that if I had not married like this, I would not be living in this kind of house now. We don't have fields or house. And I have a man who doesn't care about his children or the house or the fields. How can a woman pass her life with a man like this? If I work hard, people will say that I am from a good family. If I don't, people will feel that I am not getting enough happiness from my husband. If I should go off with someone else, I don't know where I would be. The whole village would talk about me. Just ask my neighbor what kind of person he is and what kind I am. My wedding and my neighbor Shyam's were held on the same day. His wife looks like a girl still: have you seen her? Two of her sons are married already and she has grandchildren. When we were married, she was very weak and I was strong. Look at her now. She's strong. This is the difference between happiness and sadness. Look at her and look at me.

My marriage was done with a bluff. He lied to get married to me. First, my marriage was arranged at another place. On the day of the oil massage [for the bride, about two days before the ceremony itself], those people canceled. So my mother's brother fixed my marriage here. The middleman told my uncle that my husband had twenty-five acres of land. Because there was only one night left, my uncle didn't make any inquiries about this. He didn't see the groom or the land.

My parents were so poor that they weren't able to call me back to their house for three or four months after the marriage. So my mother-in-law and father-in-law gave me a lot of trouble. My parents had nothing. They came to take me home on the day of the festival of Saluno.

My mother-in-law and father-in-law weren't very smart. When I got married, he [her husband] didn't even know what marriage meant. He didn't come to me at all even after I had traveled here four or five times. But my mother-in-law and father-in-law used to say that a barren one has come to the house. They said that I didn't know how to cook or grind or plaster the floors. So I separated just like that. They didn't give anything. We didn't have fights, we just separated. We earned our living and they theirs.

I believe when Sunita talks about being from a good family, she means that this would prove she was raised well and is bringing prosperity to her husband's house. (Recall the stories of Lakshmi and of the slovenly wife.) I am also sure that Sunita's parents never believed that her husband had twenty-five acres of land: if he had, he would not have been eager for an instant marriage. Further, despite what Sunita says, a marriage party of only eight persons is very, very small. When she talks about her parents not bringing her back to her village for several months, Sunita is commenting on another seldom-broken norm, that the bride should stay no more than a week on the first visit to her husband's house. That she was left there for three or four months was a major infraction against customary practice. Sunita's mention of the Saluno festival validates her claim, for this festival takes place in late August, while most marriages occur in May or June.

After five or six years with no children, Sunita went to a *bhagat* (a religious healer) who lives in Karimpur, who did a *pūjā* for her and gave her an amulet to wear. Shortly thereafter she became pregnant. Here she speaks of her oldest son's illness. The illness that she describes, *motījhāl*, is probably typhoid. Karimpur's residents believe that, in the case of this illness, it is vital for a rash to appear, for only if the rash comes will the patient be cured. Thus, in trying to help children believed to have *motījhāl*, I had to be sure to define my treatments (such as electrolytes) as "hot," because if I provided "cold" medicines, I would be preventing the rash from emerging and the parents wouldn't give them to the child.

Once my son was sick. The fever wouldn't leave, and then he got pneumonia [literally, "pneumonia caught him"]. He stopped urinating. There was a boil on his ear. One was on his head. He was so sick. I got an injection for him. He suffered from typhoid. He lay on a cot for fifteen days. My younger brother-in-law got another injection for him. My younger son [her ten-year-old] was in my stomach. I was thinking, "I can't carry him on my shoulders or in my arms. How can I take him to the bus stop?" I asked my son to be brave. I helped him to walk slowly to the bus stop. He reached there.

Then I went to Dr. Purusottom [an Ayurvedic doctor, or *vaidy*, who, as a traditional healer, would frown on modern cures]. He said, "You have given him an injection?"

I replied, "Yes." How could I say that I hadn't given him an injection when I had? The [other] doctor had already given him the injection. He had said that the injection was for typhoid, that the typhoid rash would come out with this injection. I was sorry then. I said, "You cure my son; the other doctor didn't help at all." I told him, "You do whatever you think is right. I don't know anything. I let him have an injection. But if you can cure him, please do. Otherwise I will suffer whatever is in my fate [*bhāgy*]."

He asked me, "How many days' medicine do you want?" I said to give me enough for a few days, because I cannot find money for the bus fare every day. He gave me medicine and said, "This is for three days. Give it three times daily." He charged three rupees. He advised me, "If this boy is hungry, give him parched grain or milk to drink."

I answered, "I don't have any milk at my house." But I bought milk and gave it to him. I fed him parched grain. Then I took him again after three days. The *vaidy* told me to give him lentil soup. So I did, and the rash appeared on his body perfectly. It came out everywhere but on his throat.

Then I took him to the *vaidy* one more time. He told me not to take him out into the air. He said that if the air touched the rash, there might be other problems. But he said that it was getting better. He said again, "Never leave him alone."

Later he felt hungry. I thought that he was better and fed him bread that evening. But as I fed him food, the *mātā kī bimārī* [the mother's—or goddess's—illness, smallpox or chicken pox] caught him. The *mātā kī bimārī* caught him badly. Then I thought, "Now I have a problem. Now I have been destroyed. The goddess's illness has also come to him."

I called the Flower Grower. He said, "Aunt, don't let him come out of the house. I am giving you this grass. You should wave this grass over him seven times and then put it on his cot. And sit by him. Do this daily." The month passed slowly. But my son became well.

See, he is the oldest. Sister, I brought them up with much trouble. Now we must arrange his marriage. But there is no fortune [*bhāgy*]. What can I do? I borrowed money for food, and now I am repaying that.

Sunita went on to lament the problems of finding a bride for her son. Her poverty made arranging the marriage difficult. Indeed, her poverty affects all aspects of her life, including her religion. One should wear a clean sari when worshiping the gods, for example, but Sunita only owns one sari and thus doesn't have a clean one to put on.

Those who have land, they can catch [a bride] on the road. But I don't have land. If you arrange to marry your daughter to my son, people will say, "Why are you marrying into that house? They don't have land. The girl will have trouble." If my son could get a job, people might come to me for his marriage.

Now I have heard about a possible marriage to be done this March. We need three thousand rupees. If someone would give me a thousand or five hundred, I wouldn't forget that person for my whole life [possibly a hint to me]. My brother has promised me a thousand rupees. He said that he didn't have that much, but he would take out a loan to help me. I have this buffalo that I raised. I shall sell it. Sister, listen to me. There are 360 days in a year. We eat well for six months and then are hungry and naked for six months. If relatives visited today, I would have to borrow flour to feed them.

.   .   .

I don't do *pūjā* every week. You can only do *pūjā* when there is enough in the house. When there is cloth in the house. I have only one sari to wear. Should I be naked for the *pūjā*? Or I should I worship only after hiding my private parts?

Sunita then spoke at length about the behavior of the younger generation. In describing the ill-behaved *bahū* or daughter-in-law, she talks about the custom when a new *bahū* is visited by the neighboring women. As she sits demurely on a jute bag spread out on the ground, her face fully veiled by her sari, each woman comes up to her, lifts the veil to inspect her, and then slips her a token sum.

I believe that both the boy and girl should respect their elders. If she is disrespectful, then they are both useless. I mean, when she is at her in-laws, she should respect her mother-in-law, her husband's sister, all the family people. Sometimes a *bahū* comes and she sits with her face uncovered. I don't like it. I like to live properly. She should hide her face. If you are bringing one or two rupees and come to see the *bahū* and she sits there with her face uncovered, you can't examine her properly or give her the money because you have already seen her. You would like to see the *bahū* properly.

A boy should be like this. He should not speak to his wife in front of everyone. I won't be in the house all of the time. So when I am not at home, he can dance with her if he likes. But not in front of me.

. . .

A girl should be married when she is nine, eleven, or thirteen years old. If you must, you can do it later, but it is very bad. Girls should be married quick, not when old. Son's marriages are not in your control. It is not necessary that he be of twelve, thirteen, or fifteen years. . . . An uneducated *bahū* is better. If an educated *bahū* comes, she will pull the hair of my head [insult me]. If a son is educated, a girl might have fifth grade. That is okay. City girls are not good. If a city *bahū* comes, she will want a sari for sixty rupees. I don't have it. I can only buy one worth twenty rupees. I might wear one worth fifteen rupees and give her one worth twenty-five. But if she wants one worth a hundred or a 125 rupees, I can't do it. It is also better if she is young. If she is older, she won't live under my control. She will live her own way. She will always be against her in-laws. If she is very young, she won't be wise. She will do as you ask. She will say that her mother-in-law has wisdom. If a younger *bahū* comes, she will respect you and obey. She will agree with how her mother-in-law and father-in-law live.

A boy should be in school or have a job before marriage.

One day, Sunita discussed her sorrows, her problems, and her thoughts about the future.

[Q: Has all your life been sad?] Sister, since I came to this house, I haven't had any happiness. Everyone advised me not to leave this place. They said, "You will find happiness when your sons are grown." Now I don't know if I will or not. I educated my sons, but none of them has a job. So it hurts me.

. . .

Now my eyes are weak because my periods have stopped. So please give me medicine so that my period will come. If a woman's period stops, she becomes blind. If you don't have a period, your eyes become weak. So if my period stops [for good], I shall be totally blind.

. . .

My husband often gets angry with me. He is very hot-tempered. He is angry if I coax him to do something. He tells me not to depend on him for

work. He tells me to get out or die. When he goes to work and brings home
nothing, my child stays hungry. I ask whether he got anything for the child
or not. He retorts that the child can die hungry; he doesn't care. Now if I
had the same outlook as he does, our children would die.

He used to beat me when he was younger. Now I can beat him if I want.
When I was young and had small children, I didn't go out. That's when he
used to beat me. When I started going out to work, then he stopped saying
anything to me. When I was inside, he used to speak to me roughly.

I work wherever I can. [Q: Do people make fun of you for working in
the fields?] No. If I were a different sort of woman, then they would make
fun. Since I am not like that, no one teases me. If there are ten men working
and I am alone, they will start teasing if I get familiar with them. If I work
quietly, they won't say a thing.

I work from eight in the morning till sunset. I cook about ten o'clock at
night. I don't cook in the morning. I eat the previous night's food. Then I
eat where I am working. Sometimes I cook at noon for the children. We
have been mostly eating potatoes. What can I do when there is no grain?
There are many expenses with three young sons. They are in school. One
has started working, and since then we have been eating regularly. But he is
becoming weak from his work.

[Q: Has the government ever helped you?] Yes, but the middlemen take
the money. The Brahmans have usurped the money. The government gave
a hundred thousand rupees for the poor people. We poor people got nothing. . . . Look, sister, I will tell you something. The money was given to the
Brahmans. That Muslim got a hundred rupees. A hundred went to the Watercarriers. A hundred to the Shepherds. I got nothing. I don't have any
connections with those who gave out the money. I was left behind. I wasn't
able to touch their feet, so I got nothing. I was not able to run after them
for ten days, so I got nothing. The money comes for the poor people, but
we have to touch their feet. We have to go with folded hands and only then
is there a chance of getting something. In my fate [*karam*], there is only half
a bread for me, never a full one. If anybody gives me one and a half or two,
it will be Bhagvan only. I have to believe only in him.

We have already met Saroj, the Brahman widow with two unmarried children. I continued to talk to Saroj throughout 1984 in Karimpur and have
seen her several times since. She told me many stories and provided me
with much insight into her views of the changing community in which
she lived. Here are some further excerpts from our conversations.

Discussing the friendships of *bahūs*, Saroj articulated a view often heard
in conversation, story, and song: women have friends in their parents' village but not in their in-laws' place.

A *bahū* doesn't need friends. Now I am an old woman, and I often meet old people here and there. But *bahū*s and daughters don't meet friends very often. After all, they have to work. I tell them to work a lot and then eat a lot. Then there will be no trouble or hardship. One has to work. Because of this I also don't have any friends.

My only advisor is Bhagvan: no one else. I have respect only for him. Ever since I started running a family, I started doing *pūjā*. I have kept friendship with the gods and nobody else. I have never asked for things from anybody. If a beggar comes, I give him bread and water. My *bahū* and daughters also do that. Everybody must follow their own *pūjā*. Whatever I do, they also do. When a beggar comes, one of us gives to him. We do the work of giving water and bread. That's our work. I don't have any friends. "The Baba [ascetic] stands alone in the bazaar and asks for good wishes." That's my stand.

Saroj's family was one of the first in the village to send their daughters to middle school and then to high school. All of her daughters are well educated by Karimpur standards, and her youngest was able to finish intercollege. For her, schooling is connected to obtaining good marriages for her daughters. The girl's family does the initial looking for a groom, and when they think they have found a proper match, they make an offer to the boy's family.

I sent my daughters to school so that they can get some intelligence. . . . So that they can go to good homes. The first thing a boy's family will ask is how far the girls have studied, whether they are good enough for them. Otherwise they won't accept the girls. Girls aren't accepted if they are not educated or if they are from a poor home. Big people won't accept them. Their boys may have a B.A. or M.A. and your girl might be nothing. That is why education is important: it allows one to marry into a good home.

Saroj constantly lamented the work ethic of modern youth. She herself has worked hard to give her children education and arrange good marriages for them. The fact that her seventeen-year-old son was sitting around not working, while their lands were sharecropped by a tenant farmer, probably contributed to her complaints about lazy young people.

Nowadays men, women, girls, and boys all think that without any work, they will have all of life's comforts. There is a saying, "Bhagvan provides the food to eat, so why should we work hard?" But you should work so that your body will grow strong. But instead they use other means to earn a living, like stealing and theft, begging, usury, or lying. In this way, they earn a livelihood. Why should they labor? But I say, work hard to satisfy your basic needs and then eat and drink merrily.

You women should work with your hands and eat the food you earn and wear cotton clothes. If you don't labor to earn your livelihood, what will you eat? Nothing at all. If you work hard, you will never stay hungry. . . . Brahman women can do any work inside the house, whether spinning or weaving cloth, so that all the family members can wear their cloth, or they should make quilts or carpets.

Service is better [than farming]. The farmer has no life. He is full of sadness. They sweat all the time. There is satisfaction in service. It is fulfilling. The farmer will always be eating lentils, while the man of service will eat vegetables. He earns and eats what he wants.

. . .

A mother's love and affection for her son or daughter is unique and matchless. Even if the children mistreat her or beat and abuse her, the mother can never do the same in return. Her affection is in the heart. The mother is always ready to help her son and daughter. There was a teacher who told a student, "If you will cut your mother's head off, I will admit you to this school." So the son immediately cut off his mother's head and ran to the teacher. On the way, he fell down, and the head fell out of his hand. As he fell, the head said, "Dear son, did you get hurt falling? Are you happy? Be happy forever." This is nothing but the mother's love and affection for her children. There is no one else like the mother. If a wife dies, you can marry another. If a husband dies, a wife can get another husband. If the mother dies, you can never replace her.

Saroj also spoke of her hopes and her future, as well as of her widowhood.

At present my life is miserable. I have insomnia because of the worries that fill my mind. After the death of her husband, no woman can be happy, even if she has property or children and grandchildren. She can never be happy. For a woman, the greatest delight is her husband. The husband is her source of joy. After her husband's death, a widow is like a fish out of water. So a widow mourns a lot when her husband dies. And the greatest sorrow is old age. So how can I be happy? There are two sorrows, a husband's death and old age.

All my children try to make me happy, but I still grieve. But my duty is to educate them properly and get them married. Then my duty ends. [Then it is up to them] whether they heed me or not. My children's duty is to make me comfortable in my old age, keeping in mind the contributions that I made to their future. I am fulfilling my duty to them. Either they remember it or not. The saying is for both, "As you sow, so shall you reap." There are still two unmarried. As soon as I get them married, my duty to them is over. Then I can breathe a sigh of relief. And I can wander and do as I like without any worries. So that is why I am unhappy. There can never again be happiness in my life.

The husband is the main pillar of life. When he dies, there is nothing for women. Other supports are like the small branches of a tree. These always break at will. But when the main pillar of life falls, then it is most sad.

Like Mohan, Raghunath, Shankar, and others whose stories are presented here, Saroj returned repeatedly to the question of old age and her fears and expectations regarding it. Without the support of her husband, her future is uncertain. Saroj's generation is the first in Karimpur to face on a large scale the insecurities of old age. Although the cultural norms are clear, the future behavior and attitudes of this generation's offspring remain an open question.

CHAPTER SIX

"Now Love Is Totally Lost"

To comprehend the significance that the vast and rapidly occurring socioeconomic changes described above hold for residents of Karimpur, we must return to the paradigms of order and control outlined initially. "Understanding" was shown to be fundamental to Karimpur conceptions of the control of women, of families, of the lower-ranked *jāti*s, and of the village itself. Yet for members of the village community to function according to this paradigm, this understanding—which is based on the innate qualities of those more highly ranked, whether by *jāti*, age, or gender—must be accepted by those below, who gain from the knowledge of their superiors. This acceptance leads to unity and cooperation, both necessary in order for family and community to function properly. Yet in the 1980s the expansion of education began to challenge the right of the old elite to have control of knowledge and understanding. Both unity and cooperation, whether at the village level or within the family, are threatened by the knowledge now held by those once considered low.

In addition to education, shifts in economic resources and the political advances made possible under the policies of a democratic India have altered the relationships between classes (and *jāti*s) and within the family. As we have seen, the forms of subordination of those ranked lower by *jāti* and those ranked low by gender are similar. In addition to the ideology of understanding outlined above, they include the denial of access to economic resources and to the sites of power, constraints on physical mobility, silencing and other forms of denying voice, as well as symbolic manifestations of domination such as gestures of obeisance and patterns of food distribution. It is precisely these symbolic manifestations of subordination that are most challenged today, especially within the realm of *jāti*/class relations. Overt challenges to household authorities are fewer, but covert challenges are certainly appearing.

In the 1980s the many voices interpreting Karimpur's history and current situation often presented different viewpoints on the social, political, and economic changes of the previous sixty years. Brahmans saw the decline of their dominance in decidedly negative terms, while the former *kamīn*s proudly told of their successes in the continuing battle for status that envelops Karimpur life. Some poor also lamented the loss of security that *jajmānī* provided, especially those few *kamīn*s who had prospered under the system. The young, seeking new familial arrangements that focus on the married couple, applauded the changes in family life. However, when the moral climate of the community was discussed, Karimpur's residents largely spoke with one voice. The complex network of rights and obligations that linked Karimpur's residents to one another no longer is operative. The old cultural blueprints are unworkable, yet new ones have not replaced them. Only the authority of the gods and goddesses remains, and hence Karimpur's residents have begun to turn to religious authority to regain a sense of order in the face of an increasingly chaotic world.

"THOSE PEOPLE HAVE BECOME BIG MEN NOW"

With this comment, Mohan captured the Brahman viewpoint on the changing class and occupational structures of Karimpur. What the Brahmans perceive as their own loss of status and the uppityness of the poor is related to the changing class structure in the village. New occupational patterns reflect a decline in the long-term relationships that marked agricultural employment as well as in *jajmānī* relationships in Karimpur and a move toward the contractual bonds of urban labor markets. These in turn have an impact on the perceived *jāti* hierarchy.

Although it was an essential component of Karimpur's economic life through the 1960s, by 1984 the *jajmānī* system had become largely inactive. In 1984 only three Karimpur families out of 327 derived their primary income from traditional *jajmānī* relationships—two Washerman families and one Carpenter. While others follow their traditional occupations, *jajmānī* ties no longer provide the primary source of income. In some instances, the inherited link between the families of *jajmān*s and *kamīn*s has been lost. Many services formerly provided by *kamīn*s are now obtained in the nearby market town. The Leatherworkers, who in 1925 were essentially bonded laborers, have been freed of their servitude. The land-rich but labor-poor *jajmān*s/farmers of the 1920s are now themselves often labor-rich because of the fragmentation of land holdings and their ability to rely on their own families for labor owing to the increasing population. Those *kamīn*s who had been peripheral to the *jajmānī* system (Shepherd, Flower Grower, Midwife, and Tailor) had been extensively employed as laborers in the 1920s but by 1984 they had often been displaced by the landlord's sons. Mohan's comments in chapter 3 on the *jajmānī* system point to the changes for many *jāti*s.

The turning point in the *jajmānī* system appears to have come in the 1960s. The reasons underlying the landowner/*jajmān*'s decision to opt out of the system are many. In the labor-rich situation of the late 1960s, a landowner no longer needed to maintain laborers who were obligated to work for him when called. It was cheaper to hire labor by the day than it was to keep making annual payments. Furthermore, the traditional grain payment had acquired a monetary value, and it was now cheaper for the landowner/*jajmān* to pay for labor in cash than in grain. By 1968 only seventy-one families (of 246) gave semiannual payments to *kamīn*s; even the major landowning *jāti*s (the Brahmans and Cultivators) no longer participated extensively in the practice. But, for most *kamīn*s, these payments had been the primary way that the maintenance of traditional hereditary *jajmānī* ties were marked.

By the 1970s, moreover, many services were simply no longer needed. Most rich farmers now had hand pumps in their courtyards, so the Watercarrier was rendered obsolete. In a curious shift in behavior, most Brahman wives now use the fields as a latrine, obviating the need for the daily services of the Sweeper (Wiser reported thirteen latrines in Brahman houses in the 1920s, none existed in the 1960s, and a few were found in 1984). The traditional occupation of the Oil Presser was eliminated by the establishment of oil mills in Mainpuri. The richer farmers prefer the Washermen in Mainpuri—with their soap powder, starch, and irons—to the Karimpur Washermen, in addition to which their wives wash more of their own clothes with the water supplied by their new hand pumps and detergents purchased in the market.

In 1984 a few *kamīn*s still received regular semiannual payments. Otherwise, payments to *kamīn*s, when given, were for services rendered on specific occasions. Moreover, only a few families used daily services—half a dozen rich Brahmans still had a Sweeper clean daily, while two or three households often used a Watercarrier to help the women scrub pots. The

Washerwomen visited the wealthier families every one or two weeks and the poorer ones only at the birth of a child or when clothes were polluted. These services continued to be hereditary, with fixed ties between *jajmān* and *kamīn* families. One Carpenter still had hereditary *jajmān*s, while the others worked for cash customers. The Tailors, now augmented by men of other *jāti*s who had learned tailoring, no longer served traditional patrons but were chosen on the basis of need and skill.

One man explained the breakdown of *jajmānī* by saying:

> *Jajmānī* has ended since these allotments of land were made. Now everyone has land. Previously we used to ask, "Where can we go? Where will we get green vegetables? Where can we shit?" Because they had all the land. . . . Previously the Brahmans had the wells. They said, "First water my fields. Then do yours." But now we farm with tube wells. Now we govern our own house.

For weddings, childbirth, funerals, and yearly festivals, *kamīn*s continue to provide ritual services. But here, too, payment is usually by the event, not by yearly subsidies. While ritual services will continue to be offered and accepted without doubt into the next century, they were not the most valued components of *jajmānī* as manifested in Karimpur during the 1970s and 1980s.[1]

When we look at the nonritual services that continue in Karimpur, one factor stands out: almost all are services primarily utilized by women or the poor—those who, for cultural or economic reasons, have little access to the services provided in the nearby market town. The Midwives, Sweepers, Washermen, Flower Growers, Watercarriers, and even Tailors all provide services accessible to the upper-class women in purdah. A few other services, such as those of the Barber, are taken advantage of in the village by poorer men because they are less expensive than in Mainpuri and more readily available to those who do not visit town regularly. But the rich farmers and their schoolboy sons get their hair cut, their carpentry done, and their clothes washed in Mainpuri. Their wives, however, are cut off from the services of the market economy by restrictions on their mobility and hence continue to patronize village *kamīn*s. Thus, cultural norms for female behavior have been nearly as influential on modern *jajmānī* practices as has the development of the market.

Aside from *jajmānī*, other occupational changes are evident in Karimpur. In 1925 nearly three-quarters—72 percent—of Karimpur men relied on farming as their principal occupation, whereas by 1984 only 51 percent relied on agriculture for their primary income (see table 8). There has

17.   The village Barber plying his traditional craft for a poorer farmer

been a diversification of jobs at all levels, with both rich and poor shifting away from agriculture, although the landed continue to work their fields.

Sharecropping remains prevalent in Karimpur, but less land is given on shares than was previously. The large landlords now have larger families and cultivate more of their land themselves. But modern farming is expensive, so the marginal farmers, those owning two acres or less, often give their lands on shares rather than invest in animals and tools. Hence those owning two to five acres continue to receive lands to sharecrop, allowing them to profit as farmers. However, modern laws have led to some instability: if a sharecropper farms the same piece of land for three years or more, he has a legal right to that land. Thus landowners are continuously shifting tenants and parcels of land, loosening the longer-term bonds that existed prior to the 1970s.

Looking at outside employment, the number of workers whose primary income comes from service rose from eight (1.0 percent of the total village population) in 1925 to fifty-four (2.6 percent of the population) in 1984. Yet this minor rise makes a crucial difference. In 1925 the

TABLE 8   MEN'S PRIMARY AND SECONDARY OCCUPATIONS
IN KARIMPUR

Occupation	Number Employed					
	1925		1975		1984	
	Primary	*Secondary*	*Primary*	*Secondary*	*Primary*	*Secondary*
Agricultural Labor	191	44	236	17	258	38
internal	20	65	45	111	39	25
external	0	0	2	15	84	15
Traditional jobs	37	18	14	36	21	18
Service jobs						
internal	0	3	1	3	4	1
external	8	1	41[a]	0	53[a]	5
Shopkeeping						
internal	7	3	7	11	23	2
external	0	0	0	0	6	0
Milk selling	0	10	6	10	16	9
TOTAL	266	146	352	203	504	113[b]

[a]In addition, there was one woman employed in this category.
[b]A greater number of men were more fully employed in 1984, which led to a noticeable decline in secondary occupations.

service jobs were held by the poor—typically by untouchable Sweepers working in Calcutta. By 1984, however, service jobs had become the desired occupation of the wealthier families: fifteen Brahmans, nine Watercarriers, four Accountants, and six Cultivators, in addition to eight Sweepers and a variety of others, held service jobs. Another two dozen educated men were seeking such work, albeit unsuccessfully. Whereas earlier, farming and *jajmānī* ties had served the employment needs of Karimpur's inhabitants, they now regularly seek jobs in the wider urban market.

Over time more and more people have opened their own shops, whether they are repairing bicycles, doing tailoring, or selling basics like soap and cigarettes. Many landowning families see setting up a shop as a way of employing educated sons, while at the same time adding a small amount to the family income. For others, their shops provide basic subsistence.

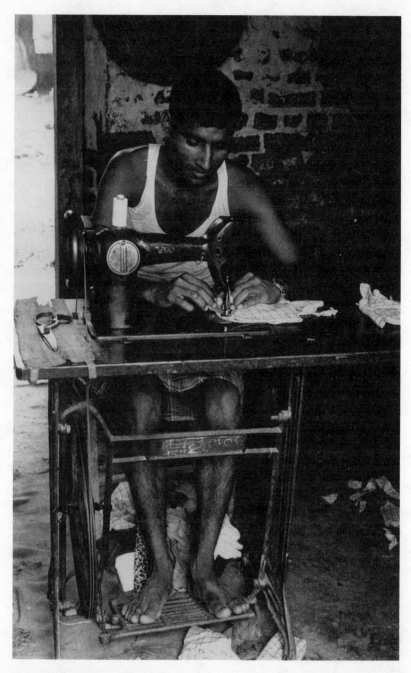

18.   An Oil Presser turned tailor

Equally important, six men now have shops in Mainpuri—for bicycle repair, radio repair, and bangle selling. Another occupation that reflects a new orientation toward the urban market is milk selling. Sixteen men, primarily Shepherds and Watercarriers, now collect milk in Karimpur and nearby villages and sell it in Mainpuri. Some use milk selling as a supplement to farm income; for others it is a full-time occupation. For those willing to work hard, this can be a lucrative business, and several have prospered. As we have noted, however, milk selling has a detrimental effect on village nutrition, as more and more families now sell their milk to supplement family incomes rather than retaining it for family consumption.[2]

Meanwhile, the poor have shifted away from agricultural employment to outside labor jobs. The number of men whose primary occupation involves labor outside of Karimpur has risen dramatically since 1975, from two to eighty-four. These men drive rickshaws, carry bags of grain for mills, load brick kilns, unload trucks, work in construction, or do any other of the many labor-intensive jobs that one finds in India. Having no land and no education, their bodies are their only resource, and even without an industrial base, Mainpuri provides such jobs for those willing to seek them. In 1975 this shift in the labor pattern had not yet occurred: there were 111 men working part time in Karimpur itself, hoping to get jobs as farm laborers that no longer existed. Currently, urban labor is preferred to agricultural labor in Karimpur for two reasons. First, casual daily wages are higher, ranging from ten to twenty-five rupees per day, while agricultural wages ran eight to twelve rupees per day in 1984. Second, payment is immediate, rather than up to six months later: working for Brahman landlords continues to be demeaning, because it still requires repeated begging before wages are paid.

With the decline of *jajmānī* over the past several decades, many of the women who had been able to make contributions to family income through their participation in the system have been displaced. Moreover, high population increases among the *kamīn jāti*s have created a surplus of women vis-à-vis the remaining *jajmānī* demands. Many formerly *kamīn* women are now jobless or work only occasionally. Females are also increasingly excluded from agriculture as their men move into urban-based labor jobs. Women whose husbands are employed in agriculture are usually themselves involved in agricultural production, either directly in the fields or in postharvesting activities such as threshing.[3] Even secluded women process enormous quantities of agricultural produce. But women can only work in the fields when partnered by a male—a father, brother, or son. Thus, as men choose to work outside the village, their women are automatically cut off from agricultural participation since they can no longer be properly accompanied. Further, their men are no longer paid with agricultural produce that the women must process: men who work as laborers in the city do not buy raw grains with their wages but already ground flour. Thus the women who were once employed in Karimpur in agriculture or through extended *kamīn* ties are now without work. Many in fact have little to do, sitting idle throughout the day. Their lack of employment, moreover, often means the loss of a voice in the household, for these women are no longer seen as contributing to the family income. One Midwife put it forcefully: "Our men are earning more than before, but we have nothing!"

These occupational changes are related to changes in economic class. To facilitate discussion of these changes in class over time, I have distinguished four economic groups: (A) the affluent, (B) those who can live reasonably comfortably, (C) those eking out a bare subsistence living, and (D) the very poor. In 1984 the characteristics of these groups differed from those in earlier periods but still offer some insight into each group.[4]

In 1984 group A included forty-five families: the affluent, richer landowners. They possess on average more than ten acres of land, in addition to having well-educated sons in service jobs. One owns a tractor, another a truck, a third a motorcycle. These families live in brick houses with several rooms. A few have electricity, and almost all have a hand pump for water in their courtyards. They are knowledgeable about health care facilities, give large dowries for their daughters, and receive equally large ones for their sons. They value education; their children are all educated, most reaching at least eighth grade. They are also most likely to live in joint families. The Brahmans Mohan, Shankar, and Saroj are representative of this group.

Group B consists of the eighty-three families who sometimes manage a surplus over their subsistence needs. Many own small plots of land, averaging four acres; some have men working in regularly paid jobs. A few are in the military. These families rarely if ever face hunger. Many have well-educated sons and daughters. They, too, often live in joint families but are not as likely to educate all their sons and daughters. Brijpal, the Accountant, is a member of this group.

Those eighty families barely managing to feed themselves but without real hunger form group C. Some men are laborers; others farm their own small plots and sharecrop for richer farmers. Their average landholding is 1.2 acres. Most manage semiregular meals; a change of clothes is common; and children and adults receive frequent health care. Education for males is saved for, and sometimes managed, but few girls go to school and never past fifth grade. Only a third live in joint families. Raghunath, the Cultivator, is from this group.

Group D comprises the 119 very poor families. The men are laborers, and some of the women work in the fields, cut grass, make cow-dung cakes to sell, or maintain low-paying *jajmānī* ties. Few of these families own any land. Most are nuclear families: less than 10 percent belong to joint households. These are families where hunger is common, adequate warm bedding for the cold January nights exceptional, a change of clothing rare, and health care minimal. Education is a luxury most cannot afford. Sheila, the Washerwoman, Sunita, the Shepherd, and Santoshi, the Midwife, belong to this group.

Karimpur's population has become increasingly poor over time, although the percentage of families in group D, the very poor, has not increased in the last ten years (see table 9). Nevertheless, owing to population increases, the actual number of poor has increased. Both groups B and C have remained proportionally rather consistent over time. What is most marked is the drop in the percentage of families who are affluent, from 28.6 percent in 1925 to 13.8 percent in 1984. These families are largely Brahman (see table 10). Hence it is not surprising that Brahmans as a whole see themselves as worse off now, despite the relative educational and material gains in their lives.

Mohan's family history illustrates how population pressures are related to the decline in Brahman dominance. Mohan's father, Jagdish, was one of two brothers who reached adulthood, but Jagdish's brother had no surviving children. (The average life span in the 1920s was less than twenty-five years.) Jagdish had tenancy rights to sixty-five acres of land, which became his own land when zamindars were outlawed in the 1950s. He had six sons, all of whom were educated through at least eighth grade and all of whom married. Five of the six brothers had sons, although two brothers died rather young and in 1968 their widows were living with Mohan's large joint family. Mohan and his brothers have a total of ten sons. When Jagdish died, each of his sons received a share of ten acres. When Mohan and his brothers die, each of their shares will be split amongst their sons. For example, the four sons of the youngest brother will each receive two and a half acres: this small landholding will put them below subsistence levels if they rely on land alone for their livelihood. Furthermore, in 1984 the six brothers already had eighteen grandsons. Unless this family is successful in business endeavors or in finding jobs for their sons, they will soon join the ranks of subsistence farmers in Karimpur.

TABLE 9   DISTRIBUTION OF KARIMPUR FAMILIES BY
ECONOMIC GROUP

Economic Group	1925	1968	1984
A	46 (28.6%)	44 (17.9%)	45 (13.8%)
B	35 (21.7%)	62 (25.2%)	83 (25.4%)
C	46 (28.6%)	55 (22.4%)	80 (24.5%)
D	34 (21.1%)	83 (33.7%)	119 (36.4%)

The changing class structure has made the tensions between Brahmans and those from the lower *jāti*s more contentious. The Brahman leaders find the strictures of a liberal government and the increasingly high status of the poor unwelcome. As the elderly Brahman Mohan said:

These people don't work that much any more. Moreover, in former times these people were poor and weak. So they were happy with what we gave to them. They were satisfied. But now the government has moved these people ahead and we have been pulled back. Now these people have reached where we were and we have reached where they were. Now they have no need for us. Just suppose—earlier, if a Midwife man or Shepherd came to my door in the evening, and the poor fellow was hungry and I was cutting fodder for the animals, I would say, "All right, sit down, cut the fodder." I would go inside and bring out some vegetables, lentils, and four breads to give him. He would cut my fodder and throw it to the animals. But nowadays, those who used to come to us for two breads don't need to. They don't need the breads. This is because their seats [in schools and government jobs] have been reserved [set aside for the scheduled castes]. Because of Jagjivan Ram [a leader of the untouchables], they got their seats reserved. We are small in numbers, so we get only one seat while these people get ten or fifteen seats. So these people have become big men now, and they know that they are big. They get money; they help in reading and writing. So why would they cut our fodder for our two breads? This is the situation.

The wife of the Flower Grower confirmed Mohan's statement, saying:

Now the lower *jāti*s have all the power. They now own fields, so they do their own work. They don't come to do yours and mine. The workers are not available. They do their own work and eat.

The poor are not seen as lazy but as working for themselves instead of the Brahmans. As a Leatherworker noted prior to the festival of Holi, when everyone spruces up their houses with fresh mud plaster and whitewash, "Now the Brahmans are having to do their own, when previously we had to do it." While Brahmans deny that the custom of bonded labor was ever prevalent in Karimpur, there were always men like Raghunath

TABLE 10   KARIMPUR FAMILIES BELOW SUBSISTENCE
LEVEL, GROUPED BY *JĀTI*

Jāti	Percent of Families			Percent of Population		
	1925	1968	1984	1925	1968	1984
HIGHEST						
Brahman	7.3	7.0	8.1	6.9	5.1	2.9
MID TO HIGH						
Bard	100.0	0.0	0.0	100.0	0.0	0.0
Accountant	0.0	50.0	66.7	0.0	77.4	60.0
Goldsmith	0.0	0.0		0.0	0.0	
Cultivator	34.6	32.6	35.6	25.0	30.0	29.9
Rice Cultivator	0.0	33.3	0.0	0.0	29.4	0.0
MID						
Carpenter	12.5	25.0	54.5	21.4	38.6	69.7
Shepherd	33.3	23.5	35.0	46.2	27.3	37.4
Grain Parcher	0.0	50.0	25.0	0.0	38.9	20.7
Watercarrier	26.3	48.6	51.1	36.1	48.2	48.3
Flower Grower	0.0	33.3	0.0	0.0	5.3	0.0
Shopkeeper	66.7	0.0	40.0	71.4	0.0	26.3[a]
Barber	0.0			0.0		
Thakur			100.0			100.0
LOW						
Potter	0.0	66.7	0.0	0.0	90.0	0.0
Washerperson	0.0	66.7	100.0	0.0	66.7	100.0
Tailor	0.0	66.7	50.0	0.0	66.7	50.0
Bangle Seller	0.0	33.3	100.0	0.0	58.3	100.0
Oil Presser	50.0	83.3	72.7	80.0	92.3	74.5
LOWEST						
Midwife	0.0	70.6	56.7	0.0	76.2	62.3
Cotton Carder	100.0	80.0	80.0	100.0	80.0	84.2
Faqir	87.5	83.3	92.3	86.4	91.3	91.5
Acrobat		0.0			0.0	
Dancing Girl	50.0		66.7			
Leatherworker	37.5	61.5	75.0	41.4	57.5	71.9
Sweeper	37.5	64.3	78.9	40.0	75.3	74.6
TOTAL	25.5	41.1	44.6	25.3	40.1	40.4
N =	*41*	*101*	*146*	*191*	*602*	*827*

[a]This caste has a bifurcated economic situation: three families are very wealthy and two families (one in-migrant) very poor.

whose families were so in debt to the landlord that they could be called
to work at any time. And *jajmānī* duties (and the resulting payments)
were mandatory. One of the Watercarrier men said:

> I think that the people who were backward twenty years ago are prosperous
> now because of assistance from the government and because of their own la-
> bor. From the time that we stopped working for those people [Brahmans],
> we have prospered. Twenty years ago, whatever you earned was taken from
> you after the harvest [in loan repayments or sharecropping]. Now all earn
> for themselves.

Shankar agreed that the poor now labored hard for themselves:

> They used to work hard before also, but now they work harder. They did
> not work so hard before. They would come for your work, do whatever was
> there, and go away. Now they have work of their own, land that they work
> very hard at. . . . Now they work hard and we don't. We are *harāmi* [an in-
> vective that signifies one who eats without working for it]. We were depen-
> dent on them. Now we can't depend on them, but our work has become lax
> and theirs has picked up.

So despite a 300 percent increase in population, laborers are now hard to find.

The poor are clear about their options: they would rather work in the
city and be paid in cash on a daily basis than work for a Karimpur
landowner for payments at some future time. Further, the city labor market sometimes pays well enough that a man can earn enough in three or
four days to feed his family for a week. Karimpur wages are lower. As one
young Carpenter put it, "Most men run to the city because of cash."

"WE WERE NOT ABLE PERSONS"

Education has been a key factor in changing the relationships among the
"big people" and the "small people" in Karimpur because it has loosened
the bonds of Brahman patronage. Granted, even today, educated Brahman
men, still bound to specific *kamīn* families through old ties of solidarity if
not of actual employment, are called upon to take their *kamīns* to the government hospital, to a local doctor, to find a lawyer, to arrange a tractor to
convey a marriage party to the bride's house, to accompany a man to the
law court, and so on. With the spread of local government agencies, cooperative banks and seed stores, development offices, and new medical facilities have come greater demands for help in dealing with these agencies.

Nowadays, however, men from other *jāti*s with fifth- or eighth-grade
educations often feel able to deal with banks, lawyers, or government development officers on their own: they no longer find the Brahman inter-

mediary so essential. As Raghunath said, "At first, only Brahmans benefited from the government, but now all the other *jāti*s are educated . . .
so they are aware of government benefits." If a mediator is needed, a man
can often find an educated friend from his *jāti*. Through this dwindling
of the need for patrons, the Brahmans are losing their ability to control
the lower *jāti*s. As a Watercarrier man explained:

> They [the Brahmans] were powerful in both money and strength. Their minds
> were good. They were educated men. We people were not educated. We were
> not able persons. Whenever a letter came, we had to go to them to read it. We
> were not educated because of poverty. We didn't have what they had. They
> had property and they had everything. Our lands were all with them.

He then added:

> Now the chief thing is that society has changed. Now the boys are educated
> [*parhe-likhe*]. They have some knowledge and our strength [*tākat*] has also
> increased. Previously the Brahmans used to go to the collectorate* [the dis-
> trict headquarters]. Without a Brahman, I could not go there. But now they
> sit at home: I myself can do all the work at the collectorate*. . . . Previously
> these Brahman people used to say, "Do this work," and the old men used to
> go and do it. But nowadays the boys are educated, so they refuse to go.
> They are righteous [*sīdhe*].

The elderly Accountant confirmed this position, saying:

> As soon as they [the poor] become educated, they become sensible about
> their poor condition. If you say to a foolish man, "Sit here," he will sit there.
> But an educated man will stand or sit. He will think, "Why should I sit?
> What is the reason?"

Education, facilitated by government initiatives as well as by higher incomes resulting from increased crop yields and urban wages, has thus
played a major role in the loss of Brahman dominance in Karimpur. While
education is cited as the most potent factor in giving Karimpur's poor a
voice, literacy per se has probably not been the sole cause. The lack of po-
tency felt by Karimpur's illiterate poor was the result of much more than
a lack of reading and writing skills. The social forces that kept the poor illiterate, and hence "without understanding," were many. Nevertheless,
illiteracy was a primary symbol of powerlessness.

"NOW YOU AND I ARE EQUAL"

One of the tenets by which Karimpur's residents had lived for generations
was the notion of an inherent inequality amongst *jāti*s. But the changes
of the recent decades, including the rhetoric of democracy, have thrown

this inequality into question. As a young Watercarrier man said, "Now you and I are equal: we are both walking parallel." Here he speaks for many in Karimpur today who espouse the slogans of a democratic government, while knowing that equality does not truly exist. While no Brahman would knowingly (or visibly) eat with an untouchable even today, nor do Brahmans attend feasts at the homes of most of Karimpur's *jāti*s, *jāti* ranks have increasingly become points of contention, especially among the men.

Brijpal, the Accountant, said, "The biggest change is that *jāti* rigidities are less." He added, "If they [untouchables] are not allowed to draw water, then section 44 is all ready. If they draw water, you cannot stop them." Brijpal is referring to the Indian constitution and laws that mandate equality: a Brahman can no longer legally prevent an untouchable from getting water at a public well. Eating habits are affected by this law, too. Brijpal offered this example:

> If the tea-shop owner gives him tea in a clay vessel, the Sweeper throws it away. "Tish, give it to me in a proper glass." And if the owner doesn't, then a charge is made about him. Look at every station: the latrine sweeper gives you water to drink. Look in every hotel: untouchables cook the food. And you and I eat it.

Village-based *jāti* hierarchies derive from combination of factors: beliefs about the innate status of a particular *jāti*, related to occupation; ritual activities that mark both purity and auspiciousness; and economic well-being and economic interactions, especially in the realm of *jajmānī* relationships. These various factors, which interact in complex ways, are reflected in two primary areas: attitudes about ranking and the daily interactions that manifest status.[5] Both attitudes about *jāti* hierarchies and daily interactions are constantly changing. Yet, overall, both show a strong inertia to change, so that while there are many beliefs about the changing status of rich and poor in Karimpur, the *jāti* hierarchy, whether measured by attitudes or interactions, actually shows relatively little change over time. Further, neither of these measures is strongly responsive to economic change.

In 1984 Bruce asked sixty Karimpur men and women for their rankings of Karimpur's twenty-four *jāti*s. Only two of the men could not or would not provide rankings (one saying, "It's all Indira's raj now, so why should I?"). In 1968 I had conducted a similar exercise with twenty men and women. The results of these surveys do reflect certain minor changes over time (see table 1, on page 15). While in both instances Brahmans ranked highest on everyone's scale and Sweepers usually ranked lowest, there is some variation at the middle levels. In particular, the Carpenters, a *jāti* that has lost most of its ties to *jajmān*s and whose men now fitfully find work in the local markets or as woodcutters, have moved down. The Accountants, with the highest literacy rates in the village, some children in service jobs, and some land, have moved up. And both the Shopkeepers and the Grain Parchers have moved up slightly, probably because some families in both *jāti*s are prospering. But a sharp distinction between those *jāti*s from whom most can or cannot take food still exists and is manifested in the attitudinal rankings.

Indeed, there is very little variation over time with regard to hierarchy as determined by food transactions that occur within the village. As we shall see below, it is true that some crucial interactional markers of status have changed: for example, lower-*jāti* men may now sit on their cots as the Brahmans walk by. But the primary exchanges that mark status are food and water. Remember that *pakkā* foods, those fried in ghee, are exchanged more freely than are *kaccā* foods, those cooked in water. Uncooked grains, fruit, and flour are exchanged even more freely. An analysis of these interactions reveals only minute changes in status in the village, although behavior outside that locale may show greater shifts, as men, especially, increasingly eat in a variety of settings.[6] In the 1960s most Brahmans started eating in the Shopkeeper houses as long as the food had been cooked by acceptable *jāti*s (such as the Barber or Watercarrier), although some Brahmans still refuse such food. Two other *jāti*s that fall on the line between widespread acceptance and nonacceptance of their *pakkā* food are the Shepherds and Grain Parchers, two *jāti*s that have recently gained economically: recently some Brahmans have begun taking their *pakkā* foods, but many have not. In a countermove, and possibly because of one-upmanship amongst those in the middle of the hierarchy, many Cultivators no longer take *pakkā* food from the Watercarriers. So on an scale based on food transactions, change in *jāti* hierarchies has been almost nonexistent. Those few changes that have occurred, moreover, are reflective of changing economic situations. It is evident that the high feel threatened by the low but are able to assert enough dominance to preserve the old interactional patterns, at least within the confines of the village. Certainly those in the middle of the hierarchy, who wish to demonstrate their own achievements, also gain from not admitting lower *jāti*s into the acceptable circle by eating their *pakkā* foods.

At the same time, although the Shopkeepers as a *jāti* are better off economically than are the Brahmans (Brahman dominance is, after all, also built on numerical strength), to this day well over half the village still does not accept food or water from the Shopkeepers. Hence dominance is not merely a function of economic prosperity but is founded on firmly entrenched beliefs about the worth of certain kinds of persons. Even as they disparage the Karimpur Brahmans, the poor often still treat them as gods on earth, albeit lesser gods than they were sixty years ago.

"THESE PEOPLE WON'T LET US RISE UP"

With this phrase, Sonu, the Washerman, captured the thoughts of the poor as he was discussing the Brahman unwillingness to change either their habits of oppression or the basic structures that have kept the poor under their control. Nevertheless, changes have occurred. Many of the more oppressive strictures—whether largely material, as in demands for labor, or largely symbolic, as in greetings—had been modified by 1984, sixty years since the Wisers were first in Karimpur. Many of these changes occurred in response to protests by the poor. Some protests took place in the 1920s; others now occur, although the specific controversies have shifted.

Despite the overwhelming dominance of the Brahmans and zamindars in the period prior to Independence, the poor did in fact rebel against what they felt to be unfair treatment. These early protests, however, did not focus directly on the dominance of the Brahmans or on the symbolic forms of subservience they demanded, but rather on actions by the Brahmans that the poor found threatening to their livelihoods. Most directly, the poor revolted when their subsistence needs were not met. They did not rebel against the fact that they were ruled but against mistreatment by those rulers. These early revolts also came from those least dominated— the Shepherds and Watercarriers, who had some options other than working for the landlords. The Leatherworkers, Midwives, and other almost landless *kamīn*s did not provide the leadership for these early rebellions.[7]

The removal of grain from the village, grain that was owed in payment there and that was necessary for survival in the village, triggered two confrontations between high and low in Karimpur. The first incident occurred in the 1920s when Mohan's rich Brahman father tried to take a bullock cart full of grain to Mainpuri to sell when he had not yet paid his *kamīn*s and laborers in the village. The cart was stopped and the workers paid. Nonetheless, this event added fuel to rising resentment, which some years later overflowed and led to a strike by the *kamīn*s in the village. Supposedly the strike, which probably took place in the late 1930s, involved all of the Karimpur *kamīn*s and lasted six months. A silver rupee was collected from each non-Brahman family to set up a strike fund. One Brahman family, that of an in-marrying son-in-law, supported the workers. The Brahman landlord Mohan reported that he was ready to beat the strikers publicly but was stopped by his brother. The strike was finally broken when one of the Brahman landlords persuaded his Carpenter neighbor and friend to cross over and begin working with the farmers' ploughs. It is hard to gauge the gains of the strike, but clearly it was one round in an increasingly contentious relationship between Brahmans and the rest of Karimpur.

A second cartload of grain led to another drawn-out battle between Brahmans and their lesser neighbors. A Watercarrier had a loan of grain to sell in Mainpuri, but he owed a large debt to Mohan's family. So Mohan's brother stopped the cart on the road and forcibly took it to his house, where he removed the grain. This led to the formation of a "committee" of lower-ranked men who negotiated with the Brahmans over a series of rights, including seating arrangements and Brahman visits to the homes of the poor. As the poor put it, "Today he has stolen my bullock cart; tomorrow he will steal yours." Every *jāti* had someone in debt to the Brahmans, so unity could be achieved.

Festivals are prominent arenas in which resistance to dominance can be articulated.[8] The Holi festival, held annually on the first day of the second half of the Hindu month of Phagun (about mid-March), has been the vehicle for a variety of confrontations over the past thirty years. This festival, one of the two major festivals of the year and the only one that literally involves everyone in the community, is comprised of a series of events, each permitting different kinds of resistance.

Holi celebrates the triumph of good over evil: devotion to the gods will overcome unrighteous and vain actions. The story told about the festival is this. There once was a king who was so vain that he believed himself immortal and equal to god. His sister, Holika, was equally vain. The king had a son named Prahlad who argued that the power of the true gods was greater than that of his father. In order to prove to his son that he, the king, was indeed greater than god, the king first had the boy thrown off a cliff and then locked in an iron box, only to have the child saved each time by his god, Bhagvan. Then one day the king commanded that a huge bonfire be built. He asked his sister, Holika, who had been told by a wise sage that she would never be burnt by fire, to hold the child in her lap until the boy was burnt. But once in the fire, Holika had a change of heart and prayed to Bhagvan that the child be saved. He emerged from the fire unscathed, while Holika burned to death. This central story of Holi is celebrated with bonfires in most communities in northern India.[9]

Holi is also a festival that celebrates love—love between humans and god, especially as seen metaphorically in love between male and female—so that many of the songs, particularly those of the men, are based on the exploits of Krishna, the Hindu god noted for his amorous adventures. It is also a time, people say, when enemies should put their fights behind them and meet once again. This does not always happen, but it is the goal of one major Holi ritual. Further, even those in mourning should discard their sorrows and sing once again. In the days before Holi, a group of Cultivator men go to the gate of each house where there was a death in the previous year and sing *anrayā*, songs to "cut" the grief and allow happiness once more in that household.

Preparations for Holi begin several weeks before the auspicious date, when wood and other combustibles are gathered, in any way possible, by village youth to build the Holi fires. Complaints arise daily about missing trees (some cut down for this purpose), beams, or other items that the boys have stolen for the fire. But once an item is put on the fire, it cannot be removed. Karimpur has three fires, two in the main village (one for each of the two major Brahman lineages and their neighbors) and a third at the Cultivator settlement on the main road. Meanwhile, new clothes are bought; houses are repaired and whitewashed; the Bangle Seller makes the rounds selling new bangles to purdah-bound women; the Potter brings new pots to each family; and special foods are cooked—lentil cakes, potato chips and other salty snacks, sweets, and, for the day itself, *pūrī*s. Groups of men gather nightly to sing the special songs of Holi, while the women may sing separately in their courtyards after their long hours of work have ended. The men celebrate too with liquor and *bhāng* (a drink made with marijuana), adding to the gaiety and increasing the spiciness of some songs. Even the cattle are bathed in the village pond to ready them for the festivities.

The actual festivities begin with the lighting of the Holi fires by a low-ranking Brahman from a nearby village whose ritual job is to light these fires. (In earlier days a Karimpur Brahman had lit the fires, but he came to feel this work beneath him as it involves killing all the animal life, such as insects or mice, that are living in the piles of brush and wood.) At the auspicious hour the fires are lit, and the men who have gathered circle them, shouting "Long live Holika Mother!" They also roast stalks of new-ripened barley, whose grains are tossed in the four directions as well as eaten, for Holi also marks the beginning of the spring harvest and barley is a traditional symbol of fertility and prosperity in Karimpur rituals.

The Holi fire is one scene of confrontation. In 1968, for example, the Sweepers, who are expected to circle the fire last as they are thought in Karimpur to have the lowest of low ranks, attempted to circle the fire first, before the Brahmans. Several times these actions almost ended the proceedings, but eventually the Sweepers desisted. Here, though, the assertion of rights was as critical as whether these rights were actually achieved. Then in the early 1970s, under the leadership of the village headman at the time, Bahadur, the Sweepers were allowed to circle the fire at the same time as the other men of the village. But another Brahman political leader later protested and that right was again denied the Sweepers: in the early 1980s they chose not to circle the fire at all. In 1984, however, the Sweepers also refused to accept the offerings made to the fire, offerings put there earlier in the day by young women from each household. These offerings, shared with the village dogs and the living creatures in the pile of brush, are offerings made downward, to remove inauspiciousness. To accept them is to acknowledge lowness.

After the bonfire has burned down, someone from each household collects a few embers from the main fire and the women light their own Holi fires, made with cow-dung cakes (some saved from the Divali rituals some six months earlier), in their courtyards. Here the women too roast barley, celebrate Holika's victory over evil ways, and sing songs honoring the gods and goddesses.

Later that same day or perhaps on the next, depending on the times set by the astrologers, is the "Holi greeting," *holī milānā*. Men from the main houses of the village spread mats on their verandahs, obtain betel leaves (*pān*) and cigarettes, and prepare to greet their kin and village mates. Everyone dresses in their new finery and by mid-afternoon long lines of men traverse the village, moving from house to house greeting one another with a ritual embrace, bending to touch the feet of those higher, and stopping for snacks and cigarettes if appropriate. Some men, close kin or *kamīn*s, enter the courtyards to greet the women waiting there. One of my favorite memories of Karimpur is of an elderly Brahman man coming into the courtyard where I was staying in 1975 to greet the women there. The youngest daughter, then about eleven, was dressed for the first time in a sari and was clearly delighted with herself. Smiling at her broadly, her relative bent to touch her feet, commenting that she surely was grown up enough now for him to acknowledge her.[10] Through the early 1970s some families also fed the men of whole *jāti*s. For example, Prakash's household, where I lived, fed all the Watercarrier men every

Holi. This ability to provide sustenance at Holi is a mark of the economic and social superiority of that family: to no longer be able to make these downward food offerings, comparable to the *prasād* of the gods, is a blow to family prestige.

The Holi greetings present a second focal point for dispute in Karimpur. Over the past thirty years there has been a slow opening of different parts of the village to visits from the Brahman landlords. Earlier, the poor would visit the Brahmans, but not vice versa. Now Brahmans are expected to visit all the houses except those of the Sweepers, and a few even go there. One way to mark a political dispute or to dishonor a group or family is not to visit them on Holi. Hence in 1984 no greetings were exchanged between the two major political factions of the Cultivators.

The final event of Holi is the throwing of colored water. Usually the day after the greetings, everyone dons their oldest, most threadbare clothes and begins to mix packets of color dyes into buckets of water. This colored water (and sometimes mud, bricks, or urine) is then thrown at one's friends and enemies, but especially on those who are higher, whether mother-in-law, husband, or father. In Karimpur, unlike some communities, the rules are somewhat rigid, so that some elderly men escape the day untouched by color. But most people end up drenched, with bright red faces and multicolored clothes. In 1984 the men of the Midwife *jāti* began throwing mud, which angered their neighbors, the Shepherds. At that point the village headman, also a neighbor, intervened, saying that if you are too poor to buy colors, you can throw mud: he then joined in an hour-long mud throwing escapade. In the color throwing, the rules are meant to be broken: the high expect to be turned on by the low. As a result, it is only by moving outside of the limits set in Karimpur that the poor can manage to voice their resistance on this occasion. As far as the festival of Holi is concerned, it is the other two major events, the fire and the greetings, that provide the main focal points of antagonism.

After Independence, the poor began to engage in further symbolic confrontations of the Brahman landlords, confrontations that if successful would give them greater stature within Karimpur society. A Shepherd in his mid-forties claimed that the Independence movement led by Mahatma Gandhi was a key component of their resistance:

> As soon as the movement against British domination was started, everyone belonging to the lower groups joined Mahatma Gandhi. All the jails were filled. They were badly treated. However, Bhagvan heard his cry and the landlord system was destroyed. Gradually we began to rise. If the Leatherworker did not plaster the Brahman's houses at Holi and Divali, they used

to beat him badly. [Allowing the low] to sit on a cot was another issue at that time. And if the Sweepers did not sweep, they would give them trouble.

The movement to permit the low to sit on a cot in the presence of a Brahman is vividly remembered, for who can sit where in front of whom is a key marker of status in much of India. In the case here, men of the lower *jātis* were not allowed to be sitting on a cot on their own verandah when a Brahman passed by. Another way of marking status is to give the position at the head of a cot to the highest-ranking person present. Those lower sit near the foot of the cot, stand or squat nearby, or, if a Sweeper, squat at some distance from the landlords on the cot. Sometime shortly after the abolition of zamindars in the 1950s, the higher-ranking of the low forced the issue and demanded the right to sit on cots in the presence of Brahmans, an incident that was recounted by a group of Shepherd men to Bruce and his Muslim research assistant. Critical to understanding this story is that the Brahmans and Shepherds live on the same lane, one of the major paths leading to the main road. Hence Brahmans going elsewhere in the village are likely to pass by Shepherd homes and see the Shepherd men on their cots.

> Mukesh and Naresh [both Shepherds] were strong and quarrelsome. If someone caused stupid [*anarth kī bāt*] problems, they would give lots of help. And they were always ready for a fight. Whenever a Brahman observed someone low sitting on a cot, he would complain about that person. The small people were never allowed to sit on cots. So the complaints became numerous, and two or perhaps three times the two Shepherd men started a quarrel. So the Brahmans stopped on their own accord. Having stopped, they said, "Our honor was based on our suppressing those people. If we do not suppress them, they will come to understand that their honor has increased."
> [Q: The Brahmans thought this way?]
> Yes, the Brahmans thought like this. I mean their power [*śakti*] decreased. Afterwards, we began to sit on the cots.
>
> ·   ·   ·
>
> The fight was fought with *lāthī*s [long poles, often carried by men as walking sticks or weapons]. I personally didn't see it; I only know from hearing the story told. They charged one another with *lāthī*s. Both groups were wounded, some badly. The blood flowed out of their bodies. Ultimately, they stopped quarreling with us.
>
> ·   ·   ·
>
> There were Karnu and Jagdish [Brahmans]: they were smart men. They constantly complained. Consequently the Shepherds decided to fight. As

soon as the Brahmans passed by that side [indicating the direction of the Brahman enclave], they picked a quarrel. They quarreled several times. Then the Brahmans became peaceful and began to stop suppressing the smaller people. The Brahmans decided: "If we fight them, we will be dishonored [veīijatī]. So we should be peaceful. There is honor in this."

In a discussion with Watercarriers, the same issue arose. They claimed that now everyone's honor is equal and then added, "Now if you pass by this street and I am sitting, I stand or not according to my will, not by pressure. You [a superior] may remain standing at the gate, while we are sitting on the cot."

The Brahmans often attempted to suppress behavior that they saw as uppity or as challenging to their position. Many of the most direct challenges came from younger men who were less schooled in the old norms of conduct and more ready to be combative than their fathers. As the following story from a Shepherd man demonstrates, the fathers were then viewed as a tool of suppression, so that any success by the challenger not only succeeded in destroying the authority of the Brahman but also that of his father.

> There is an interesting story about Shiv and me. I, Shiv, and other men used to go to Rajpura to purchase buffalo milk, which we then sold. I used to be well dressed: I had perfumed oil in my hair and I wore costly clothes. So a Brahman grabbed a handful of dust and threw it at my head. As soon as he had thrown the dust on me, I was furious. And them, they began to say, "Where is the stench flowing from? Is it coming from the drains?" This incident took place only a few years ago, not a long time ago. So in return I grabbed a handful of dust and threw it at him. Fortunately, they moved away. Afterwards somebody complained about me to Gopalan [a Brahman leader], saying that he chased the Brahmans away from his gate in this way. The Shepherds are becoming big. They are thinking that they are superior because of their good condition. So the Brahmans called my father to a meeting. My father begged them for forgiveness, and he said, "I will bring my son before you." Then my father called me. But I replied that they had started it, so why should I ask for forgiveness? For four days they exhorted my father. At last I decided that I would leave the village before I would beg their forgiveness. So you tell me who was wrong. I never went to the meeting. Then my father said, "My son has gone out of control; he did not accept my proposal, so pardon me [on behalf of him]." Once a bunch of them chased me. Thinking I would receive assistance, I ran to the shop of Bhim Sen. As soon as I reached there, those people turned away and went to their homes.

On another day the Watercarriers told of another Shepherd who was abused by a Brahman for wearing expensive shoes. The following story speaks to the same point:

There was a feast in a nearby village. One of the men of the Midwife *jāti* put on a turban. He wore it very well tied and was riding on a mare. He was going to the feast. Two Brahman brothers were sitting by the road and he passed that way, wearing his turban. He sat proudly on the back of the mare. Now he might have been uncle [through village kinship] to those two, so he asked, "Will you come to the feast?" They cried, "You sister-fucker! Why are you riding on that horse? Am I your servant? Am I a Leatherworker?" We always used to have to live with this kind of thing.

Clearly the Brahmans were opposed to being outclassed by well-dressed "small" people.

Issues like the exchange of greetings in the lane have become contentious, as well as affording points of resistance for the poor. The Brahmans complain that they are no longer greeted with respect. One Brahman landlord said that people no longer greet him with *jai rāmji kī* ("Long live Lord Ram"). Previously he added, the low "were always dependent on you [literally, "always lived behind you," *āp ke pīche rahte the*]. When you gave grain, then they would eat bread. . . . But today those who own land, they produce a lot, have begun to wear good clothes, and have stopped saying *namaste* [to us]."

It is important to recognize that the standard of living in Karimpur has improved since the 1920s. If we look at health care or mortality rates, quality of housing, sources of water, quality of clothing, educational levels, or consumer goods (watches, radios, cycles, and so on), the village as a whole has prospered. Yet there are many whose families have seen none of this increased prosperity. As one elderly Leatherworker stated, "The condition of our house is the same as before. There is difficulty all the time: there is no rest."

Yet Shankar and others claim that the Brahmans are worse off than before. It is true that average landholding per Brahman family has declined over time, what with the partition of lands among many sons. And many are heavily in debt, especially to the government. They also have connections to urban areas, where their daughters now cook on gas stoves and watch videos. When compared to their urban neighbors, they have not prospered. Neither do they feel they have prospered when they compare themselves to their old *kamīns* and tenants. Their economic and political control of the village has eroded. So whether they look inside or outside of the village, the Brahmans see themselves having lost, while the poor, despite the large numbers that barely survive, see their situation as better than it was before. Indeed, the increased political power of the poor became obvious in the late 1980s, when a non-Brahman was finally elected headman of the village.

"THERE IS NO DISCIPLINE"

Turmoil exists not only in the village but also in the household. As sons and daughters become educated and as sons are no longer bound to family farms, dependent upon their fathers' connections for a livelihood, parental authority is challenged. Shankar expressed a common opinion on current relations between fathers and sons:

> [My father] had control* over us. Now nobody has control* over anyone. . . .
> There is no discipline [*anuśāsan*]. That is, boys say that they are going to
> the market but see movies there. Had they been afraid of us—that their fa-
> ther would beat them or punish them—they would not do such things. But
> there is no discipline. They don't have any fear [*daryā bhay*] in their hearts.
> While seeing a movie or doing other bad things [*vuś karam*], they are not
> afraid of what their father will say. So they do whatever they want.

A forty-year-old Cultivator concurred, saying: "The boys who are under my discipline [*anuśāsan*], they don't wander. But those who escape my discipline, they cause trouble."

While amongst men, fathers lament the loss of control of their sons, amongst women, it is mothers-in-law who are most threatened by modern times. Saroj, as usual, was outspoken on this topic:

> Women who used to live inside the house, in purdah, nowadays those very
> women are wandering outside on the road and in the fields to collect fuel or
> cut grass or get dung for cooking. . . . Does honor lie in these activities?
> Dung should be gathered by the boys, and men should do the field work.

Women are increasingly challenging the constraints on their freedom of movement and their control over economic resources, however meagre they may be. Now younger educated women, both *bahū*s and daughters, move rather freely between village and town, often without a male escort. The enveloping shawl worn outside the house is discarded as soon as the *bahū* leaves the village boundaries and will only be grabbed if someone points to an older village man. And poor women have made arrangements to roll *bīḍī*s—cheap, locally made cigarettes—in their houses, regardless of the propriety of a woman working.

Women's songs address these issues as well. A Muslim girl sang these lines:

> The girls of today, they follow new fashions,
> Wearing churridar or pajamas, they study English,
> And on their wrists, wristwatches.
> Don't blame fate [*takdīr*].

> Look at today's daughters-in-law: they follow new fashions,
> Not covered, even their chins show,
> And on their lips, lipstick.
> Don't blame fate.

An increased desire for more consumer goods also brings problems for Karimpur's residents. Brijpal, the Accountant, defined prosperity in terms of laborers who want their houses painted, even if there are rats scurrying about all night long and their children's stomachs are empty. Shankar, the headman, says that he and others learn these new habits by watching others. Hence everyone wants money. As he put it:

> Does any man, whether rich or poor, want to wear poor quality clothes? Earlier people did not spend money on *bīḍīs*. Now they spend money on *bīḍīs*. They spend money on tobacco. They spend money on movies, which weren't there before. Now boys from the countryside dress up and go to see movies. . . . If one person indulges, then he acts as an inspiration for others, because the world moves by looking at others.

Moreover, the cinema presents the wrong moral message. Shankar also commented that "in the cinema they show people kissing, meeting girls. We regard that as very bad. . . . We should keep away from things like the movies."

The Brahman widow Saroj was another who lamented the changes in clothing and behavior: she felt that the younger women were "spreading poverty. They ask for clothes made of synthetic fabrics. These ladies want cream and powder for makeup and chairs to sit on." She was especially vehement about synthetic clothes:

> These synthetic clothes have led to hardship in every house. Previously people used to wear cotton clothes and use cotton sheets. Hence there was no pinching poverty. But these synthetic clothes have led to debts and loans. . . . The fact is that synthetic fabrics are so thin and light that if women put them on, all their body parts can be seen, even from far away. Women are so immodest in putting on synthetic saris: they don't care that their bodies are visible!

The middle-aged wife of the Flower Grower related clothing to other forms of authority within the household:

> There were many persons, so each used to be given one set of clothes for the whole year. If they got torn, they were patched. [But now] if you ask daughters-in-law to patch up their clothes and wear them, they will say all kinds of bad things. The times have changed. In former times, daughters-in-law used to patch their clothes. The father-in-law and mother-in-law used to beat and abuse them. That was the time then, daughter. That was a very strange time.

They would say, invest in the field, invest in the house. If the clothes are
torn, let them be torn. My son, now the daughters-in-law cannot tolerate it
or suffer as they did then. If they delayed a little in serving the food, then
their father-in-law used to abuse and beat them. But not now.

The songs sung by women also reiterate a new consumerist ethic and
a related concern with material goods. In one childbirth song the mother
asks the father to "play the radio, for the son cries for it," while in another
the news of the birth is to be given to the husband's mother "by making
a phone call." In a marriage song the groom's grandfather is described as
dressed and ready, "standing under an electric fan." In other songs modern boys are said "to wear pants or trousers, ride cycles, and go to the cinema." These references to modern consumer goods can only work to create greater demand for such things among Karimpur families. But, above
all, education has been most responsible for the shifts in women's behavior. A young Midwife commented, "Earlier people did not have such self-
ish minds. Now all the girls are clever, they are literate. Earlier, no one
was literate. So they never used to live alone." A middle-aged Cultivator
said that girls should not be educated past the eighth grade because "those
girls who belong to the lower groups will only end up doing housework.
What use is it getting a high school diploma when she won't be getting
a job?"

It is the daughter-in-law's demand to live alone, or at least to have
some control over her life and belongings, that has proved most challenging to mothers-in-law and family organization in Karimpur. Among
the poor, family separations have become prevalent, with young couples
frequently setting up their own households within a year of marriage.[11]
But even the poor, whose women have always had greater mobility than
rich women, lament the implications of separation. Women who live alone
no longer stay at home but go in and out. As a Midwife woman said, "She
would stay at home if she were with her mother-in-law. Living alone is
not right." But keeping families together is not always possible: families
break up because of fights between sisters-in-law or between brothers. Al-
locating expenses is also easier if families are separate, especially if one
brother has greater earnings than another. Santoshi, from the Midwife
jāti, described her family's decision to split the households of two brothers and have her mother-in-law stay with her husband's brother this way:

My mother-in-law separated because of my children, saying, "You have lots
of children. You live hungry. We will live with the other son. That son is in

service." So because of my poverty, we separated. . . . Now that son is in service. He sends money home. At my place there is nothing. Now that she has left, I have to raise the children alone. Before she used to look after them [while I went with the grazing animals to make cow-dung cakes].

Among those families who remain joint families, other forms of "separation" occur. As Karimpur families become more couple-oriented, new allocations of space develop. In 1968 only one couple, a young Brahman and his wife, had their "own room"—and only over the strenuous objections of the man's mother. But by 1984 many couples in joint families were allocated their own space to set up and use as they liked. This space, often a room of their own, was clearly off limits to the mother-in-law, who thus lost her control of her son's sexuality. Indeed, as I was frequently told, one result of both separate families and "rooms of their own" was a shortening in the time span between children, from about three years in the 1960s to barely two years in the 1980s. Women over the age of thirty felt it highly inappropriate for children to be spaced so closely.

Women express their new concerns about familial relationships in the same context that they express other concerns: stories and songs. In these public documents, private familial issues are presented in a neutral arena. Songs sung in the 1980s continually spoke of new kinship patterns. For example, in one song a bridegroom is described as very clever because he took his bride to see a movie without asking any of his kin. The following song, sung by Brahman girls in March 1984 at the wedding of Saroj's son, directly addresses the issue of new household authority patterns:

> Mother-in-law, gone, gone is your rule,
> The age of the daughter-in-law has come.
> The mother-in-law grinds with the grinding stone,
> The daughter-in-law watches.
> "Your flour is very coarse, my mother-in-law."
> The age of the daughter-in-law has come.
>
> Mother-in-law, gone, gone is your rule,
> The age of the daughter-in-law has come.
> The mother-in-law cooks the food,
> The daughter-in-law serves it.
> Serving, serving to my father-in-law a plate:
> The age of the daughter-in-law has come.
>
> Mother-in-law, gone, gone is your rule,
> The age of the daughter-in-law has come.
> The mother-in-law draws the water,

> The daughter-in-law bathes.
> "Mother-in-law, please scrub my back."
> The age of the daughter-in-law has come.
>
> Mother-in-law, gone, gone is your rule,
> The age of the daughter-in-law has come.
> The mother-in-law spreads a bed,
> The daughter-in-law lies down.
> "Mother-in-law, please massage my feet."
> The age of the daughter-in-law has come.

Another song, which was sung by Muslim girls in January 1984, addressed a topic also of concern to Saroj, namely, the incompetence of the "English-educated" girl to do household work:

> I am English-educated, but my luck [*bhāgy*] is bad, oh dearest mommy.
> My mother-in-law said, "*Bahū*, cook the breads."
> So I cooked the breads, oh dearest mommy.
> My sari worth thousands of rupees,
> It was burned up, oh dearest mommy.
> I am English-educated, but my luck is bad, oh dearest mommy.
>
> My mother-in-law said, "*Bahū*, scrub the pots."
> So I scrubbed the pots, oh dearest mommy.
> My watch worth thousands of rupees,
> The water ruined it, oh dearest mommy.
> I am English-educated, but my luck is bad, oh dearest mommy.[12]

Men's songs address other issues related to family and marriage in modern times, especially the cost of providing dowries for one's daughters. A Brahman family can now anticipate spending a minimum of twenty thousand rupees on a daughter's wedding, and most spend considerably more. Even the poorest Karimpur families have to spend two thousand rupees on a daughter's wedding, at a time when fathers can anticipate earning ten to twelve rupees a day. As we have seen, one result is a continually declining sex ratio, as daughters continue to be discriminated against in childhood. This is especially evident among the poor, whose girl children are now less likely to survive than they were sixty years ago. In contrast, as the birthrate among the poor has gone up, sons have survived at higher rates than previously. Sons are desirable, for by the age of ten they can pay their own way, but daughters only bring worry and the burden of a dowry.[13]

The extraordinary costs of weddings affect everyone. Subash, a Brahman man in his late twenties, sang this song in November 1984:

Even now it happens, but think, brother:
this system of dowry, it is ruining our country.
It's everywhere in India, our eyes
are blind to it.
Surely we must throw light on this cause of poverty.
It's because of money: it quickly causes death.
It quickly causes death.
A young girl sits in the house;
day and night the worry never ceases.
Mother and father are distressed;
mother and father are distressed.
"How can we get her married?
How can we get her married?
Which way?
We don't have the money, crying we shall die.
Somehow we must find a horse and groom."
The boy's father says this,
"I am demanding ten thousand rupees for the marriage."
This is happening in India;
no one pays it any heed.
At the boy's place, they treat you as they like.
Weddings are like cattle markets.
"We will take five thousand in *lagun*";[14]
then they do the engagement.
The girl's people are helpless.
How can they have courage?
A grownup daughter waits,
"How can we get her married?"
This is the problem with daughters;
This sin [*pāp*, namely, dowries] is very great.
This sin is very great.
Where can I find this much money?
Thousands are needed.
Destroy this giving and taking:
we must improve conditions in India.
Now with folded hands, Raghuvir speaks.
Shri Ram is our solace.

Without doubt modern families worry more about marrying daughters than about any other issue. In Karimpur, all daughters do marry, although many men remain unmarried. But whether one is rich or poor, the demands of dowry are ever present. The Midwife Santoshi, whose daughter is only thirteen but is marriageable in her eyes, has not yet paid off the debts of her husband's brother's wedding years ago, but now she is faced with a "grown" daughter. Brahman families, unable to accumulate the necessary monies, wait until their daughters are in their twenties,

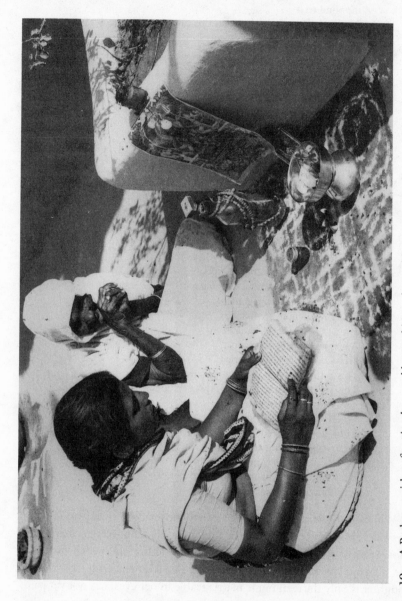

19.   A Brahman girl performing her weekly worship to the goddess in her family courtyard

making the task of finding a groom all the more difficult. But a girl must be married, and her family seeks a marriage that will be successful enough that she will have no cause to return to them. Providing a good home for a daughter or sister is an onerous task, and it may take months of traveling to locate an acceptable boy. Factors taken into account include the landholdings of the boy, including the size of his share when the father's lands are split among the brothers; farming implements, including tube wells and pump sets; the reputation of the family; the value that they place on education; the boy's prospects for earning (does he have a job?); the temperament of the mother-in-law and other daughters-in-law; and the reputations of the daughter-in-laws' families. Most critically, the rules for a good marriage have changed: education and salaried jobs are valued more than landholdings. An urban connection is also desirable. But the relative value to put on these new qualifications is hard to determine. What if a family has lied about a boy's job? A family's reputation in their home village can be checked, but this is harder in urban areas. So arranging marriages is more fraught with difficulties than in previous times.

Not surprisingly, marriages often bring tragedy. Wives are abused; and while dowry deaths such as those in Delhi are not an issue in Karimpur, as we saw earlier, two women of the village, including Raghunath's wife, have killed themselves by fire in the past twenty-five years, when the abuse became too much. Sons' marriages, too, are controversial. A Hindu family loses honor if they are forced to search for a bride for their sons, so they must await families seeking unions with them. But as Shankar said repeatedly, "Marriages now aren't even conducted on the basis of *jāti*. These days marriages are made if a boy is in service. Even if my son has an M.A., if he isn't in service, it is difficult to marry him, even when he has property."

Saroj once commented on wives' lack of obedience to their husbands, saying:

> Listen. Indian people have lost their religion. Earlier, women used to serve their husbands. Nowadays, women are more likely to break their husband's head. Indian brothers have lost their religion. Perhaps only one or two in a hundred [women] are controlled by their husbands. . . . It is the aim of Indira to bring women forward and push men back. To make them self-dependent. To give women more comforts. And to give them rights.

Here Saroj both blames women for independence and advocates it. As a female leader herself, she was often ambivalent about the position of women, proclaiming a traditional morality one minute and seeking new roles for women the next. She represents a woman balancing between old and new, seeking new patterns.

Men and women both worry about the new selfishness of children when they begin to think of their own aging. Mohan, Saroj, Santoshi, Raghunath, and others all expressed fears of being old in this new age. Typically, the youngest son in a family would care for his parents, as parents are most likely to remain in a joint family with their youngest son. But this care is no longer assured. The wife of the Accountant said, "The saddest thing is that you bring up your children, and they in turn don't look after you when you get old."[15]

"NOW THERE IS A HEADMAN IN EVERY HOUSE"

This comment, made by Aditya, one of the few Carpenters still plying his traditional trade, captures the essence of Karimpur opinion about the village community today. Whereas before there was one village headman who exercised a firm rule over all, now each household is on its own: each has its own headman, its own *mukhiyā;* each rules itself.

In village opinion, ultimately what is most damaging—because of the new domination of Indira, the advent of democracy, and economic change—is a loss of the village morality that was based on a complex web of mutual obligations. The mutual dependency of *jajmānī* and tenancy relations provided security for both rich and poor. The *jajmāns* knew that labor was available and that their wider family of *kamīns* and tenants would support them. The *kamīns* likewise could count on receiving the basic necessities from their *jajmāns*. In short, the insecurities of a contract labor market were absent. Rather, there was a moral order based on long-term, enduring solidarity. Brijpal put it thus: "Now mutual understanding is not there. Earlier, there was a lot of love between people." A young Watercarrier had similar sentiments: "Previously you and I were happy together. Now there is not as much caring as before. Suppose a brawl had taken place between us: we would still smoke together at night. Now everybody is on his own. No one cares about anyone else."

An elderly Grain Parcher elaborated on this theme:

In fact, we were very happy before and we loved each other [in the village], but slowly that love [*prem*] is being lost. There are some old people who want to love others. Really I am afraid that this kind of selfishness [*apanatv*] is going to increase and increase and increase. . . . Before people wanted to help one another. They liked to help. Before they worked together cooperatively. If someone was suffering from some difficulty, another came to help.

But now love is totally lost. . . . Now those who can work hard are happy; they are having a good life. And those who can't or won't work hard are suffering. Everyone wants everything for free.

The Cotton Carder said that now people increasingly rely on guns, that there is no love [*mauhavvat*] anymore. He added, "Now men have degenerated [literally, are 'less,' *kam*], they have no regulations [*kāydā*]." His viewpoint was supported by Brahmans as well. Sundar, a Brahman in his mid-fifties, had this to say:

Previously there was a lot of affection [*prem*] in eating and drinking, in coming and going, in speaking and talking. There was a great deal of good feeling. Now there is not much. Now men become angry over the smallest thing. . . . Previously there was not so much selfishness [*apanatv*]. We used to think about others. If they were troubled, why were they troubled? Now we don't care . . . because each man has become a leader [*netā*]. . . . Previously men used to be more righteous [literally, "straight," *sīdhā*]. They had a simple mind, simple food, simple clothing, and great affection [*prem*] for all. Now there isn't as much love.

One man explained that when only the Brahmans were rich, then politics was an issue only between the Brahmans, but now everyone is politicking and hence there is less love in the village. Shankar, the headman, also felt this way:

In earlier times when there was enmity between people, it was in the open. Everything was clean and honest. But now politics has come in. Even if you don't like someone, you will greet them, shake hands with them, and pretend to be friends—and at the same time hope some disaster befalls them.

The Brahman widow Saroj used the example of a *jāti* from a place foreign to her, the Punjab, to explain what is currently wrong with village life:

There is a *jāti* called Punjabi. You never see a beggar among them, nor do you ever find a Punjabi man in prison. There is so much cooperation among them that if someone is in a poor condition or misfortune befalls him, the other people of the Punjabi *jāti* go to him and help in every possible way to pull him out of his misery and difficulty. But here if misfortune comes to someone, nobody comes to help. Rather they may say, "Good, he has a lot of trouble. Because of his bad situation, I can satisfy my old grudge."

In the opinions of many, democratic politics is part of the problem. Democracy, land allotments, wage labor, and education have all contributed to breaking the bonds that used to unite the members of the Karimpur community. In this view the past is reevaluated positively, by both rich

20.   A young Flower Grower groom and his bride, newly returned to his village, going to worship the village goddess

and poor. As the Midwife Santoshi said, the past was the period of support. In the switchover from the time of domination to the time of democracy, from the landlord to Indira, mutual support, albeit that of a punishing mother-father, has eroded.[16] The new authority of an intrusive government pits the landlord against the poor, the rich against the rich, and the poor against the poor, rather than reinforcing their mutual bonding.

In seeing disorder in their world, and in wishing for the good old days, whatever their faults, Karimpur's residents are little different from many others around the world. England of the 1500s and 1600s is widely described in terms of disorder, while people in postcolonial, postcommunist, and postindustrial societies are today reacting to the "disorder" caused by changing patterns of life.[17] Karimpur shares with many communities around the world a breaking of the multifaceted bonds that used to link residents, as well as an increase in individualistic behavior, as men compete for jobs and other resources in a capitalist marketplace. In this village, as elsewhere, there is a dynamic tension between searching for a new rule book and clinging to old rules that might still work.

THE RESPONSE TO DISORDER

One aspect of the cultural rule book according to which Karimpur villagers have acted for generations has not been directly threatened by the social, political, and economic changes that have occurred since the 1920s: their belief in their gods and goddesses and in the affects of meritorious actions on their lives.[18] Indeed, as Karimpur's residents struggle with their destinies in the latter decades of the twentieth century, and as they attempt to deal with the disorder that affects their daily lives, they have increasingly turned to their gods and goddesses for answers.

The cultural code that supported a hierarchy whereby the high had knowledge and might and the right to control the low also supports a religious hierarchy in which the deities have greater power than humans—they are *śakti-sanpann*, power-filled—and are able to reward humans for acts of service and devotion. Those individuals who act according to their *dharma* are also rewarded, either with a better life in the near future or in a subsequent birth. But *dharma* is being redefined, I would argue, to exclude acts supportive of neighbors and the mutual obligations that once existed between *jāti* groups or within the family. In fact, I would suggest, *dharma* is now more specifically linked to actions that we Westerners have traditionally defined as religious: going on a pilgrimage, performing worship, singing religious songs.

Nevertheless, there is an outward religiosity that pervaded Karimpur life in the 1980s. Part of this religious fervor was due, I am convinced, to the increase of wealth in the village and the accompanying leisure time this made possible. As a poor woman told me many years ago, "I don't do those rituals because I can't afford them." At a minimum, to honor the gods usually requires cooking special foods, and sometimes other goods are also necessary. Further, daily devotion to the gods is time-consuming. The men and women laboring in the fields or herding cattle or processing grains in their courtyards do not have time to devote to daily service. But as they gain in prosperity and as electrical threshers and other mechanical aids cut into their work load, more time becomes available. Now, like their kin in the urban areas, they can devote an hour a day to maintaining a house shrine and bathing and feeding the images there. Further, there is money to travel to visit a guru or a newly proclaimed living "mother" in a nearby village. There has also been an increase in the

21. Brahman women worshiping Khan Bahadur, the Muslim guardian of the village, by performing the Muslim rite of "spreading a sheet" on his tomb atop the hill near the village

population of the elderly, who have both the time and the inclination for religious acts. Mohan, for example, is seldom without his prayer beads and performs several fasts every month. The Cultivator men frequently hold a twenty-four-hour *kīrtan*, a form of worship characterized by continual singing. Women may save for months and then feast numerous female kin after a vow has been fulfilled by a goddess. Two temples have been built in the village since 1967, themselves a reflection of the new commitment to religion. All of these factors have contributed to an increase in manifest religiosity in Karimpur.

But religion in the 1980s was not what it was sixty years previously. Much to the consternation of the Brahmans, one of the Cultivator men now performs weddings, something he learned from a pandit who was his guru while he was a young man. In 1966, shortly after he started performing marriages, there was a major altercation with the Brahmans, which led to the final agreement that the two groups (Brahmans and Cultivators) would go their own way.

There have been changes, too, in the deities that are worshiped. Santoshi Ma, the goddess of peace and benevolence but also a goddess whose story speaks directly to women whose husbands are working and living outside the village, has become especially popular. In the story that lies behind her worship, a young *bahū* has a worthless husband, who finally leaves home to seek his fortune. She is left alone with his family. As his absence grows longer, she is treated more and more cruelly, forced to gather firewood from the forest and given rags to wear. On one of her excursions into the forest, she comes upon a group of women worshiping Santoshi Ma. Hearing the story of the goddess, she too begins to worship her every Friday. The husband thus begins to prosper and eventually returns home. Arriving at his house, he asks after his wife, who is in the forest. When he discovers how she has been treated, he builds a lavish home for her with the help of the goddess. So those who worship the goddess will prosper, as did the young wife. This story speaks to many issues facing modern Indians: work, family relationships, and ultimately the breakup of the joint family. It is not surprising that this goddess has become one of the most popular in north India over the last thirty years or so.

There has also been a growing recognition of the differences between Hindu and Muslim. (There were no practicing Christians in the village in the 1980s.) When I first went to Karimpur in 1967, it was impossible to tell Muslim and Hindu women apart, for they both dressed in the same homespun cotton saris.[19] (Hindu and Muslim men dress alike: often only their headgear marks their religion.) By 1984, however, many Muslim women wore *silvār-kurtā* (a long shirt with baggy pants) instead of the sari worn by Hindu women. Further, now the Muslim women might don a *burkā* when going out of the village, rather than wear a shawl as the Hindu women do. In the late 1980s I was invited to a Muslim prayer ceremony held in front of one of the Muslim houses in the village, a public declaration of identity that was unheard of before, when there were only slight differences in marriage ceremonies and little other manifest Muslim religiosity.

Although Karimpur villagers are aware of and act on their religious identities, they do draw together when threatened from outside. In 1990, at the height of the first major dispute over Ram's birthplace in Ayodhya, the shrine of the Muslim village guardian, Khan Bahadur, was broken. To this day, Hindus and Muslims alike worship Khan Bahadur to alleviate troubles. That his shrine was defaced was an insult to all. On this point there was unity, and the village supported its rapid repair by the district magistrate.

Nevertheless, tensions between high and low and between Muslim and Hindu are increasing, as they are throughout India itself. The evidence in the preceding pages points to the sources of the great discomfort that those in rural India face today, lacking jobs for their sons and facing expensive marriages for their daughters. Moreover, the high know only too well that even if their sons succeed in school, government policies designed to promote the disadvantaged may preclude their entrance into more advanced training or their obtaining of the treasured service job. To the old landlords, current government policies that advance the cause of the former poor are the final affront. For the poor, however, the gains that have led to education and given them their own lands still do not guarantee jobs or prosperity. Further, both rich and poor are challenged by sons and daughters seeking to alter the rules by which families are organized. There is indeed chaos in the world of Karimpur's residents. They no longer know the rules by which life is to be ordered. They are now struggling to create a new destiny for themselves and their families, but they are on a course yet to be charted.

Epilogue

Sitting here while the blizzard of 1993 rages outside and listening to reports of yet further violence in Bombay, I find myself compelled to comment on the analysis presented above.

First of all, let me address a commonly asked question: to what extent is Karimpur "typical"? How representative is it of the many thousands of villages found throughout India? I would argue that the patterns of mutuality and hereditary rights and obligations, and of the oppression and exploitation of both women and the low, that are presented above are representative of many, if not most, rural communities throughout India. Further, the kinds of changes that have been made in those patterns are similar to changes occurring elsewhere. Many communities, especially those nearer to urban centers or those that received an earlier infusion of agricultural inputs, made such changes earlier. Others—for example, villages in eastern Uttar Pradesh, in Bihar, or in parts of Orissa—have yet to face many of these changes.

Without doubt, Karimpur's location has been critical to the specific types of socioeconomic change that it has undergone, especially in the past twenty years, but I do not believe that it is critical to the generalized patterns of these changes. Karimpur is not near a big city or an urban area with any extensive industry. The urban marketplace in Mainpuri offers few opportunities for employment aside from jobs demanding physical labor. Only since the 1980s has Delhi become a desirable point for migration, but even now most wives are left behind in Karimpur. Further, the village was not near any early irrigation facilities, such as the canals that permitted intensive sugarcane production in parts of northern Uttar Pradesh (such as Muzzafanagar), the Punjab, or Maharashtra. Hence, only in the 1980s did cash crops such as garlic and fennel come to play a significant role in Karimpur farming practices. As a result, the village is not prosperous, especially when compared to the regions mentioned above. But it is also better off than many communities that are only now receiving irrigation facilities and new agricultural inputs.

The dominance in Karimpur of Brahmans who are economically powerful is somewhat unique for Uttar Pradesh. Many feel that this has hurt the village, for the Brahmans do not work as hard as the landowners in nearby villages dominated by lower-ranked *jāti*s.[1] Certainly the consolidation of ritual and economic power in one group has had an effect on Karimpur. Educational levels were, for example, relatively high very early on because of the value that Brahman families placed on education for both males and females. But the strict purdah restrictions with which Brahman women must live have excluded them from participation in agriculture and other income-generating jobs, a model that has, moreover, been emulated by the lower *jāti*s in this community. Thus we do not find women participating in agriculture to the same degree that we often do in Jat or Gujar communities in northern India or in many South Indian communities.

Having lived in Karimpur at various times since 1967, I am convinced that the village as a whole is more prosperous than it was in the 1960s and that for most people life is somewhat better. Despite its continuing deficiencies, health care is still better than at any other time, and mortality rates for both young and old are lower. Nevertheless, the health care infrastructure is poor. Many illnesses go untreated or are not properly treated, and for many even the low quality of care available is affordable only for men and male children. Certainly the increase in a female-specific child mortality is of major concern.

Material prosperity is now evident in many homes, with hand pumps, electricity, watches, radios, fans, bicycles, better bedding, and other goods all contributing to a higher standard of living. But this increase in material prosperity is not spread evenly throughout the village: those families who make up the 44 percent living below the poverty line have few of these amenities. For them, the benefits of the 1980s are visible primarily in health care and the possibility of an education. Many rural communities in India have significantly higher standards of living; many have lower. My best guess is that Karimpur would fall somewhere in the middle range of community prosperity if we were to compare it to communities throughout India.

Finally, what about the loss of love, of mutual cooperation and caring? At the outset, we must recognize that the network of mutual obligations and dependencies related to *jajmānī* and large landlords was based on exploitation of those who did not have primary tenancy rights. Unfortunately, a modern democratic India has not yet provided opportunities for many of those who were most oppressed by the *jajmānī* system and landlordship. (Nor, of course, has a democratic United States provided opportunities for many of the descendants of those we once enslaved.) For the very poor who did have security because of those mutual obligations, life is now sometimes worse. For those who have been able to obtain an education and decent independent livelihoods, things are undoubtedly better. But for both groups, however, there are uncertainties, for the rules guiding these new lifestyles are still unclear. The dowry deaths found in northern urban areas are one manifestation of those uncertainties, as the marginal new urban middle class tries to gain in a game whose rules have yet to be clarified. That women are the objects of this new form of subjugation is not surprising, for they are the group still most strictly controlled in villages like Karimpur: they are, if you like, the last bastion of the patterns of control based on the old cultural blueprints.[2]

I recently reread a comment that Mohan made during a lengthy conversation in January 1987. Some six years before the advent of the present chaos engulfing India as a nation, Mohan spoke of his concerns about the issues facing his country. While I do not support his implicit desire for authoritarian rule, his words seem an appropriate final comment on the issues discussed in this book.

There is no longer any discipline. . . . There is anarchy. The government is not that strong. Earlier, if one constable came to the village, then everyone would shut themselves inside their houses. A few respected people would talk to the constable. Today, the superintendent of police's car comes, but the women are still bathing; some boy is honking its horn; someone else is pushing the car. Nobody has any fear. There is no discipline. A country that has no discipline is immoral; a district that has no discipline is immoral; a home, a village that have no discipline, they are immoral. If people living in a home agree to the decisions of one man, that home will never fall. A village that listens and agrees to one or two respected people, that village will never fall. They never need seek justice in court. . . . In my day, no one would touch you, even if you carried silver coins worth two or four thousand rupees. But today, I will pick your pocket if I know that you have even a hundred or two hundred rupees in your pocket. And if [the money is] in

your shoes, I will steal your shoes. And if it's in your hand, I will cut off your
hand. This is the situation. The government is lax. There is no leader who
doesn't have several criminals with him, who hasn't murdered several people. . . . Without fear, no one tells the truth. [The leaders won't let the mur-
derers be beaten in order to get at the truth, because then the issue reaches
parliament.] As a result nothing happens. So people are disorderly. Because
of this disorder, the country is suffering.

Violence, greed, lack of respect: Mohan eloquently sums up his view of
the disintegration of the old order. It is especially difficult for him as a
Brahman male, for his position had traditionally been one of enforcing
order, no matter what inequalities resulted. The new order has already al-
terd those old inequalities, as well as creating new ones. But there can be
no going back. One way or another, the villagers of Karimpur must find
a way to cope with what destiny has brought to them.

Glossary

adharma   Unrighteousness, improper behavior.

Alakshmi (*alakṣmī*)   "Nonprosperity," the name of the sister of the goddess of prosperity.

Asharh (*āsāṛh*)   The Hindu month comparable to June–July.

ātmā   The soul.

bahū   A term of address for a daughter-in-law, commonly used to refer as well to a wife, either one's own or the wife of someone junior in the household.

Baisakh (*baisākh*)   The Hindu month comparable to April–May, when weddings are most often celebrated.

Basuk Dev (*bāsuk dev*)   The snake king, also known as *vāsuki*.

Bhadon (*bhādon*)   The Hindu month comparable to August–September, a monsoon month.

Bhagvan (*bhagvān*)   A term used by Hindus for "god" in the most generic sense.

bhāgy   A term meaning "fortune" or "fate." Not as inclusive as *karma*.

bhakti   A form of Hinduism that developed from about the tenth century onward that celebrates the personal loving relationship between devotee and god.

bīḍī   A hand-rolled cigarette, made out of a leaf and cheap tobacco and tied with a short thread. Commonly smoked by men.

Brahma (*brahmā*)   One of the three major Hindu gods.

Brahman (*brāhman*)   The topmost *varṇa* among Hindus. Also a term used for the priestly *jāti*.

Brother's Second (*bhaiyā dūj*)   A festival day, falling during the autumn month of Kartik, on which women worship for the long life and good fortune of their brothers, in return for which they receive gifts.

Candi (*caṇḍī*)   A Hindu goddess, known to be easily angered and to attack those who offend her.

Chattri   A term used in Karimpur for the Kshatriya *varṇa*.

chotī   Literally meaning "small," a term used in Karimpur for those of low rank.

Damayanti (*damayantī*)   The wife of Raja Nal, a hero in both the *Mahabharata* and the epic *Dhola* sung in Karimpur.

ḍānk   A ritual of snake possession, during which the snake king, Basuk Dev, cures snakebite and answers questions.

Dashahra (*daśahrā*)   The fall festival in which the *Ramayana* is enacted and Ram's victory celebrated throughout northern India.

Dashrath (*daśrath*)   The father of Ram, hero of the *Ramayana*.

devatā   A generic term for a deity.

devī   A generic term for the goddess.

dharma   Righteousness, proper behavior.

Dharmaraj Yudhisthir (*dharmarāj yudhisthir*)   The oldest of the five brothers who are the heroes of the *Mahabharata*. Dharmaraj is an honorific title meaning "the righteous king."

Dhola (*dholā*)   An oral epic performed throughout western Uttar Pradesh and eastern Rajasthan, which tells the story of Raja Nal and his son Dhola.

Divali (*dīvālī*)   The festival of lights, taking place in mid-fall in the month of Kartik.

Draupadi (*draupadī*)   The wife of the five heroes of the *Mahabharata*. In a well-known incident, her husbands' enemies attempt to rip Draupadi's sari off her, but she is protected by Krishna, who provides her with an endless sari.

gālī   Obscene and lewd songs sung by women, most commonly at marriages, where they are addressed to the groom's kin.

Garuda (*garuḍa*)   The bird that serves as a messenger for the gods.

gaunā   The consummation ceremony that occurs some months after the actual marriage ceremony. It requires additional gifts from the girl's family.

Green Third (*hariyālī tīj*)   A festival day that occurs during the monsoon month of Savan, during which a daughter ideally returns to her parents' home. On Green Third, daughters worship Shiva and Parvati.

hakīm   A traditional medical practitioner.

Hanuman (*hanumān*)   The monkey king who is a devotee of Ram and a favorite deity throughout northern India.

Harishchand (*hariścand*)   The hero of a well-known legend, Harishchand faces his fate and lets his wife and son be sold, while he becomes a beggar at the cremation grounds.

Holi (*holī*)   A spring festival of reversal and renewal occurring in the month of Phagun.

Holika (*holīkā*)   The goddess whose deeds are celebrated at the festival of Holi.

ijjat   Honor.

Ishvar (*īśvar*)   Another term for "god."

jajmān   The patron in the traditional hereditary economic relationship that links service castes with landlords.

jajmānī   The system linking *jajmān* and *kamīn*.

Jamghantu (*jamghaṇṭu*)   A god who causes children to die. Associated with deaths from tetanus.

Janak (*janak*)   The king who finds the goddess Sita in a furrow and raises her. She marries Ram.

jāti   The Hindi word for what is often termed caste. Etymologically related to the Latin *genus*, it implies birth into a named social group, usually endogamous and associated with an occupation. There are thousands of *jāti*s throughout India, some loosely associated with one of the four *varṇa*s. Each locale has its own ranking of its resident *jāti*s.

Jaykayan (*jaykayan*)   A local god whose shrine is often the site for a child's first haircut.

Jeth (*jeth*)   A very hot month, comparable to May–June.

kaccā   Literally meaning "unripe" or "raw," this term is also used for foods that are cooked in water and not easily shared with those of unequal rank.

Kaikeyi (*kaikeyī*)   One of Raja Dashrath's three wives, who is jealous of Ram and causes him to be banished to the forest for fourteen years so that her son may ascend the throne.

Kalika (*kālikā*)   A Hindu goddess, easily angered.

kamīn   The client or laborer in the hereditary relationship defined by the *jajmānī* system.

kanyādān   The gift of the virgin, one of the most important gifts a Hindu can make.

karam   The word in the Karimpur dialect for *karma*.

karma   Based on the verbal root *kar*, "to do," this is the term for fate, that which is caused by your previous actions, whether in a past life or this one.

Kartik (*kartik*)   The Hindu month that falls in October–November. Many festivals take place during this month, including Divali.

kāydā   Regulations or customs.

Khan Bahadur   The guardian deity of Karimpur, a Muslim hero from the 1700s whose shrine is located on a nearby hilltop.

kharīf   The rainy-season crop.

kīrtan   A song event, usually characterized by continuous singing for a specified period of time, such as twenty-four hours.

Krishna (*kṛṣṇa*)   One of the most beloved of Hindu gods, Krishna took birth as an incarnation of Vishnu some eighty miles from Karimpur in order to destroy the evil king Kans. His birth and childhood and his love for the milkmaids of his community are celebrated in song and ritual.

Kshatriya (*kṣatriya*)   The second highest of the Hindu *varṇa*s, the Kshatriyas are warriors and protectors.

Kuar (*kuar*)   The Hindu month that falls in September–October. The Dashahra festival takes place during this month.

Kulakshani (*kulakṣanī*)   Literally, the one born with inauspicious characteristics, or the misfortuned one.

Kush (*kuś*)   One of the twin sons of Ram.

Kuvidya (*kuvidyā*)   The one without knowledge, a name for an inauspicious goddess.

Lakshmi (*lakṣmī*)   The goddess of prosperity. A bride is often likened to her.

Lav (*lav*)   One of the twin sons of Ram.

Mahabharata (*mahābhārata*)   Along with the *Ramayana*, one of the two earliest epic traditions in India. Its central plot, around which many legends and teachings have accreted, focuses on a cataclysmic internecine conflict between the five brothers who are its heros and their conniving cousins.

Mahadev (*mahādev*)   The great god, a epithet for Shiva.

Mandodari (*mandodarī*)   The beautiful wife of the demon-king Ravan in the *Ramayana*.

Motini (*motinī*)   The daughter of a demon, she is the first of Raja Nal's two wives in the epic *Dhola*.

mukhiyā   The traditional headman of a village.

Nakul (*nakul*)   The fourth of the five brothers who are the heroes of the *Mahabharata*.

Nal (*nal*)   The hero of the epic *Dhola* and also the hero of an episode in the *Mahabharata*.

namaste   The Hindu greeting, spoken with folded palms.

pakkā   Literally meaning "ripe," this term also refers to foods cooked in milk or milk products. These foods are purer than *kaccā* foods and hence more easily exchanged amongst social groups.

pān   Betel leaves, eaten with spices.

pāp   Sin, evil action.

pativrat   Literally, "worshiper of the husband," a woman who honors her husband continually.

patvārī   The keeper of land records, one of the most important jobs in rural India.

Phagun (*phāgun*)   The Hindu month that falls in March–April. The time of the beginning of the spring harvest, it is the month during which the festival of Holi occurs.

Pitcher Fourth (*karva cauth*)   A festival day in the autumn month of Kartik, on which a woman is supposed to present her husband with a pitcher full of sweets.

Prahlad (*prahlād*)   The boy whose is saved from fire by his devotion to the true gods.

prasād   Foods offered to the gods, which are then eaten by the devotees as the god's leftovers.

pūjā   The ritual of worship associated with *bhakti* devotionalism, in which services of various kinds (a bath, new clothes, offerings) are made to the deity in return for his or her mercy.

puṇya   Merit, meritorious actions.

pūrī   Fried unleavened breads.

Purusha (*puruṣa*)   The first man, celebrated in a Vedic hymn that describes the origin of the four *varṇa*s.

rabī   The dry-season (winter) crop.

Rajput   Literally, "son of a king," the term refers primarily to royal lineages from what is now the state of Rajasthan.

Ram (*rām*)   The hero of the *Ramayana*, who is also a reincarnation of the god Vishnu.

Ramayana (rāmāyaṇa)   An epic tradition known through many retellings in numerous languages throughout India. Its hero, Ram, is one of the most popular deities in Karimpur.

Ravan (*rāvaṇ*)   The demon-king whose evil acts lead to the birth of Ram.

śakti   Literally "power" or "energy," this is the feminine principle that activates the universe.

Saluno (*salūno*)   A festival that takes place at the end of the month of Bhadon.

samajhdār   A term meaning "sensible" or "having understanding."

samajhnā   Literally, "to have understanding; to be knowledgeable," a quality often thought not to be present in women and members of lower-ranked *jāti*s.

Santoshi Ma (*santoṣī mā*)   The goddess of benevolence and peace.

Savan (*sāvan*)   The Hindu month comparable to July–August, a rainy-season month.

Savitri (*sāvitrī*)   A goddess whose devotion to her husband saved him from the grasp of the god of death.

Shiva (*śiva*)   One of the three major gods of Hinduism, Shiva is both destroyer and creator.

Shudra (*śūdra*)   The lowest of the four *varṇa*s, the workers.

Sita (*sītā*)   Daughter of Janak and wife of Ram.

Siyao Mata (*siyāo*)   "Lampblack Mother," whose ritual takes place the day after Divali.

Snake's Fifth (*nāg pancmī*)   A festival day during the monsoon month of Savan, on which women worship snakes, especially Basuk Dev.

Thakur (*thākur*)   A term used to refer to a landlord. In Karimpur, it is used like a *jāti* name.

tulsī   The basil plant, believed to be associated with Vishnu.

vaidy   A traditional healer.

Vaishya (*vaiśya*)   The third of the four *varṇa*s, traders or merchants.

varṇa   One of the four social groups that formed the structure for the earliest Hindu social organization.

vidhātā   The Arranger (i.e., the Creator), a deity.

Vishnu (*viṣṇu*)   One of the three major Hindu gods, Vishnu is the protector. Krishna and Ram are reincarnations of Vishnu, born to destroy evil on earth.

Yama (*yama*)   The god of death.

Notes

PREFACE

1. See Foster et al., eds., 1979 for a discussion of long-term studies. As this volume points out, part of the value of such studies lies in the fact that they reveal how "a transformation that would have looked impossible a generation ago happens" (p. 326). See also Wadley and Derr 1989b for a consideration of the methodological problems involved in restudying Karimpur. Other restudies or long-term studies of Indian communities include Epstein 1973 and 1979; Leaf 1984; Ullrich 1987a and 1987b; Das Gupta 1977; Dreze 1988; and Saith and Tankha 1992.

2. The village of Karimpur that is the object of study here is not coterminous with the revenue village of which it is the administrative center. The village of this study is composed of three hamlets, understood by their inhabitants jointly to constitute the village "Karimpur." Their understanding of these boundaries is demonstrated both ritually and behaviorally. While I am aware of criticisms of the concept of "village" for Asia and of using it as a unit of analysis (Breman 1987), I believe that to Karimpur residents, the village, despite its many links to the outside, remains a discrete place in their conceptual schemes.

3. In the 1920s the Wisers collected hundreds of pages of Karimpur oral traditions, primarily by paying teenage boys a rupee a page for any texts that they brought. These were then transcribed into roman script, and some were translated. The Hindi originals, on large sheets of brown paper, are archived at the Divinity School Library, Yale University. Beginning in 1967, I have recorded numerous oral traditions, both sung and narrated. The original audio recordings and copies of all transcriptions and translations are available at the Archive for Traditional Music, Indiana University, and at the Archive and Research Center for Ethnomusicology in New Delhi. I have also indexed the two collections by genre. Items collected by the Wisers are prefixed WC; those that I collected are prefaced Wa.

4. On the move from all-inclusive to disaggregated naming, see, for example, Shostak 1981; Johnson 1992. On multiple histories and spurious traditions, see Guha 1980; and Handler and Linnekan 1984. For the new concern with anthropological praxis, see Wulff and Fiske, eds., 1987; Parajuli and Enslin 1990; and Harrison 1991.

5. All the taped interviews were then transcribed in Hindi by Ant Ram Batham, whose dedication to our endeavor was prodigious, as anyone who has been involved in the work of transcribing can well imagine. (Sadly, Ant Ram died of tuberculosis in January 1986, at the age of twenty-five, leaving a wife and son.) We didn't have the space or the supplies to keep tapes of every last interview, but some particularly important ones were saved, as were all those containing folk narratives. All the translations in this book are mine.

6. For more on the role of an informed outsider, see Rosaldo 1986 on Ilongut narratives.

7. As Rosaldo noted for the Ilonguts, "hunting becomes history; gardening never does" (1986, 134).

8. It is difficult to judge the role of age, level of status, and personality characteristics in this outcome. Roger Jeffery found that his younger male assistant was often allowed in on in sexual joking, whereas he as a married male was not. I heard little from the villagers about sex before my marriage, but more afterwards. Bruce found a reluctance to talk about sexual matters among all but his closest friends. Some of the more sexual songs sung by the men at Holi were explicitly considered inappropriate for "filling the machine to go to America," so there was clearly some self-censorship occurring.

9. For more on issues of interpretation and translation, see Mills 1991; Bruner 1988.

10. Works that consider issues of ethics and and the role of the anthropologist include Stacey 1988; Abu-Lughod 1990b; Patai 1991; and Wolf 1992.

11. See Marcus and Fischer 1986; Clifford 1988; and Fabian 1990.

CHAPTER 1:   "TELL THEM TO LISTEN WITH THEIR EARS OPEN"

1. Kulakshani literally means "she who is born with inauspicious characteristics."

2. Discourse refers not only to the texts themselves but also to the activities involved in their production and use. For further discussion, see Smith 1984.

3. I have translated *karma* as both "destiny" and "fate." Other closely related terms, such as *bhāgy*, are also sometimes translated as fate, with the Hindi indicated in the text.

4. On the Purusha hymn, see Dimmitt and van Buitenen 1978, 35; on the worship paradigm, see Wadley 1975a; on inauspiciousness, see Raheja 1988; on order in Hindu kingdoms, see Dirks 1989; and for males and females, see Wadley 1977a and Bennett 1983. See also Marriott 1989.

5. On caste, see in particular Dumont 1970; Marriott and Inden 1974; and Marriott 1976. I will have more to say on the position of Dumont in chap. 3, where the political and religious connections of *śakti*, power, to hierarchy and *jāti* status are demonstrated.

6. Exceptions to this norm for India are U. Sharma 1980a; M. Sharma 1985; Jeffery, Jeffery, and Lyon 1989; and Agrawal 1986, 1988. The term patriarchal is problematic: some scholars find it too laden with Eurocentric meanings while others question its validity for all castes and classes in India. I maintain that the Sweeper woman working outside of her home is still embedded in a system of male dominance as long as her husband has the fundamental right to rule her (and beat her), even if her voice in household affairs carries more weight than that of her landlord's wife. See Omvedt 1986 for a discussion of patriarchy as entailing a subordination of women that is rooted in the family.

7. I use gender to imply the process by which meaning is given to the perceived biological differences between men and women, a process that turns biological facts into social relationships. See also J. W. Scott 1986; Ortner and Whitehead, eds., 1981.

8. On this issue as it relates to the contemporary United States, see Rapp 1982.

9. Throughout this book, I have translated *jāti* names by their nearest English equivalent, usually an occupational designation, although most Karimpur residents in fact farm for a significant portion of their livelihood. *Jāti* names in English are capitalized; uncapitalized, these designations refer to someone who does the same work, but not as a traditional *jāti* occupation.

10. My thoughts on culture have been most extensively influenced by Geertz 1973; Wagner 1981; and Tambiah 1985. For performance theory, see Bauman 1977; Schieffelin 1985; and Brenneis 1987.

11. Geertz's work (1977) on Balinese and Moroccan personhood and Marriott's writings (1980) on the Hindu person have been critical to my thinking on this subject. With regard to the point about the verb "to be," it is interesting to contrast English and Hindi with Navajo, in which "to go" is the principal verb (Witherspoon 1977).

12. It is important to note that while Hindi grammar emphasizes action rather than state of being (and thus that the person is constantly in flux), Hindi grammar also emphasizes action *on* the person, rather than *by* the person. What we call the passive voice is accordingly much more common in Hindi than in English. Whether this syntactical pattern is truly "passive" or rather more complexly related to how different conceptions of personhood are manifested in grammar requires a study not possible here. Nevertheless, the pervasiveness of this grammatical pattern was forcibly brought home to me as I tried to rid the translations in this book of "Indian English"—to make them as true to idiom in the English as they were in the original Hindi. I found myself continually restructuring sentences to delete the passive voice.

13. See Ortner 1984 and Comaroff 1985 on the role of history and protest in human lives.

14. Bernard Cohn's classic article, "The Pasts of an Indian Village" (1961) contains the first mention of this issue for India. Here, I am expanding on Sahlins's notion of "different cultures, different historicities" (1985, viii) to include different groups within one larger social frame.

15. See Shankar 1987.

16. Derived from the Hindi word *ḍāku*, the British English term *dacoit* refers to a robber or thief. Some of these achieve legendary fame and are heralded in

myth and song. The fame of its dacoits was indeed Mainpuri District's sole source of renown elsewhere in North India.

17. At that time Mainpuri was the headquarters of the extensive district of Etawah, later subdivided into Etah, Mainpuri, and Etawah Districts.

18. In 1977–78 the Planning Commission set the poverty line at Rs. 65 per capita per month. By 1984 this figure was Rs. 80.

FOUR LIVES

1. The term *bahū* literally means daughter-in-law but also is the most common word in Karimpur for wife.

2. About $42.00 at the time (circa 1970).

3. *Gaunā* is the ceremony of the consummation of a marriage. Until recently, the *śādī*, the actual ceremony of marriage, took place some three years before the *gaunā*. At the *śādī*, the bride would visit the groom's house for only four to five days, then return to her parents until the *gaunā*, normally not celebrated until she reached menarche. At the time of *gaunā*, the bride would often stay a month or more at the husband's house. Thus, even though brides were often very young at the time of their *śādī*, the marriage was in name only for some years. More recently, however, with older brides the *gaunā* may occur within a year, or even at the time of the *śādī* itself. A third ceremony known as *ronā*, literally, "to cry," marks the bride's departure to stay more or less permanently with her husband's family.

4. Shankar is a rich Brahman landlord and farmer, who was also the village headman in the early 1980s.

5. That is, there were the four cousins sharing their father's land, while Raghunath, as sole heir to his father, had a share equal to the total of theirs.

6. "Engine" has now become a Hindi word, used to refer to a diesel-powered tube-well pump.

7. Raghunath used the local measure of *bīghā*: in the Karimpur area there are five *bīghā*s to an acre. I have translated the local measures into acres throughout this book.

8. Raghunath always spoke of his uncle's children as if they were his real brothers and sister.

9. An asterisk indicates that a term was in English in the original.

10. A panchayat is a council of elders, either of one's own *jāti* or of respected men in the village. The same term is used for the elected village council, which is what Raghunath is referring to here.

11. The Indian grading system gives the marks First Class (or Division), Second Class, Third Class, and Fail. Here Raghunath indicates that his boyhood friends were not good students.

12. North Indian villages are a nucleus of closely packed houses, often raised above the surrounding terrain, with fields spreading out toward the horizon. Members of similar castes, or *jāti*s, usually live adjacent to one another. The Wisers termed Raghunath's section of the village "Humble Lane" (Wiser and Wiser 1989).

13. See Wadley 1976b for a full discussion of this ritual and Raghunath's role in it.

14. In 1984, one rupee was worth about seven or eight cents.

15. It is inappropriate to eat sitting on a cot. A purified section of ground near the cooking hearth is the proper place to eat.

16. See Wadley 1992 for more on Saroj's political balancing act.

17. He was probably born in 1914. On the day of this interview, he and his older brother had a lengthy discussion of his date of birth. Other evidence is consistent with a 1914 birth date.

18. The anna was a coin in circulation prior to Independence. There were sixteen annas to a rupee.

19. In the 1920s the Karimpur school had only grades one and two. Bicchwan is a larger village located on the Grand Trunk Road, several miles to the east of Karimpur. Students walked there by a dirt path.

20. He married at age sixteen. His bride was ten.

CHAPTER 2: "THERE SHOULD BE CONTROL"

1. There is a resemblance between some of these concepts and those explored by Marriott (1989), especially in the relationships he notes between matching and coherence/unity and between control and unmarking. While I have difficulty applying all of the elements of his cube to the Karimpur data, I find the concepts of matching and unmarking particularly useful, especially in that they reinforce the hierarchical nature of control (unmarking) and the cohesion implied by matching.

2. Cultures, of course, embrace a range of conceptual models, associations, and prescriptions. Humans, in building their own social identities, link these elements in idiosyncratic ways, depending upon their own (complex) social relationships. The elements available are often presented in a given culture's public discourses, which present multiple, varying cultural images for people to work with. Images of women—complex, sometimes contradictory—are one such realm of Hindu culture, a realm that articulates a range of female identities and behavioral patterns out of which individuals can shape their own understandings of gender. See also Wiltenburg 1992.

3. Various authors have discussed the nature of women as defined in classical Hindu texts (Wadley 1977a) or by current belief (Bennett 1983). None of these discussions contradicts the argument here, although the Karimpur evidence reveals a greater complexity and contestation of viewpoints than earlier writers, including myself, recognized. Raheja and Gold (1994) also address this complexity, especially the distinction between fertility and sexuality.

4. This is a modified translation originally published in Wadley 1981a. This particular item is WC 017–27.

5. Sung by Surendra Dube, December 11, 1990, on the verandah of Umesh Pandey.

6. See Raheja 1988 for a detailed discussion related to inauspiciousness and its removal in North India.

7. See Babb 1981.

8. Thus, for example, like many others working in India, I have been able to interact with strange men with minimal harassment by calling them "brother."

9. On the subject of food and bodily harmony, see Pugh 1981.

10. See Toomey 1990.

11. See especially Marriott 1968 on this topic. See also Harper 1964; Dumont 1970. I rely in the following discussion on the ideas of the "open" Hindu person, the "mutable membranes" that form human beings and the objects of their material world. The work of McKim Marriott has been especially influential.

12. Early on, British observers noted the purification rites of Hindus that require the five products of the cow (dung, urine, milk, yoghurt, ghee). Milk, yoghurt, and ghee continue to be basic to Karimpur food habits, while a thin layer of dung is used on every festival day to purify family courtyards. Objects and materials also transmit the pollution of a person's touch. Thus, brass pots, the most easily polluted vessels, are never used in serving guests of lower rank. As a semi-untouchable outsider, I was never allowed to touch brassware, and women would often send for a glass or china cup from a neighbor's when serving me tea.

13. *Karva cauth* takes place on the fourth day of the dark half of Kartik, usually in early November. See Wadley 1980a for more details.

14. Trawick 1990b notes that in South India as well, sexual displays between spouses should be hidden.

15. In addition to the inter-*jāti* marriage that he proposes, he is also seeking a woman of higher social status than himself, which is even more problematic. Men are allowed sexual relations with women lower than themselves, but women should not have sexual relations with a lower man, as they will become polluted from his semen. For the girl, then, this proposed marriage is especially distasteful.

16. In other stories on the same theme, this place is clearly a *bāgh*, usually translated "garden" but in fact a grove of trees, a geographical space on the boundary of nature and culture, of cultivated and uncultivated.

17. The original is WC 017–38. Ann Gold (Raheja and Gold 1994) provides several vivid illustrations of the link between food and sex. In one *gālī* (abusive or lewd songs sung only by women, usually at weddings), a woman's excessive craving for sugarcane is equated with her desire to copulate.

18. Ashes are used to clean pots; hence the mother is being rubbed on pots in this construction.

19. On the subject of women's versus men's narratives, see Ramanujan 1991.

20. The ascetic holy man who entertains female visitors is a frequent figure in Karimpur folk tales. See also Narayan 1989.

21. Mohan tells a version of this story for the *ekādaśī vrat kathā* (the story of the fast of the eleventh day of each fortnight of the lunar month). Another variant is found in the opening segment of the epic *Dhola*.

22. See U. Sharma 1980b and Jacobson 1982 for more details on patterns of female seclusion and their implications for female access to material and cultural resources. See also Agrawal 1986 and 1988.

23. Compare this comment to the scene in Brijpal's earlier story where the Thakur takes his wife to the fair. Again, the fair provides an arena for male-female interactions and gazing. As the primary excursion and entertainment for women and children in rural north India, the yearly fair remains a major event. Further, since women do not frequent the daily markets, the fair is the one time in a year when secluded women can be seen by others.

24. Rapp 1982 has proved most critical to my understanding of this issue as it relates to India.

25. Brahmans are often considered *bhūdevatā*, gods on earth.

26. On the control of women's speech and its role in Karimpur musical events, see Wadley 1991b.

27. The right of the swami to remain silent was brought home to me in an encounter with one of India's more eminent gurus, Bhagvan Das of the Kine Rami sect, when he was visiting a friend in upstate New York. Although I speak rather fluent Hindi, everything that I said was interpreted through a disciple, to whom Bhagvan Das then responded in a low tone, slowly and very quietly. His words were finally relayed via the disciple back to me. Only after about an hour did he deign to speak directly to me. I am told that he uses a "translator" for all encounters, thereby putting great distance between the guru and devotee and also giving greater weight to his pronouncements.

28. Silence as a form of "language as power" deserves further study, although I found Bottigheimer 1986 and Elshtain 1982 to be particularly useful; see also Gal 1991. It is also possible that women must be silent in order to obtain the power to curse, as a swami obtains his powers through *tapas*, ascetic practices. But I never heard this explanation given in Karimpur. On some occasions, however, silence is a form of resistance, a refusal to accede to the norms.

29. Likewise, Shweder and Bourne (1982) note that Oriyas place little value on differentiating the person from the role.

30. See Wadley 1977a for further discussion of these specific rituals. Other sources crucial to understanding women's ritual roles in India include Bennett 1983; Thompson 1985; and Raheja 1989.

31. On this point, see Alan Roland's discussion of the "we-self" regard (Roland 1988). Roland states: "The feelings of inner regard or esteem are experienced not only around oneself and one's body image, but equally around the 'we' of the extended family, the particular community (*jati*) and other groups one belongs to. . . . Since there are powerful and pervasive feelings of esteem around the honor and reputation of one's family, particularly in relation to other families in one's community, public behavior always reflects on family reputation and affects other family members" (p. 242).

32. My thoughts on these matters have been influenced by, among others, Gilligan 1982; Ullrich 1987a and 1987b; and Kakar 1979 and 1981. Further, as Roland (1988, 249–50) points out, the daughter obtains her sense of "we-self" regard by adhering to the customs and traditions that uphold family honor.

33. These payments do add up, and many women cherish this small stash of cash for years afterwards.

34. Not surprisingly, this disregard for women is manifested in behavior toward them that includes lack of celebrations for female births, neglect of female children, and no extended period of mourning at the death of females. These issues are dealt with in later chapters. See also Miller 1981; Wadley and Derr 1986; and Wadley 1989b and 1993b.

35. For an excellent, if brief, discussion of family politics, see Davis 1976. Trawick 1990a provides another rich glimpse of South Indian family life, as does Hobson 1978.

36. For a good introduction to the subject of male sexuality in India, see Carstairs 1961. Other discussions include Kakar 1979 and 1981.

37. On the festival of Holi, see Marriott 1966.

38. *Bīḍīs* are local, hand-rolled cigarettes. *Pān* is betel leaves rolled with spices and tobacco, a favorite treat throughout India.

39. See Wadley and Derr 1989a for a fuller discussion of this fire as it related to Karimpur political economy and the concepts of sin (*pāp*) and fate (*karma*). The subject of fate will be further explored in chapter 4.

SHANKAR, THE VILLAGE HEADMAN, AND SUDHIR, A POOR BRAHMAN

1. Shankar is wrong here, as many Sweepers had jobs in Calcutta even in the early 1920s. But no one of his rank or education had had a job outside of the village.

2. According to the Uttar Pradesh Imposition of Ceiling on Land Holdings Act (1960), no one person is allowed to hold the title to more than forty acres of land (George 1972). If a family exceeds five members, though, an additional eight acres for each additional person could be added, up to a maximum of twenty acres (p. 13). Shankar thus feels that if he had had more children, he would not have lost any land because his holdings exceeded the legal limits when zamindars were abolished.

3. Here Shankar refers to a key component of the Hindu concept of fate, namely, that the fates of one's kin (and village) are interconnected with one's own. So Shankar wonders what he has done to bring this catastrophe on his daughter. See also Wadley and Derr 1989a.

CHAPTER 3:   "POWER COMES THROUGH MONEY"

1. The *Ramayana* is a major epic poem, with an attendant religious tradition, that is read and heard by Hindus in North India in a variety of retellings and per-formance styles. To touch someone's feet is a sign of respect.

2. In 1925 they controlled 74 percent of the agricultural land.

3. Although his story began with four sons, Raghunath never discussed the status and *jāti* of the fourth.

4. In other words, class relations are marked more by *jāti* membership than by actual economic situation: in Karimpur, belonging to a high class is a matter not of wealth but of being a Brahman. Thus, one almost comparably wealthy but small *jāti*, the Accountants, align themselves with the *chotī jāti*s. See also J. C. Scott 1986, 44–45, for a discussion of class as it is lived in Malaysia.

5. These reforms were mandated by the central government, but their imple-mentation was left as a matter for the individual state governments. In the case of Karimpur, land reform was enacted in the Uttar Pradesh Zamindari Abolition and Land Reforms Act (1950). For more details on this process, see Derr 1979a; Wadley and Derr 1989b.

6. There are one hundred *paise* in a rupee. In 1984, fifty *paise* were equiva-lent to about four cents.

7. Among other things, Leatherworkers had the responsibility to remove the carcasses of dead animals, but in Karimpur they were also full-time laborers for their *jajmān*s.

8. Holi and Divali are the major festivals celebrated in Karimpur. Each occurs around the time of a major harvest—Holi, the festival of color-throwing and revelry, in the spring, and Divali, the festival of lights, in the fall. For both, houses are cleaned and whitewashed. For more on Karimpur festival cycles, see Wadley 1975a (= 1986c).

9. Workers were often entitled to go to the fields at each harvest and claim a given amount of grain or other produce. Mohan mentions these payments regularly.

10. For ease of comprehension, I have transformed all weights into pounds.

11. Mohan used the male pronoun, but in fact about half of those who do this work are women.

12. On Pitcher Fourth, a woman is supposed to present her husband with a pitcher full of sweets.

13. Each *jāti* is, of course, composed of both men and women, but only some have specifically female jobs. The traditional daily work of the Sweepers is almost entirely performed by women. Although male sweepers can do outdoor cleaning chores, they more often engage in some other lowly occupation, such as raising pigs or making baskets, as well as working as hired field laborers (like members of many *jāti*s).

14. They received a portion of the grain sent for parching as payment, but Brahmans paid a lesser share than did others in the village.

15. The Cotton Carder (*dhunā*), Bangle Seller (*manihār*), and Faqir are all Muslim *jāti*s. They do not intermarry among themselves and are separately ranked in Karimpur. Muslims constitute about 6.5 percent of the Karimpur population.

16. The language of giving and receiving in Karimpur is complex and requires an analysis in its own right. According to Karimpur informants, *dān-dakṣiṇā* can be given only to those who are high or Brahman (the *rāy jāti* is considered a low Brahman group). *Bainā* are gifts made to *kamīn*s who work for you. Offerings to remove inauspiciousness, such as the small pots of grain circled over the heads of a singer, bride, or groom, are called *nyeochār*. In wedding ceremonies, the *dān-dakṣiṇā* given the Brahman priest is kept separate from the *nyeochār* given the serving *jāti*s (Barber, Watercarrier, Washerman, etc.), and the *dān* for the priest is *not* circled over the couple. Both the language of gift giving in Karimpur and the concepts and rules governing it differ markedly from the language and rules found by Raheja (1988). Two factors seem critical: Karimpur is a village dominated by a single high caste, so that gifts that mark hierarchy may be more critical. Second, *bhakti*—devotional religion—is significant in this area, unlike the area in which Raheja worked.

17. The husband-wife relationship is also seen as one of halves, where the wife is said to be the half-body of her husband. It is revealing that the same concept underlies *jajmān-kamīn* and husband-wife.

18. W. Wiser 1958, 120–21.

19. Ibid., 118–19.

20. Ibid., xxlv.

21. For more on the power of Hindu deities, see Wadley 1975a (= 1986c).

22. See Pugh 1981 for more on this topic.

23. Ravan is the antihero of the popular epic, the *Ramayana*. He is destroyed by the gods after he uses his powers against society.

24. Honor, like fate, *karma*, is shared among the group to which one belongs. Recall, too, Roland's concept of we-self regard as it pertains to Indians (Roland 1988).

25. See Wadley 1981a for the complete story.

26. *Sanskritization* is a term first used by Srinivas (1956) to describe the process whereby the lifestyles of the lower groups are changed so as to match what are perceived as the "Sanskritic" and hence more proper lifestyles of those higher in the *jāti* hierarchy. Sanskritization is contrasted to Westernization, the copying of lifestyles brought by the British and more recently through other channels.

SHEILA, THE WASHERWOMAN

1. Brother's Second is a ritual during which girls and women worship their brothers. Taking place after Divali in the fall festival cycle, it is a time when women often go to their natal homes.

2. The implication is that she was not sent empty-handed but in fact took minor gifts for the ritual with her. Nevertheless, in the next sentence she tells us that they improperly sent her without a male escort.

3. Sheila almost always used the term *kismat* for fate. This Urdu-derived word is sometimes understood to mean luck rather than a fate with which your are born, but it is clear from Sheila's use, as in *merī kismat men likhī hai*, "it is written in my *kismat*," that she intended *kismat* to be almost if not fully synonymous with *karma*, for it is *karma* that is written at birth by the goddess of fate, Behmata.

4. *Harīrā* is a dish served to new mothers to replace the heat in their bodies that they have lost through childbirth and is their primary food for the first days after birth. It also contains jaggery, ginger, and other spices. (*Harīrā* means "happiness," so we might translate the name of this dish as "food of happiness.") Since Sheila had no female relatives around, her husband made it. She also says that he cooks whenever she cannot.

5. Births, especially of sons, are celebrated with rituals and songs. *Satiyā* is an auspicious design, the Hindu version of the swastika, made in cow dung on the housefront. *Caruvā* is a milk pot decorated with cow dung and barley seeds (a symbol of fertility) in which water for the new mother is heated.

6. Sheila here identifies a woman from another *jāti*, a Midwife, as her honorary mother-in-law, as there are no Washerwomen in the village who could have that relationship to her, even fictively.

7. Most families in Karimpur eat only twice a day, usually at about 10 A.M. and again in the evening. A few wealthier families may serve tea in the early morning, at least for the adult men.

8. These are foods categorized as "cold" but are not literally cold in our sense of unheated. Cold foods include those she has listed plus things like refined sugar (whereas raw sugar, jaggery, is "hot"). The idea is that one should eat foods that provide balance to one's bodily state. Thus, during the hot season or when feverish, one should eat "cold" foods. There is no a priori rationale for the categorization of foods as hot or cold. However, most foods harvested during the cold season (such as peanuts, fennel, and jaggery) are considered "hot," while those harvested in the hot season (carrots, chick-peas, melons, and cucumbers, for example) are "cold."

9. Note that Sheila is not allowed to say her husband's name, so she must use pronouns or circumlocutions like "this one's father."

CHAPTER 4: "POVERTY IS WRITTEN IN MY DESTINY"

1. WC, song 42.

2. This song, an old *kīrtan*, was sung to me by Mr. Adranji, a teacher at the junior school, December 10, 1983.

3. WC, song 187.

4. For a fuller explication of fate, sin, and merit in the context of the Karimpur fire, see Wadley and Derr 1989a.

5. Classical Indian philosophy acknowledges three kinds of *karma*: *prārabdha karma*, which has already begun to yield its fruit and has resulted in your present birth; stored *karma* from the past, or *sancita karma*, which has not yet begun to yield its fruit; and *kriyamāna karma*, the *karma* that you perform in the present life. The only types of *karma* that can be changed by religious ritual or knowledge are *sancita* and *kriyamāna*; *prārabdha* must be lived out in its entirety (Dasgupta 1961, 414). Karimpur residents believe, however, that the fruits of all *karma* start accruing immediately: the categories of *prārabdha* and *sancita* essentially do not exist. Thus all kinds of *karma* can be changed in this lifetime. (See also Wadley 1983.) I am grateful to Phyllis Granoff for her help in untangling this web.

6. Note that Saroj does not count her son's daughter as a child in this statement. For her, a marriage that has, in over seventeen years, resulted in only one child, a mere girl, is essentially infertile.

7. See Wadley 1975a, 110–12, for a fuller explanation of sorrow and distress in relationship to the actions of the gods.

8. Wadley 1983 deals specifically with the role of ritual behavior in altering one's fate. For more on the story of Shiva and the son, see Wadley 1975a and 1983.

9. Likewise, J. C. Scott (1985, 2) notes that being poor in Malaysia, without proper housing, is equated with living like chickens.

10. In her study of the elderly in Delhi, Vatuk (1990) found a similar refrain of "working with my hands" to be a mark of fitness.

11. In the imagery here, the mother has become the goddess Durga, who rides a lion, while the father is Yamraj, the god of death. The excerpt is taken from Wadley 1989a, 88–89.

12. The song was sung by Watercarrier women on the occasion of Shiv Teras, a festival honoring Shiva and Parvati, February 29, 1984. It is an old *kīrtan*.

13. The term *chaumāsī* derives from two facets of the religious calendar. The gods are believed to sleep for four months, from mid-Asharh until mid-Kartik (July through October). Further, gurus, sadhus, and other holy men retreat to their ashrams for the four months of the rainy season, primarily because of the difficulty of traveling at that time.

14. This is a song known and sung only by males. Perhaps by putting its words in the wife's mouth, poor men are able to rebel without being seen as rebelling and are thus able safely to state resistance.

15. *Kājal* is the lampblack used as eyeliner. An auspicious substance, it protects children from the evil eye.

16. Here she implies that her husband bribed him for the land.

17. Occurring on the third day of the dark half of Savan, Green Third is a festival for daughters, who ideally visit their parents' home during this month. On this day, they worship Shiva and Parvati.

18. The work of Robert Chambers led me to think seriously about various aspects of seasonality: see Chambers, Longhurst, and Pacey, eds., 1981. For more on disease and ecology in northern India, see Arnold 1989.

19. Snake's Fifth (nāg pancmī) takes place on the fifth day of the bright half of Savan (July–August). During the monsoon, snakes are a greater threat than at other times, since their normal habitats are flooded. Women worship snakes on this day, especially Basuk Dev, the king of snakes.

20. For more on Karimpur births and their relationship to fertility, see Wadley 1993b; and Wadley and Derr 1986. For more on issues of childhood mortality in northern India, see Smucker at al. 1980; Miller 1981; Caldwell, Reddy, and Caldwell 1982 and 1984; Nag and Kak 1984; Jain 1985; and Das Gupta 1987.

21. These figures are based on retrospective fertility histories of all women living in the village who were ever married, which yielded a sample of 2,324 children. These fertility records were then used to generate a tentative year of birth and death for each child, using census data as a check. Women were reinterviewed to eliminate discrepancies. The results, I believe, are more accurate retrospective fertility histories than are normally the case.

Parents were asked what they understood to be the cause of death. The resulting data are by no means medically accurate, especially since most of these children died without seeing a doctor. However, the parent's belief is certainly better than no answer at all and in most cases represents, I believe, a modicum of truth.

In addition, Indian data on fertility are always suspect because of a bias toward the underreporting of female births and deaths. After closely examining the data developed from the retrospective fertility histories, I believe that there was indeed some such underreporting. For the purposes of this analysis, however, I have used the unadjusted figures, but I should issue the caution that the number of female births and deaths, especially neonatal deaths caused by tetanus, may be understated.

22. See Wadley (In press) for a fuller discussion of widows' options in Karimpur.

23. My knowledge of the limitations of these units comes from my experience in trying to obtain medical care for sick villagers. These included a teenage girl who died of childbirth fever, and Santoshi's nephew, who was hit by a car on the main road in Karimpur. Because of the dangers of traveling at night, it was impossible to get this child to Agra (and the probability of his surviving the trip was in any event minuscule). In addition, we took numerous women and children to the government clinics for everything ranging from malaria to worm infestations to ear infections. One group taken to the Christian hospital in Kasganj included a man with leprosy, a barren women, and a man with kidney stones (who later had an operation there). One night Prakash's fourteen-year-old grandson arrived at our rooms in Mainpuri in the midst of a monsoon downpour, with his mother and two sisters in a rickshaw, all ill. We put them in the car and took them to the quarters of the government doctor: two had pneumonia and one complications from malaria. After purchasing the necessary drugs and marking them so that this young boy could administer them to the right individual in the right dosages, we sent them all home by car.

Despite the prevalence of dysentery, it was impossible to get a stool test for amoebas in Mainpuri. And my faith in doctors there died when I went to one for diarrhea and was given a pill with a glass of water drawn directly from the faucet to swallow it with. I suffer from serious recurrent ear infections and yet never found a doctor in Mainpuri who used an otoscope. Worse yet, needles used by doctors both in the village and in Mainpuri were rarely sterilized. Unless health practices change dramatically, the AIDS epidemic now threatening India will be very serious, spreading rapidly to all segments of the population.

24. I have argued elsewhere (Wadley 1993b) that the desire for male children who can quickly begin to earn their keep is a key factor in the increased fertility and the growing disparity in the survival rates of male and female children amongst the poor. In order to have more sons, poor families are having more children. But since this also increases the number of female children, more daughters fail to thrive.

25. See Wadley 1976b for more on this ritual.

26. *Kīrtan* as term describing a singing event has different meanings depending upon its context and class associations. Middle- and lower-ranked men often use the word to mean an event in which they sing continuously for some stated period of time (such as twenty-four hours), while Brahman men usually use it to refer to a event in which there is a lot of solo singing, with numerous instruments and a competitive element as well.

27. I shall always regret the 1968 fair when I purchased whistles for all seven small children in my village family! For days, shrill blasts penetrated every corner of our village home.

28. My debt to J. C. Scott 1985 is obvious here. Abu-Lughod's recent article (1990a) has also clarified my thoughts on peasant resistance.

29. *Hari*, greenness, is a symbol of prosperity and good fortune. A bride wears green bangles, and the monsoon festival discussed earlier is called Green Third.

30. Midwifery is not always hereditary. Jeffery, Jeffery, and Lyon (1989) report on villages several hundred miles to the north of Karimpur where midwives have chosen to attain those skills, often out of economic necessity. But in Karimpur the families of the *dhānuk jāti* have always provided midwives for the rest of the village (except Sweepers), with hereditary ties linking each *dhānuk* family to its *jajmān*s. Like other *jajmānī* relations, these links could be broken only through mutual consent and permission from *jāti* panchayats. These hereditary links between midwives and patrons were still largely in place in 1984.

31. See also Harper 1968 on long-term indentured servants whose work was shabbily done.

32. See J. C. Scott 1985 for further discussion of the meaning of being poor.

CHAPTER 5: "THE DOMINATION OF INDIRA"

1. In 1984, when this research was carried out, Indira Gandhi was prime minister of India. In this statement, she symbolically represents "government" in all its many manifestations.

2. For more on these issues, see Bardhan 1984; Desai, Rudolph, and Rudra, eds., 1984; Herring 1984; and Gupta 1987.

3. For an analysis of rural change, especially agricultural change, in north India, see Etienne 1982 and 1988; and Gupta 1987. The communities in Uttar Pradesh examined by these authors are about a hundred miles northeast of Karimpur. Jeffery, Jeffery, and Lyon 1989 contains many insights into rural social structure and change, particularly as it affects women. Kessinger 1974 discusses a community in the Punjab; Chakravarti 1975 a village in Rajasthan; and Harriss 1982 and Mencher 1978 communities in Tamil Nadu.

4. Derr (1979a, 21) reports this story, which an older Muslim man told him in 1974:

> There were four or six houses of Thakurs in Karimpur. The Thakurs and Brahmans here fought, with the result that the Thakurs sent the Brahmans out of the village. The Brahmans went to Aliganj, where the main house of Khan Bahadur was. The Brahmans complained in this way: "The Thakurs beat us and threw us out." Then Khan Bahadur came riding his elephant to the village. Beating the Thakurs, he sent them away. Some of the Thakurs live in Laharipur, Singharpur, and Bagholi—on all four sides [of Karimpur]. Not one single Thakur was left in Karimpur. Then Khan Bahadur said, "I am putting the foundation of this village, and if here will live a single Brahman he will be powerful in this village."

Another version of the story appears in C. Wiser 1978, 144–45. To this day, a shrine to Khan Bahadur located on the top of the ruined fort to the west of the village is worshiped on most Thursdays by Hindu and Muslim residents who seek his aid in some predicament. Khan Bahadur was probably one Yaqut Khan, alias Khan Bahadur Khan, founder of Aliganj, who was killed in battle in 1748 (Derr 1979a, 22).

5. I have calculated a generation at twenty years: given the early marriage age of Karimpur residents, the period separating father from oldest child is rarely more than twenty years. This calculation also fits with the period in which Khan Bahadur lived.

6. W. Wiser 1933, 233. For a fuller discussion of the history of land ownership in Karimpur, see Derr 1979a, 20–29; 100–120. Neale 1962, Metcalf 1979, Stokes 1975, and Whitcombe 1971 provide further insight into the history of land tenure in India, and in North India specifically.

7. Since the Agra Tenancy Act protected tenants from arbitrary rent increases, proprietors started levying an additional tribute called *nazrānā* from tenants, with rates up to forty or fifty rupees per acre in the subdistrict (*tahsil*) to which Karimpur belongs. An Accountant in the village, who himself worked as land record-keeper elsewhere, said that "*nazrānā* was a kind of tip for them, which the landlords used to levy as a fine." It was levied on behalf of the raja, but no receipts were given. Moreover, while a hundred rupees might be demanded from the farmer, the raja would see only a portion, perhaps fifty rupees, the rest being "eaten" by his agents.

8. Permanent tenants were one of seven classes of tenants defined by the Agra Tenancy Act (Local Act III of 1926): permanent tenure holders, fixed-rate tenants, exproprietary tenants, occupancy tenants, statutory tenants, heirs of statutory tenants, and nonoccupancy tenants (W. Wiser 1933, 239). See also Derr 1979a, 105–10.

9. Other rental and sharecropping systems are also found. A common form was *chautāī*, quarter shares, in which a man worked for the whole year with a

given farmer, putting in a quarter of the inputs (but no animals or tools) and receiving a quarter of the crop in return. Rent (*agotārā*) was on the increase in 1984, with rates ranging from Rs. 300 to Rs. 700 per 0.2 acres.

10. On the loss of common property resources throughout India, see Jodha 1990. Land redistribution, like land sales, also points up the increased necessity of dealing with government officials, as opposed to the zamindar and his agents. For the importance of the shift from psychological relationships with the landlord to those with the government, see Kakar 1981.

11. See Derr 1979a, 151–59. See also Oldenberg 1987 and 1990 for a discussion of land consolidation as land reform in Uttar Pradesh and also of corruption in relation to land consolidation.

12. The 1968 figure comes from an interview that I conducted with the tube-well operator in July 1968. The 1975 figure is from an interview by Derr with the operator in April 1975. The tube-well operator attributed the decrease in the command area to the increase in private tube wells. Further, most villagers said that the tube well served at most one-third of the village fields (about three hundred acres). This figure is confirmed by the fact that in 1975, of the 3.18 miles of lined channels, only 1.42 were frequently used, 0.69 miles rarely used, and 1.07 miles never used.

13. We were told by some farmers that no loans were available to purchase electric motors, although I was unable to confirm this allegation.

14. Blair 1981 compares the Indian block development program to participatory programs in Bangladesh, Pakistan, and the United States. See also Heginbotham 1975 for an insightful discussion of the community development model as implemented in South India. Franda 1979 discusses the success of cooperative ventures in India.

15. For more on Saroj's leadership role, see Wadley 1992.

16. Following J. C. Scott (1985), this manipulation could also be considered a form of resistance. Certainly it involves a blatant disregard of stated rules.

17. This jump in food grain production occurred throughout India. For all of India, production went from more than 54 million tons in 1949–50, to 89 million tons in 1964–65, to 108.4 million tons in 1970–71, 131.9 million tons in 1978–79, and 152.4 million tons in 1983–84 (Sharma and Dak 1989, 2–3). Likewise, the productivity per hectare in India as a whole rose from 653 kilos in 1952 to 1,851 kilos in 1985, and in the Punjab yields were as high as 3,200 kilos per hectare (ibid., 3).

18. The Mainpuri region, lacking canal irrigation, did not have an adequate supply of water in the 1960s and 1970s for large-scale sugarcane production. Hence there are no sugar mills in the area, nor is there the intensive sugarcane cultivation that one finds in Bijnor and Muzzafnagar Districts north of Delhi.

19. See Derr 1979a, 178–79, for more on cash crops in Karimpur. Manwar 1990 points to the importance of family labor in the subsistence farming of South Asia. In particular, he shows that if labor costs were counted, Bangladeshi farmers would find farming totally unprofitable.

20. If we assume that a set of the least expensive clothing costs maybe one hundred rupees, each member of this fictional family could afford three sets of clothes per year—but this would leave nothing for medical bills, bedding, school-books, bus fares, and so on.

21. Rath 1985 provides a description of the hopes and failures of this program and a critical analysis of its various components. For further discussion of development projects, and of outside aid to India, see Chakravarty 1987; and Lipton and Toye 1990.

22. The following analysis is based on an unpublished paper by Bruce Derr (Derr 1984).

23. In *vapāsī benāmā* a landowner signs an agreement with another person to the effect that the landowner will receive a sum of money and that the loan is to be repaid in a certain amount of time or the lender will receive the title to whatever land is stipulated in the agreement.

24. See Cohn 1959 and 1965 for an analysis of consensual dispute settlement in India.

25. Literally, that the Thakur "would do justice" (*nyāy kariye*). As in most comparable Hindi phrases, here an action is implied but the Thakur per se is not said to be just—in contrast to the English emphasis on "states of being." Note, too, that over time what is meant by "justice" can and does change. The same story, up to this point, is discussed in Moore 1990. Her informants, whose version of the tale apparently did not include the conclusion that appears here, said that the story illustrates the blindness of the big men who arbitrate justice.

26. This was not a dowry death, in that the boy's family was not seeking additional money from her family. Nor did anyone think that there was exceptional abuse, beyond what "normally" occurred in this household. As we learned earlier, Raghunath's wife also burned herself to death on account of abusive in-laws, so that there is a history of such incidents in Karimpur prior to the so-called dowry deaths current in Delhi and other North Indian cities.

27. The dispute over who would accompany the injured girl revolved around who was willing to be present and hence responsible if and when she died: all of the adult males refused to go, for they knew that they would be held accountable if she died.

28. In 1976 Indira Gandhi claimed emergency powers and disbanded parliament. During this period of authoritarian rule, under the influence of her son Sanjay, family planning programs were intensified and many forced into unwanted procedures.

29. There is also the argument that if women are to have control of their bodies, this means that they have the right to choose to have children as well as the right to choose not to have children. Governments that mandate family planning for their own purposes are, moreover, denying families the right to choose their own lifestyles. For Karimpur's poor, more children, especially sons, are desirable. See Wadley 1993b; Cain 1981. On family planning policies in Bijnor District, Uttar Pradesh, see Jeffery, Jeffery, and Lyon 1989.

30. For more on the quality of soil and its relationship to what is grown, see Daniel 1984. In an unpublished article, Vasavi (n.d.) notes that in Karnataka "hybrid" seeds are believed to lead to "hybrid" people, people who are weak and have moral and physical defects.

CHAPTER 6:   "NOW LOVE IS TOTALLY LOST"

1. It is the ritual aspects of *jajmānī*, however, that have been the focus of earlier discussions of the endurance of the *jajmānī* system. See Beidelman 1959; Gould 1964; and Elder 1970; see also Commander 1983, for an overview.

2. As we were leaving in 1984, the milk sellers were beginning to feel the effects of new inspection measures designed to cut down on the watering down of milk that had been taking place between the villages and the cities. New regulations were also being promulgated that would require milk sellers to be licensed. Such measures will undoubtedly affect the popularity of this source of income in the future.

3. Boserup 1990 surveys the literature on women and agricultural development.

4. See Wadley and Derr 1989b for a detailed analysis of this issue.

5. The literature on *jāti* hierarchies is extensive. See especially Marriott 1968 and 1976; Dumont 1970; Raheja 1988.

6. Women have fewer opportunities to eat outside of their homes. Further, they frequently carry cooked food when traveling or bring along their own pots and grain to cook for themselves. Men's eating behavior also seems to change by distance: in Mainpuri, for example, a Brahman would not eat food cooked by a Muslim, but in Delhi he might.

7. In terming these "early" rebellions, I am not denying that there was resistance to the landlords prior to the 1920s. However, I heard no stories of events prior to this time, when elders like Mohan were young children and hence could presumably remember events that had taken place during their lifetimes. On the point about revolts over subsistence needs, see J. C. Scott 1986.

8. Rituals can be considered modes of exercising or seeking to exercise power symbolically. Certainly the actions discussed here, whether forms of greeting or the events of the Holi festival, are rituals in which Brahmans seek to exercise, and the poor seek to undercut, power as it is symbolically manifested. See also Prakash 1990.

9. The most critical work on Holi is Marriott 1966. Several events in Karimpur are different than those in the village where Marriott worked, Kishan Garhi, a hundred or so miles away, but the essential elements of the festival are similar.

10. In Karimpur the explanation for this practice is that a daughter is considered "higher" than the males of her patriline, as she will marry out, into a higher status family. Hence, even unmarried girls are higher than the older male kin and should be honored by having their feet touched.

11. There is thus a greater percentage of nuclear families among the poor than among those more affluent. In actual fact, however, although the proportion of joint families has decreased slightly over the past decade, larger families have meant that the actual percentage of the population living in joint families has increased. Moreover, these joint families are more likely now than in the 1920s to be lineal families, that is, a father and mother living with their married sons and their families. The short life spans in the early part of the century usually prevented a lineal joint family from developing, as at least one parent would typically die at a relatively young age. See Wadley and Derr 1988 for an analysis of Karimpur family structures over time. See also Freed and Freed 1982 and 1983 for a similar discussion.

12. "Mommy" is in English in the original text, with the addition of an honorific *jī: māmmijī*, which I have translated as "dearest mommy."

13. See Wadley 1993b for a fuller discussion of this issue.

14. *Lagun* is a ceremony that proceeds the actual marriage by several weeks. The major cash portion of the dowry is given then.

15. In an excellent article on social security for North Indian families, Dreze (1988) notes that his informants felt that respect and care by sons of parents was diminishing rapidly, something that they attributed to the spread of individualistic values.

16. See Kakar 1981, chap. 6.

17. See Ahmed 1992. On disorder in early modern Europe, see Fletcher and Stevenson, eds., 1985; and Amussen 1988. Wiltenburg 1992 discusses disorder and females in this same period.

18. I do not have any evidence to suggest that the secularism preached by India's leaders throughout the twentieth century ever really reached the ears of my friends in Karimpur.

19. In Karimpur, these are actually termed *dhotī*. They are half a yard shorter than the sari and themselves reflect a change from the full gathered skirt and loose shirt worn sixty years ago. The woman's *dhotī* is also wrapped differently than a sari. Nowadays, though, the younger women will don the longer sari on festive occasions: one of my fondest memories of my days in Karimpur is of teaching the teenage girls in my family there how to wrap a sari "Delhi-style" for the Holi festival in 1975.

EPILOGUE

1. This conclusion, which is based on personal observation and comments made by friends in Karimpur, was affirmed by David Sopher when he visited Karimpur and nearby villages in the mid-1970s.

2. This is not to deny that there are many communities in India where control of the low remains rigid, often enforced with violence. But in those communities—and urban areas—where the low have begun to break the bonds of oppression, most women continue to be bound by rules and practices of subordination.

Bibliography

Abu-Lughod, Lila
    1990a   "The Romance of Resistance: Tracing Transformations of Power through Bedouin Women." *American Ethnologist* 17: 41–55.
    1990b   "Can There Be a Feminist Ethnography?" *Women and Performance* 5: 7–27.

Agarwal, Bina
    1986   "Women, Poverty, and Agricultural Growth in India." *Journal of Peasant Studies* 13: 165–220.
    1988   "Who Sows? Who Reaps? Women and Land Rights in India." *Journal of Peasant Studies* 15: 531–81.

Ahmed, Akbar S.
    1992   *Postmodernism and Islam: Predicament and Promise.* New York: Routledge.

Amussen, Susan Dwyer
    1988   *An Ordered Society: Gender and Class in Early Modern England.* New York: Basil Blackwell.

Arnold, David
    1989   "The Ecology and Cosmology of Disease in the Banaras Region." In Sandria B. Freitag, ed., *Culture and Power in Banaras: Community, Performance, and Environment, 1800–1980,* 246–67. Berkeley: University of California Press.

Babb, Lawrence Alan
    1981   "Glancing: Visual Interaction in Hinduism." *Journal of Anthropological Research* 37: 47–64.

Bardhan, Pranab K.
    1984   *Land, Labor, and Rural Poverty: Essays in Development Economics.* Delhi: Oxford University Press.

Bauman, Richard
    1977   *Verbal Art as Performance*. Rawley, Mass.: Newbury House
                Publishers.
Beidelman, Thomas O.
    1959   *A Comparative Analysis of the Jajmani System*. Locust Valley,
                N.Y.: J. J. Augustin.
Bennett, Lynn
    1983   *Dangerous Wives and Sacred Sisters: Social and Symbolic Roles of
                High-Caste Women in Nepal*. New York: Columbia University
                Press.
Blair, Harry W.
    1981   *The Political Economy of Participation in Local Development Pro-
                grams: Short-Term Impasse and Long-Term Change in South Asia
                and the United States from the 1950s to the 1970s*. Ithaca: Rural
                Development Committee, Cornell University.
Boserup, Ester
    1990   "Population, the Status of Women, and Rural Development." In
                Geoffrey McNicoll and Mead Cain, eds., *Rural Development and
                Population: Institutions and Policy*, 45–60. New York: Oxford
                University Press.
Bottigheimer, Ruth B.
    1986   "Silenced Women in Grimms' Tales: The 'Fit' between Fairy Tales
                and Society in Their Historical Context." In Ruth B. Bottigheimer,
                ed., *Fairy Tales and Society: Illusion, Allusion, and Paradigm*,
                115–32. Philadelphia: University of Pennsylvania Press.
Breman, Jan
    1987   *The Shattered Image: Construction and Deconstruction of the Vil-
                lage in Colonial Asia*. Amsterdam: Center for Asian Studies.
Brenneis, Donald
    1987   "Performing Passions: Aesthetics and Politics in an Occasionally
                Egalitarian Community." *American Ethnologist* 14: 236–50.
Bruner, Edward M., ed.
    1988   *Text, Play, and Story: The Construction and Reconstruction of Self
                and Society*. Prospect Heights, Ill.: Waveland Press. Orig. publ.
                Washington, D.C.: American Ethnological Society, 1984.
Cain, Mead
    1981   "Risk and Insurance: Perspectives on Fertility and Agrarian
                Change in India and Bangladesh." *Population and Development
                Review* 7: 435–74.
Caldwell, John C., P. H. Reddy, and Pat Caldwell
    1982   "The Causes of Demographic Change in Rural South India."
                Population and Development Review 8: 689–727.
    1984   "The Determinants of Fertility Decline in Rural South India." In
                Tim Dyson and Nigel Crook, eds., *India's Demography: Essays on
                the Contemporary Population*, 187–207. New Delhi: South Asian
                Publishers.

Carstairs, G. Morris
    1961   *The Twice-Born: A Study of a Community of High-Caste Hindus.*
                Bloomington: Indiana University Press.
Chakravarti, Anand
    1975   *Contradiction and Change: Emerging Patterns of Authority in a*
                Rajasthan Village. Delhi: Oxford University Press.
Chakravarty, Sukhamoy
    1987   *Development Planning: The Indian Experience.* Oxford: Claren-
                don Press.
Chambers, Robert, Richard Longhurst, and Arnold Pacey, eds.
    1981   *Seasonal Dimensions to Rural Poverty.* London: Frances Pinter.
Clifford, James
    1988   *The Predicament of Culture: Twentieth-Century Ethnography, Lit-*
                erature, and Art. Cambridge, Mass.: Harvard University Press.
Cohn, Barnard S.
    1959   "Some Notes on Law and Change in North India." *Economic De-*
                velopment and Cultural Change 8: 79–93.
    1961   "The Pasts of an Indian Village." *Comparative Studies in Society*
                and History 3: 241–49.
    1965   "Anthropological Notes on Disputes and Law in India." *Ameri-*
                can Anthropologist 67: 82–122.
Comaroff, Jean
    1985   *Body of Power, Spirit of Resistance: The Culture and History of a*
                South African People. Chicago: University of Chicago Press.
Commander, Simon
    1983   "The Jajmani System in North India: An Examination of Its Logic
                and Status across Two Centuries." *Modern Asian Studies* 17:
                283–311.
Daniel, E. Valentine
    1984   *Fluid Signs: Being a Person the Tamil Way.* Berkeley: University
                of California Press.
Das, Arvind N.
    1986   *The "Longue Durée": Continuity and Change in Changel. Exercise*
                in Undocumented, Local, Oral Historiography of an Indian Vil-
                lage from the 18th towards the 21st Century. Rotterdam: Compar-
                ative Asian Studies Programme, Erasmus University.
Das Gupta, Monica
    1977   "From a Closed to an Open System: Fertility Behavior in a Chang-
                ing Indian Village." In T. Scarlett Epstein and Darrell Jackson,
                eds., *The Feasibility of Fertility Planning: Micro-Perspectives,*
                97–121. Oxford: Pergammon Press.
    1987   "Selective Discrimination against Female Children in Rural Pun-
                jab, India." *Population and Development Review* 13: 77–100.
Dasgupta, S.
    1961   *A History of Indian Philosophy,* vol. 3. Cambridge: Cambridge
                University Press.

Davis, Marvin
   1976   "The Politics of Family Life in Rural West Bengal." *Ethnology* 15: 189–200.
Derr, Bruce W.
   1976   "The Illiterate Peasant Farmer: A Misunderstood Expert." Paper presented at the New York State Conference on Asian Studies, Albany.
   1977   "More People, More Food, More Poverty: Karimpur, 1925–1975." Paper presented at the annual meeting of the North India Studies Association in conjunction with the annual meeting of the Association for Asian Studies, New York City.
   1979a   *The Growing Abundance of Food and Poverty in a North Indian Village: Karimpur, 1925–1975.* Ph.D. diss., Syracuse University.
   1979b   "Karimpur Kids: Economic and Demographic Aspects of Population Growth in Karimpur." Paper presented at the Eighth Annual Conference on South Asia, Madison, Wisconsin.
   1980   "Jajmani in Karimpur: Fifty Years after Wiser." Paper presented at the Ninth Annual Conference on South Asia, Madison, Wisconsin.
   1981a   "Sharecropping in Karimpur: Contemporary Forms and Tendencies." In *Proceedings of the Second International Symposium on Asian Studies 1980*, vol. 4, *South and Southwest Asia*, 589–99. Hong Kong: Asian Research Service.
   1981b   "Farmers at the Edge of Subsistence." Paper presented at the annual meeting of the Association for Asian Studies, Toronto.
   1984   " 'Ham Garibi Log': The 'New Poor' in Karimpur." Paper presented at the Thirteenth Annual Conference on South Asia, Madison, Wisconsin.
Desai, Meghnad, Susanne Rudolph, and Ashok Rudra, eds.
   1984   *Agrarian Power and Agricultural Productivity in South Asia.* Delhi: Oxford University Press.
Dimmitt, Cornelia, and J.A.B. van Buitenen
   1978   *Classical Hindu Mythology: A Reader in the Sanskrit Purāṇas.* Philadelphia: Temple University Press.
Dirks, Nicholas B.
   1989   "The Original Caste: Power, History and Hierarchy in South Asia." *Contributions to Indian Sociology* 23: 59–78.
Dreze, Jean
   1988   "Social Insecurity in India: A Case Study." Paper presented at the Workshop on Social Security in Developing Countries, London School of Economics, London.
Dumont, Louis
   1970   *Homo Hierarchicus: An Essay on the Caste System.* Chicago: University of Chicago Press.
Elder, Joseph W.
   1970   "Rajpur: Change in the Jajmānī System of an Uttar Pradesh Village." In K. Ishwaran, ed., *Change and Continuity in India's Villages*, 105–28. New York: Columbia University Press.

Elshtain, Jean Bethke
  1982   "Feminist Discourse and Its Discontents: Language, Power, and
            Meaning." *Signs: Journal of Women in Culture and Society* 7:
            603–21.
Epstein, T. Scarlett
  1973   *South India, Yesterday, Today, and Tomorrow: Mysore Villages
            Revisited.* New York: Holmes and Meier.
  1979   "Mysore Villages Revisited." In George M. Foster et al., eds.,
            Long-Term Field Research in Social Anthropology, 209–26. New
            York: Academic Press.
Etienne, Gilbert
  1982   *India's Changing Rural Scene, 1963–1979.* Delhi: Oxford Uni-
            versity Press.
  1988   *Food and Poverty: India's Half-Won Battle.* New Delhi: Sage Pub-
            lications.
Fabian, Johannes
  1990   "Presence and Representation: The Other and Anthropological
            Writing." *Critical Inquiry* 16: 753–72.
Fletcher, Anthony, and John Stevenson, eds.
  1985   *Order and Disorder in Early Modern England.* Cambridge: Cam-
            bridge University Press.
Foster, George M., et al., eds.
  1979   *Long-Term Field Research in Social Anthropology.* New York: Aca-
            demic Press.
Franda, Marcus F.
  1979   *India's Rural Development: An Assessment of Alternatives.* Bloom-
            ington: Indiana University Press.
Freed, Stanley A., and Ruth S. Freed
  1982   "Changing Family Types in India." *Ethnology* 21: 189–202.
  1983   "The Domestic Cycle in India: Natural History of a Will-o'-the-
            Wisp." *American Ethnologist* 10: 312–27.
Gal, Susan.
  1991   "Between Speech and Silence: The Problematics of Research on
            Language and Gender." In Micaela di Leonardo, ed., *Gender at
            the Crossroads of Knowledge: Feminist Anthropology in the Post-
            modern Era*, 175–203. Berkeley: University of California Press.
Geertz, Clifford
  1973   *The Interpretation of Cultures.* New York: Basic Books.
  1977   " 'From the Native's Point of View': On the Nature of Anthro-
            pological Understanding." In Janet L. Dolgin, David S. Kem-
            nitzer, and David M. Schneider, eds., *Symbolic Anthropology: A
            Reader in the Study of Symbols and Meanings*, 480–92. New York:
            Columbia University Press.
George, P. T.
  1972   *Terminology in Indian Land Reforms.* Poona: Gokhale Institute
            of Politics and Economics.

Gilligan, Carol
    1982   *In a Different Voice: Psychological Theory and Women's Develop-ment.* Cambridge, Mass.: Harvard University Press.
Gould, Harold
    1964   "A Jajmani System of North India: Its Structure, Magnitude, and Meaning." *Ethnology* 3: 12–41.
Guha, Ranajit, ed.
    1980   *Subaltern Studies I: Writings in South Asian History and Society.* Delhi: Oxford University Press.
Gupta, Akhil
    1987   *Technology, Power, and the State in a Complex Agricultural Soci-ety: The Green Revolution in a North Indian Village.* Ph.D. diss., Stanford University.
Handler, Richard, and Jocelyn Linnekan
    1984   "Tradition, Genuine or Spurious." *Journal of American Folklore* 97: 273–90.
Harper, Edward B.
    1964   "Ritual Pollution as an Integrator of Caste and Religion." *Jour-nal of Asian Studies* 2: 151–97.
    1968   "Social Consequences of an 'Unsuccessful' Low-Caste Move-ment." In *Comparative Studies in Society and History, Supplement III,* ed. James Silverberg, 36–65.
Harrison, Faye V., ed.
    1991   *Decolonizing Anthropology: Moving Further toward an Anthro-pology of Liberation.* Washington D.C.: American Anthropologi-cal Association.
Harriss, John
    1982   *Capitalism and Peasant Farming: Agrarian Structure and Ideol-ogy in Northern Tamil Nadu.* Bombay: Oxford University Press.
Heginbotham, Stanley J.
    1975   *Cultures in Conflict: The Four Faces of Indian Bureaucracy.* New York: Columbia University Press.
Herring, Ronald J.
    1983   *Land to the Tiller.* New Haven: Yale University Press.
    1984   "Economic Consequences of Local Power Configurations in Rural South Asia." In Meghnad Desai, Susanne Rudolph, and Ashok Rudra, eds., *Agrarian Power and Agricultural Productiv-ity in South Asia,* 198–249. Delhi: Oxford University Press.
Hershman, Paul
    1977   "Virgin and Mother." In Ian M. Lewis, ed., *Symbols and Senti-ment: Cross-cultural Studies in Symbolism,* 269–92. New York: Academic Press.
Hiebert, Paul G.
    1981   "Old Age in a South Indian Village." In Pamela T. Amoss and Stevan Harrell, eds., *Others Ways of Growing Old: Anthropologi-cal Perspectives,* 211–26. Stanford: Stanford University Press.

Hobson, Sarah
    1978   *Family Web: A Story of India*. London: John Murray.
Inden, Ronald B.
    1986   "Orientalist Constructions of India." *Modern Asian Studies* 20:
                401–46.
Jacobson, Doranne
    1982   "Purdah and the Hindu Family in Central India." In Hannah Pa-
                panek and Gail Minault, eds., *Separate Worlds: Studies of Purdah
                in South Asia*, 81–109. Columbia, Mo: South Asia Books.
Jain, A. K.
    1985   "Determinants of Regional Variations in Infant Mortality in Rural
                India." *Population Studies* 39: 407–24.
Jeffery, Patricia, Roger Jeffery, and Andrew Lyon
    1989   *Labour Pains and Labour Power: Women and Childbearing in
                India*. London: Zed Books.
Jodha, N. S.
    1990   "Depletion of Common Property Resources in India: Micro-
                Level Evidence." In Geoffrey McNicoll and Mead Cain, eds.,
                Rural Development and Population: Institutions and Policy,
                261–83. New York: Oxford University Press.
Johnson, Patricia Lyons, ed.
    1992   *Balancing Acts: Women and the Process of Social Change*. Boulder,
                Colo.: Westview Press.
Kakar, Sudhir
    1979   *Identity and Adulthood*. Delhi: Oxford University Press.
    1981   *The Inner World: A Psycho-analytic Study of Childhood and Soci-
                ety in India*. Delhi: Oxford University Press.
Kessinger, Tom G.
    1974   *Vilyatpur, 1848–1968: Social and Economic Change in a North In-
                dian Village*. Berkeley: University of California Press.
Leaf, Murray J.
    1984   *Song of Hope: The Green Revolution in a Panjab Village*. New
                Brunswick, N.J.: Rutgers University Press.
Lipton, Michael, and John Toye
    1990   *Does Aid Work in India? A Country Study of the Impact of Offi-
                cial Development Assistance*. London: Routledge.
Manwar, Ali
    1990   "Social Structure of Capital Formation in Bangladesh: A Micro-
                Level Study in the Village Community." Ph.D. diss., Syracuse
                University.
Marcus, George E., and Michael M. J. Fischer
    1986   *Anthropology as Cultural Critique: An Experimental Moment in
                the Human Sciences*. Chicago: University of Chicago Press.
Marriott, McKim
    1966   "The Feast of Love." In Milton Singer, ed., *Krishna: Myths, Rites,
                and Attitudes*, 200–212. Honolulu: East-West Center Press, Uni-
                versity of Hawaii.

1968   "Caste Ranking and Food Transactions: A Matrix Analysis." In
            Milton Singer and Barnard S. Cohn, eds., *Structure and Change
            in Indian Society*, 133–72. Chicago: Aldine Publishing.
1976   "Hindu Transactions: Diversity without Dualism." In Bruce D.
            Kapferer, ed., *Transaction and Meaning: Directions in the An-
            thropology of Exchange and Symbolic Behavior*, 109–42. Philadel-
            phia: Institute for the Study of Human Issues.
1980   "The Open Hindu Person." Unpublished paper.
1989   "Constructing an Indian Ethnosociology." *Contributions to
            Indian Sociology* 23: 1–41.
Marriott, McKim, and Ronald B. Inden
1974   "Caste Systems." In *Encyclopaedia Britannica*, 15th ed.
Mencher, Joan P.
1978   *Agriculture and Social Structure in Tamil Nadu: Past Origins,
            Present Transformations, and Future Prospects*. Bombay: Allied
            Publishers.
Metcalf, Thomas R.
1979   *Land, Landlords, and the British Raj: Northern India in the Nine-
            teenth Century*. Berkeley: University of California Press.
Miller, Barbara D.
1981   *The Endangered Sex: Neglect of Female Children in Rural North
            India*. Ithaca: Cornell University Press.
Mills, Margaret
1991   *Rhetorics and Politics in Afghan Traditional Storytelling*. Philadel-
            phia: University of Pennsylvania Press.
Moore, Erin
1990   "Dream Bread: An Exemplum in a Rajasthani Panchayat." *Jour-
            nal of American Folklore* 103: 301–23.
Nag, Moni, and Neeraj Kak
1984   "Demographic Transition in a Punjab Village." *Population and
            Development Review* 10: 661–78.
Nair, Kusum
1979   *In Defense of the Irrational Peasant: Indian Agriculture after the
            Green Revolution*. Chicago: University of Chicago Press.
Narayan, Kirin
1989   *Storytellers, Saints, and Scoundrels: Folk Narrative in Hindu Re-
            ligious Teaching*. Philadelphia: University of Pennsylvania Press.
Neale, Walter C.
1962   *Economic Change in Rural India: Land Tenure and Reform in
            Uttar Pradesh, 1800–1955*. New Haven: Yale University Press.
Oldenberg, Philip
1987   "Middlemen in Third-World Corruption: Implications of an In-
            dian Case." *World Politics* 32: 508–35.
1990   "Land Consolidation as Land Reform in India." *World Develop-
            ment* 18: 183–95.
Omvedt, Gail
1986   " 'Patriarchy': The Analysis of Women's Oppression." *Insurgent
            Sociologist* 13: 30–50.

Ortner, Sherry B.
  1984   "Anthropology in the Sixties." *Comparative Studies in Society and History* 26: 126–66.
Ortner, Sherry B., and Harriet Whitehead, eds.
  1981   *Sexual Meanings: The Cultural Construction of Gender and Sexuality.* Cambridge: Cambridge University Press.
Parajuli, Pramod, and Elizabeth Enslin
  1990   "From Learning Literacy to Regenerating Women's Spaces: A Story of Women's Empowerment in Nepal." *Convergence* 23: 44–56.
Patai, Daphne
  1991   "U.S. Academics and Third World Women: Is Ethical Research Possible?" In Sherna Berger Gluck and Daphne Patai, eds., *Women's Words: The Feminist Practice of Oral History*, 137–53. New York: Routledge.
Prakash, Gyan
  1990   *Bonded Histories: Genealogies of Labor Servitude in Colonial India.* Cambridge: Cambridge University Press.
Pugh, Judy F.
  1981   *Person and Experience: The Astrological System of North India.* Ph.D. diss., University of Chicago.
Raheja, Gloria Goodwin
  1988   *The Poison in the Gift: Ritual, Prestation, and the Dominant Caste in a North Indian Village.* Chicago: University of Chicago Press.
  1989   "Centrality, Mutuality and Hierarchy: Shifting Aspects of Inter-caste Relationships in North India." *Contributions to Indian Sociology* 23: 79–102.
Raheja, Gloria Goodwin, and Ann Grodzins Gold
  1994   *Listen to the Heron's Words: Reimagining Gender and Kinship in North India.* Berkeley: University of California Press.
Ramanujan, A. K.
  1991   "Toward a Counter-system: Women's Tales." In Arjun Appadurai, Frank J. Korom, and Margaret A. Mills, eds., *Gender, Genre, and Power in South Asian Expressive Traditions*, 33–55. Philadelphia: University of Pennsylvania Press.
Rapp, Rayna
  1982   "Family and Class in Contemporary America: Notes toward an Understanding of Ideology." In Barrie Thorne and Marilyn Yalom, eds., *Rethinking the Family*, 168–87. New York: Longman.
Rath, Nilakantha
  1985   " 'Garibi Hatao': Can IRDP Do It?" *Economic and Political Weekly* 20: 238–46.
Roland, Alan
  1988   *In Search of Self in India and Japan: Toward a Cross-cultural Psychology.* Princeton: Princeton University Press.
Rosaldo, Renato
  1986   "Ilongot Hunting as Story and Experience." In Edward Bruner and Victor Turner, eds., *The Anthropology of Experience*, 97–138. Urbana: University of Illinois Press.

Sahlins, Marshall David
1985   *Islands of History.* Chicago: University of Chicago Press.
Saith, Athwani, and Ajay Tankha
1992   "Longitudinal Analysis of Structural Change in a North Indian
            Village: 1970–1978." Working Paper Series, no. 128, Institute
            of Social Studies, The Hague.
Schieffelin, Edward L.
1985   "Performance and the Cultural Construction of Reality." *Amer-
            ican Ethnologist* 12: 707–24.
Scott, James C.
1985   *Weapons of the Weak: Everyday Forms of Peasant Resistance.* New
            Haven: Yale University Press.
1986   "Everyday Forms of Peasant Resistance." *Journal of Peasant
            Studies* 13: 5–35.
Scott, Joan W.
1986   "Gender: A Useful Category of Historical Analysis." *American
            Historical Review* 91: 1053–75.
Sen, Gita
1982   "Women Workers and the Green Revolution." In Lourdes Bene-
            ria, ed., *Women and Development: The Sexual Division of Labor in
            Rural Societies,* 29–64. New York: Praeger.
1984   "Subordination and Sexual Control: A Comparative View of the
            Control of Women." *Review of Radical Political Economics* 16:
            133–42.
Shankar, Kripa
1987   *Uttar Pradesh in Statistics.* New Delhi: Ashish Publishing House.
Sharma, Madan Lal, and T. M. Dak
1989   *Green Revolution and Social Change.* Delhi: Ajanta Publications.
Sharma, Miriam
1985   "Caste, Class, and Gender: Production and Reproduction in
            North India." *Journal of Peasant Studies* 12: 57–88.
Sharma, Ursula
1980a   *Women, Work and Property in Northwest India.* London: Tavi-
            stock.
1980b   "Purdah and Public Space." In Alfred DeSouza, ed., *Women in
            Contemporary India and South Asia,* 213–39. New Delhi:
            Manohar Books.
Shostak, Marjorie
1981   *Nisa: The Life and Words of a !Kung Woman.* Cambridge, Mass.:
            Harvard University Press.
Shweder, Richard A., and E. Bourne
1982   "Does the Concept of the Person Vary Cross-culturally?" In An-
            thony J. Marsella and Geoffrey M. White, eds., *Cultural Concep-
            tions of Mental Health and Therapy,* 97–137. Boston: D. Reidel.
Siddiqi, Majid Hayat
1978   *Agrarian Unrest in Northern India: The United Provinces,
            1918–22.* New Delhi: Vikas Publishing House.

Smith, Dorothy E.
    1984   "Textually Mediated Social Organization." *International Social
                Science Journal* 36: 59–75.
Smucker, Celeste M., et al.
    1980   "Neo-natal Mortality in South Asia: The Special Role of Tetanus."
                Population Studies 34: 321–35.
Srinivas, M. N.
    1956   "A Note on Sanskritization and Westernization." *Far Eastern
                Quarterly* 15: 481–96.
Stacey, Judith
    1988   "Can There Be a Feminist Ethnography?" *Women's Studies In-
                ternational Forum* 11: 21–27.
Stokes, Eric
    1975   "The Structure of Land Holding in Uttar Pradesh, 1860–1948."
                Indian Economic and Social History Review 12: 113–32.
Tambiah, Stanley J.
    1985   *Culture, Thought, and Social Action.* Cambridge, Mass.: Harvard
                University Press.
Thompson, Catherine
    1985   "The Power to Pollute and the Power to Preserve: Perceptions of
                Female Power in a Hindu Village." *Social Science and Medicine*
                21: 701–11.
Toomey, Paul M.
    1990   "Krishna's Consuming Passions: Food as Metaphor and
                Metonym for Emotion at Mount Govardhan." In Owen M.
                Lynch, ed., *Divine Passions: The Social Construction of Emotion in
                India*, 157–81. Berkeley: University of California Press.
Trawick, Margaret
    1990a   *Notes on Love in a Tamil Family.* Berkeley: University of Califor-
                nia Press.
    1990b   "The Ideology of Love in a Tamil Family." In Owen M. Lynch,
                ed., *Divine Passions: The Social Construction of Emotion in India*,
                37–63. Berkeley: University of California Press.
Tual, Anny
    1986   "Speech and Silence: Women in Iran." In Leela Dube, Eleanor
                Leacock, and Shirley Ardener, eds., *Visibility and Power: Essays on
                Women in Society and Development*, 54–69. Delhi: Oxford Uni-
                versity Press.
Ullrich, Helen
    1987a   "Marriage Patterns among Havik Brahmins: A Twenty-Year Study
                of Change." *Sex Roles* 16: 615–35.
    1987b   "A Study of Change and Depression among Havik Brahmin
                Women in a South Indian Village." *Culture, Medicine and Psy-
                chiatry* 11: 261–87.
Vasavi, A. R.
    n.d.   "From 'Appropriateness' to 'System': Shifts in the Agrarian Pre-
                cepts of a Semi-arid Region." Unpublished paper, Michigan State
                University.

Vatuk, Sylvia
1990   " 'To Be a Burden on Others': Dependency Anxiety among the Elderly in India." In Owen M. Lynch, ed., *Divine Passions: The Social Construction of Emotion in India*, 64–88. Berkeley: University of California Press.

Wadley, Susan S.
1975a   *Shakti: Power in the Conceptual Structure of Karimpur Religion.* University of Chicago Studies in Anthropology: Series in Social, Cultural, and Linguistic Anthropology, no. 2. Department of Anthropology, University of Chicago.

1975b   "Folk Literature in Karimpur: A Catalogue of Types." *Journal of South Asian Literature* 11: 7–17.

1976a   "Brothers, Husbands and Sometimes Sons: Kinsmen in North Indian Ritual." *Eastern Anthropologist* 29: 149–70.

1976b   "The Spirit 'Rides' or the Spirit 'Comes': Possession in a North Indian Village." In Agehananda Bharati, ed., *Rituals, Cults and Shamanism: The Realm of the Extrahuman*, 233–51. The Hague: Mouton.

1977a   "Women and the Hindu Tradition." *Signs: Journal of Women in Culture and Society* 3: 113–25.

1977b   "Power in Hindu Ideology and Practice." In Kenneth David, ed., *The New Wind: Changing Identities in South Asia*, 134–57. The Hague: Mouton.

1978   "Texts in Contexts: Oral Traditions and the Study of Religion in Karimpur." In Sylvia Vatuk, ed., *American Studies in the Anthropology of India*, 309–41. New Delhi: Manohar.

1980a   "Women's Family and Household Rites in a North Indian Village." In Nancy Auer Falk and Rita M. Gross, eds., *Unspoken Worlds: Women's Religious Lives in Non-Western Cultures*, 94–109. New York: Harper and Row.

1980b   "Women's Songs, Music, and the Seasons in a North Indian Village." Paper presented at the annual meeting of the Society for Ethnomusicology, Bloomington, Indiana.

1981a   "Women as Mothers, Wives and Daughters in North Indian Folklore." *Asian Thought and Society* 6: 4–24.

1981b   "Cunning in the Courtyard: Women in Karimpur Folktales." Paper presented at the annual meeting of the Association for Asian Studies, Toronto.

1983   "Vrats: Transformers of Destiny." In Val Daniel and Charles Keyes, eds., *Karma: An Anthropological Inquiry*, 147–62. Berkeley: University of California Press.

1986a   "The *Kathā* of Sakat: Two Tellings." In Stuart H. Blackburn and A. K. Ramanujan, eds., *Another Harmony: New Essays on the Folklore of India*, 195–232. Berkeley: University of California Press.

1986b   "Survey Research or Intensive Field Studies? A Review of the Debate with Special Reference to South Asia." *Journal of Social Studies* 33: 19–34.

1986c   *Shakti: Power in the Conceptual Structure of Karimpur Religion.*
             New Delhi: Munshiram Manoharlal. (Reprint of Wadley 1975a.)

1989a   "Choosing a Path: Performance Strategies in a North India Epic."
             In Stuart H. Blackburn et al., eds., *Oral Epics in India*, 75–101.
             Berkeley: University of California Press.

1989b   "Female Survival Changes in Rural North India." *Cultural Survival Quarterly* 13: 35–39.

1991a   "Why Does Ram Swarup Sing? Song and Speech in the North Indian Epic Dhola." In A. Appadurai, Frank J. Korom, and Margaret
             A. Mills, eds., *Gender, Genre, and Power in South Asian Expressive Traditions*, 201–23. Philadelphia: University of Pennsylvania Press.

1991b   "A Women's *Bulua* and a Men's *Kirtan*: Enacting Honor, Community, and Gender in Cultural Performances in Rural North India." Paper presented at the Conference on Language, Gender,
             and the Subaltern Voice: Framing Identities in South Asia, University of Minnesota.

1992   "The 'Village Indira': A Brahman Widow and Political Action in
             Rural North India." In Patricia Lyons Johnson, ed., *Balancing Acts: Women and the Process of Social Change*, 65–87. Boulder,
             Colo.: Westview Press.

1993a   "Beyond Texts: Tunes and Contexts in Indian Folk Music." In
             Bonnie C. Wade, ed., *Texts, Tunes and Tones: Parameters of Music in Multicultural Perspective*, 71–106. New Delhi: Oxford and
             IBH Publishing Co.

1993b   "Family Composition Strategies in Rural North India." *Social Science and Medicine* 37: 1367–76.

In press   "No Longer a Wife: Widows in Rural North India." In Paul Courtright and Lindsay Harlan, eds., *From the Margins of Hindu Marriage: Essays on Gender, Religion, and Culture*. New York: Oxford
             University Press.

Wadley, Susan S., and Bruce W. Derr

1978   "Introduction," in *Four Families of Karimpur*, by Charlotte V.
             Wiser. Foreign and Comparative Studies Program, South Asian
             Series, no. 3, Syracuse University, Syracuse, New York.

1986   "Child Survival and Economic Status in a North Indian Village."
             Paper presented at the Ninth European Conference on Modern
             South Asian Studies, Heidelberg.

1988   "Karimpur Families over 60 Years." *South Asian Anthropologist*
             9: 119–32.

1989a   "Eating Sins in Karimpur." *Contributions to Indian Sociology* 23:
             131–48.

1989b   "Karimpur, 1925–1984: Understanding Rural India through
             Restudies." In Pranab Bardhan, ed., *Conversations between Anthropologists and Economists: Methodological Issues in Measuring Economic Change in Rural India*, 76–126. Delhi: Oxford University Press.

Wagner, Roy
    1981   *The Invention of Culture.* Chicago: University of Chicago Press.
Whitcombe, Charlotte
    1971   *Agrarian Conditions in Northern India,* vol. 1, *The United
                  Provinces under British Rule, 1860–1900.* New Delhi: Thomson
                  Press.
Wiltenburg, Joy
    1992   *Disorderly Women and Female Power in the Street Literature of
                  Early Modern England and Germany.* Charlottesville: University
                  Press of Virginia.
Wiser, Charlotte V.
    1929   "A Hindu Village Home in North India." *International Review
                  of Missions,* July. London.
    1936   *The Foods of a Hindu Village in North India.* Allahabad: Superin-
                  tendent, Printing and Stationery, United Provinces.
    1978   *Four Families of Karimpur.* Foreign and Comparative Studies
                  Program, South Asian Series, no. 3, Syracuse University, Syracuse,
                  New York..
    1980   "Time Perspectives in Village India." In Priscilla Reining and Bar-
                  bara Lenkerd, eds., *Village Viability in Contemporary Society.* AAS
                  Selected Symposium, no. 34, 123–59. Boulder, Colo.: Westview
                  Press.
Wiser, William H.
    1933   *Social Institutions of a Hindu Village in North India.* Ph.D. diss.,
                  Cornell University.
    1958   *The Hindu Jajmani System: A Socio-economic System Interrelating
                  Members of a Hindu Village Community in Services.* Lucknow:
                  Lucknow Publishing House. Orig. publ. 1936.
Wiser, William H., and Charlotte V. Wiser
    1989   *Behind Mud Walls, 1930–1960.* With a sequel, "The Village in
                  1970," and a new chapter by Susan S. Wadley, "The Village in
                  1984." Berkeley: University of California Press. First ed., *Behind
                  Mud Walls,* 1930.
Witherspoon, Gary
    1977   *Language and Art in the Navajo Universe.* Ann Arbor: University
                  of Michigan Press.
Wolf, Margery
    1992   *A Thrice-Told Tale: Feminism, Postmodernism, and Ethnographic
                  Responsibility.* Stanford: Stanford University Press.
Wulff, Robert M., and Shirley J. Fiske, eds.
    1987   *Anthropological Praxis: Translating Knowledge into Action.* Boul-
                  der, Colo.: Westview Press.

Index

298

Index

176–77; and sexuality, 41–52, 101; silencing of, 55–59; songs of, 49–50,
58, 101, 146, 229, 234–35, 236,
237–38; subordination of, 59; and
voting, 189; Watercarrier, 114, 135.
See also Fertility; Marriage; Midwives;
Purdah; Widows
Worship. *See* Religion

Yama, 56, 124, 258
Yamraj, 127, 269n.11
Yaqut Khan, 272n.4

Zamindars, 10, 91, 163, 165, 167, 168,
189, 219, 226, 231. *See also* Landlords; Landowners

Compositor: BookMasters, Inc.
Text: 10/13 Galliard
Display: Galliard
Printer: Maple-Vail Book Manufacturing Group
Binder: Maple-Vail Book Manufacturing Group